BIPOLAR DISORDERS

Guide to Helping Children & Adolescents

BIPOLAR DISORDERS

Guide to Helping Children & Adolescents

Mitzi Waltz

Beijing • Cambridge • Farnham • Köln • Paris • Sebastopol • Taipei • Tokyo

Bipolar Disorders: A Guide to Helping Children and Adolescents
by Mitzi Waltz

Copyright © 2000 by Mitzi Waltz. All rights reserved.
Printed in the United States of America.

Published by O'Reilly & Associates, Inc., 101 Morris Street, Sebastopol, CA 95472.

Editor: Linda Lamb

Production Editor: Sarah Jane Shangraw

Cover Design: Edie Freedman

Printing History:

      January 2000: First Edition

Library of Congress Cataloging-in-Publication Data:

Waltz, Mitzi.
    Bipolar disorders : a guide to helping children and adolescents / Mitzi Waltz.— 1st ed.
      p. cm.
    Includes bibliographical references and index.
    ISBN 1-56592-656-0 (pbk. : acid-free paper)
    1. Depression in children. 2. Depression in adolescents. 3. Manic-depressive illness in children. 4. Manic-depressive illness in adolescence. 5. Adolescent psychopathology. I. Title.

RJ506.D4 W35 2000
618.92'895—dc21

For Carmen

Table of Contents

Preface   ix

1. What Are Bipolar Disorders?   1

2. Getting a Diagnosis   31

3. Living with Bipolar Disorders   66

4. Medical Interventions   115

5. Therapeutic Interventions   206

6. Other Interventions   234

7. Insurance   278

8. School   316

9. Transitions   372

Resources   389

Notes   423

Index   427

Preface

THERE ARE TWO SIDES to every story, and the tale of my daughter's experience with childhood-onset bipolar disorder is no exception. The difference in age, experience, priorities, and perceptions between child and parent can create two very different versions of the same events.

Carmen knew at a very young age that her brain worked differently—and I did not. She sometimes saw things that weren't there and was afraid. As a young single mother, I dismissed her hallucinations as bad dreams, wiped away her tears, soothed over her moods, and relished her joy for life. She was a lovable, bright, pretty girl with a passionate disposition that seemed no more important a quirk than her enthusiasm for the Barbies and girlish clothes I had disdained in my tomboy childhood. That was just Carmen: quick to laugh, quick to cry, always dramatic, curious, and on the move.

A neurological difference becomes a neurological disorder gradually. It can happen so quietly that parents are shocked when difficult symptoms emerge, even though problems have been bubbling under the surface for years. As Carmen came closer to puberty, others were quicker to notice than I. A concerned fifth-grade teacher thought an alternative school known for its creative bent might be a better fit than our neighborhood elementary, so we transferred her. Carmen's new stepfather raged over her sassy, smart-mouth attitude and bouts of tears, so we sought marriage counseling. At her new school, reports of misbehavior filtered home—fighting, moodiness, crying, oppositional behavior in the classroom, rumors of an eating disorder—so we stuck up for our daughter, angry that the school blamed our parenting skills and stepfamily blending problems.

But as such things progress, there comes a time when you can no longer deny that something is wrong. Perhaps you are at that stage right now: your child has just been diagnosed with a bipolar disorder, or you fear that he or she will be. Perhaps you're a professional who works with children and teens affected by these extremes of mood and emotion. I hope that my experience—my daughter's experience, our family's experience—can help you understand and cope with the trials you face.

In the rest of this preface, the words in italics are Carmen's own.

Maybe the first thing we should have noticed was that Carmen saw the world differently than most people. She took things very personally, and always assumed the worst (therapists call this "catastrophizing"—thinking of the worst possible outcome in any situation, and fully expecting it to occur).

> *To be quite honest, I have always been pretty self-absorbed, in the sense that everything going on in the world that I know of is affecting me somehow. Even if that situation is completely unrelated to me, I still have the knowledge of it, therefore it affects me. I can't remember how many times I was told: "The world does not revolve around you, Carmen."*

> *Maybe it was this way of thinking that made the mood swings so hard on me. I wanted them to come from something else. I was too ready to blame everyone else around me. I over-analyzed every thought in my head, and found some way for it to relate to a situation in my life.*

I had known for a long time that Carmen had very definite mood swings that seemed to come and go suddenly, but I never thought of them as a symptom of mental illness. I groped around for an explanation (a bad day at school, too much sugar, puberty, chaos on the home front), and I could usually latch onto something. What I now know is that hypomania was such a frequent state for her that it had come to seem perfectly normal. And even though I now know what her hypomania can become when unchecked, I would never want to take this away from her.

> *Realistically speaking, who takes notice when you're happy? Happiness is socially acceptable. Sure, it's true that when I'm happy it can be a bit overwhelming, but after the sadness I'd felt, any form of good feelings was welcome.*

> *In a weird way, having bipolar disorder is almost like having two personalities. One is great: motivated, happy, and entirely energetic. Wonderful things can be accomplished in this mindset. However, no matter how fantastic it seems, there are always down sides. For one, you have no idea why you feel this way, which can ultimately suppress any of the positive aspects, and two, it doesn't last forever.*

It was depression that finally made me realize something was wrong—but I didn't recognize it as depression at first. Neither did Carmen's teachers, the school counselor, or the first therapist she saw.

I thought I knew depression intimately. I've suffered several episodes of depression myself, including a fairly severe postpartum depression after the birth of Carmen's younger brother. To me, depression meant feeling bleak, listless, self-pitying, and tired. What was I to make of this child who was irritable and angry, unable to sleep at night, screaming at me one minute and giggling over the phone with her friends the next? Depression didn't even cross my mind.

Our home became increasingly tense as Carmen moved through middle school. Her morning moods seemed to set the tone for the entire day, and it usually wasn't good. Differences of opinion on how to discipline her almost ended my marriage. And it didn't help that much of my attention was on my toddler, who was showing the early signs of autism (he has since been diagnosed with a pervasive developmental disorder and other neurological problems).

My memories of those early adolescent years are blurred, even though they weren't that long ago. Many hateful words were exchanged, and like most mothers, I've chosen to forget as much as I can. There were fears about friends who might be a bad influence, about smoking, about drugs and alcohol. And emerging from all of it was the clear knowledge that my daughter was in serious trouble. She locked herself in her room most afternoons, barely acknowledging the rest of the family except to yell at us. Her appearance changed, she fought with her old friends, and her school performance slid from stellar to nonexistent.

By high school, Carmen's life was undeniably falling apart. She couldn't even get up in the morning. Nothing was going right for her, least of all school. She dropped out, dropped in again, and worked my last nerve with her dramatic behavior, including running away from home and substance abuse. One evening her brother walked into her room and found her cutting her wrists. I took her to two different hospitals that night in an effort to get her immediate help. She was hospitalized on an adolescent psychiatric ward for a week.

I was first diagnosed with clinical depression. When I received that diagnosis it seemed fitting to both myself and those around me. Depres-

*sion hits you in different ways. It can be anything from extreme irritation
to deep sadness. Sometimes you just want to start crying for no reason.
Insecurities build up. The people around you don't seem to be able to
relate to you, let alone care, and you end up feeling very alone.*

*I think the fact that it came out of nowhere is why I felt the need to
blame everyone and everything around me. I felt so isolated in my
thoughts and feelings that I ended up pushing a lot of people away.*

Hospitalization wasn't a quick fix, especially since she was discharged too
early, misdiagnosed, and given the wrong medication. There followed two
years in which I was afraid we would lose Carmen to the streets. We tried to
get a special education program started after she got out of the hospital, but
the process dragged on for months. She was never able to re-enter high
school successfully. We were faced with continued angry outbursts, and even
violent behavior. Still much too young to get a job, she left home and stayed
with a succession of friends. All we could do was offer help from a distance,
and hang on to that thin thread of hope.

*I started using drugs to relieve myself of what was going on in my
head. At the time I thought I was just using drugs for fun. But of course it
was fun for me not to have to deal with the feelings I was having.*

*Eventually the drugs stopped doing what they used to. I started see-
ing what they were doing to the people around me. So I quit. I quit alone.
For awhile I sort of used that to keep me happy: if I could do that by
myself, then I could deal with everything else by myself. Of course that
didn't really work for long, and I sought help.*

*I was finally diagnosed with bipolar disorder and began taking medi-
cation and going to therapy.*

It seemed like no one had answers for us. The family counselor we saw
emphasized tough love, telling us we shouldn't even see or talk to Carmen
unless she promised to come home and obey our rules. My heart said otherwise, and eventually, with help from a counselor more knowledgeable about
mental illness, we began to put our family back together. We set ground
rules that protected us, without laying down ultimatums. Our relationship
was better, but her symptoms were not.

Carmen tried several medications during this period, and each one seemed to be worse than the last.

> *You can't explain to people how it feels to be on the wrong medication. On Zoloft, I felt like a zombie, like I was not myself at all. My thoughts were really, really slow, and by the time they came out of my mouth they didn't make any sense.*

> *Paxil didn't have as drastic an effect as Zoloft, but I still didn't feel like I was thinking normally. I was just kind of groggy all the time.*

> *On Depakote I was violent and wanted to smash windows. My body felt like I just really needed to punch something—all the time. I was very manic, I needed to move, to listen to lots of loud music, and just scream!*

Thankfully, when she finally tried lithium it was successful: in fact, Carmen was eventually so stable that she decided to stop taking it—a typical mistake for a bipolar teen. She has had only one major relapse since, which also responded rapidly to medication. She still experiences milder mood swings and related physical symptoms, particularly anxiety and panic attacks, and continues to look for a medication that can help her weather these better.

Attending talk therapy and addressing a hormone imbalance that was affecting her mood were also important in helping Carmen become more stable. In turn, stabilization has helped Carmen make lasting lifestyle changes on her own initiative. These changes have improved how she feels and functions each day. She is now able to choose and pursue her own goals, including earning her GED, attending trade school, working, living independently, and even studying abroad.

> *I think living with bipolar disorder is easier if you have a little more structure in what you're doing. I'm very structured in my work schedule. One thing that really improved my symptoms is when I started going to school again and had to get up at the same time every day.*

> *I've been doing fine. I've finished the first part of my education, traveled, and supported myself for over a year now.*

> *I've basically been using this illness as a creative outlet. I can use the good side with work and with friends. However, the other side is still*

present. I highly doubt that it will ever completely disappear, even with
medication. It's something that I'll have to deal with for the rest of my life.
And the fact that I have accepted this is what has helped me the most.

Sometimes it's hard for me to let Carmen take full control of her life. Every parent of a young adult worries, but transition to self-sufficiency for a person who has been disabled by illness in the past is especially difficult. I try to maintain a balance between being a resource, and letting her find her own wings. We've made a family plan about how we would handle a serious relapse, and we've taken steps to make sure she has continued medical coverage and good doctors. We've supported her efforts to pursue an education and a career, and although there have been bad days along the way, her decisions so far have shown more maturity than you would expect for someone her age.

As tough as Carmen's experiences over the past six years or so have been, I believe they've also strengthened her in many ways. She has developed compassion for other people's differences, and thought more deeply about what she wants out of life than many adults who are in their mid-20s. She is focused on her strengths rather than her weaknesses now, able to use her creativity and quick mind to reach her goals. We have high hopes for her future—and based on what we've learned, we know that even if new obstacles crop up in her way, we'll be able to get past them together.

I hope this book will help you find that same sense of hope and confidence. It is a compilation of everything I have learned along the way—everything I wish I had known at the beginning of this journey.

A few notes about the text

This book is intended to bring together all the basic information needed by parents of a child or teenager diagnosed with a bipolar disorder. Professionals who work with bipolar youth should also find it useful. The first two chapters provide a broad overview of the entire bipolar disorders family, and explain how they are diagnosed. Subsequent chapters cover family issues, treatment options, dealing with insurance problems and the healthcare system, school, and transition planning for bipolar teens.

The appendix, *Resources*, lists books, web sites, organizations, special diagnostic and treatment centers, and more to help you find the help your child needs.

Bipolar disorders occur in both girls and boys, so this book alternates between pronouns when talking about patients. Many adults with mental illnesses and their advocates do not like the practice of putting their disability first in constructions such as "bipolar child" or "bipolar patients." These terms are sometimes used in the text, but hopefully everyone reading this book understands that patients are always people first, and that a diagnosis is just an adjective to describe a part of who they are.

Every effort has been made to provide accurate information about resources in the English-speaking world, including North America, the UK, the Republic of Ireland, Australia, and New Zealand. Bipolar disorders are a universal phenomenon, however, and occur in all races and nationalities. Readers in other parts of the world may be able to find local resources and current information in languages other than English on the World Wide Web. Some of the web sites and email discussion groups listed in the appendix to this book can point you toward resources in your part of the world. Simply because this book was written in the US, some information will be skewed toward American readers. Most, however, will be useful to all.

Findings from the latest medical research are presented throughout the text. This information is not intended as medical advice. Please consult your physician before starting, stopping, or changing any medical treatment. Some of the health information provided comes from small studies or is controversial in nature. No endorsement of any particular medical or therapeutic approach to bipolar disorders is intended, and readers are encouraged to carefully examine any claims made by healthcare facilities, pharmaceutical firms, supplement manufacturers, therapists, and others before implementing new treatments.

Throughout the book, you will find the words of other parents and patients. Their quotes are offset from the rest of the text and presented in italics. In many cases their names and other identifying details have been changed at their request.

Acknowledgments

Many teenagers and young adults with bipolar disorders, and more than 20 parents of children with bipolar disorders, took the time to answer questions about their personal experiences. They deserve much of the credit for this book, as their replies guided its structure and contents.

A draft of the manuscript was reviewed by Tomie Burke, a parent of a bipolar child as well as owner and founder of the BPParent listserv, an Internet-based mailing list for parents of bipolar children; Martha Hellander, executive director of the Child and Adolescent Bipolar Foundation and the parent of a bipolar child; Dr. Robert L. Findling, director of the Division of Child and Adolescent Psychiatry and co-director of the Stanley Clinical Research Center at Case Western Reserve University/University Hospitals of Cleveland; Dr. Marv Rosen, a highly experienced child psychiatrist with Network Behavioral Health in Portland, Oregon; Sally Mink, RN, of the Depression and Related Affective Disorders Association (DRADA); parent Stephanie Kirk; and Troy Mott, an adult with bipolar disorder, among others. Their comments and criticisms were invaluable and much appreciated.

The National Alliance for the Mentally Ill has also been a primary, and extraordinarily valuable, resource. Created by parents, this organization gives voice to the concerns of families and patients affected by mental illness. It works in the nation's legislatures, in the media, online, in its excellent annual conference, and in hundreds of community support groups to provide information, help, and hope.

Linda Lamb, Carol Wenmoth, Claire Cloutier, Edie Freedman, and all of the extraordinarily professional editorial and production staff at O'Reilly & Associates have my utmost respect and admiration, as does my agent, Karen Nazor.

And Carmen, who inadvertently introduced me to this topic, gets the most thanks of all, especially for putting up with my nosy questions and busy schedule over the past year.

—Mitzi Waltz

If you would like to comment on this book or offer suggestions for future editions, please send email to *patientguides@oreilly.com*, or write to O'Reilly & Associates Inc. at 101 Morris Street, Sebastopol, CA 95472.

CHAPTER 1

What Are Bipolar Disorders?

ALTHOUGH THE EXACT CAUSE of bipolar disorders is not yet known, they are treatable medical illnesses. Evidence indicates that the genes for bipolar disorders can be inherited, although not everyone who carries the genes develops difficulties.

In this chapter, we look at the states of mind and behaviors that characterize bipolar disorders, with special attention to differences seen in young patients. We discuss the diagnostic system used by most psychiatrists, and explain what is currently known about causes, including genetics, nervous system differences, and factors that may cause bipolar disorders to begin or become worse. We also look at gender, culture, and other factors that can relate to diagnosis.

Mood swings

Everyone experiences the occasional unexplained mood swing. Maybe it's the weather, PMS, or just a bad day that throws you into the blue zone. Maybe it's sunny skies, hearing your favorite song first thing in the morning, or looking forward to a special event that kicks off one of those "good vibration" days when nothing can go wrong. The important thing is that the blues go away before too long, and the enjoyable sense of euphoria doesn't get you in trouble. People with bipolar disorders, however, experience mood swings that go far beyond the norm. Their moods swing low and keep dropping until life doesn't feel worth living anymore. They swing so high that they lose touch with reality, making rash decisions and behaving wildly. Moods may cycle so rapidly that the person literally can't function. When these symptoms occur during the all-important years of childhood and adolescence, they can be especially devastating, disrupting normal development.

A sample case history

The following story illustrates the wide mood swings that can be experienced by someone with a bipolar disorder. Although the teen in the story is fictional, his symptoms, feelings, and behavior are drawn from real life.

Fifteen-year-old Adam's drawings of complex, highly detailed robots fill several notebooks—notebooks that should have been used for homework. He has another set of notebooks hidden under his bed. These notebooks contain a disjointed diary of his day-to-day feelings.

In these secret volumes, Adam confesses that he often feels like he's outside himself, watching his body go through the motions of everyday life. He sometimes feels suspicious of others, even paranoid. "My life sucks, and it keeps on getting worse!" he writes one day, adding that no one understands the confusion, even terror, that he feels daily. On another day, his entry fills the page with exuberance and high-minded plans for inventing a new kind of computer. In other entries, he writes of—and, lately, makes concrete plans for—suicide.

Adam was diagnosed with attention deficit hyperactivity disorder (ADHD) at age 5, but Ritalin seemed to lose its effectiveness rapidly. So far, he has performed well enough in school, despite some unusual outbursts in class. These have happened on days when he was especially hyperactive. He became agitated, angry, and loud. Once he even attacked another boy in the hall who had laughed at Adam's behavior in the classroom. Adam was suspended, and returned to school calmly after a week.

Home is another matter. When Adam talks to his mother, he jumps from idea to idea. Sometimes his ideas are obviously bright or funny, but other times they seem quite strange.

Of late, however, his mother is literally afraid of—and for—her son. Always stubborn, Adam has become outrageously defiant. In the past three months, he has shoved her several times and threatened to hit her. His language is foul, and he openly shows his contempt for adult authority. He refuses to do his chores or his homework, yet expects the respect accorded to adults. She can't get him to wake up for school in the morning, but he's up at all hours of the night.

This is more than typical teenage rebellion. Adam's mother fears that he may be using drugs—he's always been a risk-taker, and he has stayed out overnight without calling home recently. Once she went looking for him and found him walking quickly down the middle of a nearby street at four in the morning. On the way home, he rambled at rapid speed on a hundred different topics before finally crashing on the living room couch. When he woke the next day, he seemed flat and emotionless, as if the night's activity had sapped all his energy.

His mother just never knows what to expect. Will Adam lock himself in his room in a blue funk, or will he be bouncing off the walls, full of a million ideas and plans? Will he finish high school? Will he survive high school? What can she do to help?

His mother doesn't know it yet, but Adam is suffering from bipolar disorder, also known as manic depression. It's a disorder of the brain and nervous system that causes severe mood swings, from the deepest suicidal depression to the most elated highs. Some of the most famous artists, musicians, politicians, and writers of our time have been bipolar and, sadly, so have a disproportionate number of the inmates in our juvenile facilities, psychiatric hospitals, and prisons.

The importance of diagnosis and treatment

Left untreated, bipolar disorders can plunge an adult into absolute hell. When disorders emerge in childhood, the ravages can be even more severe, for educational and vocational opportunities, self-esteem, and family support may be lost. According to Dr. Gary R. Spivack, a child psychiatrist affiliated with Dominion Hospital of Falls Church, Virginia, "Development of personality disorder—notably narcissistic, antisocial, and borderline personality disorders—along with substance abuse, is almost inevitable without proper treatment."[1]

Patients, their families, and their communities pay a heavy toll when these disorders are not recognized and treated. Suicide is a common outcome, as are school failure, limited job prospects, dependence on public assistance, legal difficulties, and expensive hospitalizations.

Until very recently, bipolar disorders were almost never diagnosed in children and only rarely recognized in adolescents, although of the two million or more adults diagnosed with a bipolar disorder in the US, between 20 and 40 percent experienced onset of the illness in their teen years or before. A groundbreaking survey of bipolar adults who are members of the National Depressive and Manic Depressive Association, a support and advocacy group in the US, found that fully 60 percent of the respondents reported onset of the disorder's symptoms before 19 years of age.[2]

Psychiatrists now recognize that bipolar disorders in children can be misdiagnosed as ADHD, which shares certain characteristics (see the section "Differential diagnosis" in Chapter 2, *Getting a Diagnosis*). According to recent data published in the *Journal of the American Academy of Child and Adolescent Psychiatry (JAACAP)*, 23 percent of the children currently diagnosed with ADHD will eventually be diagnosed as having a bipolar disorder, either by itself or in combination with ADHD.[3] Between 3 and 5 percent of American children fit the criteria for ADHD—accordingly, as many as a million children in the US alone may have a childhood-onset bipolar disorder. Of course, not all child psychiatrists agree with these statistics.

Today, we know that bipolar disorders are medical problems, not the result of faulty thinking, lack of willpower, or poor parenting. While inconsistent, abusive, or absent parents may worsen the course of bipolar disorders, they cannot cause them. Medications and other interventions are available that can help most people with bipolar disorders.

Types of bipolar disorders

There is more than one kind of bipolar disorder, although all of them include the basic symptom of drastic and debilitating mood swings. In the US, diagnosis is confirmed when the patient's inner feelings and outward behavior fit the criteria for one of the bipolar disorders listed in the fourth edition of the *Diagnostic and Statistical Manual of Mental Disorders* (*DSM-IV*), the book used by psychiatrists and other physicians to define brain-based medical problems. The *DSM-IV* assigns a number to each disorder and subtype.

In Europe and most other parts of the world, diagnosis is made when the patient fits the criteria for one of the similar classifications in the World Health Organization's *ICD-10 Classification of Mental and Behavioural Disorders*. The *ICD-10* also assigns numbers to each psychiatric condition it lists.

We present the *DSM-IV* criteria in this book, as they vary only slightly from those in the *ICD-10*, and they have been updated more recently.

Note for readers outside the US: If you need to take a look at the *ICD-10* criteria for bipolar disorders, they are available at *http://www.mentalhealth. com/icd/p22-md02.html*. You can also look through the *ICD-10* classification book itself at most public, university, medical, and private libraries that have a medical reference section.

We'll discuss the unusual moods associated with bipolar disorders—depression, hypomania, mania, and mixed states—later in this chapter (see "States of mind in bipolar disorders"). Depending on which of these moods the person experiences and how often they occur, a diagnosis will be chosen from one of the following major types.

Bipolar I disorder (BPI)

Bipolar I disorder is what used to be described as "manic depression." People with BPI swing into depression and have had at least one manic episode. Many also have hypomanic or mixed episodes.

> *He had been out of control for a long time and I just dealt with it, it never sunk in my head that this was a more than normal tantrum. He got to the point of wanting to commit suicide, so we had him hospitalized and it was the best thing we could ever have done. He was diagnosed, put on the correct meds and safe.* —Lynn, *mother of 11-year-old Michael (diagnosed BPI with mixed states and psychosis, obsessive-compulsive disorder, tic disorder)*

This is considered to be the most serious form of bipolar disorder, but paradoxically, it can be easier to treat than bipolar II disorder because the mood swings are wider, and sometimes they are further apart from each other and more predictable. The diagnosis should be followed by one of these modifiers:

- Most recent episode depressed (*DSM-IV* 296.5)
- Most recent episode hypomanic (*DSM-IV* 296.40)
- Most recent episode manic (*DSM-IV* 296.4x)
- Most recent episode mixed (*DSM-IV* 296.6x)

- Most recent episode unspecified (*DSM-IV* 296.7)
- Single manic episode (*DSM-IV* 296.0x)

Bipolar II disorder (BPII)

Bipolar II disorder (*DSM-IV* 296.89) is defined as recurrent depression with hypomania, but not mania or mixed states. People with BPII also tend to be more emotionally labile (moody) in between actual mood swings.

Although BPII is sometimes described as milder than bipolar I, these patients can actually be harder to treat because they may have fewer periods of normal mood in between their depressed and hypomanic periods.

> *Selena has only been manic when she took Prozac, before we knew she was bipolar. Hypomania, however, we know all too well. At first she's just a little giddy and can't get to sleep at night, but before long she's driving everyone bananas. And as soon as this stage passes she is depressed, where she refuses to get up for school and grumps around constantly. We definitely cherish any moods that are more normal. —Estella, mother of 8-year-old Selena (diagnosed BPII and ADHD)*

Cyclothymic disorder (cyclothymia)

Cyclothymic disorder (*DSM-IV* 301.13) in children is described as a chronic mood disturbance for at least a year. Both depressed and hypomanic moods are present, but there are no major depressive, manic, or mixed episodes. The patient must have gone without a period of normal mood for more than two months during the year. The cycles and moods are not as severe as those seen in bipolar II. If you were in a joking mood, you might call cyclothymia "bipolar lite."

Although it comes from a milder version of the same chemical imbalance that causes bipolar I and bipolar II, some psychiatrists feel cyclothymia is more like one of the personality disorders: an ingrained personality trait that causes difficulty for the person who has it and for those around him. That doesn't make it much easier to handle for the affected child, and may make accessing treatment resources more difficult.

> *Ben specifically complained about the loss of feeling tired. It really disturbed him. He would go look in the mirror and say, "I look tired, so my body must be tired. But I don't feel tired." He could not fall asleep. He*

asked me to make an appointment with his psychiatrist, [saying clearly that] "Something is wrong, Mom." —Marlene, mother of 8-year-old Billy (diagnosed cyclothymic disorder)

Mood disorder NOS (not otherwise specified)

If your child has some characteristics of bipolar I, bipolar II, or cyclothymic disorder but does not fit all the requirements, your doctor might use the diagnosis "mood disorder NOS" (*DSM-IV* 296.80). For some patients, this term is a stop-gap measure that ensures they receive needed services until a final diagnosis can be figured out. Some other patients are a "diagnosis of one": they have a mood disorder, but it just refuses to obey the *DSM-IV* rules.

Other mood disorders

You may also hear about bipolar III disorder. This isn't an official *DSM-IV* diagnosis yet, but it has been proposed as a separate category by Dr. Hagop Akiskal, a major researcher who is director of the International Mood Center at the University of California in San Diego.

Dr. Akiskal defines bipolar III as "recurrent depressions without spontaneous hypomania, but often with hyperthymic temperament and/or bipolar family history."[4] Such people may have mood swings, or a stable mood of hypomania on a regular basis, but without major disruptions in their lives as a result. Like others with bipolar disorders, these patients are in danger of becoming hypomanic or even manic if they take antidepressants without a mood stabilizer.

Seasonal affective disorder (SAD) is a mood disorder that follows the seasons of the year. People with SAD tend to get depressed in the dark months of winter, and some also experience hypomania or mania in the sunnier times of year. Others may have a different pattern. As many as 85 percent of people with seasonal mood swings may actually warrant a bipolar II diagnosis. Indeed, most people with bipolar disorders are slightly more sensitive than the average person to changes in the amount of light, the weather, even their latitude on the planet. Psychiatrists have been known to joke about "the manic month of May," but it's not funny to those whose moods swing way too far up with the spring sunshine. Identifying cyclical patterns of any sort can help you design a good treatment plan.

Some researchers feel that the severest form of premenstrual syndrome (PMS), called premenstrual dysphoric disorder, is a type of cyclothymic disorder caused by inability to regulate hormonal fluctuations.

Some children with mood disorders might also fall into the "regulatory disorders" categories proposed by Dr. Stanley Greenspan, a prominent researcher into the neurological and psychiatric problems of children. Dr. Greenspan describes these children as having "differences in responsiveness to sensations, in processing sensations, and in motor planning."[5] They may be anxious and fearful, aggressive and defiant, self-absorbed, hyperactive, and/or inattentive as a result of the confusion they experience. In the study of bipolar disorders, most of the research has focused on difficulties in regulating mood. Dr. Greenspan's work has looked at difficulties in regulating other neurological systems that may in turn affect mood. It's likely that there is overlap between the regulatory disorders and bipolar disorders, particularly in children. This research may also help in the development of new treatments.

The axis system

The American Psychiatric Association uses a special diagnostic system to assess the patient in five areas of function, each of which it calls an "axis": a center line about which something (in this case, psychiatric and behavioral symptoms) revolves. Each area is considered individually, and then graphed as a separate part of the diagnosis. These are:

- Axis I. Major psychiatric disorders, such as bipolar disorder or schizophrenia

- Axis II. Personality disorders (ingrained personality traits that cause the patient difficulty in life), mental retardation, or developmental delay

- Axis III. Physical disorders that can affect thought or behavior, such as epilepsy

- Axis IV. Stresses in the patient's life, such as being the victim of child abuse

- Axis V. Level of function described on a scale of 0 (minimal function) to 100 (perfect function)

Any disorders listed on Axes I, II, and III will be taken from the *DSM-IV.*

Items listed on Axis IV come from interviews with the patient or his parents.

The "score" listed on Axis V is based on everything the doctor has learned. It is a subjective measure of how well the patient is able to handle everyday life at home and at school, and of how well the patient is able to handle stressful situations.

If the doctor isn't sure that your child has a bipolar disorder, he may put the Axis I code for a single episode of depression, mania, or hypomania on the chart, and continue to observe for future mood swings before making a diagnosis. If this is the case, the *DSM-IV* code for the episode in question may be followed by one of these modifiers:

- .x1 (mild)
- .x2 (moderate)
- .x3 (severe without psychotic features)
- .x4 (severe with psychotic features)
    - mood-congruent psychotic features
    - mood-incongruent psychotic features
- .x5 (in partial remission)
- .x6 (in full remission)
- .x0 (unspecified)

States of mind in bipolar disorders

As the definitions above suggest, the type of bipolar disorder with which a person is diagnosed is based on which states of mind he has been in—depressive, hypomanic, manic, or mixed—and how often. All four of these are extremes of mood. When they are anything other than transitory states of mind, they can cause dangerous lapses in judgment. These lapses can be serious enough to put the patient's life in danger.

The *DSM-IV* defines these states of mind fairly precisely. Real life is not always so clear cut, especially where the moods of children and adolescents are concerned. The normal moods of the young are mercurial, and so are their abnormal moods. You are more likely to see mixed moods or rapid cycling between states in children. This can be confusing for the doctor, and maddening for the patient and her parents.

Depression

Most people have experienced a depressed mood due to a sad event, such as the death of a relative or friend. Clinical depression is characterized by a depressed mood that does not go away after a week or two, or after the normal period of grieving (usually about two months, although this can depend on the situation and the mourner's cultural background). Symptoms of clinical depression include:

- Sadness that does not go away
- Crying for no reason, or for very small reasons
- Change in appetite (lack of appetite, gorging on food)
- Change in sleep pattern (insomnia, oversleeping, sleeping at unusual times)
- Irritability and agitation
- Anger
- Worrying and anxiety
- Pessimism or a "who cares?" attitude
- Lack of energy for normal activities
- Feelings of guilt and worthlessness
- Inability to concentrate or make decisions
- Loss of pleasure in usual interests
- Withdrawal from friendships and other relationships
- Aches and pains, seemingly without medical cause
- Recurring thoughts of death, suicide, or other frightening possibilities

You may be surprised to see irritability, agitation, and anger listed above. When most people say "I'm feeling depressed," they mean "I'm feeling really down in the dumps." Clinical depression can show up in other kinds of down feelings, though—and this is especially true in children. This difference between child and adult depression has caused many a misdiagnosis. The tantrum-throwing, raging child may be suffering from depression, not oppositional defiant disorder or plain old bad attitude. Like Adam, the 15-year-old in the story at the beginning of this chapter, the angry, out-of-control teenager's behavior may be coming from depression, not the hormone storms of puberty or a conduct disorder.

In fact, if there's any one characteristic of childhood depression that stands out when it is compared to typical adult depression, it's extreme irritability. Parents report that long before they realized their child was depressed, the child was extraordinarily irritable and moody. Small disappointments seemed to be major heartbreaks, and the everyday irritants at school and home no longer rolled off their backs. Parents often describe themselves as walking on eggshells when their child is in this irritable/depressed state, as the slightest frustration can set off a firestorm of anger or a torrent of tears.

To meet the *DSM-IV* criteria for an episode of clinical depression, the depressed mood must last for at least two weeks, and cannot meet the criteria for a mixed state, as described later in this chapter. The symptoms must not be due to a medical condition, drug use or abuse, or normal bereavement. The symptoms must also cause the patient significant emotional distress, or impact on how well he can carry out daily life activities. The patient must have at least five of the following symptoms, and two of them must be (1) depressed mood and (2) loss of interest or pleasure in former pursuits:

- Depressed (or irritable/depressed) mood most of the day, nearly every day, according to the patient or observers.

- Dramatically diminished interest or pleasure in all, or almost all, customary activities for most of the day, nearly every day, according to the patient or observers.

- Significant weight loss when not dieting, or weight gain of more than 5 percent of previous body weight in a month, or decrease or increase in appetite nearly every day. In children, failure to make expected weight gains.

- Insomnia or oversleeping nearly every day. (Sometimes there will be a pattern of insomnia for one or more nights, followed by oversleeping for one or more nights and/or days.)

- A visibly higher or lower level of activity, thought, and possibly speech, than usual.

- Feelings of fatigue or low energy levels nearly every day.

- Feelings of worthlessness, or excessive or inappropriate guilt feelings, nearly every day.

- A noticeably diminished ability to think, pay attention, or make decisions, nearly every day.

- Recurrent thoughts of death or suicidal ideation, with or without an actual plan for committing suicide. (In children these thoughts may be expressed as talking constantly about dead pets, dead relatives or friends, or having a general morbid preoccupation with things having to do with death and dying.)

Some people who are depressed have delusions that fit their mood—for example, they may have delusional feelings of guilt or worthlessness, or have auditory hallucinations that include voices telling them they deserve to die or similar negative messages. Delusions that don't fit with the depressed mood (such as thinking you have been sent by God to save the world) indicate that something else is going on, as do visual hallucinations.

Mania

Clinical mania occurs when manic thoughts and behavior continue over a period of time, and impair how the person functions socially, at work, or in school. The child can't complete his usual activities, and may require hospitalization. Symptoms of a manic episode can include:

- An abnormally euphoric, optimistic mood that is not a transitory state
- Exaggerated sense of self-confidence
- Decreased need for sleep
- Compulsively cleaning or doing other tasks, often into the wee hours
- Grandiosity: a delusional sense of self-importance and superiority over others
- Excessive irritability
- Aggression
- Increased level of mental and physical activity (hyperactivity)
- Pressured speech: speaking at a rapid pace, often loudly, and almost constantly ("motormouth")
- Flight of ideas: thoughts race through the mind, jumping from topic to topic
- Missing steps in logical thinking
- Extreme impulsiveness and distractibility
- Poor judgment

- Reckless, out-of-character behavior, which may include compulsive sexual behavior, gambling, substance abuse, and other risky pursuits
- Changes in style of dress, in the direction of the wild and unusual
- In some severe cases, hallucinations (auditory or visual)

You'll note that irritability is a characteristic symptom of both depression and mania. Aggression, too, can be seen in either state. In bipolar children, irritability and aggression may take the form of tantrums or rages, which can seemingly be triggered by the smallest request or mistake. Apart from suicidal behavior, aggression and rages are probably the most difficult aspects of childhood bipolar disorder for parents to handle. This is undesirable behavior, of course, but until the child has his own brakes to apply in the form of mental tools or medication, it is also out of the child's control. As the adult, you have to keep the child and others safe, and yet avoid punishing behavior that can't be easily controlled. It's a tough balancing act, and will be discussed in greater detail in Chapter 3, *Living with Bipolar Disorders*.

To meet the *DSM-IV* criteria for a manic episode, three of the following symptoms must be present for at least a week (four if the mood is mostly irritable):

- Inflated self-esteem or grandiosity
- Decreased need for sleep
- Pressured speech
- Flight of ideas
- Increased distractibility
- Increased hyperactivity or increased goal-directed activity
- Increased reckless, thrill-seeking behavior

The manic mood must be serious enough to cause the child major problems at home and at school, or to require hospitalization, or it must include psychotic features such as delusions or hallucinations. It must not meet the criteria for a mixed episode, nor should it be due to drug use, medication, or another medical condition.

Hypomania

When most adults think of a manic mood, they think of a day when they've been in a frenzy of purposeful but exhilarating activity, such as frantically furnishing a nursery the night before a new baby's anticipated arrival. Most people do have the ability to gear up for an occasional day like this, but we all know the crash effect that usually follows on its heels. This perfectly normal and useful frame of mind is very much like the mood called hypomania in people with bipolar disorders. It's a sense of heightened awareness and activity that, unfortunately, has a tendency to spin out of control to become a full-blown mania.

This ability to sustain a hypomanic state is the main reason that bipolar disorders are often associated with creative, driven personalities. A hypomanic artist may be able to focus intently on a painting or musical composition, working through the night to create a masterpiece. A hypomanic businesswoman may come up with a long list of fabulous ideas for new products. A hypomanic construction worker may pour on the juice to finish a project in record time. The burst of activity may be followed by 24 hours in bed, but as long as the finished product is appreciated, the hypomanic state is seen as a gift, not a curse.

When it's controllable, hypomania may well be a gift to those with a creative temperament and a willingness to keep their activities strictly within bounds. The problem is that it's very hard to control your behavior in a hypomanic state, and much of the activity that takes place can be reckless. Without an appropriate outlet for this excess energy, it may be translated into fast driving, hard drinking, drug-taking, sexual promiscuity, profligate spending, and a host of other risky behaviors that children in particular should avoid.

In fact, hypomanic states may be far more dangerous for children than they are for adults. Children are natural risk-takers. Think of all the foolish stunts you pulled as a child, unaware of the dangers involved. From shoplifting sweets to climbing tall trees, children are less likely to stop their own risky behavior.

Parents and other adult authority figures act as the brakes for young children, and we try to do so for risk-taking teens as well. Because we can usually stop wild, risky behavior before it goes too far, hypomania and mania in children can be hard to recognize.

> The core symptoms [of these states] should still be the same, but there
> may be developmental differences in the way they present. The kind of
> reckless behavior an adult might present with would be different than an

8-year-old would present with. Kids can still have grandiose delusions, but may not go on long spending sprees or take trips across the country because adults won't let them. Just being a kid limits what you can do as far as reckless behavior. —Dr. Jon McClellan, co-author of JAACAP's "Practice Parameters for the Assessment and Treatment of Children and Adolescents with Bipolar Disorder"

To meet the *DSM-IV* criteria for a hypomanic episode, the state must be uncharacteristic of the child's normal behavior, last for at least four days, and be obvious to outside observers such as parents or teachers. It must not be due to another medical condition, to drug use or abuse, or to some form of antidepressant treatment. It must not be so severe that the person cannot manage most normal functions or that it requires hospitalization, nor can psychotic features be present. At least three of these symptoms must be seen:

- Inflated self-esteem or grandiosity
- Decreased need for sleep
- Pressured speech
- Flight of ideas
- Difficulty paying attention
- Agitation, hyperactivity, feeling driven to pursue activities
- Involvement in reckless activities

Mixed state (mixed mania)

A mixed state has features of both mania and depression. These symptoms may occur at the same time, or the person may cycle back and forth between depression, hypomania, and mania over a period of days. Technically, the latter is called ultra-rapid cycling. The symptoms should not be caused by drug or alcohol use, medication, or another medical condition.

To meet the *DSM-IV* criteria for a mixed episode, the patient must meet the criteria listed previously for a manic episode and the criteria listed previously for a depressed episode, for almost every day of a one-week period. This disturbed mood must be serious enough that it prevents the person from carrying out normal activities or causes him to require hospitalization, or it must have psychotic features.

Mixed episodes are more common in children and adolescents than in adults. They are hard to treat, and hard for the patient (especially the very young patient) to adequately explain. In fact, it is thought that most adolescents, particularly young adolescents, first present the symptoms of a mixed state or depression, rather than simple hypomania or mania. That's one of the reasons that childhood bipolar disorders tend to be confused with ADHD, especially if the mixed state involves agitation, irritation, a high activity level, and oppositional behavior.

Rapid cycling

People who are rapid cyclers have had four or more mood swings resulting in depression, hypomania, mania, or mixed states in a twelve-month period. Children and women are more likely to be rapid cyclers. Ultra-rapid cyclers swing between moods so quickly that they may seem to be in a near-constant mixed state.

Rapid cyclers are the most difficult bipolar patients to treat. They tend to be more sensitive to some medications, and to get no benefit from others. Because their behavior and thought patterns are very unpredictable, they can also be difficult to work with in therapy sessions.

Psychosis

A person in a psychotic state is out of touch with objective reality in some way. He may be cataleptic (unresponsive) or catatonic (responding to the environment with unusual physical activity, which may be agitated or aggressive). He may experience auditory hallucinations (sounds or voices that are not there), visual hallucinations (seeing things that are not there), or sensory hallucinations (smelling, tasting, or feeling things that are not there). He may be completely swept away from reality by delusions, such as believing that he is a supernatural being, or that he is under attack by unseen forces. When most people think of insanity, it is psychosis that they think of.

It's important to note that a person can appear to be functioning normally while experiencing psychotic symptoms. In fact, patients report that they can sometimes make these symptoms go away for a little while by throwing themselves into a frenzy of cleaning or exercising, or by deliberately filling their mind with other thoughts. These stop-gap measures eventually fail, but it's important for patients to identify activities that may help shut out these scary symptoms temporarily while they seek medical attention.

Psychosis is a medical phenomenon. It can be temporarily induced in perfectly normal people by stimulating certain regions of the brain with electricity, or by administering hallucinogenic drugs like LSD. When a person has psychotic symptoms, some kind of chemical or electrical process in the brain has gone terribly wrong. This cannot be fixed by psychotherapy, although therapy may be a useful part of a total treatment plan. Therapists can help patients identify the beginning of a psychotic thought pattern or behavior, so that they can develop coping skills and know when to seek help. The therapist can also provide reassurance; as you can imagine, psychosis can be intensely frightening to the person who experiences it.

There are many medications available that can alleviate psychotic symptoms.

Bipolar children

Physicians are only now beginning to understand how bipolar disorders look when they occur during childhood and adolescence, and how they affect the lives of young patients. The *DSM-IV* criteria were designed for adults, and are based on the way adults with bipolar disorders feel and act. There are diagnostic criteria that are unique to children, but they are still not widely known. As we learn more about the developmental course of bipolar disorders in children, we may be able to develop new tools for recognizing and treating bipolar disorders earlier. Until then, diagnosis will remain a difficult and uncertain process, particularly for the youngest patients.

Early signs of bipolar disorders

Many parents of bipolar children and teenagers report that they knew the child was "different" from infancy. These babies were more difficult to care for and less predictable than others. They may not have established a regular sleep schedule, resisted weaning or the introduction of new foods, and violently disliked transitions and new situations. They may have cried more than other babies and toddlers, had more temper tantrums, and continued to tantrum into the later years of childhood.

Severe separation anxiety—clinging to a parent and refusing to be separated, even for a moment—is also reported by many parents.

These harbingers of later mood disorder are not seen in all bipolar children, of course, but they are common enough to offer clues about the roots of bipolar disorders. They add to the mounting evidence for innate, genetic causes.

Unique symptoms

Children with bipolar disorders may have different symptoms simply because they are still developing physically and emotionally. Symptoms of childhood bipolar disorders wax and wane, sometimes very rapidly. Hallmark symptoms may include disruptive behavior that gets worse, extreme moodiness and irritability, insomnia and sleep problems, angry or aggressive episodes followed by periods of remorse and guilt, declining academic performance, increasing impulsiveness and hyperactivity, decreasing ability to concentrate and pay attention, and a decreasing ability to handle frustration.[6]

Children who are later diagnosed with bipolar disorder seem to share a common temperament. They are very emotional, swinging from extreme happiness to extreme anger. They are often uninhibited and impulsive, and may have signs of a general lack of regulation in one or more body systems (for example, bedwetting or daytime accidents past the usual age). Sometimes they may seem to think and move slowly and want to sleep constantly. At other times they may stay up late, wake early and often, and bounce off the walls with endless energy. They may have episodes of delusional thinking.

In these children, strange behaviors and moods occur out of the blue. This pattern of waxing and waning, and of changing moods and behavior, is the key to diagnosis. Children with ADHD or a conduct disorder have difficult behaviors that are relatively consistent (see the sections on these conditions in Chapter 2). If they are hyperactive, they are hyper almost all the time, at home and at school, in summer and winter. Children with bipolar disorders seem to shift their behaviors and moods in unpredictable ways, becoming hyper and then withdrawn, irritable and then deliriously happy.[7]

Specific events may trigger unusual behaviors or mood swings, but the response to these events is far out of proportion or extremely prolonged.

Diagnosticians know that a family history of bipolar disorder is a strong marker for childhood bipolar disorders. Another is mania induced by taking a drug or medication, particularly if the child becomes manic from taking an antidepressant. Doctors have to be careful not to mistake delays in regulatory system development for bipolar episodes, however, and diagnosis is often a process of eliminating other possible causes.

Long-term consequences

The ongoing effects of untreated childhood bipolar disorder are many—and they can be severe. Teen suicide and self-injurious behavior are clear and obvious dangers, but the daily disruption bipolar disorders cause in a child's education and personal development can also cause long-lasting harm.

Childhood is when most of us learn to govern our emotions and behaviors. When emotions and behaviors are beyond our ability to control, even with great effort, self-righting skills may never be gained. Children with bipolar disorders may miss large chunks of their schooling, preventing them from pursuing higher education or a good job as an adult. They may have difficulty forming friendships and building good relationships with family members. Many will run afoul of the law due to impulsive, reckless, aggressive behavior. Many will experiment with drugs and alcohol in an effort to self-medicate, to fit in with peers, or simply in pursuit of bigger and better highs.

All of these effects cause children and adolescents harm when they occur, and they also affect the course of their adult lives. Reckless decisions made by a 15-year-old during a manic or depressed episode can end in incarceration, expulsion from school, serious injury, or death. Long-term cognitive problems are sometimes associated with untreated bipolar disorder, as well as with misuse of drugs while ill, and with improperly prescribed psychiatric medications. These problems can include slow thinking, difficulty in working through logic problems, and errors in comprehension and retention of information. These sorts of difficulties are especially frustrating for otherwise intelligent people.

Another difference between bipolar adolescents and bipolar adults is their level of resistance to treatment. It's fairly easy for parents to insist that young children take their medication regularly, attend school, and see their therapist. Adolescent development includes increasing independence, however. Many teenagers experiment with behaviors, belief systems, and appearance changes that are tailor-made to shock or annoy their parents—and that's normal. Unfortunately, some also begin to refuse education, medication, and therapy. This is probably a very normal thing for a developing teen to try, but the consequences can be dire. Parents have to do whatever it takes to ensure compliance.

They also need to listen to their teenagers' concerns. Medication that helped four years ago may not be so effective after puberty, or may be having new side effects. Your teenager may need a different kind of school program than the one that used to work. He might prefer to see a different psychiatrist or therapist.

Family therapy can be very useful for helping teens and parents balance issues of healthcare and independence. The ultimate goal should be ensuring that your teenager is well-informed about his diagnosis and treatment options, and capable of self-care by young adulthood. We'll talk more about this process in Chapter 9, *Transitions*.

What causes bipolar disorders?

Bipolar disorders are caused by differences in how a person's brain and nervous system regulate basic behaviors.

The human nervous system is an amazing organic machine, creating and reacting to a complex stew of chemical, electrical, and magnetic impulses. It's constantly humming away, taking in information from all of our senses and reacting to it in ways that control every bodily activity, from basic breathing and circulation on up.

A single misstep in one of these processes can set a chain of events in motion that leads to a neurological event, such as a memory lapse, a seizure, or a manic episode. If such missteps occur constantly, the person has a neurological disorder.

Circadian rhythms

The nervous systems of people with bipolar disorders frequently make specific types of regulatory errors. Many of them involve the body's internal clock, which controls the phenomena known as circadian rhythms. These are the regular rhythmic changes in waking and sleeping, waxing and waning activity levels, even sensations of hunger or thirst and their satisfaction. The chemical clock that governs these rhythms is located in a part of the hypothalamus gland called the suprachiasmatic nucleus, which (among other things) regulates the pineal gland's secretion of the hormone melatonin.

You've probably heard about melatonin supplements sold as a cure for insomnia. Indeed, this hormone is the body's own shut-down mechanism, and production of it usually kicks in as dusk begins. The suprachiasmatic nucleus sets itself based on the past several days' pattern of light and dark, slowly adjusting itself in pace with the seasons. It does seem important for people to be exposed to at least some strong, direct light (sunlight or artificial) around mid-day, and for the overall patterns of dark and light to change slowly and naturally. People with bipolar disorders appear to have more difficulty in regulating this system. It's a chicken-and-egg situation: the rhythms are disordered, so sleep, waking, and other patterns are disturbed. As insomnia, oversleeping, changes in eating habits, and higher or lower activity levels set in, the clock gets harder to reset, and person becomes more and more ill.[8]

The production of the neurotransmitter serotonin is also affected by a reduced amount of light in the environment. Neurotransmitters are hormone-like chemicals that send signals to all parts of the nervous system. Serotonin affects mood, appetite, and much more. In people with bipolar disorders, serotonin and other neurotransmitters may be created in the wrong amounts, absorbed by the wrong parts of the brain or other sites, or refused admittance at sites that should accept them.

With each regulatory error, the person's symptoms become more noticeable, and more serious. It's like a snowball rolling downhill: eventually the circadian rhythms and other regulatory systems are completely off track, resulting in extreme mood swings, and bringing on depression, mania, or other abnormal states of mind. The affected person may start to have noticeable errors in thinking. He may even hear sounds or voices that aren't there, feel that he's being watched, or think that he is a special person with a great mission to accomplish.

The nervous system's disordered condition will eventually show up outwardly as well. Movements may become rapid or very slow, jerky or superprecise. The tone and pace of speech may change. For example, speedy, disjointed speech is associated with mania.

What is it about people with bipolar disorders that permits this devastating chain reaction to occur? As of this writing, no one can point to a specific gene or brain difference with certainty, but bipolar disorders are probably caused by a complicated mix of inherited genetic differences, differences in brain structure and chemistry, unusual electrical or magnetic activity in the brain, and environmental factors.

Genetic differences

There is currently no doubt that bipolar disorders run in families. Several studies have made the genetic links clear, even though the exact mechanism isn't understood.[9] As with other psychiatric disorders known to have genetic underpinnings, the inheritance pattern of bipolar disorders probably involves a complex interaction of several different genes.

> *My husband was the only one who was skipped on the paternal side from getting bipolar disorder. He has seen his sister and many uncles, etc., die as a result of this illness, and his dad is still alive with it. —Lynn, mother of 11-year-old Michael (diagnosed BPI, mixed states with psychosis)*

Clues are emerging. One of the most interesting is the link between bipolar disorder and velo-cardio-facial syndrome (VCFS), as reported by a team headed by psychiatric researcher Dr. Demetri Papolos. VCFS is a fairly common set of physical abnormalities that includes a characteristically long face with a large nose, small ears with a folded portion, narrow "squinty" eyes, and a relatively expressionless mouth. People with VCFS have very nasal vocal tone, may be born with a cleft palate, have heart problems, and have learning disabilities. A deletion on chromosome 22 causes VCFS.[10]

Other researchers have proposed possible chromosomal differences on chromosomes 5, 12, 18, 21, and the X chromosome in people with bipolar disorders.

Brain differences

A deletion on chromosome 22 is probably at least part of the problem, likely leading to structural differences in the developing brain. There may also be differences in how the eyes (which are a sense organ tightly bound to the brain) absorb light.

The brain is the most complex and least understood organ in the body. It is the focal point of the central nervous system, which also includes the nerves of the spine. The central nervous system receives, processes, and sends billions of signals every day by way of chemicals and electrical impulses. Scientists are only starting to identify how these chemicals and power surges work, and what we know right now is woefully inadequate for helping when these processes go awry.

The brain is mostly made up of two kinds of cells. The first kind, neurons, do the hard work of transmitting all that information. The second kind, glial cells, are twice as numerous as neurons. Glial cells have the less glamorous jobs of making sure the neurons have enough nutrients and other chemicals, repairing the brain if it is injured, and confronting bacteria that try to attack the brain.

These cells combine to form a vastly intricate architecture. The brain is made up of several complex parts, all of which work together to control body functions, produce thought and emotion, and store and retrieve memories. Researchers are not absolutely sure which parts of the central nervous system are affected by bipolar disorders, although a clearer picture is emerging every year thanks to brain-imaging technologies. These include computer tomography (CAT), magnetic resonance imagery (MRI), and single photon emission computed tomography (SPECT or neuroSPECT) scans.

Although they can't be used to diagnose bipolar disorders just yet, brain scans can show where abnormal activity is occurring, or whether the brain is structured differently than usual. The Bipolar Disorders Clinic at Stanford University has been at the forefront of brain imaging research, and its preliminary findings implicate differences in the prefrontal and anterior paralimbic areas of the brain, including the almond-shaped portion called the amygdala.[11]

Prefrontal areas have also been found to be different in patients with ADHD. Other specific differences found in ADHD via MRI scans are significant loss of normal right/left asymmetry in the caudate nucleus, smaller right globus, smaller right anterior frontal region, smaller cerebellum, and reversal of normal lateral ventricular asymmetry, among others.[12]

The amygdala is one of several small structures deep within the brain that are called the basal ganglia. These structures are involved with governing automatic movements and behaviors, and are connected to the hypothalamus gland by nerve fibers. The basal ganglia are part of the brain's inhibitory system, and when they're not working properly, compulsive movements (tics), compulsive or obsessive thoughts and behaviors, and disinhibition can occur. There is a higher prevalence of bipolar disorder among people diagnosed with Tourette syndrome, a neurological disorder known to involve differences in the basal ganglia.[13]

More bipolar-specific findings from brain scans include an enlarged caudate nucleus, and white matter hyperintensities ("white spots" of unknown origin that show up on the scans).[14] Imaging studies are not in total agreement, and the number of studies done is still fairly small. No one is sure what these brain differences really mean, nor are they leading medicine in new diagnostic or treatment directions as yet.

Neurotransmitters: The brain's telephone system

Neurons are the brain's internal communication centers, but they don't trade messages directly. Neurons have a central cell body with long "arms" called axons, and smaller tentacle-like structures called dendrites (see Figure 1-1). Inside a neuron, all the messages are sent via electrical impulses. Where two neurons meet to swap information, however, there's a small space between them called the synaptic cleft. Electrical impulses have to be translated into neurotransmitters like those mentioned earlier in this chapter, chemicals that cross the synaptic cleft and are then retranslated into electrical signals on the other side (see Figure 1-2).

There are many different neurotransmitters and related hormones running around in the human brain, the central nervous system, and the gastrointestinal system. They're all site-specific chemicals that can be absorbed only by certain cells, and only at certain spots. This ensures that the right kinds of messages get through. They are also used and absorbed differently in various areas of the body, and sometimes turned into other kinds of chemicals.

Along with the hormone melatonin, several neurotransmitters appear to be involved in bipolar disorders, including:

- Serotonin. Also called 5-hydroxytryptamine or 5-HT, Serotonin controls sleep, mood, some types of sensory perception, body-temperature regulation, and appetite. It affects the rate at which hormones are released, and has something to do with inflammation.

- Dopamine. Sometimes abbreviated as DA, this neurotransmitter helps control body movements and thought patterns, and also regulates how hormones are released.

- Norepinephrine. Used by both the central nervous system and the peripheral sympathetic nervous system (the nerves that communicate with the rest of the body), it governs arousal, the "fight or flight" response, anxiety, and memory.

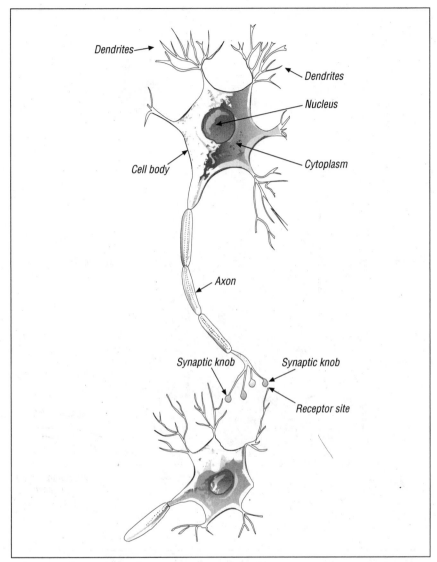

Figure 1-1. The structure of a neuron

Medications that change how much of certain hormones and neurotransmitters are produced, or how these chemicals are absorbed in the brain, produce changes in symptoms—that's one of the clues that have let researchers know which chemicals have something to do with various health conditions. These medicines don't cure the underlying disorder, but in some people they can create major improvements in behavior and emotional stability. It's a bit like taking the hormone insulin for diabetes: you're still a diabetic,

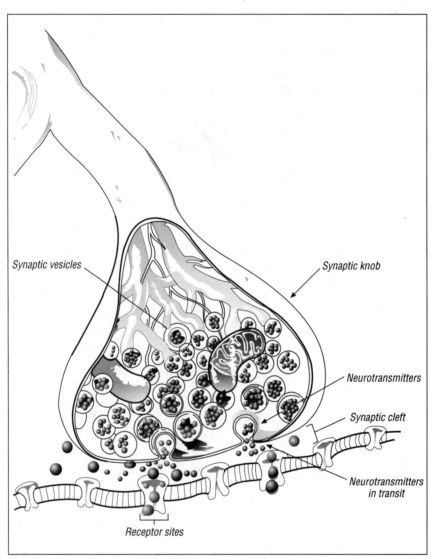

Figure 1-2. *Neurotransmitters crossing the synaptic cleft*

Labels on figure:
Synaptic vesicles
Synaptic knob
Neurotransmitters
Synaptic cleft
Neurotransmitters in transit
Receptor sites

and you still must watch your diet, but the insulin injections help you control the illness and prevent its most debilitating effects. See Chapter 4, *Medical Interventions,* for more information about these medications and how they work.

Physical activity, exercise, diet, vitamins, and herbal supplements can also affect these neurotransmitters. That's one of the reasons parents and professionals should be as careful about choosing alternative treatments as they would be about prescription drugs. For more information about nonpharmaceutical treatments for bipolar disorders, see Chapter 6, *Other Interventions*.

There is even some evidence that positive or negative life experiences, including talk therapy and behavior modification, can help make actual neurological change over a period of time. Therapy is definitely very helpful for learning to handle the negative aspects that can occur with these disorders, from embarrassing public behavior to difficulties in personal relationships. A good relationship with a therapist is often the key to ensuring that patients keep on their medication and maintain a healthy lifestyle. For more about therapy and related concepts, see Chapter 5, *Therapeutic Interventions*.

Electrical miswiring

The brain's electrical system is intimately intertwined with its chemical messaging system. Problems can occur during the electrical side of the communication process when uncontrolled surges of electricity, called seizures, take place inside the brain. Seizure disorders (epilepsy) are somewhat more common in people with bipolar disorders. That's a clue that abnormal electrical activity may sometimes be involved in causing mood swings, or may happen as a result of mood swings.

Some types of seizures are hard to recognize, even with sophisticated equipment. For example, some doctors believe that the inexplicable temper tantrums and rages characteristic of children and some adults with bipolar disorders may be related to seizures occurring deep within the brain. Others suspect that an increase in a phenomenon called kindling—sort of an electrical "blip" in brain activity that can be caused by environmental triggers—may be at fault. In people with epilepsy, the kindling process leads to a seizure, while in those with migraine, kindling precedes a migraine headache or other symptom. Perhaps in some people with bipolar disorders, the result of kindling is behavioral or psychiatric disturbances. No one really knows just yet.

If epileptic seizures are suspected, neurologists usually rely on evidence gathered via an electroencephalogram (EEG). Unfortunately, EEG equipment is not sensitive enough to detect all types of seizures in all parts of the brain. Chapter 4 presents more information about the connection between bipolar disorders and epilepsy, and about how seizure disorders can be diagnosed and treated.

Immune-system impairment

It's not a totally mainstream idea, but some scientists theorize that bipolar disorders may include an immune system problem. There's a certain amount of good sense to this idea, since the immune system is tightly bound to the endocrine (hormonal) system. In addition, people with known immune disorders, such as lupus, often experience mood swings.

Interestingly, lithium, the most popular medication for bipolar disorders, also seems to have some antiviral effects. There hasn't been enough research done on this angle yet, but for at least some patients, immune-system problems could be a cause or a side effect of manic-depressive illness. Chapter 6 will take a look at the latest information in this area of inquiry.

Dual and multiple diagnoses

When psychiatrists say the words "dual diagnosis," they are almost always referring to a person who has a mental illness and a substance abuse problem. Drug and alcohol abuse are far more common among people with bipolar disorder than any other Axis I psychiatric disorder—and the lifetime prevalence is an astonishing 60 percent or more among those who have childhood- or adolescent-onset bipolar disorders. Drug and alcohol use also usually starts during the teenage years, sometimes even earlier.

Choice of drug may even be a diagnostic clue: up to 30 percent of cocaine addicts fit the criteria for bipolar disorder, as do a sizable portion of alcoholics and amphetamine users. It is not yet known whether these individuals abuse drugs as a result of their bipolar illness, or have bipolar-like symptoms as a result of their drug use. There is some pretty compelling evidence that the former, rather than the latter, is usually the case.

Substance abuse can complicate diagnosis and treatment. In the past, the conventional wisdom was that the alcoholic or drug addict had to be clean and sober before psychiatric treatment could succeed, but current clinical experience indicates that it's essential to treat the underlying bipolar disorder along with the substance abuse problem. In fact, mood stabilization may be a very necessary part of substance-abuse treatment for this population. Medication and therapy can greatly reduce the relapse rate. [15]

Many people with bipolar disorder have other psychiatric or medical problems to contend with, a fact that can complicate their treatment and even contribute to mood swings. Several neurological and physical problems occur more often in people with bipolar disorder than in the general population. The list includes migraines, seizure disorders, ADHD, developmental delays, obsessive-compulsive disorder (OCD), Tourette syndrome, anxiety disorders, autism and other pervasive developmental disorders, autoimmune disorders, and gastrointestinal disorders. Many of these conditions have symptoms that can be mistaken for those of bipolar disorder (see the "Differential diagnosis" section in Chapter 2 for more information).

Other factors in bipolar disorders

Gender can influence medical diagnosis more than one might expect. Women are diagnosed more often with depressive disorders in general, although childhood bipolar diagnoses are balanced fairly evenly between males and females. There is some evidence that childhood bipolar disorder is diagnosed more commonly among males.[16] Other studies have found more diagnoses of adolescent bipolar disorder among females.[17]

It seems likely that women and girls are sometimes misdiagnosed as bipolar due to problems that are actually caused by hormonal cycles—although men, too, can have hormonal disorders that cause mood swings. Culture has an impact as well: the bias and stress experienced by women and girls in a sexist culture can produce emotional problems, and normal behavior for a particular girl or woman can be "pathologized" when seen through certain cultural lenses. A female with a tempestuous, artistic, assertive, even aggressive temperament might be called mentally ill in a culture that does not value these attributes in females. Girls and women may also seek medical help more often than males with similar symptoms.

Bipolar women do seem to be more prone to rapid cycling than male patients, and to have more depressed and mixed moods. Hormonal activity definitely plays a role in how and when bipolar illness expresses itself, particularly right after pregnancy.[18]

Males can also be affected by gender bias. A man or boy with undiagnosed bipolar disorder may come to the attention of the criminal justice system before he sees a mental health professional. He may find himself with a police record rather than a treatment plan, simply because moody, unpredictable, aggressive behavior in males is generally seen as a personal problem, not a medical one. Statistically, males with bipolar disorder are more likely to get involved in potentially criminal, aggressive, assaultive, or risky behavior than females. This may be because males often have greater access to tools that make such behavior more dangerous, such as weapons and fast cars. There may also be more cultural acceptance of aggressive, risky, and even assaultive behavior among males, leading to missed diagnosis, and missed opportunities for intervention. Even though females are more likely to attempt suicide, males are more likely to actually kill themselves.

Other cultural issues, including race, religion, economic status, and nationality, can have an impact on diagnosis as well. Psychiatric professionals, school officials, and families all carry some cultural baggage, ranging from assumptions about what is proper behavior to stereotypes about the behavior of other cultural or racial groups. These ideas can play a role in who gets diagnosed, how they are treated, and what resources are made available.

Although bipolar disorders run in families, there is no evidence that any ethnic group is immune, nor is there evidence that members of any particular group have a far higher chance of developing bipolar disorder. Characteristics that often accompany these disorders, such as the ability to hyperfocus, enhanced creativity, and (within bounds) aggressiveness, are so valuable that despite the disorder's down side, individuals with bipolar disorders have been desirable as mates, and so are found in every community.

And as parents and professionals dealing with childhood bipolar disorders, it's those good characteristics that we must keep in mind. It's not right to think of everything about bipolar disorders as bad, nor should we try to turn youth with these challenges into carbon copies of their peers. Along with their illness they have often received special gifts, and these gifts can actually help them overcome their difficulties. Whether it's a creative streak, an ability to produce massive amounts of work in short bursts, or simply the wacky sense of humor and gift of gab that characterize many people with bipolar disorder, we need to recognize and build upon what's special and wonderful in these individuals. Then they can not only achieve mental health, but reach their full creative potential as individuals.

CHAPTER 2

Getting a Diagnosis

D<small>IAGNOSING BIPOLAR DISORDERS</small> is not an exact science. They can be obscured by or mistaken for other disorders of the mind or body. There's no blood test, brain imaging machine, or written exam that can provide certainty. Careful observation of the patient's mood, demeanor (affect), and behavior is the key.

In this chapter, we talk about how to find an expert in child and adolescent bipolar disorders, and how a diagnosis is made. Topics include the diagnostic process, and other medical conditions that can mimic the symptoms of bipolar disorders.

Where to begin

Most parents begin their search for help with their child's pediatrician. That's a good place to start, but while most pediatricians are experts in strep throat, stomachaches, and other typical childhood medical problems, they receive very little training in neurology or psychiatry. In fact, a study by Elizabeth Costello, PhD, associate professor of child and adolescent psychiatry at Duke University, found that a large HMO's pediatricians were able to identify only 17 percent of the children who presented with psychiatric disorders. That 17 percent tended to be children with the most common problems, including bedwetting and learning disabilities.[1]

> *My son was first diagnosed at the age of 15. He was hospitalized because he was so unstable and out of control. This is when they diagnosed him with bipolar disorder. His first doctor was not too sure about the bipolar diagnosis because he did not have the typical symptoms.*
> —*Cindy, mother of 16-year-old Craig (diagnosed bipolar disorder)*

Diagnosing bipolar disorders in children and teens can be especially difficult. You need to see not just any psychiatrist or psychologist, but one who is knowledgeable about the latest research in this area. To have a chance of seeing someone who fits this description, you will probably have to personally identify one or more such doctors in your area in advance. You might begin your search for an expert by calling a support or advocacy group, like the National Alliance for the Mentally Ill (NAMI). Several are listed in the appendix, *Resources*.

Internet discussion groups like BPparent, BPSO, and Riders can also be a good source of tips and advice about doctors in your area. We'll talk more about the value of support groups, both traditional and online, in Chapter 3, *Living with Bipolar Disorders*, but the best time to make first contact with these is when you are still in search of a diagnosis and help. You can avoid dead ends, unqualified doctors, and much heartache by tapping into these resources right away. Even if it turns out that your child's problems are due to another condition, you'll be glad to have found out so quickly.

A third source for referrals is the psychiatry or neurology department of a nearby medical school. Many medical schools have excellent clinics staffed by both experienced doctors and residents who are learning the ropes. Some of the foremost experts in child and adolescent bipolar disorders are affiliated with university programs. These doctors are often (but not always!) aware of the latest research findings and treatments. Several university-affiliated programs with special expertise in bipolar disorders are listed in the appendix.

Your very best bet is a board-certified child psychiatrist who has a working relationship with a good hospital, preferably one affiliated with a university medical school. "Board-certified" means that the doctor has completed a very rigorous training program, has already practiced child psychiatry for some years, and meets the most rigorous qualifications in the field as set by an official board of his peers. Of course, the best doctors are also the busiest and the hardest to get an appointment with. Make sure you have a second-best choice in the wings, just in case.

Once you have identified your experts, call them to make sure they are currently taking new patients. Ask specifically if they see bipolar patients who are your child's age. You may also want to ask if they have worked with your health plan or HMO before. Insurance regulations, or the rules of your national health plan, usually govern just how you go about accessing a specialist. We'll discuss problems that frequently occur and provide ideas for dealing with them in Chapter 7, *Insurance*.

Consultation appointment

Now that you know who your child should eventually see, you have to go back to square one. Usually you must put the diagnostic process in motion by requesting a consultation appointment with your child's pediatrician or general practitioner (GP). This kind of appointment is a little different from the typical "height check, weight check, immunization booster, your throat looks fine" visit. In fact, it may take place in a meeting room or office rather than in an examination room. It should also be longer in length: a half-hour at least, preferably an hour.

Accurate, detailed records are the most important thing parents can contribute at this appointment. These should include the usual "baby book" milestones (first step, first word, etc.) as well as notes about anything unusual that parents have observed. Areas the pediatrician is likely to ask about include patient and family medical history, the child's relationships with family members and peers, and the child's play patterns and interests.

Your doctor will want to know a lot of details about your family's mental health history. Take the time to ask older relatives what they know. Often people with bipolar disorder were never officially diagnosed, but will be described by those who remember them as moody, depressed, hyper, wild, bad-tempered, alcoholic, married and divorced multiple times, or difficult. You may get some surprises at this stage of the game, such as tales of a grandparent's secret trips to the hospital or sanitarium. On the other hand, some people are very reluctant to tell the truth about mental illness in the family. You may even need to sleuth through medical records or diaries in the attic, check public records to see if family members have been institutionalized or imprisoned for behavior that could have been due to a bipolar disorder, or question doctors who may have known older family members. Physicians are duty-bound not to give you personal information about living persons, but they can generally be more forthcoming about patients who are deceased. Once you have this family history in hand, you might want to put it in very simple "family tree" form for your physician.

Keeping a daily diary is also an excellent way to prepare for the consultation appointment. Many families have learned a great deal during this process. Use your diary to record activities, diet, and behaviors each day for a period of two weeks or more, with the time and duration of activities and behaviors noted. Not only can this diary provide a very complete picture of the child to a professional, it can also help to identify patterns. Some families have identified food allergies this way, or gotten data they needed to create the most beneficial daily routine for their child. If you can, use a calendar, personal diaries, medical notes, and your own recollections to create a rough chart of your child's major mood swings over the past year or so. That can help a doctor find out if there is a seasonal pattern to the patient's mood swings, or if there are other identifiable triggers, such as holidays, times of particular stress, or use of medication for another condition.

If your child has seen other doctors, you must sign releases to have her medical records transferred to the pediatrician before the consultation appointment, and to the expert later on. School records that would be helpful can also be transferred if a signed release is on file. Transfers always seem to take longer than you would expect, so get releases taken care of early, and make sure the records were actually sent and received. Alternatively, if you have your own copies of these records (and you should), you may photocopy and deliver them yourself.

Parents should also summarize their concerns in writing. The records already mentioned can help you gather your thoughts. You don't have to be an eloquent writer to express what worries you. You can jot down a simple numbered list rather than writing whole paragraphs if you prefer. It may help to compare your child to his or her siblings, or to other children in the day-care center or school. Be sure to include specific information about episodes of suspected depression, hypomania, mania, and mixed moods, including the symptoms you have seen, and the timing and length of these episodes. Also list any behaviors, such as suicide threats or attempts, aggressive behaviors, self-mutilation, sudden onset of school phobia or other fears, anxiety or panic attacks, and possible substance abuse that you want to make sure the pediatrician knows about. Some parents send their summary of concerns to the doctor in advance; others prefer to use it as an agenda for discussion during the consultation.

You might also want to talk to a nurse or physician's assistant who works closely with the pediatrician. In large medical practices and HMOs, nurses and assistants are an important part of the organization. They can be allies for parents who need referrals to specialists, or even just a listening ear. If you are lucky enough to find a knowledgeable and sympathetic nurse, her input can help greatly, even if it's just comments she makes during office chit-chat with the doctor.

If possible, your information and your child's complete medical file should be available to the pediatrician at least a week before the consultation appointment. These should be accompanied by a request that she read the material in advance, and review the patient's file before the meeting. You want to ensure that your child's case is fresh in your doctor's mind at the consultation appointment.

When you arrive for the consultation, bring any additional records you have gathered, copies of your earlier letter (just in case it never reached the doctor), your summary of concerns, and any questions you want to ask. It's a good idea to bring a small notebook or tape recorder as well, so you can keep a record of the discussion. If your child tends to be difficult to manage, bring a bag of toys or books that are likely to help keep him occupied.

Diagnostic tools

Medical practitioners use a variety of tools to make diagnosis easier. These include the *DSM-IV* or *ICD-10* criteria (see Chapter 1), structured interviews where the patient or parent answers a list of questions, less-structured discussions in therapy sessions, direct observation of the patient in a medical setting, direct observation of the patient in a more natural setting (such as at home or at school), and standardized questionnaires for the doctor, the patient, or the patient's family to fill out. Sometimes a doctor or psychiatrist will also order certain medical tests to rule out health conditions that affect mood.

It's important to use more than one kind of diagnostic tool, and especially so with children. That's because a bipolar child's behavior may not fit the *DSM-IV* or *ICD-10* criteria as precisely as that of a bipolar adult. Children are less able to put their feelings into words than adults, and they're more likely to agree with statements made by adults, regardless of how they actually feel. They may not be able to come forward with information about medical symptoms that could lead in a different diagnostic direction. Children may also be uncooperative due to shyness, fear, or the unfamiliarity of the diagnostic process. Some behavior that would be considered highly unusual in an adult is normal for a child, and vice versa.

That's why parents, who have been their child's closest observers, are so essential for helping professionals find a correct diagnosis. They can provide information about the child's development, normal behavior and departures from it, normal and unusual moods, and medical problems.

If the consultation seems to be getting off to an awkward start, start with your summary of concerns or list of questions. Always keep your goal in mind: referral to one of the experts you have already identified. You're there to make a case for this referral, and your observations are the evidence you'll need to convince the pediatrician. Think of yourself as a salesperson trying to convince a customer. You want to be the one in charge of this meeting, and keeping that image in your mind can help.

Referral roadblocks

Most pediatricians will simply listen, discuss the issues you raise, and recommend the next course of action. Some will use a set of standard questions about behavior and development to screen your child. Checklists and guidelines are great, but there's really no substitute for knowledge and experience. As parents interviewed for this book make clear, some pediatricians are reluctant to even consider the possibility of bipolar disorder in a child or teenager. You may hear phrases like "your child just needs to be disciplined more strictly," "he'll grow out of it," or "let's wait and see." There are several responses you can make:

- Go back over your evidence, explaining how her difficult behaviors and mood swings are affecting her at school, at home, and in the community. If you feel comfortable doing so, you may also want to mention how it is affecting your family life. If you believe that your child's life or your family's safety are in danger, make this fact very clear.

- Let the doctor know what interventions you've already tried, such as parenting classes, disciplinary measures, treatment for ADHD or other disorders, counseling, or school changes.

- Emphasize any special factors that you feel support the possibility that your child could have bipolar disorder. These include knowledge that other people in your family have been diagnosed as bipolar; presence in your family of other disorders with strong links to bipolar disorder, such as migraine, ADHD, or epilepsy; and suggestions by a previous doctor or other professional (teacher, social worker, etc.) that the child should be evaluated for bipolar disorder.

- Ask the doctor to put his refusal to refer in writing. This may not be something he'd like to commit to paper, so you might end up getting the referral after all.

- If the doctor does put his refusal in writing, you can choose to call your diagnostic facility of choice and set up an appointment directly. Be prepared to pay for this visit out-of-pocket. However, if the specialist confirms your suspicions, you should be able to bill your insurance company for reimbursement due to refusal of an appropriate referral.

- If the pediatrician won't refer but won't put his refusal in writing either, you can still "self-refer," but it will be harder to get reimbursed. You should send a letter to the pediatrician explaining why you have made this choice over his objections. Send a copy to your insurance company as well. This creates a paper record, allowing you to pursue a claim for improper refusal later on, if warranted.

- Go up the chain of command, if your doctor is in a managed care organization or HMO. These medical groups have boards that consider patient complaints. You can petition the board to approve your referral even if the pediatrician refuses. Usually this is done in writing, not in person.

In the US, most doctors share the risks and expenses of caring for special-needs patients, including specialist referrals, with business partners or an HMO group. Doctors who make too many referrals can face financial penalties, even if the extra services were absolutely necessary. Physicians may also feel constrained by directives from insurance companies, which want to minimize expenses.

Low-income Americans who are uninsured face the biggest barrier of all: lack of access to healthcare. Your county health or mental health department should be your first stop. Your school district may also provide some diagnostic and therapeutic assistance in areas related to classroom behavior and performance. There are special medical programs and facilities available for low-income families and for children with handicapping conditions, although they often have long waiting lists. Chapter 7 provides many ideas for getting diagnostic help and ongoing care if your child is not covered by private insurance.

In Canada and Europe, where the single-payer system of nationalized health-care predominates, doctors have a different set of constraints on their ability to make referrals. Resources are focused on providing basic healthcare to everyone, so specialists are rarer and harder to access than in the US. Parents who want prompt care for their children may be forced to pay out-of-pocket to doctors who practice outside the national healthcare scheme. The expenses can be considerable. Some families have been able to gain more timely access with help from a sympathetic social worker or health visitor, or have called on advocacy groups for assistance.

In countries where neither private insurance nor the single-payer model predominates, parents should seek out—and pay for—a specialist directly, without going through a preliminary consultation appointment. Reduced-fee or free help may be available through state-run hospitals and clinics, medical facilities owned by religious orders or charities, or individual physicians who are willing to take a case at a lower cost than usual.

Seeing a specialist

Technically, psychologists, neuropsychologists (psychologists with special training in neurological disorders), and psychiatrists are the appropriate professionals for diagnosing bipolar disorders. You may end up seeing a neurologist instead, especially if the diagnosis is complicated by another neurological problem, such as epilepsy.

In areas with limited medical resources, you may be able to see only a therapist, social worker, or counselor. These professionals are not legally qualified to diagnose bipolar disorders, but there are some who have ample experience in this area, and can at least help you get started. They may be able to consult with a medical doctor at a distance, or arrange for a visit to the closest qualified physician for the final diagnosis.

In some health plans, a therapist or counselor acts as a gatekeeper; you must see this person before you are allowed to see a psychiatrist. Therapists, counselors, and social workers can administer many of the standardized tests used in the diagnostic process, observe the patient and take notes, and talk to patients and families about the child's family, medical, social, and educational history. A good therapist, counselor, or social worker can be a very important part of the diagnostic team by handling the paperwork and finding out what needs the patient and his family have.

While therapists, counselors, and social workers can offer suggestions to the psychiatrist, psychologist, or neurologist, they should not give the child a diagnosis themselves. They also cannot prescribe medication—and neither can a psychologist. In practice, however, these professionals often know quite a lot about medication, and can work productively with a psychiatrist, neurologist, or other medical doctor. After the diagnosis has been made, they can provide more information, offer therapy sessions, help families locate resources in the community, and be a listening ear when needed.

When you finally see a psychiatrist, psychologist, or neurologist, your visit is unlikely to resemble the stereotypical trip to the shrink as seen in a Woody Allen film. Neurologists usually work in a medical office, complete with examining table. Psychiatrists and psychologists who work with children usually have an office with a desk, comfortable chairs and perhaps a sofa, and toys. They'll probably want to talk to the parents first, with or without the child present, then spend some time with the child alone, and finally with both parents and child. They may administer standardized tests, or you may simply chat together about your concerns.

Pay attention to your feelings in this meeting. Sometimes a particular doctor is not a good fit for your child or your family. Just as some people respond best to the fatherly Marcus Welby-style family doctor, others prefer a no-nonsense clinical manner, and still others do best in a collaborative relationship with their physician.

> We saw about three doctors and two therapists before we finally found someone who clicked with our daughter, and with us. Dr. B-- listened to all of us, and made it clear to our daughter that her health, safety, and happiness was the primary concern. That made her feel much more comfortable. Some of the other people we had seen seemed bent on turning her into a perfect, conformist teenager, and focused on minor things like her hair or clothes when we were worried about far greater problems. Dr. B-- was willing to hear her out about some health worries she had, and as it turned out, these were very important to helping her recover. Because this doctor gained her trust, our daughter was willing to tell her about symptoms she had not revealed to the others. She was also more willing to listen to the doctor about taking medication.

Regardless of her personal style, a psychiatrist or psychologist should always be a good listener. She should be willing to answer questions, whether it's the patient or the parents who ask. Sometimes it's comforting when a professional takes charge of everything right away, but in reality you must have the ability to communicate freely and without fear of having your queries brushed aside. The psychiatrist or psychologist may see your child only once, she may see your child on a monthly basis for medication management, or in a few cases she may see your child for weekly or more frequent therapy sessions. You, however, will see your child every day of the year, in all sorts of situations. A smart doctor knows that your observations and input will be essential at every stage of your child's treatment.

It may take awhile for the doctor to make a diagnosis. This can be frustrating, but it's much better than having a doctor who jumps to conclusions! If your child or family is in danger, of course, you shouldn't be forced to wait for months while the doctor decides. It's possible to treat dangerous symptoms, such as suicidal or assaultive behavior, without knowing the psychiatric diagnosis for certain. Day treatment or hospitalization are also options that can keep everyone safe while the diagnostic process drags on.

Tests for bipolar disorders

As noted earlier in this chapter, the most important tools for diagnosing bipolar disorders are direct observation, personal interviews, and your family history. Many evaluators will also use some standardized questionnaires to find out about and assess symptoms. You may hear these referred to as "tests" for bipolar disorders, but please understand that they're really just questionnaires. You can't accurately diagnose someone with a mental illness because of answers they gave on a piece of paper. They're helpful for screening new patients, and sometimes the questions asked will help a patient bring forward new information about symptoms they haven't talked about before, but they're not a sure thing.

Psychologists and psychiatrists working for school districts seem to be especially fond of tests, probably because academics use them to assess students in most other areas. Many evaluators will take a holistic approach, using tests for learning disabilities, sensory problems, functional differences in the nervous system, and other factors.

Some tests are screening instruments: simple lists of questions for the patient or the patient's parent that can identify red flags for mental or neurological disorders in general. Others are targeted more precisely, such as the Attention Deficit Disorders Evaluation Scale. The information you gain from tests, if properly administered, can be truly invaluable for designing school and treatment programs.

Tools for gauging emotional disturbance that ask patients to draw pictures or interpret the pictures or words of others are highly subjective. These so-called projective tests are routinely administered nonetheless, especially in school settings. This includes the well-known Rorschach blot interpretation test, the House-Tree-Person test, and many variations on the same theme. Pediatricians certainly don't have the expertise to interpret these, and many therapists and counselors interpret them right out of dated textbooks. Although these assessments sometimes give an evaluator a better feel for a child's problems than the child's answers to questions, using them well requires a level of intuition that not all possess. In other words, you are far more likely to get useful, reliable information from interviews, direct observation, and objective diagnostic tools.

Psychiatric and neurological assessments

There are many tools that can help doctors uncover and measure the severity of behavioral, psychiatric, and neurological symptoms. Some that you may encounter include:

Achenbach Child Behavior Checklist (CBC)
> The CBC is available in versions for girls and boys of various ages. Six different inventories are used, including a parent report, teacher report, youth report (if practical), and structured direct observation report. It looks at the child's behaviors in several areas, including withdrawal, anxiety, etc. The results are classified as clinically significant or normal.

Attention Deficit Disorders Evaluation Scale
> Versions of this questionnaire about behaviors linked with ADD/ADHD are available for parents to fill out at home or in a clinical setting, as well as for direct use with older children and adults. Scores are expressed as a scale.

Behavior Assessment System for Children (BASC)
> This set of tests includes a teacher rating scale, parent rating scale, and self-report of personality. The BASC attempts to measure both problem and adaptive behaviors, as well as behaviors linked to ADD/ADHD. Scores are expressed as a scale keyed to a norm.

Connors Rating Scales (CRS)
> Parent and teacher versions of this scale-based test are available. It is intended to uncover behaviors linked to ADD/ADHD (Connors ADHD/

DSM-IV Scales, also known as CADS), conduct disorders, learning disabilities, psychosomatic complaints, and anxiety, among other conditions. Scores are plotted graphically.

Draw-a-Person

This is a projective psychological screening procedure in which the child is asked to draw three human figures: a man, a woman, and himself. The drawing is then rated on a scale, with differences in ratings according to gender and age. Ratings are subjective interpretations, not objective measures.

Halstead-Reitan Neuropsychological Test Battery for Children (HNTBC)

This may be the most widely used neuropsychological test for signs of brain damage. It is comprised of about a dozen tests covering things like grip strength, the ability to match pictures, and the ability to follow a rhythmic pattern. Results are usually expressed as a scale (the Halstead Impairment Index). Additional information about right-left dominance or performance patterns may also be derived.

House-Tree-Person Projective Drawing Technique

In this projective test, the child is asked to draw a house, a tree, and a person, and then is asked a series of questions about these drawings. Sometimes these drawings are separate, sometimes they are done on a single page. Ratings are subjective interpretations, not objective measures.

Kiddie-SADS-Present and Lifetime Version (K-SADS-PL)

This test is designed to obtain severity ratings of symptoms, and to assess current and lifetime history of psychiatric disorders in children and adolescents. It includes a questionnaire and a structured interview. There are supplemental tests for various types of disorders, including ADHD and affective disorders. Results are scaled.

Kinetic Family Drawing System for Family and School

In this projective test, the child draws her family doing something, or her class doing something. Then the child is asked questions about what's going on in the drawing. Ratings are subjective interpretations, not objective measures.

Luria-Nebraska Neuropsychological Battery, Children's Revision (LNNB-CR)

The LNNB-CR contains 11 scales with a total of 149 test items, which are intended to measure motor skills, rhythm, tactile, visual, receptive speech, expressive language, writing, reading, arithmetic, memory, and intelligence. Each test item is scored on a scale, and a total scale for all items is also derived.

Pediatric Symptom Checklist (PSC)

One of the most common screening tools used by pediatricians when they consult with parents, the PSC is a list of 35 questions created by Dr. Michael S. Jellinek of Harvard Medical School. It has proven to be about 95 percent effective at catching psychiatric disorders in children.

Vineland Adaptive Behavior Scales

These tests measure personal and social skills from birth to adulthood, using a semi-structured interview with a parent or other caregiver. Versions are available for children of all ages. Social and behavioral maturity in four major areas—communication, daily living skills, socialization, and motor skills—is assessed. Responses are rated on a 100-point scale for each area, and a composite score is also provided. Scores can be translated into developmental or mental ages.

IQ, development, and academic tests

Other tests attempt to measure intelligence, developmental level, and academic ability or progress. Intelligence testing is an especially tricky concept, as repeated studies have shown that children's IQs can and do change when they are measured differently, or when the child is taught differently and then re-tested. Most IQ tests also carry some cultural, racial, language, and/or gender bias, although testing companies are certainly trying to create better tests. However, because this bias has inappropriately placed non-handicapped students from ethnic minorities into Special Education in the past, it is no longer legal to use IQ tests alone as an evaluation tool in US schools.

In fact, as a result of misuse, IQ testing is beginning to fall out of favor. It has been supplanted in some school districts and medical practices by tests that measure adaptive behavior, which can be loosely described as how well and how quickly a person can come up with a solution to a problem and carry it out. These provide a more realistic measure of intelligence as most people think of it, as opposed to measuring cultural knowledge.

Developmental tests rank the individual's development against the norm, often resulting in a "mental age" or "developmental age" score. Some of the tests listed in the "Psychiatric and neurological tests" section earlier in this chapter can also be used to chart a child's developmental age.

Academic testing is a must during the Special Education evaluation process, and many psychiatrists and psychologists working independently of schools also use these tests. That's because school is the most important life activity for school-age children, and often an arena for substantial stress due to learning disabilities or neurological problems. If these can be identified and addressed, the child will likely have a better treatment outcome. Stress contributes mightily to mood swings.

Some clinicians like to compare the results of intelligence, developmental, and academic tests. This practice can provide a picture of actual achievement against the background of supposed innate capability.

Intelligence, developmental, and academic tests your child may be given include:

Adaptive Behavior Inventory for Children (ABIC)
> This standardized measure of adaptive behavior uses a questionnaire format, with a parent or other caregiver providing the answers. It includes subtests called Family, Community, Peer Relations, Nonacademic School Roles, Earner/Consumer, and Self-Maintenance. Used with the WISC-III IQ test and a special grading scale, ABIC is part of the System of Multicultural Pluralistic Assessment used by some districts to make more-sensitive assessments of racial minority children. Results are expressed on a scale.

Battelle Developmental Inventory
> This test ranks children's self-adaptive skills (self-feeding, dressing, etc.) as a percentage of his chronological age. The score may be expressed as a percentage, such as "between 40 percent and 55 percent of his/her chronological age," or as a single-number standard deviation.

Children's Memory Scale (CMS)
> The CMS test is intended to provide a complete picture of a child or adolescent's cognitive ability, and is often used with children who have acquired or innate neurological problems. Areas screened in six subtests include verbal and visual memory; short-delay and long-delay memory; recall, recognition, and working memory; learning characteristics; and ability to focus and maintain attention. It rates skills in all areas, and links them to an IQ score.

Developmental Assessment Screening Inventory II (DASI-II)

This screening and assessment tool for preschool children does not rely heavily on verbal or language-based skills. Its scores rate the child's developmental level.

Developmental Profile II

This developmental skill inventory for children up to 9 years old is based on an interview with a parent or other caregiver. It covers physical, self-help, social-emotional, communication, and academic skills. Scores are provided as an individual profile depicting the functional developmental age level in each area.

Learning Potential Assessment Device (LPAD)

This test of cognitive function uses different assumptions from some of the other IQ tests, and was designed for use primarily with learning disabled or developmentally disabled children. It provides several scaled scores, with interesting ideas about interpreting and using them.

Leiter International Performance Scale, Revised (Leiter-R)

This nonverbal IQ test has puzzle-type problems for the areas of visual, spatial, and language-based reasoning. It produces scaled results.

Peabody Developmental and Motor Scales (PDMS)

These tests use activities, such as threading beads or catching a ball, to gauge the level of physical development, as well as motor capabilities and coordination. They can be used to test large groups of children. Scores are expressed on a scale interpreted as an age level, so raw numbers may be followed by notations like "below age level by 5 percentiles" or "above age level."

Peabody Individual Achievement Test (PIAT)

These short tests measure performance in reading, writing, spelling, and math. Scores are expressed as a grade level.

Stanford-Binet Intelligence Test, Fourth Edition (S-B IV)

An intelligence test sometimes used with young or nonverbal children, although not preferred by most clinicians. The score is expressed as an IQ number or as a scale.

Test of Nonverbal Intelligence 2 (TONI-2)

This short, nonverbal IQ test for children over five presents a series of increasingly difficult problem-solving tasks, such as locating the missing part of a figure. The score is expressed as an IQ number or age equivalent.

Vineland Adaptive Behavior Scales
A standardized measure of adaptive behavior, the Vineland scale tests problem-solving and cognitive skills. Scores are presented as a scale, IQ-style number, or age equivalent.

Weschler Intelligence Scale for Children, Revised (WISC-R), Weschler Intelligence Scale for Children, Third Edition (WISC-III)
The Weschler scales are intelligence tests that use age-appropriate word-based activities as well as mechanical, puzzle-like activities to test problem-solving skills. They return scores for verbal IQ and performance IQ, which can be broken down into several categories.

Wide Range of Assessment Test, Revision 3 (WRAT 3)
This standardized test determines academic level in reading, writing, spelling, and math. Scores are expressed as raw numbers or grade level equivalents.

Woodcock-Johnson Psycho-Educational Battery, Revised (WJPEB-R, WJ-R)
An individual test of educational achievement in reading, writing, spelling, and math, the WJ-R has many subtests that can be given as a group or separately. Standard scores are derived that compare the test-taker against US norms, and that can also be expressed as an age or grade-level equivalency. One popular subtest, the Scales of Independent Behavior, Revised (SIB-R/Woodcock, Johnson Battery, Part IV) is a standardized measure of adaptive behavior. SIB-R scores are raw numbers similar to IQ scores, but may be shown as a grade or age equivalency.

Sometimes a standardized local, state, or national academic test is used to rate a child by grade level instead of one of the commercial tests listed.

The diagnostic report

Once the psychiatrist, psychologist, or neurologist has completed his observations, interviews, and testing, he'll be ready to make a diagnosis. This will probably be done in a report that describes the child; summarizes the events, observations, and tests that led up to the diagnosis; and finally presents the doctor's diagnosis. Most practitioners will also include suggestions for therapy, medications, or schooling based on what was learned.

Sometimes you'll see notes in the report about specific manic, hypomanic, mixed, or depressive episodes. Often these describe the most recent episode (usually the one that brought your child in for treatment). Sometimes there will be notes on several episodes.

Some parents interviewed for this book noted that they were never given a copy of the diagnostic report. Instead, they may have been informed of the diagnosis verbally—even over the phone—without getting much information or a chance to ask questions. This is not an acceptable practice. Bipolar disorder is a chronic medical condition that can be hard to treat. A good diagnostician knows that a label alone isn't much help. It must be accompanied by information about what should happen next, and what the family can expect in the future. If your diagnosing professional isn't forthcoming with this level of information, move on to someone else who is more committed to working closely with you and your child. Insist on getting copies of any reports, including scores on standardized tests.

Other parents said the diagnostic report was hard to read. Usually the doctor will write out the diagnosis in full, either on an Axis chart or elsewhere on the report. If she uses numbers instead, ask her to give you the full definition for them. If the doctor is too busy to explain the report to you, seek out someone who can. This is another area where a therapist or social worker can come in handy. They have a background in psychiatric jargon and the mumbo-jumbo of testing, but they're also accustomed to using real-world language with their clients.

One thing to ask for in the evaluation report is a prognosis. Doctors are often reluctant to give this information—after all, they don't have a crystal ball, and they don't want to raise false hopes. Simply explain that you want to know what might be possible with the interventions they recommend.

Also ask how progress in areas of deficit might best be measured. For example, if your child is re-evaluated, his Axis V score should inch upward if treatment has been successful. It's possible for a person diagnosed with a major mental disorder to end up with a perfectly adequate Axis V score, meaning that he is coping well with life despite the disorder.

To measure progress, your practitioner may want to use the same checklists and observations again after a certain period of time.

Differential diagnosis

There are a number of emotional disturbances, neurological problems, and medical illnesses that can look like bipolar disorders—or that can occur along with bipolar disorders, masking symptoms and making treatment more complicated. For these reasons, making a diagnosis is often a process of elimination. Doctors call this process "differential diagnosis," which means finding the right medical label by eliminating others that don't fit.

Every medical professional has his own frame of reference. A pediatrician tends to think of parenting and developmental issues when a child comes in with behavior problems. A psychiatrist thumbs through the *DSM-IV* for a diagnosis that seems to fit. A neurologist thinks about seizures and brain damage. It's not feasible to consider every single possibility, but you do need to rule out (or rule in) certain common causes for symptoms.

First-year medical students are always taught the old saw, "If you hear hoof-beats, think horses, not zebras." That means that one should consider common problems first when trouble emerges, rather than investigating rare and unusual diseases. It's good basic advice, but some of our kids really do have stripes! If your bipolar child or patient does not respond to the usual treatment options, it can be worthwhile to consider other causes for her difficulties, especially if particular symptoms or family history indicate that you should.

ADHD

As discussed at the beginning of the chapter, bipolar disorder in children is frequently misdiagnosed as attention deficit hyperactivity disorder (ADHD). To fit the *DSM-IV* criteria for ADHD, some hyperactive, inattentive, or impulsive symptoms must appear before the age of seven; symptoms must be present in two or more settings (such as at school and at home); and the symptoms must cause real difficulty for the child.

The official ADHD criteria also state that symptoms must not be due to another mental disorder, including bipolar disorder. This either/or position is controversial with some clinicians, who see ADHD and bipolar disorder in children as overlapping, but separate, conditions. An investigation by Dr. Jane Wozniak at Harvard Medical School, found that while 20 percent of the children in her study diagnosed with ADHD also met the criteria for mania,

98 percent of the children who had been diagnosed with manic features fit the criteria for ADHD.[2] These two disorders are usually treated with different types of medication and other interventions.

To meet the criteria for ADHD, the patient must fall into one of the following two categories:

1. The patient has six or more of the following symptoms, persisting for at least six months, occurring frequently, and occurring to a degree inconsistent with the child's developmental level:

   - Fails to pay attention to details, makes careless mistakes in schoolwork or other activities

   - Has difficulty sustaining attention in schoolwork, chores, or play activities

   - Does not seem to listen when spoken to directly

   - Fails to follow instructions, does not finish schoolwork or chores (not due to deliberate oppositional behavior or failure to understand instructions)

   - Has difficulty organizing tasks and activities

   - Avoids, dislikes, or is reluctant to try tasks that require sustained mental effort, such as homework

   - Loses things needed for tasks or activities, such as toys, homework assignments, or books

   - Is easily distracted by noise or other external stimuli

   - Is forgetful in daily activities

2. The patient has six or more of the following symptoms of hyperactivity/impulsivity, persisting for at least six months, and to a degree that is inconsistent with developmental level.

   Hyperactivity:

   - Fidgets with hands or feet, squirms in seat

   - Can't seem to remain seated in the classroom or other places where it is expected

   - Runs and climbs excessively in inappropriate situations and places (in adolescents, this can be subjective feelings of restlessness)

   - Has difficulty playing quietly

- Is physically very active—acts as if "driven by a motor"
- Talks excessively

Impulsivity:

- Blurts out answers out of turn or before questions are completed
- Can't seem to wait for turn in play or at school
- Interrupts or intrudes on others by butting into conversations or games, invading others' personal space, etc.

Based on these criteria, the *DSM-IV* separates ADHD into four categories:

- **ADHD, Predominantly Inattentive Type (314.00).** Child meets the criteria in section 1, but not in section 2.

- **ADHD, Predominantly Hyperactive-Impulsive Type (314.01).** Child meets the criteria in section 2, but not in section 1.

- **ADHD, Combined Type (314.01).** Child meets the criteria in both section 1 and section 2.

- **ADHD NOS (314.9).** Child has prominent symptoms of hyperactivity/impulsivity and/or attention deficit, but doesn't meet all of the required criteria for any of the other three types. This diagnosis is sometimes used when the child has another primary condition, such as bipolar disorder, but also has symptoms of ADHD that are not fully explained by that disorder.

As you can see, there's a great deal of overlap between the features of ADHD and bipolar disorder. Diagnosticians trying to tell one from the other look for features like psychosis, depression, rapid mood swings, waxing and waning of symptoms, inappropriate affect, and disregard for the feelings of others. These are more characteristic of bipolar disorders than of ADHD.

Other telltale factors can include angry destructiveness seen in bipolar disorders, as opposed to careless destructiveness in ADHD; temper tantrums or rages that can last for hours in bipolar disorders, as opposed to 30 to 40 minutes in ADHD; and a level of energy expended during manic episodes or bipolar rages that is far beyond what an adult could duplicate on purpose. Although both bipolar and ADHD children can have severe tantrums, bipolar children are less likely to be set off by overstimulation or insults than by simple adult boundary-setting. Bipolar children may move, talk, and think differently than usual during and after a rage, while the behavior and affect of tantruming ADHD children is relatively consistent. Some bipolar children will not even remember the event, giving it a seizure-like quality. It should be noted that similar types of tantrum/rage behaviors are also seen in Tourette syndrome and autistic spectrum disorders.

Another difference is seen mostly in the morning. Children with ADHD tend to bounce out of bed, ready to take on the world with an overabundant supply of energy. Bipolar children are more likely to be hard to wake up and slow to get going. They may complain bitterly, be irritable, and malinger with stomachaches, headaches, and other phantom illnesses.

There are also differences in the classroom. Although some children with ADHD also have the ability to hyperfocus, it's more characteristic of bipolar disorders. That means you're more likely to see an uneven pattern of attention in bipolar children. Bipolar children are also less likely to be diagnosed with specific learning disabilities. Many are early talkers and readers, and use language with special skill. They may be quite brilliant conversationalists at early ages, able to tell jokes effectively, use puns and plays on words, and employ expressive body language to full effect. There is often an evident flair for the dramatic.

A troubling symptom that may be noticed in bipolar children as early as preschool is sexual precociousness. Bipolar children seem to become aware of gender differences early, and some may have difficult-to-manage crushes or even touch other children inappropriately. Several parents of bipolar girls interviewed for this book noted that their daughters were unusually giggly, flirtatious, and ultra-feminine, even as toddlers.

Other personality traits that may emerge very early in bipolar children include a rebellious streak that seems to bring them into deliberate conflict with authority figures, and reckless behavior based on grandiose thinking (such as leaping from the playground climbing structure because they believe they can fly, or coming into conflict with teachers because they believe they know best how a class should be taught).[3]

One surprising difference involves dreams: many bipolar children and adolescents are traumatized by unusually violent, gory nightmares. Clinicians report that these dreams are so horrible that children are usually very reluctant to talk about them. Nightmares may explain the pattern of frequent waking throughout the night, morning tiredness, and the literal fear of going to sleep seen in many bipolar children. These dreams may result in part from interruptions in circadian rhythms caused by sleep disturbances, or from neurotransmitter differences—it has long been known that certain medications that affect the brain have the side effect of causing more vivid dreams.

Children with ADHD, on the other hand, aren't afraid of bedtime so much as they are too full of energy to relax.[4]

If the child has more behavior problems at home than at school, that can also be an indicator. Children with bipolar disorders have more difficulties in situations that involve strong relationships with others, so their home behavior may be much worse than it is in the classroom. Children with ADHD, on the other hand, tend to have more problems at school, where their inattentiveness and impulsiveness are harder to manage and redirect.[5]

Remember, *DSM-IV* criteria to the contrary, there are people who appear to have both a bipolar disorder and ADHD.

Substance abuse

As noted earlier in this chapter, the use of illegal drugs and alcohol by children can produce personality changes, unusual behavior, mood swings, and even psychotic symptoms. If there is any question that the child may have ingested drugs or alcohol, a full drug screen (not just marijuana) should be done.

Illegal steroids are one substance that physicians sometimes forget to screen for in teenagers. That's unfortunate, because studies show that they are used far too often, especially by teens who are interested in athletics or bodybuilding. Illegal steroids can cause major mood swings, including states that mimic depression, as well as sudden angry, aggressive, manic-like behavior (colloquially known as 'roid rage).

Substance abuse can also be a symptom of bipolar disorders, however, as teens or adults may find that drinking or drugging masks their problems for a little while. For that reason, the discovery that a patient has been abusing drugs or alcohol does not rule out a bipolar diagnosis.

Medication side effects

Both prescription and over-the-counter medications can cause severe behavioral side effects in some people. Parents should be sure to mention all medications, including herbal medicines and vitamin supplements, to their child's psychiatrist when a diagnosis of bipolar disorder is under consideration. Even long-term medication users can suddenly have new side effects, as maturing bodies begin to react differently to medicines that were previously helpful.

Professionals should carefully question teens about their use of over-the-counter drugs and herbal remedies. For example, large doses of B vitamins cause increased hyperactivity in some children. Stimulants like Vivarin and NoDoz, antihistamines containing ephedra, ephedrine, pseudoephedrine, and similar stimulants, corticosteroids such as prednisone, and stimulant-based "diet pills" can seriously disturb moods and the sleep cycle.

The discovery that medication side effects may play a role in the problems a person is experiencing does not rule out bipolar disorder. In fact, some undiagnosed bipolar teens and adults self-medicate with over-the-counter stimulants, herbal remedies, and other legal substances. Unfortunately, these substances can also kick off mood swings.

Unipolar depression

Unipolar, or simple, depression is just that: depressed mood that lasts longer than two weeks, and is not due to another medical condition, the side effects of medication, or normal reaction to a major life event (such as grieving after a parent's death). It is the most common form of depression. Most people with unipolar depression have periods of feeling normal, including feeling happy. These shouldn't be confused with hypomania, but occasionally they are.

Many people with bipolar disorders first seek help during or because of a depressive episode. Doctors then prescribe one of the antidepressant drugs commonly used to treat unipolar depression: selective serotonin uptake inhibitors (SSRIs) such as Paxil, Prozac, and Effexor; or tricyclic antidepressants, such as Anafranil or Tofranil. If the patient is actually bipolar, the result may be a manic episode. Often this is the first clue to the correct diagnosis.

Unfortunately, this clue is all too often overlooked. Parents report that their bipolar children have endured mania-producing trials on several antidepressants in succession before finally getting a correct diagnosis. Because the behavior that occurs during manic episodes can be so dangerous to the patient and to others, anyone taking an antidepressant for the first time or switching to a new antidepressant should be carefully monitored for the signs of hypomania or mania.

SSRIs, and sometimes tricyclic antidepressants, do have a place in the treatment of bipolar disorders for some patients. Normally the person's mood swings must be controlled by a mood stabilizer like lithium or Depakote before these drugs can be safely given, however.

Schizophrenia

Bipolar children and adolescents are more likely to have psychotic features, such as hallucinations, grandiose thinking, or delusions, than bipolar adults. This is probably because children have a less fully developed sense of reality and fantasy; even normal children occasionally confuse the two. These symptoms sometimes cause bipolar children and teens to be misdiagnosed as schizophrenic or schizoaffective (see "Schizoaffective," below).

Schizophrenia is a major mental illness characterized by psychotic symptoms, often including complete loss of connection with reality. One difference between schizophrenia and bipolar disorder is affect: schizophrenics usually have what's called a blunt affect. They don't react much to outside stimuli, and they don't have much personality. It can be hard to tell this from the demeanor of a person who's in a depressed state, however, which can bring on an apathetic attitude and delayed response to stimuli.

Another difference between schizophrenia and bipolar disorder is that bipolar mood swings can be sudden, but schizophrenia almost always has a slow, gradually worsening onset. It also does not normally wax and wane like bipolar disorders. Schizophrenics rarely have the characteristic signs of true mania, namely hyperactivity and pressured speech.

A third difference is that schizophrenics are more likely to suffer from a thought disorder. While patients in either group may hallucinate or be delusional, the bipolar patient is more likely to realize, at least intermittently, that the phenomena they are experiencing are not normal. For example, the bipolar person may hear voices and fully realize some of the time that the voices are not real, that they are a psychiatric symptom. The schizophrenic person is not connected enough with objective reality to tell the voices in their head from voices on the radio. Schizophrenics are also more likely to have truly bizarre delusions, including psychotic symptoms that don't jibe with their outward mood. For example, they may seem quite cheerful while informing you that the walls are dripping with blood.

Sometimes differential diagnosis is made via medication: schizophrenia does not respond to lithium, and bipolar mood swings are not well-controlled by the neuroleptic drugs most useful for schizophrenia (some people with bipolar disorder do benefit from neuroleptics, however, usually in addition to a mood stabilizer).

Note to African-American families: In the US, some recent studies indicate that African-Americans with bipolar disorders run a higher risk of being misdiagnosed as schizophrenic than other patients do. No one is quite sure why. Minority parents who are told their child is schizophrenic or schizoaffective need to be aware of this potential for error.

Schizoaffective

The terms schizoaffective disorder or schizoaffective depression indicate that the patient has some characteristics of a mood disorder, such as bipolar disorder or unipolar depression, and some characteristics of schizophrenia.

This diagnosis is probably applied too often to children and teens with bipolar disorder. As noted previously, psychotic symptoms in bipolar youth are not necessarily signs of schizophrenia.

Anxiety

Anxiety disorders are common enough that almost everyone knows someone who suffers from them. They include panic disorders and extreme phobias of all sorts, from claustrophobia (fear of being in small, enclosed places) to arachnophobia (fear of spiders). Basically put, they all involve an extreme reaction to certain situations or stimuli, as the body puts its "fight or flight" system in motion for no good reason.

Some people with anxiety disorders have panic attacks so severe that they could almost be mistaken for mania. They may make rapid movements, have an increased heartbeat, and talk a lot to calm themselves down. Panic attacks and phobias are embarrassing and can limit your activities, so it's only natural that people with severe anxiety disorders may have low self-esteem or feel depressed.

Anxiety disorders are more common in people with bipolar disorders than in the general population. Often it's the anxiety disorder, with its totally debilitating panic attacks or phobias, that will bring a bipolar person into treatment for the first time.

Oppositional defiant disorder and conduct disorder

Oppositional defiant disorder (ODD) is the *DSM-IV*'s diagnosis for the classic schoolyard bully: the child who deliberately hurts others, destroys property, willfully clashes with authority at every turn, and seems to get great satisfaction out of his behavior. Children with ODD tend to be vindictive, seeking revenge for real or perceived wrongs. They blame others for all their problems—and often for their own actions as well. They are truly the juvenile version of the antisocial adult and gleefully gravitate toward gangs, violent crime, and eventually prison.

As the child with ODD gets older, he is usually tagged with the conduct disorder (CD) label. He may be selected for special programs that can help the "at-risk" teenager—or he may be selected for a stint in a juvenile corrections facility. There is hope for these kids, of course, and medical studies show their behavior may have medical causes as well as environmental ones.

The difference between ODD and conduct disorder on one hand, and bipolar disorder on the other, is that the ODD or conduct disorder child usually has at least a perceived reason for his tantrums, aggression, and assaultive behavior. (The real reason may be an abusive situation at home, or feelings of inferiority.)

Children with ODD or conduct disorder often operate under the bad influence of peers. This is less frequently the case in bipolar disorders, even when the behavior (shoplifting, substance abuse, fighting) looks the same on the surface.

Bipolar children tend to have an elevated or irritable mood along with their antisocial outbursts, while the ODD or conduct disorder child is mostly mad, or just plain mean. Psychotic symptoms are also not a part of ODD or conduct disorder.

Many clinicians—and parents—feel that these labels are dispensed far too frequently, and that children tagged as ODD or CD are quickly rejected by schools and by many treatment programs. On later review, a great many children diagnosed with ODD or a conduct disorder prove to be bipolar.

Personality disorders

There are two major ways of looking at personality disorders. The official view is that they are maladaptive ways of seeing the world, reacting to events, and relating to people, and that they cause problems for the people who have them. Most psychiatrists believe that personality disorders arise from childhood difficulties and conflicts, so they are rarely diagnosed in young children. Symptoms must be present before early adulthood, however.

A second view is that personality disorders are, at least in part, shadows of major mental or neurological disorders.

The *DSM-IV* identifies ten major personality disorders (PDs), which it divides into three groups, Clusters A, B, and C (or I, II, and III). It is believed that some personality disorders—particularly borderline personality disorder—can arise from untreated bipolar disorders. Studies indicate that the PDs listed under Cluster B are more common in people with bipolar disorders.[6] Depending on which of the two views (presented above) you hold, that may be because bipolar children and adolescents miss out on healthy personality development due to their illness, or because some personality characteristics are determined by the same genes or other influences that cause bipolar disorders.

Cluster A personality disorders include:

- **Paranoid.** Distrustful, suspicious of others and their motives.

- **Schizoid.** Very limited social and emotional range.

- **Schizotypal.** Limited social and emotional range coupled with unusual thought and behavior patterns.

Cluster B personality disorders include:

- **Antisocial.** Unconcerned about rules, laws, or the rights of others; often violent, aggressive, destructive. The adult version of ODD or conduct disorder. Also called sociopathic or psychopathic personality.

- **Borderline.** Unstable relationships, values, self-image, and emotions; reckless and impulsive; episodes of aggressive or highly emotional behavior.

- **Histrionic.** Attention-seeking, highly emotional.

- **Narcissistic.** Self-absorbed, self-important, demanding, limited understanding of other people's perspectives.

Cluster C personality disorders include:

- **Avoidant.** Feels inadequate, overly sensitive to criticism, avoids social interaction.

- **Dependent.** Overly dependent on others for approval or care, clinging and submissive.

- **Obsessive-Compulsive.** Overly controlled (and controlling), orderly, and perfectionistic.

You may hear about other personality disorders that are not currently listed in the *DSM-IV*. One of these is depressive personality disorder, which can be defined as having a chronically gloomy outlook on life without being clinically depressed. Another is passive-aggressive personality disorder, which involves using passive resistance to express anger (for example, playing the long-suffering martyr rather than telling your husband off). To ensure that any other personality problems have a clinical label, some psychiatrists may employ the term "personality disorder, not otherwise specified."

Thyroid disorders

Hyperthyroidism is overactivity of the thyroid gland; hypothyroidism is underactivity of the thyroid gland. According to the Thyroid Society, about 10 percent of patients with diagnosed depression have thyroid dysfunction. It's hard to tell whether the thyroid dysfunction caused the depression or simply coexists with it, but treating the thyroid condition often helps depressive symptoms.

Some people have a fluctuating level of thyroid function, and may present with bipolar-like symptoms.

Hormonal disorders

First among these is puberty: not a disorder, but a time when mood swings, changes in personality, and oppositional behavior are common. These symptoms are part of growing up. They're caused by surges of hormones, and exacerbated by the normal process of the child emotionally maturing and striving for independence. Puberty can begin surprisingly early, and seems to be coming earlier today than it did 50 or 100 years ago. It's not uncommon today for girls to begin puberty at 11, or even at 10. That can cause problems, because even though a girl's (or boy's) body may be surging ahead, emotional development is usually not in step.

Some people have more than the usual behavior problems in puberty. Their hormone levels don't ebb and flow, they surge wildly and stop suddenly. These individuals may have very noticeable and debilitating mood swings, including depression, lethargy, irritability, and even aggression. Girls with hormonal imbalances may also have serious menstrual irregularities. Because most girls do not menstruate as regularly as adult women, these problems may be brushed aside by pediatricians. And in fact, the majority of girls with early menstrual irregularity are just fine. A few, however, have hormonal disorders that will not disappear, and that cause mood swings that can be mistaken for the beginnings of bipolar disorder. Hormonal disorders can be identified, and can be treated with hormone supplements. Some girls will find relief by taking birth control pills, getting injections of Depo-Provera, or getting Norplant implants. All of these are conveniently available ways to change the hormonal imbalance (and all also have a potential for side effects that must be carefully balanced against possible benefits).

Thyroid and pituitary disorders are also hormonal disorders—and so, one might argue, are bipolar disorders! That's because the neurotransmitters that are believed to be working improperly or being produced in the wrong amounts in bipolar disorders are substances related to hormones, and are also affected by hormone production. In other words, if there's a problem with the sex-linked hormones, such as estrogen, progesterone, or testosterone, that problem may also affect the production, transmission, or use of neurotransmitters such as serotonin and dopamine. This may be one of the reasons that bipolar disorders tend to emerge, worsen, or improve (depending on the patient) just before or during periods of special hormonal activity, such as menstruation, puberty, the transition from adolescence to adulthood, pregnancy, the period just after giving birth, and menopause.

In some patients, hormonal disorders may mimic the symptoms of bipolar disorders. In others, they may be intimately intertwined. Getting treatment for an underlying hormonal disorder has contributed greatly to the stability of many people with bipolar disorders. Of course, some medications used to treat hormonal disorders, including hormone supplements, can also cause mood swings.

Cushing's disease

This disease can result from a tumor on the pituitary gland. A related condition, Cushing's disorder, can be caused by a tumor on the adrenal gland, lung, or elsewhere—or by overuse of corticosteroid medications or illegal steroids. The adrenal gland becomes overstimulated by the hormone ACTH, causing symptoms that can include mood swings and other mental disturbances, raised blood glucose levels, high blood pressure, excess growth of facial and body hair, weight gain, and reddening of the face and neck.

Rheumatoid arthritis

Rheumatoid arthritis is an autoimmune disorder that causes inflammation and degeneration of the joints. It does occur in children and teenagers, but may not be suspected as the cause for lethargy, unexplained aches and pains, and mood swings. These symptoms may come and go, making diagnosis difficult. Rheumatoid arthritis can range from very mild to completely disabling—even in children.

Hypoglycemia

Hypoglycemia is a deficiency of glucose in the bloodstream: low blood sugar. It can cause confusion, weakness, fainting, sudden loss of energy or fatigue—all symptoms that can mimic depression. It is treated by ingesting or injecting glucose, and since the results of suddenly ingesting lots of sugar can mimic hyperactivity, the yo-yo behavior and mood swings of the hypoglycemic child could be mistaken for a bipolar pattern. Hypoglycemia is a common side effect of diabetes, but can occur without it.

Diabetes mellitus

Diabetes is a metabolic disorder with autoimmune and genetic components. The body is unable to use carbohydrates and sugars to produce energy due to lack of the pancreatic hormone insulin. The body tries to use fats as an energy source instead, but the by-products of metabolizing fats build up in the bloodstream. This can cause convulsions or even diabetic coma.

Diabetics can have problems with high blood sugar (hyperglycemia) or with hypoglycemia (see previous entry) unless they follow a careful diet. Diabetes can usually be controlled with diet and medication. Symptoms of uncontrolled diabetes can include mood swings.

Lupus

Lupus erythematosus (LE, also called systemic lupus) is an autoimmune disorder that causes chronic inflammation of the connective tissue, including the skin, internal organs, and sometimes the nervous system and brain. Symptoms can include a scaly, red, butterfly-shaped rash on the face, joint pain, fatigue, and mood swings. It appears to have at least some genetic component, so if lupus has appeared in a patient's family before, it's important to rule it out.

Lupus can be diagnosed via a blood test. It is generally considered to be a disease of adults, but sometimes the early warning signs are seen in teenagers. It is more common in women than in men, and it may be more common in people of African or Mediterranean descent.

Some medications used to treat lupus, especially the corticosteroids, can also cause mood swings.

AIDS

Sexually active or drug-using teens are at risk for acquired immune deficiency syndrome, and over the past fifteen years many children of mothers with AIDS have been born with the virus. AIDS erodes the immune system's effectiveness, leaving the body and brain open to all sorts of infections. The Epstein-Barr virus (see "Mononucleosis," below), human herpes virus, and many others have the ability to cause mood swings and psychosis.

People with AIDS are also more susceptible to overgrowth of yeasts and fungi in the body, including Candida albicans (a yeast normally found in the digestive tract in small amounts) and cryptosporidium, which can cause unusual behaviors and physical symptoms if left untreated.

A diagnosis of AIDS or a related immune-deficiency condition does not rule out the possibility of a bipolar disorder. In fact, it's safe to assume that people with untreated bipolar disorders are at greater risk for contracting AIDS, because compulsive sexual activity and substance abuse are more common in this population. Actual psychosis is not usually seen in AIDS until the very late stages of the disease. However, disturbances in mood, sleep, and energy levels can be among the early warning signs of this illness.

Mononucleosis

Mononucleosis ("mono," also known as glandular fever) is an infection of the lymphatic system caused by the Epstein-Barr virus, a common virus in the herpes family that usually does not cause illness. Symptoms can mimic those of depression, including fatigue, loss of energy, unexplained aches and pains, and changes in sleep and mood. It is characterized by high levels of mononuclear leukocytes (white blood cells) in the blood stream, and therefore can be diagnosed with a blood test.

Mono tends to strike children and teenagers more frequently than adults, and has an affinity for people with compromised immune systems. It can be extraordinarily difficult to recover from, with episodes of illusory wellness during which the patient may try to make up for lost time. This swing from seeming depression to seeming hypomania could be mistaken for cyclothymia, SAD, or even bipolar II disorder. Untreated mono can also lead to hepatitis, which can also cause severe mood swings.

Chronic fatigue syndrome

Also known as chronic fatigue immune deficiency syndrome (CFIDS), this debilitating disorder is of unknown origin, although some sort of virus or other infection of the nervous system is the suspected cause. People with chronic fatigue syndrome have symptoms that mimic those of depression, including irritability, extreme fatigue, unexplained aches and pains, and changes in sleep and mood. During brief periods of recovery, such patients may become virtual whirlwinds of activity as they try to make up for everything they've missed while ill. This swing from seeming depression to seeming hypomania could be mistaken for cyclothymia, SAD, or even bipolar II disorder. And, of course, depression can also be mistaken for CFIDS.

Multiple sclerosis

Multiple sclerosis (MS) is a progressive disease of the nervous system characterized by damage to the myelin sheath, the tissue that surrounds and protects the spinal cord and nerves. Early symptoms can include fatigue, irritability, shaky movements, sudden muscle weakness, sleep disturbances, and mood swings.

MS normally affects young and middle-aged adults, not children—although its early warning signs are sometimes identified in teenagers. The cause of MS is currently unknown. It may be caused by viral or bacterial infection of the nervous system, or it may be an abnormal autoimmune response.

The medication Interferon is sometimes used to treat MS, and can cause mood and sleep disturbances.

Hepatitis

Hepatitis is an inflammation of the liver. It is caused by infection with one of several hepatitis viruses (hepatitis A, B, C, etc.) or can be a side effect of other diseases, including mononucleosis and lupus. Like AIDS, hepatitis infection can be spread via sexual activity, IV drug use, accidental contact with bodily fluids, or infected blood products. Infectious hepatitis can even be spread in foods prepared by or shared with an infected person.

Because the liver is the body's center for eliminating toxic substances, all sorts of symptoms occur when it isn't working properly. The most common include fever, nausea, weakness, persistent headache, and jaundice (a yellow discoloration of the skin, and sometimes of the whites of the eyes). People with untreated hepatitis, or with one of the forms of infectious hepatitis that cannot currently be easily treated, may also experience mood swings. These are generally in the direction of depression, although some patients also experience grandiose thinking, aggression, and other symptoms that could look like hypomania or mania.

Medications used to treat resistant forms of hepatitis, such as Interferon, can also cause mood and sleep disturbances.

Tay-Sachs disease

When Tay-Sachs disease strikes in adolescence, there is a strong correlation with bipolar-like psychiatric symptoms. A blood test is available to screen possible cases. This inherited neurological disorder, which is normally fatal in infancy, occurs in people with northern European, Jewish, and French-Canadian ancestry.

Is it psychosis?

One area where differential diagnosis is particularly crucial is psychotic symptoms. Of course, drug use can cause a person to temporarily lose touch with reality. Hallucinogens are the most frequent offenders, although some people have had strange experiences with other drugs. Speed and cocaine can induce both psychotic symptoms and mania. Amphetamine abusers are particularly likely to have sensory hallucinations, such as feeling like something is crawling under their skin, and may become both delusional and aggressive. Long-term alcohol abuse can result in similar hallucinations (the infamous delirium tremens, or "DTs").

A few people have delayed reactions to drugs, and may experience unpleasant "flashbacks" or ongoing distortions of reality due to previous drug use. These may be caused by damage to neural circuits. Therapy can help affected individuals recognize and cope with these episodes. In some cases, medication can help.

Sometimes people with bipolar disorder have delusional thought patterns without actually being psychotic. A bipolar teenager might come to believe that he is a brilliantly talented rock musician, and lay elaborate plans for his imminent rise to stardom. For example, right after reading a magazine article about a cool record label, he might run away to Los Angeles and seek out this company, thinking it will surely sign him to a record deal on the spot. He may have actual talent, but an outsider could easily see that the rest of his assumptions are delusional. He's not psychotic, but if no one intervenes before he acts on his delusions, he may well slide into psychosis.

Sometimes other phenomena are mistaken for hallucinations. People with migraines or seizure disorders report a hallucination-like phenomenon called an *aura*. Different people experience different types of auras, but if the aura is visual it tends to include geometric patterns, or patterns of moving light. Auditory auras tend to be buzzing, ringing, or even musical sounds rather than voices. Some people report experiencing certain smells or tastes before a migraine attack or a seizure. Others may have physical auras, such as feeling a spreading warmth, a sudden stomachache, or a prickly sensation on the scalp. Both migraines and seizures are more common in people with bipolar disorders than in the general population.

It's important to take cultural differences into account, too. Some religious belief systems include rituals in which people may experience trance states and other psychosis-like phenomena, such as hearing voices, speaking in tongues, or believing that they are communicating with otherworldly beings. Professionals working with these patients need to be sensitive to their spiritual traditions, while still helping them to see where a spiritual experience ends and psychosis begins. Sometimes a particular religious practice may not be healthy for a person with a mental disorder. Other practices may be very helpful indeed.

When spiritual beliefs are intensely important to a child with bipolar disorder and/or his family, a pastor, priest, rabbi, shaman, or other spiritual counselor can become part of the evaluation and treatment team. It's difficult sometimes for psychiatric professionals to work closely with patients whose view of their illness or of the world in general is colored by strong religious beliefs. Sometimes there are also institutional barriers to cooperation with religious leaders. Parents can often be the bridge between these two healing professions.

Families should be aware that spiritual counseling alone is unlikely to cure a child's mental illness. They also need to know that otherwise valid religious beliefs can be distorted by mental illness, which can turn religious practices into obsessions and compulsions, or gateways to psychotic episodes. Taken together, good medical and spiritual help can heal the whole person.

Conversely, medical professionals who have spiritual beliefs of their own must be careful not to push them on patients and families who may have different opinions.

Evaluation should be ongoing

Diagnosis should not be a one-shot affair. The gradual physical and emotional development of a child has unique effects on how bipolar disorders and other neurological problems express themselves. As your child matures, he will gain insight and skills that can help him take advantage of different types of treatments. School and other experiences will change your concerns for your child. Physical maturity matters too. Puberty in particular is a period of great upheaval, where symptoms can change drastically—for better or for worse.

Try to ensure that your child is assessed at regular intervals for overall mood stability, response to medications, and adjustment to life. Not only treatments, but treatment goals will change as your child gets older. In periods of relative stability, for example, treatment may emphasize social, emotional, and academic development. You can take advantage of these periods to make up for lost time, and to build skills that may make future episodes easier to handle. In periods of instability, goals may be much more basic.

CHAPTER 3

Living with Bipolar Disorders

WHEN THE SYMPTOMS of a bipolar disorder strike your child, it changes everything about your family's life. Prevention must be your watchword. The best ways to minimize the life-shattering potential of bipolar disorders are to treat these conditions immediately and thoroughly, and to avoid severe mood swings whenever possible. Untreated bipolar disorders can rapidly zoom out of control, and each ensuing manic or depressive episode seems to be harder to treat.

> I wish I had known more about what to do when Jakob first started showing symptoms. He went through too much at a young age. It would have helped if we had known to focus on his health first, and worry about school second. We didn't change our priorities until he was hospitalized for a second time. —Pam, mother of 20-year-old Jakob (diagnosed bipolar I disorder)

In this chapter, we take a look at dealing with the diagnosis, the behaviors, the problems, and the disruptions that come with bipolar disorders. The emphasis is on being proactive: thinking ahead about goals and how to reach them, and avoiding common dangers.

First things first

When you're caught in the maelstrom, it seems to take all of your energy just to stay upright. The trick is to set small goals that you can reach, stringing them together to achieve those big, important goals that lie farther down the road.

If you've ever taken a college psychology course, you probably remember Maslow's hierarchy of needs (see Figure 3-1). Drawn up by behavioral scientist Abraham Maslow in 1943, it's a visual guide to the forces that motivate people, from the most basic survival instincts to the highest altruistic motives. It's also a good guide to what's most important when determining how to help a child or teenager faced with a bipolar disorder. It will help you set those goals, both small and large.

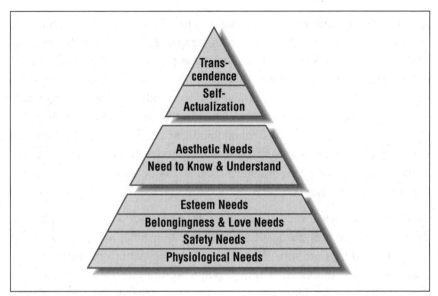

Figure 3-1. Maslow's hierarchy of needs

Maslow defined physiological needs as the basic things we need to survive: food, clothing, and shelter. Safety needs include freedom from physical danger, and the feeling that your physiological needs will be met. At the next level is the need to relate to others socially and emotionally. Esteem needs refer to the desire to feel loved and accepted by others in return, and to have adequate self-esteem.

Maslow identified additional needs that people strive for once these basic needs have been met. These include, at the top, what he called "self-actualization": the need to reach one's fullest potential as a human being.

His hierarchy is a general guide, not an absolute. Most of us can think of people who have reached their full human potential despite struggling daily to meet their most basic physical needs. But it's certainly true that when your survival needs are not being met, it's difficult to think about abstractions like the future, not to mention considering the impact of your behavior on the lives of others.

Now let's translate this hierarchy into a guideline for treatment.

Physiological needs

You must first ensure that your child is eating properly and sheltered from the elements. This may mean life changes for your family, from changing your diet to applying for public assistance if needed.

Bipolar children and teens have a higher rate of eating disorders, including anorexia and bulimia, than other young people. These are treatable medical conditions, almost certainly related to some part of the same neurological differences that cause bipolar disorders. Many other bipolar youth are extremely picky eaters, willing to ingest so few foods that you may rightfully worry about their health. Treatment for eating disorders, and work on problems that may underlie self-limited food choices, fall into the "survival needs" category. Hypersensitivity to textures and smells is a common but little-known cause for eating problems, and it can be treated (see Chapter 5, *Therapeutic Interventions*).

Another physiological need is continued treatment for any chronic physical illness your child may have, such as diabetes or asthma. Even long-standing medical conditions are sometimes ignored during periods of mental health crisis, but if left untreated they will only contribute to further destabilization. Medications for these conditions can interfere with the effects of psychiatric medications, so make sure your general practitioner and psychiatric practitioner are working together.

Because teenagers with bipolar disorder are at high risk for running away and may end up living in precarious circumstances if they do so, meeting their physiological need for shelter and basic bodily safety can mean considering hospitalization or other very strong interventions. It can also mean treating your runaway teen with bipolar disorder differently than you would a teenager who chooses to hit the road in search of thrills. You'll need to continue to be a presence in your child's life, and you'll still have a responsibility to ensure that his needs are met, wherever he may be. Don't let the "tough love" crowd tell you otherwise!

That doesn't mean sending cash that could be misused. Solutions might include purchasing food or food vouchers, meeting your child for restaurant meals, arranging for shelter, funneling financial assistance through a youth agency, and letting your child know that food and a roof are waiting for him at home when he's ready to return.

Safety needs

Young people with bipolar disorders are often their own worst enemies. They are at increased risk due to impulsive and self-destructive behaviors, including drug and alcohol abuse. Reducing, and hopefully eliminating, these behaviors should be the number one priority of psychiatric treatment and therapy. Until these crises are dealt with, other symptoms will be barely noticeable, much less treatable.

Take preventative steps to avoid the problem of drug and alcohol abuse as early as possible, including educating your child and yourself about these medical issues. Let your child know that if he's ever faced with a decision or problem related to substance abuse, your door is always open, and you will be nonjudgmental. People with bipolar disorders who avoid the trap of substance abuse have a far better prognosis than those who do not. Many teens—perhaps even most—will experiment. If they are armed with information and know where to go for help, however, they have a better chance of avoiding long-term difficulties. (See "Substance abuse" later in this chapter for more information.)

Your family and the larger community also have safety needs. If your child is acting out in ways that put you or others in danger, these aggressive or abusive behaviors must be addressed. Doing so may also protect your child from entering the criminal justice system, an arena where you may not be able to protect him from harm. (See "Criminal justice and the bipolar child" later in this chapter for additional information.)

Keeping your child's environment safe usually means keeping her at home or nearby when not in school. Some homes are not safe, however. If child or spousal abuse is occurring in your home, that's not a safe environment for your bipolar child. Take whatever steps are necessary to end these problems. If your immediate neighborhood presents serious dangers to your child's well-being, eliminating this major source of stress can have a profound impact.

For teens, watch out for the warning signs of abusive relationships with boyfriends or girlfriends, and for friends whose behavior may put your child in danger. Impulsivity and self-esteem problems can make children with bipolar disorders more susceptible to abuse, and to the lure of gangs.

You must also pay attention to hazards in your home, such as weapons, medications, and anything else that could be a means to self-harm, suicide, or harm to others. (See the section "Suicide prevention" at the end of this chapter for more on this topic.)

Safety needs also have an emotional aspect. Many children with bipolar disorders suffer from anxiety. Their thoughts spiral out of control easily, adding unnecessary stress. For example, your child may overhear you arguing with her mother about money, and assume that your family is in danger of going hungry. Let your child know early and often that you'll make sure her basic needs are met.

Don't burden a young child with worries about financial or safety problems. Make sure that teens understand the stresses your family faces, and let them see how you are actively working to solve them. Talk to them about their worries and fears. These steps should soothe overheated imaginations.

If you do have problems meeting these needs, don't hesitate to ask family members or friends for help, or to see if you or your child are eligible for public assistance.

Social needs

It's pretty hard to meet your own social needs. Others must be willing to be in a relationship with you. The social world is fraught with problems for young people with bipolar disorders, however. Their impulsive behavior and unusual outbursts can make them social pariahs, or attract the wrong element. Finding good friends—or even any friends—can be a real challenge.

> Lisa used to be one of the most popular kids in school. Once she
> started in with the depression and manic moods, she lost almost all of her
> friends. They were afraid of her and just started leaving her alone. She
> now only has about three friends that are really close and understand her.
> —Donna, mother of 16-year-old Lisa (diagnosed bipolar I disorder, post-
> traumatic stress disorder, and anxiety disorder)

Younger children and some teens with bipolar disorders can benefit from explicit training in social skills. Usually delivered in a group setting, social skills instruction covers topics like how to have a conversation, playing well with others, etiquette and proper behavior, and sometimes personal grooming issues. The group may be made up of children or teens who all have a bipolar disorder, youth with a variety of disabilities, or a mix of youth with and without special needs. These groups may be available in schools or through mental health clinics. Others are set up by psychiatrists, or are part of group therapy programs or formal mental-health support groups for kids.

Social skills are also learned through regular youth activities, of course, such as Scouting and religious groups. As manic-depressive illness progresses, it can be harder to feel comfortable in these groups without special support. Most religious denominations and national youth organizations have disability accommodation specialists, but often they are not as familiar with mental illness as with physical disability.

> Michael was in soccer, in Scouts, and involved with Brigade through the church, but over time his interest stopped. He acts much younger than he is, and plays mostly with girls because he feels more comfortable with them than with boys his age. —Lynn, mother of 11-year-old Michael (diagnosed BPI with mixed states and psychosis, OCD, tic disorder)

Some teens with bipolar disorder report that they prefer the company of adults to that of other teenagers. This type of relationship has obvious drawbacks if the adult involved is not trustworthy, but when the relationship is not exploitative, an adult friend can be a very positive role model. If you have a bipolar teen who just can't relate to high school peers, try to help him find outlets for safe social relationships outside of school that can become a positive focus. Community theater groups, service or activist organizations, mixed-age sports leagues, or an after-school job are just some of the possibilities that have worked well for others.

Parents should act as "emotion coaches" for their bipolar children, helping their children recognize and manage their own emotions more effectively. You can help your child label the feelings and behaviors that cause him social distress, and think up strategies for dealing with these difficulties. A child who withdraws from social contact can be helped out of her shell with ideas and advice that help her gradually ease back into friendships and social activities. A teenager whose social abilities have become more fragile due to manic-depressive illness may function better in short visits with one close friend.

Perhaps the two greatest social skills you can help your child develop are a sense of humor and flexibility. These will help him weather life's setbacks even better than good manners or conversation skills.

Parents can also help by ensuring access to social situations. For young children, set up play dates and other social situations for success through careful planning and parental supervision. At this age you can have a lot of say about who your child associates with. Finding one or more peers with a positive outlook and similar interests can have a long-term benefit for a child with psychiatric challenges. You may need to talk openly with the parents of your child's friends to help them understand his needs, and to make plans for what to do if any problems crop up in social situations or during visits to their homes.

Usually parents need to be more involved with a bipolar child's social life than they might otherwise be. These children have a greater need for supervision, guidance, and advice in negotiating social difficulties. One-to-one situations or structured groups like Scouting, Campfire, church youth groups, or activity clubs tend to be more comfortable for them than just hanging out.

Personality is based partly on inborn traits, and partly on how relationships with others are experienced. The person who is rejected and belittled may react by expecting rejection, avoiding social contact, or pushing others away deliberately. When these coping strategies combine to reinforce difficult inborn traits, the result can be a personality disorder, as discussed in Chapter 2, *Getting a Diagnosis*. Like substance abuse, personality disorders make manic-depressive illness harder to treat.

Esteem needs

You can think of this as the internal benefits of having your social needs met. Your goal is to raise a healthy young adult with strong self-esteem. Self-esteem is an internal perception of self-value, based in large part on the words, deeds, and reactions of others. Your child needs opportunities to see that he is socially acceptable, lovable, and cared for. He needs to see that his attachments to others are valued and returned. He needs chances to let his innate talents shine through, whatever they may be.

This may not be possible in the context of old relationships. Some members of your family may reject your child in ways that are hurtful. Peers and teachers can also be cruel, especially if they don't understand the nature of the illness.

Parents are not perfect either. Every parent of a bipolar child or teen will yell at, shame, blame, or berate him for behaviors related to his illness at some time or another. If you can walk away from heated situations before you blow your stack, that's great. If you don't always manage it, show your child the worth of an honest apology.

Loving a person with a mental illness can be hard work. Let your child know in any way you can that your love for him is not based on his accomplishments, grades, behavior, physical attractiveness, social prominence, or any other external trait, but on his intrinsic worth as a person. Help him find outlets for any special interests or abilities that he may have, whether it's art, sports, or comic antics. Success in one area of life can help him get through feelings of inadequacy or failure in other areas.

Beyond the basics

You've probably noticed what hasn't been mentioned yet: school, work, and a successful adult life. That's because getting an education, learning job skills, and reaching for the brass ring are far more likely to occur when a foundation of physical security, safety, social support, emotional stability, and self-confidence is there to support these efforts. And yet, many parents and professionals expect bipolar children to achieve academically when these needs have not yet been met.

That's setting a child up for failure.

There are many roads to adult success, and the regular freeway may be too hard for a person coping with bipolar disorder to navigate without special support. Part of that support comes from within, from a feeling of basic security, the knowledge that she is protected by loving relationships with others, and a sense of resiliency and personal ability to meet life's challenges. Another part of that support is external: the caring actions of family and friends, therapeutic relationships with professionals, medical help, and adequate planning for special educational needs.

Families have to recognize these special needs, and be flexible enough to meet them even when it means letting go of old expectations.

> When Lili quit high school, for a while I really felt like her life was over. I knew there were options—alternative school, private school, home-schooling, tutoring, the GED—but the outcome was less certain. With all of the challenges she faced, her choice seemed especially foolish.
>
> But we kept going. Option after option didn't work out, probably because too much of our attention was on school, and not enough on

holding together her fragile psyche. When we finally stepped back and said, "First, you have to be safe and healthy," things began to fall into place.

Medication helped stop the mood swings, and she was able to find the internal motivation to get an education. She earned her GED easily, entered trade school at the tender age of 16, and is now successfully employed in a career she enjoys. Her way of doing things was different from the usual way, but it worked for her. —Sarah, mother of 17-year-old Lili (diagnosed bipolar II disorder and OCD)

Taking charge of bipolar disorder

Medical care is an essential first step. For children and teens with bipolar disorders, medication is almost always the foundation of all subsequent interventions. As parents and professionals, we can research medication options, make sure medicines are taken, and watch out for side effects. We'll discuss medication in detail in Chapter 4, *Medical Interventions*.

There are other tasks to undertake as well, and these can be just as important. These include learning about the disorder, teaching the affected child about the disorder, and discerning patterns that are the key to proactive treatment.

Helping your child understand bipolar disorder

It can be hard to explain the symptoms of bipolar disorders to a young child. They experience them, but they have no frame of reference for knowing they are feeling, seeing, hearing, or doing anything unusual. You might try using pretend play to explain different moods, emotions, and behaviors. Some therapists use pictures of facial expressions, and ask young children to label the emotions these expressions show, or to act them out.

You can let your child know when strong emotions are okay, and when they should approach you or another adult for help with overwhelming feelings of sadness, anxiety, agitation, and so on. Children are usually relieved to know that you and other adults are there to help them, and that they won't be shamed or belittled for having more intense reactions or emotions than other children do. This encourages the child to observe his behavior and feelings more closely, a practice that will help him stay more stable throughout his life.

> As a child I was a worrier. I worried about things like death and change. It was always hard for me to fall asleep at night, so I would just sit in bed thinking and worrying. I had strange fears: fear of sharp objects, fear of vomiting. I had eating problems as a result of these fears when I was about 6 years old and again at 9. It was hard to think of anything else.

> Now that we have identified my symptoms, my family and friends know when it's me and not the bipolar disorder talking. My only advice is to learn about your diagnosis. Understand what you have. Be educated about your illness. —Marcia, 24 years old (diagnosed bipolar II disorder)

Older children can read simply written materials on bipolar disorder. It's important for them to understand that they have a medical condition, not an attitude problem or lack of willpower, and that help is available. There will be contradictory messages from teachers, classmates, friends, and perhaps even some relatives. The more a patient comprehends and accepts the medical nature of bipolar disorders, the more likely she is to weather this type of misguided criticism.

Teenagers can usually benefit from the same books, films, online resources, and other materials that you find helpful, including this book.

The mood and behavior diary

Teens and some older children are able to keep track of their ups and downs in a fairly methodical way. Like the more casual forms of self-observation just discussed, this is an essential skill. It may seem that asking a teenager to keep a mood and behavior diary is an encouragement for them to obsess about their disorder and its symptoms, but if the idea is correctly presented, it's an empowering activity. It can also reduce the number of serious depressive and manic episodes by signaling earlier when help is needed.

For younger children, parents can fill out a mood and behavior diary based on observation. Sometimes a teacher or other school employee can help with tracking moods and behavior during the school day.

What would this kind of diary look like? It depends on the child. Some adolescents love to write long diary entries, others might grudgingly check off a few boxes on a worksheet every day. No matter what the format is, it should hold a daily collection of information that illuminates early warning signs of incipient mania, hypomania, or depression. This data can help you and your child recognize what emotions, activities, behaviors, and seasonal changes precede mood swings, what makes mood swings stronger and longer-lasting, and what seems to make mood swings milder and shorter.

> The autumn season always seemed to be a down time for me, starting as early as age 5, while my springs and summers seem to have always been really up. Obviously, the hypomania I experience can be quite enjoyable, but my depressions are very down. I have not necessarily reached the point of suicide in my depressions, but have experienced constant sleeping, irritability, lack of interest, difficulty concentrating, obsessive thoughts, etc. —Marcia

Some typical early warning signs are listed in the official criteria for depression, hypomania, or mania—pressured speech, for example, or decreased need for sleep. Others can be personal in nature, such as menstrual cycles, being stressed out over an upcoming test at school, or athletic exertion.

Figure 3-2 shows an example of a daily mood and behavior worksheet that uses a simple Yes/No style.

If keeping a mood and behavior diary seems like a stupid chore to your child, explain that keeping track of his changing moods and symptoms may help his doctor reduce the amount of medication he needs, and will almost surely keep him out of serious trouble if he does it daily.

Preventing mood swings

The information gained from daily records can help head mood swings off at the pass. For example, many people with bipolar disorders will enter a hypomanic or manic phase if their sleep schedule is severely disturbed for two nights in a row (some doctors call this familiar pattern the "Two Day Rule"). If you see a growing pattern of sleep disturbance, you can take steps to turn things around. For some people, the solution will be as simple as a warm bath and a cup of herbal tea before bed. Others may need to try medication, either an over-the-counter preparation, a supplement like melatonin, or a prescription drug. When you know sleep deprivation is a trigger for mood swings, you can more easily be proactive.

SLEEP

Did you have a hard time getting to sleep last night? ☐ Yes ☐ No

Did you wake one or more times during the night and have a hard time getting back to sleep? ☐ Yes ☐ No

Did you have nightmares or very unusual dreams? ☐ Yes ☐ No

Was it hard to wake up on time this morning? ☐ Yes ☐ No

MEDICINE

Did you take all of your medicine on time today? ☐ Yes ☐ No

Did you start or stop taking any medication today, or change your dose? (If yes, which? _____) ☐ Yes ☐ No

FOOD

Did you eat a complete breakfast today? ☐ Yes ☐ No

Did you eat a complete lunch today? ☐ Yes ☐ No

Did you eat a complete dinner today? ☐ Yes ☐ No

Did you have snacks after school or between meals? ☐ Yes ☐ No

Did you eat anything unusual, or anything that disagreed with your digestion? (If yes, what? _____) ☐ Yes ☐ No

SCHOOL

Did you go to school today? ☐ Yes ☐ No

Did you have trouble paying attention in class? (If yes, in which classes? _____) ☐ Yes ☐ No

Did anything happen at school that made you feel sad, angry, upset, or scared? (If yes, what? _____) ☐ Yes ☐ No

Is anything coming up soon at school that's making you nervous or excited? (If yes, what? _____) ☐ Yes ☐ No

Did you find yourself talking "too much" today, or did other people say you were doing so? ☐ Yes ☐ No

Did you have a hard time staying still in class today, or did other people say you were fidgety? ☐ Yes ☐ No

Did you feel tired, "bummed out," or sick at school today? ☐ Yes ☐ No

HOME/OTHER

Did you have any special activities today? (If yes, what? _____) ☐ Yes ☐ No

Did you get in trouble at home today? (If yes, why? _____) ☐ Yes ☐ No

Is anything happening at home making you feel sad, angry, upset, or scared? (If yes, what? _____) ☐ Yes ☐ No

Were you able to relax today? ☐ Yes ☐ No

Did you keep thinking strange, depressing, or scary thoughts today? ☐ Yes ☐ No

Did you feel tired, "bummed out," or sick at home today? ☐ Yes ☐ No

Figure 3-2. Daily mood and behavior worksheet

Stress can be particularly hard to recognize in children and teens. Most parents have almost forgotten how stressful impending tests, cruel comments from other children, social worries, and unsympathetic teachers can be. Children with behavior, mood, or attentional problems have more than the usual share of stress, and this can contribute to the mood-swing roller coaster. Stress breeds anxiety, which can change eating and sleeping habits. Identifying and doing something about stressful situations can prevent problems.

Some patients also have certain dates or special events that frequently act as triggers, including holidays (which are mood-swing minefields due to schedule and diet changes, not to mention family expectations), birthdays, and the anniversaries of past traumatic events.

> *It was the seventh anniversary of my stepfather's death that coincided with my first down swing. I was 17, and I remember crying for hours and not understanding why. Even though it's been 13 years since I was diagnosed with a bipolar disorder, this date still consistently acts as a trigger for a down swing. —Troy, age 30 (diagnosed bipolar I disorder)*

The mood and behavior diary is not only a formal data collection device, it's a simple tool for starting conversations with your child about moods, emotions, and behaviors. Teenagers in particular can be hard to talk to about stress, social problems, school failures, and personal issues. The mood and behavior diary puts these problems on the table every day in a non-threatening, non-blaming way. Make it clear that everyone has these difficulties sometimes, including you, and talk about different ways people can solve their annoying little problems such as eating right, sleeping well, preparing in advance for potentially stressful situations, and avoiding negative interactions with people. Chapter 6, *Other Interventions*, offers a number of coping and non-medical treatment strategies that have worked for people with bipolar disorders.

Of course, medication changes are another important response when you see triggers emerge that tend to cause a serious mood swing.

Thinking about thinking

Some of the most persistent problems that children and adolescents with bipolar disorders have involve types of thinking that are irrational and difficult for others to understand. When young people learn to recognize and name these "thought errors," it can help them avoid making a scene, getting embarrassed, and getting in trouble. Once you can label and dissect an irrational thought, you take away some of its power. The longer these patterns are allowed to continue, however, the more likely they are to become ingrained, lifelong habits. These habits of thought contribute to development of the hard-to-treat personality disorders that often bedevil bipolar adults.

Problematic thought styles include:

- **Catastrophizing.** Seeing only the worst possible outcome in everything. For example, your child might think that because he failed his algebra test he will get an F for the semester, everyone will know he's stupid, the teacher will hate him, you will ground him, and moreover, he'll never get into college, and on and on. No matter what soothing words or solutions you try to apply, he'll insist that there's no remedy.

- **Minimization.** Another side of catastrophizing, this involves minimizing your own good qualities, or refusing to see the good (or bad) qualities of other people or situations. People who minimize may be accused of wearing rose-colored glasses, or of wearing blinders that allow them to see only the worst. If a person fails to meet the minimizer's high expectations in one way—for example, by being dishonest on a single occasion—the minimizer will suddenly write the person off forever, refusing to see any good characteristics that may exist.

- **Grandiosity.** Having an exaggerated sense of self-importance or ability. For example, your child may fancy herself the all-time expert at soccer, and act as though everyone else should see and worship her fabulous skill as well. She may think she can run the classroom better than her "stupid" teacher, or feel that she should be equal in power to her parents or other adults.

- **Personalization.** A particularly unfortunate type of grandiosity that presumes you are the center of the universe, causing events for good or ill that truly have little or nothing to do with you. A child might believe his mean thoughts made his mother ill, for example.

- **Magical thinking.** Most common in children and adults with obsessive-compulsive disorder, but seen in people with bipolar disorders as well. Magical thinkers come to believe that by doing some sort of ritual they can avoid harm to themselves or others. The ritual may or may not be connected with the perceived harm, and sufferers tend to keep their rituals secret. Children are not always sure what harm the ritual is fending off; they may simply report knowing that "something bad will happen" if they don't touch each slat of the fence or make sure their footsteps end on an even number. Others may come to feel that ritual behavior will bring about some positive event.

- **Leaps in logic.** Making seemingly logic-based statements, even though the process that led to the idea was missing obvious steps. Jumping to conclusions, often negative ones. One special type of logical leap is assuming that you know what someone else is thinking. For instance, a teenager might assume that everyone at school hates her, or that anyone who is whispering is talking about her. Another common error is assuming that other people will naturally know what you are thinking, leading to great misunderstandings when they don't seem to grasp what you're talking about or doing.

- **"All or nothing" thinking.** Being unable to see shades of gray in everyday life can lead to major misperceptions and even despair. A person who thinks only in black-and-white terms can't comprehend small successes. He's either an abject failure or a complete success, never simply on his way to doing better.

- **Paranoia.** In its extreme forms, paranoia slides into the realm of delusion. Many bipolar people experience less severe forms of paranoia because of personalizing events, catastrophizing, or making leaps in logic. A teen with mildly paranoid thoughts might feel that everyone at school is watching and judging him, when in fact he's barely on their radar screen.

- **Delusional thinking.** Most of the other thought styles mentioned above are mildly delusional. Seriously delusional thinking has even less basis in reality, and can include holding persistently strange beliefs. For example, your child may insist that he was kidnapped by aliens, and really believe that it is true.

Not only are these thought styles in error, they're intensely uncomfortable to the person who uses them—or should we say suffers from them, because no one would deliberately choose to have these anxiety-producing thoughts. When these thoughts emerge in words and deeds, the damage can be even worse. Expressing such ideas alienates friends and family, and can lead to teasing, ostracism, and severe misunderstandings.

Young children in particular don't have much of a frame of reference when it comes to thinking styles. They may well assume that everyone thinks this way! Older children and teens are usually more self-aware. Unless they're in an acute depressed, hypomanic, mixed, or manic episode, they may try hard to keep their "weird" thoughts under wraps. That's an exhausting use of mental energy, and makes the sufferer feel terribly alienated.

The same chemical imbalances that cause bipolar disorder are at the root of these thought errors, although they also have a basis in life experiences. When you have been taunted, teased, bullied, and ridiculed on a regular basis, for example, personalization and paranoia are not that farfetched. You may have been scapegoated so often that you start to feel like you really *are* the cause of all problems.

The rigidity that these problematic thought patterns have in common may also come from life experiences, at least in part. Many clinicians suspect that because people with bipolar disorders often deal with illogical waves of emotion and activity, they try to impose strict structures on their thoughts and beliefs to compensate. It's easy to get carried away with this, though, especially for children who don't have a lifetime of "normal" thinking to compare these thought patterns to.

Because these thought styles have at least some chemical basis, medication helps in many cases. Another good approach (especially when it's used in conjunction with medication) is cognitive therapy, a type of talk therapy geared precisely toward helping people identify erroneous thinking and mistaken beliefs about themselves and the world. We'll talk more about cognitive therapy in Chapter 5, *Therapeutic Interventions*, but some of the techniques used by cognitive therapists can come in handy at home.

First, you have to listen to what's being said—really listen. You might even want to take notes. Don't interrupt or make a value judgment on the thoughts your child is expressing while you're in active listening mode.

Next, ask questions about the thoughts expressed. See if you can help your child express the logic (or discover the lack of it) behind his statements. It can be hard to do, but try to avoid evaluating his words yourself. What you're trying to do is not so much to tell him the "right" way to think, but to help him discover his own thought errors, and to help him learn ways to correct or avoid these mistakes in the future.

Knowing the formal rules of logic can be extraordinarily helpful to someone with bipolar disorder. These are taught in speech classes and sometimes in writing classes, and can also be learned from books. They'll help your child know when others are trying to fool her, and also give her some clues for recognizing when her own brain is playing illogical tricks.

Kids with a visual bent may benefit from diagramming their thoughts using boxes and lines, or using computer programming-style "if-then" statements. This technique can help people see how flexible most situations and problems are, with many possible choices, solutions, and end results. "Choose your own adventure" books that let readers drive the story by making choices for the characters are another vehicle for explaining this concept. You can also ask "what do you think made him do that?" and "what if?" questions about the thoughts and choices of characters in their favorite books or movies.

Truly delusional thinking can become entrenched, sometimes very quickly. Keeping the lines of communication open should help you spot this kind of trouble before it occurs, although many people with delusional thoughts are very secretive about them. Because delusions are a type of psychosis (a loss of connection with objective reality), medication is almost always used to help break the pattern. When delusions are potentially harmful to the patient or others, full or partial hospitalization may be called for until medication can take effect.

Adding structure

You can structure your family life and community support system in ways that provide the best possible environment for a child or adolescent with a bipolar disorder. Some of these structures may be very different from what popular parenting books recommend.

First, you need to establish you and your spouse or partner, if any, as the authority at home. Being an authoritative presence in your child's life is not the same thing as being a dictator! It simply means that like a team captain, you're calling the plays based on your knowledge of the situation at hand and the input of your team members. An authority sets and enforces rules with compassion and fairness, and builds in enough flexibility to meet the needs of those in his care. An authority leads by example, not just by decree, and certainly not by force unless there's no alternative.

House rules should be the same for everyone (as you surely know already, bipolar kids will beat the issue of perceived unfairness into the ground). The rules should be prominently posted, just like they are at school or at the public pool. The list of specific rules should be as short and simple as possible, with a catch-all rule like "Treat others as you would like to be treated," to cover the gray areas. Rules should be discussed, role-played, and discussed again. You can bet that they will be tested!

You need to choose your battles carefully. Make hard and fast rules only on those items that simply can't be challenged. For most children and teens with bipolar disorder, the short list includes sleeping and waking times, eating, taking medication, avoiding dangerous behavior, and attending school. The rest of your rules—chores, activities, clothing style, avoiding profane language, even homework—need to be a little more flexible. There will be times when your child can gladly comply with your requests, and others when he needs your help to de-stress his life. Be observant and sensitive. Use the hierarchy idea presented at the beginning of this chapter to set your priorities. Safety and health come first, the rest is all gravy.

Many parenting experts recommend family meetings, but they aren't always a great idea when your child has a bipolar disorder. Family meetings foster a feeling of equality between family members. Usually, that's a good thing, but when children or teens have problems with grandiosity, one of the most visible ways it's expressed is in feeling and acting as though they are equal or even superior to their parents. Family meetings can actually contribute to this notion. You may be able to structure family meetings more carefully to ensure that children's contributions are heard and valued, while adults still retain the ability to make decisions. It's not the democratic family structure that many of us would prefer, but in this situation it may be essential to keeping peace in your home and keeping your child safe.

Many parenting experts decry the concept of scheduling children with many activities, but rigid scheduling is exactly what works best for most people with bipolar disorder. That doesn't mean every day must be a blur of activity. In fact, scheduling down time for relaxation is extremely important. Instead, each day should have a predictable pattern, from what time you get up in the morning to what you do after school. The earlier in life you begin to set these patterns, the easier it is for your child to get comfortable with them.

Older children can often help you figure out where the lines should be drawn. You might also want to check with their friends' parents about issues like bedtime, late-night weekend activities, and the like. If all of you can present a united front, it will cut off the ever-popular "but Mike's mother lets him do it" argument. It also reinforces your choices, and will probably help your child feel more comfortable with them as well.

Older children, and even some grade-schoolers, can benefit from using a daily planner to keep track of their schedule. When they can look forward to a predictable pattern of school, play, enjoyable activities, and goals, it's reassuring.

Your child should make as many choices about her schedule and activities as possible. Someday it will all be up to her, and she'll need the skills to make wise decisions about managing her time to promote optimal health. As she nears adulthood, talk often about how you handle your own scheduling conflicts and stresses.

Discipline

Discipline is difficult when a child has any type of mental or neurological illness. Not only do the old rules not always apply, you have to be flexible about behaviors that are due to your child's illness. Because bipolar disorders wax and wane, this is particularly hard to do if you want to maintain consistency. If your child is a rapid cycler, the challenge of responding properly is even bigger.

Proactive measures

The best strategy is to be proactive. Use preventative measures like the mood and behavior diary, consistent medical care, and daily structure to reduce the opportunity for mood swings and associated problem behavior. Eliminate sources of serious danger from your home, as discussed in the section "Safety matters" later in this chapter.

When your child is well, discuss measures you should take when he is not able to help acting out. Set up a system of signals he can use to let you and his teachers know when he needs extra help in controlling his behavior. These can help you gracefully remove him from a situation, such as a Little League game or classroom, before things get out of hand.

Set up a safe place at school and at home where he can take a "self time-out" when stress starts to build up too high. At school, this may be a resource room, a quiet office, or the library. At home, it may be your child's room or a cushy living-room chair. When you're out in the community, your car can become a refuge, or you can search out a public restroom, restaurant booth, or park bench. Most people prefer a feeling of being safely enclosed when they're on the verge of losing it. Some kids find that full-body pressure seems to calm the storm, and may benefit from being held by a parent, swaddled tightly in a blanket, or under a mattress, heavy blanket, or sofa cushions.

Your child's physician may be able to prescribe a tranquilizer or other medication for use as needed in emergencies. Make sure you thoroughly discuss when, how, and how often this medication can be used. If you don't have emergency medication available, an over-the-counter antihistamine like Benedryl can sometimes help calm a raging, sleepless, anxiety-plagued child temporarily. Obviously, you don't want to make this a regular practice.

Positive discipline

Most parents and school behavior experts have found that positive consequences are more effective than negative consequences at keeping kids with bipolar disorders on track. Many behavioral classrooms use a "token economy" to encourage good behavior. Each improvement or positive action merits a star or other mark on a chart, or a physical token such as a poker chip or paper chit. When a certain number of stars, chips, chits, or other tokens have been earned, there's a reward. Classroom rewards may include computer time, play time, having lunch with the teacher, or small items like stickers or nifty pencils.

You can adapt the token economy system for use at home, tying an allowance, event, special time with parents or siblings, or other desired reward to earning a certain number of tokens. Try not to set the bar too high, of course. Start out with easily achievable goals and small rewards, and work up from there. Try not to take away tokens for negative behavior—just firmly refuse to give tokens for anything but positive, desirable behavior.

Children shouldn't expect a treat for every good deed, of course. Your goal should be to eventually make a hug, smile, or positive statement about the behavior reward enough, and, in the long term, to make the warm inner feelings your child gets from behaving well and helping others to be a sufficient incentive. Giving rewards for good behavior goes against the grain for many parents. It may help to remember that bipolar kids don't always get those good feelings from good behavior. In fact, controlling their own behavior and complying with requests can be anxiety-producing, even almost painful. By adding a tangible incentive, you're chipping away at a disordered nervous system that has previously been reinforcing the wrong behavior, and working against the desired behavior.

Be sure to catch your child being good whenever you can. Too often discipline stresses and even reinforces bad behavior by giving it more attention than the positive things children and teenagers do. Be more lavish with your praise when warranted than you are with your disapproval and anger.

Sometimes parents need to take a self time-out. We've all had those days when a long string of minor misbehavior and stress adds up to a major blow-up over some little thing, like a ball thrown in the house or a spilled soda pop. Model the same stress-busting techniques that you encourage your child to use, whether it's deep breathing and counting to ten, or going to your room for five minutes (we'll talk more about these in Chapter 6). Your example is probably the best teaching tool you have.

Pick your battles

Many parents have found Ross Greene's excellent book *The Explosive Child: A New Approach for Understanding and Parenting Easily Frustrated, Chronically Inflexible Children* to be very helpful. Greene encourages parents and teachers to employ what he calls the basket system: use the mental device of several baskets to sort your rules in order of importance. Rules and chores that go in Basket A are the essentials. The rest go in Baskets B, C, and so on, in order of descending importance. Greene stresses the need to pick your battles carefully when dealing with a child who is oppositional, tantrums or rages easily, and has out-of-proportion reactions to small disagreements or requests. It's good advice, especially when your child is in the throes of a depressed, manic, or mixed state.

Another good resource for discipline ideas is a video called "Bending the Rules," available from the southern California chapter of the Tourette Syndrome Association. Like bipolar children, some children with Tourette have episodes of hard-to-handle behavior, including uncontrollable rages. The national TSA also has a well-written pamphlet available about neurologically caused rages. Ordering information for these and some other helpful materials on behavior is listed in the appendix, *Resources*.

> *We have found that listening to our child's requests, or sometimes demands, is very important! Our style of managing our children has been a complete turnaround from how we raised our children "before bipolar." We have really tried to listen and pick our battles carefully. —Bob, father of 18-year-old Shannon (diagnosed bipolar I disorder)*

The more you learn about the behaviors associated with bipolar disorders in children, the easier it will be to divide purposeful bad behavior from behaviors that are due to the illness itself. Even if the outcome of the behavior is the same—a broken window, for example—consequences may have to vary a little. For instance, whenever a window is broken, restitution is the natural and logical consequence. If the window was broken during a blind rage during a depressed or manic episode, however, a lecture or an immediate demand for payment will probably just make the situation worse. A child who is out of control is unlikely to be able to listen. Simply state what the consequence is, and mention that you'll talk about it later when the child is feeling better.

You can expect for there to be some disparity between your child's behavior at home and at school. Many kids with bipolar disorders work so hard to hold it together at school that they fall apart at home. By adding some accommodations at school that take the pressure off a bit, you may be able to achieve a happy medium. Until then, do your best to keep after-school time, weekends, and vacations structured for low stress.

Natural and logical consequences

Make sure that consequences you apply for misbehavior, willful or otherwise, fit the description of "natural and logical consequences." Bipolar children have a passion for fairness that often escalates into yet another battle if the punishment does not fit the crime. Parent Effectiveness Training (PET) and similar programs for helping parents of nondisabled children improve their discipline strategies won't fit your needs entirely, but they can help you learn more about identifying natural and logical consequences.

Physical punishments such as hitting or spanking really have no place in managing the behavior of a person with bipolar disorder, regardless of age. They simply teach that pain and force are a good way to impose your will on others, and that's not a lesson you want to teach someone who already has problems with impulsivity, limit-setting, and aggression.

If you're having a hard time managing your child's behavior without getting physical, you're not alone. Almost every parent of a child with a bipolar disorder has crossed the line sometime, and felt tempted to do so many more times. Reach out for help to increase your repertoire of techniques through consultation with a behavior expert, or with parenting training that is geared toward working with mentally ill children. You should be able to access help through your school district, a government mental health agency, a hospital with a psychiatric care department, or private programs.

Also try to build a personal support system made up of friends and family members, an online or in-person support group, or even a telephone crisis line for parents. It's tough to discipline any strong-willed child, and having someone to talk to can really help you keep up the struggle without resorting to violence. This advice goes double for single parents.

Children and teens with bipolar disorder may themselves be physically abusive when in a depressed, manic, or mixed state, or even when a regular confrontation escalates into a tantrum or rage. Your first duty is to protect yourself and others from harm. This can mean removing the child to a time-out area, sending a teenager to her room (and possibly locking her inside), using protective physical holds, and in some cases seeking emergency medical and/or law enforcement help.

Knowing how to physically control your child safely is a must. Improper physical restraint can injure or even kill. Ineffective holds only end up causing harm to you or others in the vicinity. Surprisingly, your relative size doesn't make much difference if you know the right techniques. Call the nearest colleges and find one that offers a psychiatric nursing program. Ask them about Professional Assault Response Training (PART) or similar programs that teach psychiatric nurses how to protect themselves from violent patients. The PART program is usually a two-day course, and can teach you several physical control techniques that will be both effective and safe for your child or teenager. You may also be able to access PART training or a similar course through your local mental health department, a hospital that has a psychiatric staff, or even a police department. Your child's teacher or classroom aide may also need to have this training.

Note for professionals: Professionals need to be very sensitive to the safety needs of families with aggressive, even violent bipolar children. Parents and siblings should never have to endure physical attacks, nor can they bear up under constant and extreme verbal abuse for long. When safety is at stake, it's best to treat the patient aggressively and rapidly, up to and including referring her for day treatment or hospitalization. Remember that while a child's aggressive behavior may be tolerable to you in a 45-minute office visit, the patient's family must endure the same behavior (or worse) day and night.

Don't underestimate a child's power to harm himself or others while in a depressed, manic, mixed, or psychotic state. Such children have been known to set deadly fires, injure or kill pets, attempt to stab or strangle family members, and attack with a level of violence and physical strength that surprises adults. The risk of suicide, even at ages as young as three or four, is also very real. Many parents of bipolar children report that their child has attempted to jump from a moving vehicle, run into fast-moving traffic, or leap out of a window. The same parents also report that their pleas for help have not always been taken seriously by professionals, even when they report these frightening incidents. The calm child you see in your office may indeed be the raging maniac the parent is describing—that disparity in behavior from day to day, even minute to minute, is the essence of bipolar disorders.

However, if you are using physical holds or locking your child in a room for protection, you do run the risk of being investigated by child protective services. In fact, some troubled young people use allegations of child abuse to get revenge on their parents. Your best strategy is to be proactive: consult with your child's medical team, and have them put their emergency recommendations in writing. Get training, be careful, stay calm and kind, and if you are contacted by the authorities, bring in your experts to help.

Other people with a bipolar disorder turn their violent impulses on themselves, banging their heads on walls, slicing their arms, or otherwise harming their own bodies. This isn't a discipline problem, it's a medical issue. Usually these self-injurious behaviors (SIB) are not suicide attempts, but physical expressions of inner pain. Nevertheless, they can cause serious self-harm.

Let your child know that she can talk to you about these impulses and behaviors, and that there will never be any shame or punishment attached to SIB. Medication changes can usually help, but therapeutic relationships with parents and/or professionals are the key to reducing and eventually eliminating self-injurious behaviors. Sometimes SIB in young children is related to another health condition, such as ear infections. It can be a good idea to eliminate these possibilities before you change or start psychiatric medication. (See "Handling self-injurious behavior (SIB)," later in this chapter, for more ideas and information.)

Verbal abuse is also very common during depressed or manic phases, and may occur at other times as well due to the increased impulsivity and thought errors that characterize bipolar disorders. To the best of your ability, simply end the conversation, and refuse to react to taunts and insults. Realize that these words are coming out unbidden, and that your child will probably be shocked at what he has said later. Don't demand an apology on the spot, as it will only escalate the situation. Wait to discuss the verbal abuse later, when your child is well and calm. Don't be accusatory, just let him know that your feelings were hurt—and that you love him anyway.

Disciplining teenagers is difficult under the best of circumstances, but it's doubly so when your adolescent has mood swings and the other behavioral challenges associated with bipolar disorders. The techniques that worked when your child was younger may seem babyish now, and physical control is tougher when your child is larger and more wily about telling lies, slipping out of the house at night, and acting independently in the world. Keep applying proactive measures to protect your child, family, and community as best you can. Don't be afraid to call in reinforcements—the parents of your child's friends, your neighbors, teachers and other school personnel, mental health professionals, sometimes even the juvenile authorities—if your teen's behavior is bringing him into conflict with the law.

When things get tough, don't try to go it alone.

Family relationships

Your family relationships have probably already suffered many blows due to your child's disorder. Divorce is more common in families dealing with any disability in a child, and even more so when the problem is a mental illness. Disagreements between parents on how to manage and discipline the child, or on medical treatment, are common. There are issues of guilt, blame, sorrow, and stress to work out.

It is possible to build (or rebuild) strong family relationships despite these additional challenges. Family therapy is a great place to work out problems that seem insoluble on your own. You may find that as you discuss your difficulties and work to solve them together, your relationships will become deeper and stronger. If you can face your problems with a united front, the outlook for your child's health will also be much improved.

> It has been a major strain on the entire family, but we are all closer than ever because of it. My husband and I were having some problems in the beginning, but we worked them out and made a point to find time for ourselves. —Cindy, mother of 16-year-old Craig and 19-year-old Kara (both diagnosed bipolar disorder)

Behavior isn't the only issue that pits parents and siblings against each other. The financial burden of treating bipolar disorders can be heavy. In-patient hospitalization can cost more than $1,000 per day if not covered by insurance, and therapy, medications, and regular healthcare add up to hundreds of dollars per month. We'll discuss some ways to reduce your expenses in Chapter 7, *Insurance*, but there will be bills to pay.

Sometimes the result is more than just a momentary budget problem. You or your spouse may have to give up a lot to care for your child. One of you may decide to stay at home full time, or reduce your work to a part-time schedule. Promotions that require moving to an area with inadequate medical care for your child may be turned down. The chance to further your own education or put away money for a comfortable retirement, material niceties, or even basic financial stability may be out of reach.

Siblings often resent the money spent on their brother or sister's healthcare, especially if it takes away from their own needs or desires. Siblings may indeed miss out on nice clothes, spring break trips, even college due to the cost of medical care. This is something you'll need to discuss with them in advance. Let older siblings in on budget problems, without causing unnecessary worry. Talk about and look for alternative ways to meet their needs. In some families, a grandparent, aunt, or uncle may be willing to offer some special financial and personal support for siblings.

As discussed earlier in this chapter, grandiosity can disrupt family relationships. Another way this can come out in the family structure is with the grandiose child making alliances with one parent against the other, as if he is the co-parent rather than the child. Although it's important to treat children of any age with respect, respect is a two-way street. Parents should not be ordered around or turned against each other by their children. Grandiosity in a child or teenager with bipolar disorder can erupt into power struggles over who's the boss. You've got to nip this tactic in the bud.

The ongoing chaos of life with someone whose moods swing wildly has a detrimental effect on family relationships and home life. In fact, people married to or parenting a person with a bipolar disorder often swear that the illness is contagious! The same proactive steps that work to help your bipolar child—scheduling, setting limits, and reducing opportunities for problems—can help keep the rest of your family on track, too.

You will have to put your foot down in certain areas. For example, if there is physical abuse, sexual abuse, emotional abuse, or drug or alcohol abuse going on in your home, your former spouse's home, or a relative's home, that environment is not safe for a child or teen with bipolar disorder until these issues have been addressed. In divorced families with joint custody, this may mean involving the courts or a mediator to enforce these changes. Because they are essential to your child's health and well-being, the stress of fighting these battles will be worth it in the long run.

One area where you do need to smooth over differences within the family is discipline, whether the disagreement over rules and methods is between partners, between two parents who are divorced, or between parents and grandparents or other relatives. Other family members may not be willing to accept neurological explanations for behavior, and may disagree with your discipline methods or medical treatment choices. Sometimes there's nothing you can do about this problem. In other cases, providing reading material or even bringing the family member in to talk to your child's doctor or a behavior expert can help clear the air.

No matter how you manage it, it's essential to set and enforce consistent boundaries about the most important issues. On the secondary issues, one parent's household or that of other relatives may well be more or less strict. That's just a result of being different people, and perhaps having different lifestyles. If both sides in the discipline debate can agree on the big issues and also agree not to sweat the small stuff, your child will probably learn how to negotiate both environments.

Sometimes your child's diagnosis opens up old wounds. The genetic nature of bipolar disorders dictates that other family members may have the same problems. If these individuals were not treated sympathetically, they may be especially angry about how you treat your child. It's a form of misplaced jealousy, and it may not be within your power to remedy.

Value clashes

As your child gets older, your spouse and extended family members won't be the only source of value clashes. Most teenagers act out in ways intended to get your attention, often adopting value systems and appearance choices tailor-made to shock the older generation. It's all part of growing up, and you probably did it too.

When bipolar kids act out, though, they really go all the way. Often they'll cycle through a whole series of subcultural styles and peer groups, trying on new identities and "looks" in a frantic search for a place where they fit in. One day you may send a granola-crunching hippie throwback to bed, only to find Sid Vicious Jr. snarling at you across the breakfast table the next morning. Punk, heavy metal, jock, gothic, hip-hop, skater, skinhead, mall rat, straight edge, yuppie, Rasta, boot-scootin' country boy—you might see it all before your kid settles into a fully formed adult personality.

In fact, adopting unusual styles of dress and flitting from peer group to peer group is extremely common among bipolar teens. When it happens suddenly, it can be a clue about an incipient hypomanic, manic, or depressive episode. Often it's just one of the impulsive whims common to our kids, though, an outward expression of the artistic and daring temperament that's part of the whole package. It's a symptom of the general instability they feel, not the cause of it.

After two troubled teens shot teachers and classmates in Littleton, Colorado, many pundits quickly tried to pin the blame on the shooter's supposed involvement in the "gothic" subculture, as expressed by liking gloomy, decadent music and wearing black clothing. It's essential for worried parents to remember that music and clothing themselves do not cause behavior. If a change in your child's appearance or interests has you concerned, talk to him about it. He may be trying to tell you something—or he may just be enjoying a bit of harmless adolescent rebellion.

Subcultures are attractive to young people who are unsure about their identity and values. They offer a ready-made set of friends, activities, beliefs, even clothes and music, all designed to make a new adherent feel right at home (if they'll just conform to the mores of the other nonconformists). Usually newcomers end up being more than a little disillusioned after awhile, and by adulthood identity is based less on affiliation with a prepackaged subculture than on true personal affinity.

Your teen may try out new political or religious beliefs as well as make odd lifestyle choices. Unless you have a truly good reason to be concerned (see "Gangs, cults, and other dangers" later in this chapter), these usually fall into the "if you ignore it, it will go away" category. Quite possibly you'll end up disagreeing on some very fundamental issues, as probably happened with you and your own parents. You have a right to hold your own beliefs and values, and as long as your child is a minor, he'll have to deal with that fact. You can't impose your values and beliefs on a teenager, but you certainly can express them and, more importantly, live them. Years from now, you'll be surprised at how much sunk in even as your teenager raised a ruckus.

For teens, trying out new identities and ideas is usually okay. Don't make assumptions based on appearance (or the appearance of your child's friends). There are some great young people out there wearing weird-looking outfits. There are some monsters camouflaged in seeming normalcy. Make your child's friends welcome in your home, unless you have a truly good reason not to. Although troubled young people tend to attract similar souls, having one family home that's a safe place can keep a whole group of rebels without a clue more secure. Stay involved, even if it means enduring horrible concerts or dragging yourself to the skate park every Saturday.

Don't fall into the trap of being the so-called cool parent who enables bad behavior by allowing drug use, beer bashes, or underage sex in your home, but be the truly cool parent who sees beyond outward appearance to the growing, questioning young person inside.

Of course, if your child's peer group is involved with drugs, drinking, extremely risky behavior, or violence, you need to know—and act. Talk openly with your child about your own youthful experiences, telling her what you learned from them, and what stuck with you. Talk about what was positive and negative about cultural styles you've seen in the course of your life, from hippie to yuppie. Let her know that clothes, music, and the other outward trappings are not all that important to you, but that personal values and her safety are.

Many teenagers find solace in music, one of the few venues for poetic and angst-filled expression open to young people. Talk to your child about the music and lyrics he likes. Being judgmental won't help, even if it's Marilyn Manson or something equally provocative that piques his interest. Find out what attracts him to the sound and the words. Music is so powerful because it operates almost entirely on the level of emotion and physical sensation. It can drag you down, validate your feelings, uplift you, or all three, even all at once. It can be intensely therapeutic, both for the musician and the listener. Your teen may be using "dark" music as a vehicle for expressing his own pain, or it may let him know he isn't alone. Those factors are not necessarily negative, especially if he also has a supportive relationship with you to rely on for a more positive kind of solace.

Of course, depressing music and lyrics can also validate feelings of despair and hopelessness, deepening the spiral of depression. Contrary to some lawsuits you may have heard about, pop music can't cause teen suicide. Doom and gloom tunes are a clue to an existing condition, however, and the fact that teens often externalize their affinity for this stuff by the slogans on their T-shirts and what they write on their school notebooks should let you know that it's a form of nonverbal communication with you, the parent or professional. Take that conversational gambit and run with it if you think there is cause to worry.

Bad friends

Almost every parent has blamed their child's misbehavior on bad friends at one time or another. Is there such a thing? You bet. Sociopaths have to start somewhere, and your child just might latch on to one someday. Whether it's a buddy or a budding love interest, watch out for the friend who seems to take control of your child's life and deliberately turn it in an ugly direction.

Truly bad friends are the ones who have no positive parental influence, who get your kid into trouble with the law, and who manipulate every situation to their own benefit. Some of these kids may seem to have redeeming qualities, but do what you can to minimize your child's time with them all the same. If you can, work with the friend's parents to redirect him, or simply make your child unavailable by scheduling him right out of this friend's life.

In a few extreme cases, such as a friend who is trying to involve your child in gang activity or other criminal behavior, you may have to involve school authorities or the police. Some parents have simply chosen to move out of the neighborhood or the city, or considered boarding school. Avoid making the reason for these actions obvious, of course: friends that parents hate are doubly attractive to any rebellious teen.

Gangs, cults, and other dangers

Most youth subcultures are about as dangerous as joining the 7-Up Underground instead of the Pepsi Generation. Teens with mental illness may stumble into darker regions, however. Their low self-esteem and obsessional tendencies may even make gangs, cults, and other dicey fringe elements look extra attractive.

Keep an eye out for changes in behavior and values that seem to be more than superficial, and that could be dangerous. Groups led by adults or by much older teens are usually more suspect than same-age peer groups. If your child is being excessively secretive about his activities, or if you're getting worried reports from school or the police, check up on them. Follow your intuition.

Gangs and cult-like groups actively prey on those who are least able to resist them. If you've successfully taught your child the laws of logical argument, you may be able to use that knowledge to defuse the group's appeal. You can use logic and deductive reasoning to show whether beliefs are false, and to show the likely consequences of continued involvement. You may have to take more extreme steps to remove your child from the situation if he is unable or unwilling to recognize the danger.

Children with bipolar disorders are especially vulnerable to sexual predators as well. Their neediness attracts the worst sort of manipulative person, and their emotional weakness cements the attraction. Bipolar youth are far more active sexually than their peers. Sexual precocity is considered a symptom of the disorder, and their behavior is also influenced by both the strong desire for exciting physical sensations, and the idea of creating instant (if empty) relationships by having sex with someone.

The best defense against sexual predators is a combination of education and satisfying nonsexual relationships with friends, family members, and adult mentors. If you are aware that your child has become sexually active, you may not be able to stem the primal urge that prompts this behavior. You can do your best to keep your child busy and supervised, ensure that she has plenty of information about protecting her health, make sure you are available for questions and, if needed, provide healthcare and contraceptives. An unplanned pregnancy is a disaster for any teen, but even more so if one of the youth involved has a bipolar disorder.

Safety matters

This may be the hardest part of this book for parents and professionals to read, but in many ways, it's also the most important. The hardest job we have is keeping bipolar children and teens alive. Suicide, accidents resulting from suicidal impulses or foolish risk-taking, and self-harm are large obstacles that we must carefully help them avoid. Bipolar kids are like ships tossed on crashing waves of mood and action, and these dangerous icebergs lurk just below the surface. Like seasoned sea captains, we have to hold tight to the wheel, keep careful tabs on the weather, and batten down the hatches to steer the ship through to safety.

Suicide prevention

Suicide is the third leading cause of death among US teens, and the suicide rate has climbed continuously since 1952—a sobering reminder of how stressful modern adolescence can be.

For people with a bipolar disorder, however, the suicide rate is five times higher.

The American Psychiatric Association warns parents to be on the lookout for warning signs of suicide, including:

- Withdrawal from friends and family
- Inability to concentrate

- Talk of suicide
- Dramatic changes in personal appearance
- Loss of interest in favorite activities
- Expressions of hopelessness or excessive guilt
- Self-destructive behavior (such as reckless driving, drug abuse, and promiscuity)
- Preoccupation with death
- Giving away favorite possessions
- Suddenly "cheering up" after a deep depression (the new mood may mean a plan for suicide has been made, causing the person to feel relieved)

If you noticed that some of these warning signs are common characteristics of people with bipolar disorder, you're very observant. Our children are predisposed to the despair and suffering that causes suicide because of the chemical imbalance in their brains, and because of the effect this illness has on their lives and relationships.

Never ignore the warning signs of suicide. Most people who try to kill themselves give advance notice—and this is especially true of young people. Be open to the nonverbal messages your child may be sending you, and if your suspicions are aroused, *act*. Don't be afraid to come right out and ask if suicide is on his mind.

Information and advance planning are your best allies in preventing youth suicide. If your child has already threatened to attempt suicide, or has attempted suicide, there are several resources that can get you in touch with immediate help. See the section "Suicide prevention" in the appendix.

Every parent with a bipolar child should prepare in advance to deal with a suicide crisis, just in case. Most people with a bipolar disorder do consider suicide at some time, although not all will make a serious attempt. When and if the moment comes, the prepared parent can concentrate all his energy on helping his child, rather than frantically searching for resources.

A suicide crisis is not something to keep quiet about or to handle discreetly at home. Successful suicide attempts mean death, and unsuccessful ones can cause permanent injury or brain damage. Because some teenagers make half-hearted "cry for help" suicide attempts in response to breaking up with a boyfriend or similar minor tragedies, emergency room personnel are not always as sympathetic as they should be. To protect your child from callous treatment or too-early release, you need to have a hospital admission plan set up in advance.

The most helpful person for putting this plan in place is your child's psychiatrist. Set up a private session to talk about local mental health facilities. Most psychiatrists have had to commit a patient from time to time, and almost all have worked with local facilities or members of their staffs. They can usually tell you which hospitals have the best ward for children or teens, and which staff person you should talk to in advance.

A county or provincial mental health professional or social worker may also have information about local resources, and of course parents in local support groups can tell you about their experiences as well.

Make an appointment to visit the best facility or the top two or three in advance. Try to meet the program's director if possible. Find out what the admissions process is—where you would go in case of a crisis, who you can call if you need help getting your child to the facility, and what the criteria for admission are. Tell them a little about your child and the concerns that have led you to check out their program. (Evaluating hospital programs is discussed in greater detail in Chapter 4.)

Lack of information is one of the biggest problems families face when their child needs emergency mental health help. Transferring paper medical files and even computerized files seems to take forever, and sometimes the documents that do arrive are incomplete. You may want to provide the facility you would use in a crisis with an advance copy of your child's basic medical and mental health history, a list of medications used currently and in the past, and your insurance data, just in case. Alternatively, make a copy of this information and store it where you can grab it en route to the facility.

In larger cities, there may be a crisis triage center for mental health admissions. This is usually a separate area of a hospital. If a suicide attempt has been made that caused injury, including an attempted drug overdose, you would almost certainly go to the emergency room first. If your child has swung into a severe depression, mania, or mixed state, or if he has become psychotic, you may be able to go to the crisis triage center instead. Here she can be evaluated by professionals, given emergency medications if needed, and directed to an inpatient or day treatment facility.

We had never used the crisis triage center before, but when I real-
ized that Lili was manic, that's where our insurance company sent us. We
had to wait a long time, but since the room wasn't full of injured, bleed-
ing people it was easier for her to calm down. There were several parents
there with children or teenagers; in fact, there was a play area with toys
for the little kids. When her turn came, we were interviewed separately. I
felt worried about letting her out of my sight, but once you're in the exam
rooms the place is pretty secure.

They were able to tell she was manic to the point of psychosis imme-
diately. She was paranoid, agitated, and having hallucinations. They gave
her a tranquilizer and a very large dose of Zyprexa right there, and gave
me a prescription for more. They also took care of calling her regular psy-
chiatrist and making sure she could be seen there very soon to see how the
meds were working.

One thing they didn't do is tell us what the side effects of the Zyprexa
might be. She fell asleep as soon as we got in the car and then she slept
straight through until it was time for her doctor's appointment the next
day. Here's where we had problems. When she woke up, she was disori-
ented, confused, and unable to make her body and brain work properly.
She walked with her legs and arms stiff, hunched over like an old lady. I
had to help her into the car, and practically carry her into the doctor's
office. At one point she sat down in the middle of the floor in the waiting
room, crying and moaning. It's like she had no inhibitions or self-control. I
was really scared, especially since I was afraid she might try to run off in
this state. She doesn't remember anything about this day now.

Amazingly, by the second day she was fine, as if the manic episode
had never happened. I guess the medication was a good thing, but I wish
they'd warned us to stay home for a day or two while the effects of that
big dose wore off. —Sarah, mother of 17-year-old Lili

In areas without a special intake center, you can call ahead to the emergency
room and let them know if there are special security needs or medications
that should be on hand when you arrive. In some areas you may be able to
take your child directly to a mental health facility, such as a county mental
hospital, for immediate evaluation. Be sure to call first, as some facilities will
turn you away unless they feel it is a matter of life or death. Others don't

have good assessment facilities on site, and you'll only end up waiting or being redirected.

Of course, insurance companies, HMOs, and public health policies can have a lot to do with how you go about accessing emergency mental healthcare. We'll look at these more closely in Chapter 7.

Another important step you can take to prevent youth suicide is to remove implements of self-destruction from your home, particularly guns. Guns are a terribly final choice, and they are the weapon used in more than half of all suicides. Usually when a child or teenager shoots himself, he got the gun at his own home. If you own guns, or if members of your extended family own guns, get rid of them. Locking them up is not enough to stop a person who is determined to kill himself.

If your gun is needed for your job as a police officer, soldier, or security guard, store it securely at the station house, base, or company headquarters.

If you currently keep a gun in the home for protection against criminals, get a burglar alarm, security bars, panic button, or Doberman instead.

Don't assume that your child would never use a gun. Today, suicidal girls are almost as likely as boys to use a gun—and boys who choose guns are often the quiet, gentle types you would not expect to do so.

Talk to your child's friends, babysitters, and other people whose homes he may go to about their guns. Some people are incredibly careless with firearms, leaving them loaded in unlocked drawers or even lying in plain sight. All it takes to cause disaster is a moment of curiosity or impulse coupled with access to a weapon that causes instant death.

Most conscientious people will comply with your request to keep weapons out of their home for your child's sake or, at the very least, lock up any firearms they own securely. If someone resists, you can mention the legal liability involved in leaving firearms within reach of children, especially when they have been warned about a person with suicidal impulses. If that doesn't work, you'll just have to make that home off limits to your child.

Guns aren't the only danger, of course. You may need to have a lock installed on your kitchen knife drawer, get rid of hunting knives and sharp tools, and ensure that there are no hoses around that would fit over your car's exhaust pipe. Some families have had to take very stringent measures during a suicide crisis, from removing closet bars to taking the door off their child's room. Some have had to bar windows from the outside and add keyed interior locks to keep a suicidal child from running. And nonetheless suicidal individuals will try to find a means of self-harm, from using a light fixture to hang themselves to slicing their arms with glass from a broken window.

You most certainly should lock up medications—and not just prescription ones. Aspirin and Tylenol are used very frequently in suicide attempts. Both of them are potentially fatal in large doses (in fact, Tylenol is one of the medications used most often in successful attempts). Use a daily pill reminder box to measure out each day's doses in advance, and keep the full bottles in a securely locked medicine chest. A heavy-duty cash box, available at most office supply stores, is a portable substitute. If you happen to have a safe in your home for important papers, you can use it to store medications.

Accident prevention

Bipolar kids are notoriously accident-prone. They're born daredevils, in search of new sensations. They enjoy attention, and their natural level of activity is high. These characteristics become stronger when hypomania or mania hits.

Suicidal youths may also disguise deliberately self-destructive behavior by making it look like an accident. Examples of the latter include ridiculously dangerous stunts, like trying to bungee jump off the local water tower, or attempting self-harm with reckless driving.

Picking up the pieces after an accident is draining. It's far better (and in the case of suicidal pseudo-accidents, far safer) to prevent accidents before they occur. Check your home and neighborhood for attractive nuisances: items and places that almost invite trouble. These may include high, climbable structures, abandoned buildings and cars, and bodies of water.

You should always maintain control of family vehicles, giving out car keys only when a bipolar teenager is absolutely stable and free of substance abuse problems. A car in the hands of a manic or depressed person is like a half-ton battering ram.

Another proactive way to prevent accidents is to provide opportunities for safer risk-taking. If your bipolar child craves danger, you can dole it out in acceptable amounts by providing trampolines, skateboarding or BMX bicycling ramps, trees to climb and build treehouses in, rock-climbing or skiing excursions, and supervision to make sure these exciting activities stay as safe as possible. These sensation-seeking impulses will probably be with your child for life. If you start early to channel them into acceptable outlets, he may find good ways to receive the intense sensations he craves without causing harm to himself or others.

Handling self-injurious behavior (SIB)

For a long time, self-mutilation was a dirty little secret. With the publication of widely read books like *The Scarred Soul: Understanding & Ending Self-Inflicted Violence,* by Tracy Alderman, in 1997, and both *Cutting: Understanding and Overcoming Self-Mutilation,* by Steven Levenkron, and *A Bright Red Scream: Self-Mutilation and the Language of Pain,* by Marilee Strong, in 1998, self-injurious behavior (SIB) is finally something that more people are aware of and able to talk about.

Common forms of SIB include cutting (usually this involves shallow cuts on the arms, legs, or torso), puncturing or piercing the skin (not to be confused with the cosmetic piercing so in vogue these days), hitting (including banging the head on hard objects), burning the skin with lit cigarettes or matches, and picking at the skin or at scabs. People who have had SIB describe it as a way to relieve inner pain or stress, as a form of self-punishment, or as a way to create sensations that are almost enjoyable when compared to the out-of-control feelings they had before committing the act. It can also be entirely compulsive, with seemingly no rhyme or reason behind it.

You might compare SIB to the activities of ancient saints and mystics, many of whom used mortification of the flesh via hair shirts, whips, or beds of nails to achieve ecstatic states or to drive out impure thoughts. In some religions, these activities are still practiced and revered, but modern society usually views self-mutilation as repugnant and shameful. In truth, it's just another bad coping mechanism, not unlike drinking, using drugs, or becoming a workaholic. It can be treated, particularly with medication and the same kinds of support and self-help strategies that work for substance abuse and other coping strategies gone awry.

People with bipolar disorders are at high risk for SIB, especially if they do not learn other, safer ways to deal with emotional distress at an early age. Be alert to clues that may indicate SIB, such as frequent unexplained injuries or constantly wearing long-sleeved shirts. It's important to be accepting about the person and even the behavior, although that's difficult for many parents and professionals to do. A child with SIB will continue to hide the problem and avoid help unless she feels safe talking to you about it.

Many medical people have very little experience in treating SIB, and some actually do more harm than good. If your child needs help with SIB, look for a psychiatrist who has expertise in this area and who understands the need to help the patient gradually develop safe substitute behaviors that can allay emotional pain and mood problems.

> People who self-injure generally do so because of an internal dynamic, and not in order to annoy, anger, or irritate others. Their self-injury is a behavioral response to an emotional state, and is usually not done in order to frustrate caretakers. In emergency rooms, people with self-inflicted wounds are often told, directly and indirectly, that they are not as deserving of care as someone who has an accidental injury. They are treated badly by the same doctors who would not hesitate to do everything possible to preserve the life of an overweight, sedentary heart-attack patient. —Deb Martinson, from "Self-injury: A Quick Guide to the Basics" (available online at http://www.palace.net/~llama/psych/intro.html)

Some doctors still try to psychoanalyze patients with SIB, assuming that it always arises from some secret trauma. For a person with a chemical imbalance, this approach can be more harmful than getting no treatment at all. It essentially blames the patient, and it does nothing to assuage the actual feelings and impulses that cause repetitive self-injury.

Substance abuse

According to the most recent literature on substance abuse and bipolar disorder, these two problems occur together so frequently that all young people with a bipolar diagnosis should also be assessed for drug and alcohol problems.[1] Those who experience mixed states or rapid cycling have the highest rate of danger from substance abuse—the discomfort a person feels in these chaotic moods is so great that she may be willing to do or take almost anything to make it stop.

Some drugs, including marijuana, downers, alcohol, and opiates, seem to temporarily blunt the effects of mood swings, only to cause ill effects later. Others can actively exacerbate manic depression. Speed (methamphetamine, crank, crystal) and cocaine are two that have sent many abusers into mania, often followed quickly by deep depression and psychotic symptoms. Hallucinogens, including LSD and PCP, can set off psychotic symptoms as well. These drugs are not a good idea for any child or teenager, but their effects on young people with bipolar disorders can be even worse.

As with suicide, accidents, and SIB, the best approach to substance abuse is prevention. First, take a look at your own example: if you find that drugs or alcohol have become important coping strategies for you, seek immediate treatment. Talk to your child about responsible use of alcohol, for example, a glass of wine with a special meal, or a cold beer on a hot day at the ball game. Point out examples of inappropriate or excessive use, from street alcoholics to news stories about young people in trouble due to drug use or drunken driving. You really don't have to preach, just provide a good example and accurate information to counteract the messages your child will receive from ads, pop culture, and peers.

When a person first begins to try drugs or alcohol, there's still time to stop without involving a detox center or other strong measures. She needs to think about why she has chosen to try alcohol or drugs, such as feeling self-conscious in social situations or inability to handle peer pressure; other activities that might have the same positive effects, such as improving her social skills; and ways to avoid temptation, including choosing a different peer group or steering her friends toward something other than bong hits and beer bashes. These are issues that can be discussed with a parent or a counselor.

Most teens will attend a wild party or two, out of curiosity or boredom if nothing else. You may be able to prevent them from coming to harm even when they've made a bad choice. Many families have drawn up a contract with their children, promising that they will retrieve them from a dangerous situation at any hour, with no lecture to follow. Let them know that while they may make some poor judgment calls, you're available to come to their rescue.

You may also need to actively help kids whose peers are fixated on drinking and drugs to find other ways to spend their time. This negative aspect of youth culture isn't just a big-city phenomenon by the way—small towns and rural areas, with their lack of activities and places to go, can have extraordinarily high rates of drinking and drug use among teens. The drug and alcohol problems of suburban youth are often covered up, but they're there in force, spurred by lack of supervision after school, access to cash, and easy mobility.

When substance abuse progresses in frequency or seriousness, or when highly dangerous drugs are involved, early intervention is essential. Experts in treating children and teenagers with a dual diagnosis of bipolar disorder and substance abuse or bipolar disorder and substance dependency say success depends on appropriate medication; education about their psychiatric condition, psychiatric medications, and the dangers of drug and alcohol abuse; and close monitoring. Lithium has proven to greatly reduce or eliminate substance abuse in as many as 75 percent of dual-diagnosis youth with a bipolar disorder. It can be assumed that when other types of mood stabilizers are tested, they will show at least some positive effect on substance abuse as well. Twelve-step programs such as AA are important for reaching and maintaining recovery.

Although some sources recommend treating the substance abuse first, mostly because drugs and alcohol can have severe interactions with the medication used to treat manic depression, both really need to be addressed at once. Obviously, a person who is not sober is unable to adhere to the lifestyle changes, medication regime, and therapy appointments needed to hold back mood swings. At the same time, most bipolar substance abusers drink or use drugs partly to self-medicate their symptoms, and they may misuse their prescription medications as well.

Drug treatment programs, including inpatient detox centers, are beginning to be more knowledgeable about working with bipolar patients. If your child will be going to a drug treatment program, make sure that its clinical staff is fully aware of the implications of his illness, and that appropriate medication management and psychiatric expertise will be available.

Most detox centers say that about a month is needed to break a true addiction's physical grasp, and it takes a year of sobriety before an addict can honestly feel mentally comfortable without his substance of abuse. Relapses are common until several years of sobriety have been achieved, and can present severe dangers, including suicide. The earlier a drug or alcohol user seeks effective treatment, however, the more likely he is to achieve complete freedom from substance abuse without progressing to substance dependency.

Many addicts use self-help resources like Alcoholics Anonymous (AA), Narcotics Anonymous (NA), or Rational Recovery to get and stay sober. In these programs, people attend regular meetings to talk about their addiction problems and offer each other support. Former substance abusers who have gotten clean act as mentors to newcomers. Generally speaking, these 12-step programs are an excellent resource for drug and alcohol users in recovery. There are special groups for teens, although many experts recommend teens attend mixed-age groups. Participants in 12-step programs are paired with sponsors who can help them deal with temptation, social pressure, old behavior patterns, and the stress of meeting new expectations.

There are also adjunct groups for the families of addicts. Family support groups can really help you make it through this difficult period. You'll learn many strategies for helping your child on the road to recovery. Families Anonymous is one with many local chapters.

The only down side of 12-step programs is that a few former addicts are against using prescription medications for brain disorders, seeing them as simply a legal substitute for street drugs or alcohol. This is not an official policy of AA or NA, by the way. To make sure a particular 12-step group doesn't have this orientation, talk to one of the group's long-term members or to its institutional sponsor, if any.

Several medications are available to assist in the drug and alcohol detox process. These are discussed in Chapter 4.

Criminal justice and the bipolar child

Jail can be the worst possible place for a person with a mental illness, so many families suffer through repeated abuses rather than allow their child to be arrested. Some even hide their child's criminal activities from the police, while they desperately search for more sympathetic help.

> Our family cannot enjoy anything because of my son. We have no
> extra money, and he steals whenever there is any money in the house at
> all—even when we lock it up, he will find my keys and steal it. My
> daughter is in Girl Scouts and the youngest is in Cub Scouts, and he steals
> their Scout money from cookie sales, candy bar sales, popcorn sales,
> whatever. Then we have to replace it, so it really puts a burden on us. We
> are behind in our bills now because we have had to replace so much
> money that he has stolen, and also because of the required trips for when

he was hospitalized last year at a place ten hours away in Boise, Idaho,
because it was the closest place to get him any kind of help. I had to quit
my job, and now I cannot work because I cannot leave him alone, and no
one will "babysit" a 16-year-old, especially one that steals from them.
—Cindy, mother of 16-year-old Nathan (diagnosed bipolar disorder,
OCD, ADHD, post-traumatic stress disorder, chemical dependency,
bulimia)

Young people with bipolar disorder are likely to tangle with the law one or more times. Impulsivity and sensation-seeking are a major part of the problem. Certain crimes, such as shoplifting, drug- and alcohol-related offenses, and sexual escapades, are largely crimes of impulse and sensation.

Grandiose thinking is also an issue. It's not that bipolar kids are too crazy to know right from wrong, or to know what the laws are—but when they're grandiose, they just think the laws don't apply to them! They may follow their impulses and desires without a second thought, even when they have been fully informed of the consequences.

Of course, when symptoms of psychosis are present the person is usually not aware of rules, laws, or proper behavior. A person who is in a manic, depressed, or mixed state may also attract police attention due to bizarre behavior or appearance.

Unless psychosis is present when the crime is committed, bipolar disorder rarely makes for a successful insanity defense. That means non-psychotic persons who have committed crimes, even if their bipolar symptoms had everything to do with the crime, are likely to go to a juvenile facility or prison rather than being committed to a mental hospital for treatment. Generally speaking, that's not a good thing.

Since the closure of most large public mental hospitals in the US and the UK, increasing numbers of mentally ill youth and adults are being sent to prison instead of getting appropriate healthcare. In prison they rarely receive quality psychiatric care or medication, and they find themselves in the farthest thing imaginable from a therapeutic environment. This situation has reached crisis proportions, and advocacy groups for the mentally ill are crying out for a solution. Some areas are experimenting with special courts for mentally ill offenders. Others already have special drug courts, and these can be very helpful in routing young offenders into treatment.

Until a solution is found to the problems of our criminal justice system, you must do your best to keep your child out of it. That doesn't mean allowing him to perpetrate crimes against your family or others—it means proactively finding appropriate treatment and medication that will prevent criminal behavior. Most larger cities now have therapeutic residential or day treatment programs for at-risk youth. These are kids as young as preschool age who are in danger of committing criminal acts. They may be victims of child abuse, or they may have neurological disorders. Not all of these programs are good—but some do have an understanding of childhood psychiatric problems that are not due to abuse or neglect, and these can be a godsend for families whose bipolar offspring are aggressive, assaultive, or otherwise committing criminal acts.

If your child's legal problems stem from substance abuse or dependency, seek out the help of a reputable treatment center. The juvenile justice system can often send a child with a known psychiatric condition to a day treatment, residential, or drug/alcohol treatment center rather than to jail, unless a jury decides otherwise. If you can get your child into one before his criminal behavior puts him in jeopardy for imprisonment, all the better.

If your child is incarcerated, he will face many obstacles to accessing proper mental healthcare. The worst abuses are often at the local level, in city lockups and county jails where prisoners awaiting trial and those convicted of minor offenses are usually held. These facilities were never intended for long-term prisoners, and they have few if any resources to provide even basic healthcare. Psychiatric care is minimal or nonexistent—or just really, really bad. There have been hundreds of cases of suicide, abuse of mentally ill inmates by other prisoners, and serious self-harm reported in recent years. Prescribed medications may not be given. Mental health evaluations may be scheduled but never done. There's just no way around the fact that you will need a lawyer to have any influence at all. If you don't already have one who seems able to help ensure your child's safety, call your nearest chapter of NAMI or another mental health advocacy agency to get a referral.

There are long-term juvenile facilities that have caring professionals on staff, or that are willing to work with outside psychiatrists and social workers. Simply staying involved in your incarcerated child's treatment can be an uphill struggle, however. For most children in prison, the family environment they grew up in is a big part of why they're there. This is the model that prison mental health professionals are used to dealing with. They may have programs for counseling young offenders who were sexually or physically abused, and hopefully they will have drug and alcohol treatment available (sadly, many do not, even though substance abuse is the number one predictor for crime at any age). They are less used to recognizing, accommodating, and treating mental illness, despite the fact that it is very common in young offenders.

Parents may need to use the legal system to ensure that their incarcerated child receives regular medical and psychiatric care, is properly medicated, that improper medications are not used as a chemical straitjacket, and that their child is not physically restrained or isolated as a substitute for medical care. You will probably want to take special steps to safeguard at least some of your parental rights, because you have no say without them. Technically, when a child is incarcerated those parental rights revert to the state. It seems wise to retain as much authority as you legally can, because someday your child will be released and those rights may revert back to you.

Usually the best person to talk to at a juvenile justice facility will be a social worker. The quality of prison social workers varies drastically, but a good one can be a true ally in helping your child overcome this experience.

In some cases, parents may have no alternative but to use the legal system to obtain help for their bipolar child. If you find yourself in this situation, seek out reliable allies who can support you and inform you about your options. Allies can be found in parent support groups, organizations such as NAMI and DRADA, drug and alcohol treatment programs for youth, and elsewhere.

Maintaining your sanity

A parent who is stressed to the point of burn-out has little chance of effectively parenting a difficult child. You've got to mobilize your inner and outer resources to protect your own peace of mind. That includes taking care of your physical health with regular checkups, eating right, and exercise. It also means caring for your own mental health.

It's uncomfortable for many of us to consider, but the genetic nature of bipolar disorders dictates that many parents of bipolar teens are also bipolar, or must deal with less severe versions of bipolar symptoms. Coupled with the rigors of parenting a bipolar child, this can spell disaster. Even if you're uncomfortable with medication or therapy based on past bad experiences, it's very important to do as much as you can to help yourself. Think of the analogy of airplane oxygen masks: parents are instructed to first put their own oxygen mask in place, then ensure that their child's oxygen mask is working properly. If your physical or mental health falls by the wayside, you won't be available to help your child.

You need a personal safety net just as much as your child does. A caring therapist, a family social worker who keeps your needs in the picture, and supportive family members can make a big difference.

Another great resource is access to respite care, especially for single parents and families with more than one affected member. Respite care providers are babysitters with extra training in working with the mentally or physically disabled. They can take your child for a few hours or even a few days, allowing you time to take care of other tasks, attend to your own health needs (such as a scheduled operation that may require a few days in bed), reacquaint yourself with your spouse, or even take a short vacation.

Respite care has been very hard to access in the past, but that's changing. Talk to your county or provincial mental health department, and to local support and advocacy groups for the disabled for information about respite resources in your area. Groups like the ARC (Association of Retarded Citizens), United Cerebral Palsy, Easter Seals, and Samaritans usually know where to send you.

There's still a severe shortage of respite care providers, and there are even fewer with special training in working with the mentally ill. This is an essential need for families, though. In many cases you can get respite services at no or low cost through a charitable group or through government mental health services. Be sure that providers are carefully screened, trained, and supervised.

Another thing you can do to maintain your sanity is keep careful records. There's nothing that gives parents more headaches than school systems and medical facilities that can't seem to keep track of information on medications given, treatments tried, and classroom strategies that worked or flopped. If you can keep your medical and school info neatly filed, you'll find that a major area of stress in your life will almost disappear. It's not easy, but it's really worth the trouble!

Finally, find ways to let yourself relax, even for just a few minutes while your child is sleeping. Prayer, meditation, yoga, or just a nice hot bath with a trashy novel can do wonders for your spirit. Without these stolen moments of peace, it's hard to find the energy to keep up the hard work of raising a child with bipolar disorder. When you can get 'em, grab 'em.

Support and advocacy

No family can handle bipolar disorder well on its own. Besides the many professionals who can help, there are also other families who have walked this road before. Their advice, support, and friendship can be a precious gift in your life. When you join a good support group for families coping with bipolar disorders, you'll gain shoulders to lean on, people you can call in a crisis, and a source of the latest information on services, healthcare, education, local doctors, and opportunities for your child. You'll meet parents just like yourself. You'll have people in your life that you don't have to put up a brave front with.

Another kind of helpful group concentrates on advocacy for mentally ill people and their families. In the US, NAMI is the biggest of these, with chapters in almost every part of the country. These groups work to improve services, medical treatment, and schools, and change the laws that affect people with mental illness. Many of them also have a support group component, especially in more rural areas where support and advocacy go hand in hand.

Support and advocacy groups also give people who are living with mental problems and their families a way to give back to the community, and to lift up those who are faced with a new diagnosis.

> *I turn to friends on the BPParent online support group, and to the friends who live around me that I met through the support group.*
> *—Lynn, mother of 11-year-old Michael (diagnosed BPI with mixed states and psychosis, OCD, tic disorder)*

· · · · ·

> *I rely on the National Alliance for the Mentally Ill and BPParent.*
> *—Cindy, mother of 16-year-old Craig and 19-year-old Kara*

· · · · ·

> *I turn to my close friends for support, and Billy sees a PhD psychologist for a combination of cognitive-behavioral and play therapy. The primary focus has been on coping with frustration. He also enjoys his Baha'i [religious] children's classes. —Marlene, mother of 8-year-old Billy (diagnosed cyclothymic disorder)*

A new kind of support group has arrived with the advent of the Internet: online support communities for people with mental or neurological disorders and their families. The great thing about these online groups is that they're available 24 hours a day. You can log in with your computer whenever it's convenient for you—late at night, when the kids are at school, or on your lunch break at work. All you need is a basic computer and an Internet account, either through a local Internet service provider or through a major commercial service like AOL or EOL. You can also use public computers, like those at a local library.

BPParent (*http://www.bpparent.org/*) is probably the most active online support group for parents of bipolar children. Founded by a parent in need, it is a mailing list that also maintains a web site with a great deal of useful information. Every day dozens of list members post questions, comments, answers to other list members' questions, and occasionally cries for help to the list's address. Each subscriber receives all of these email messages, either individually or combined in a single digest. You can answer messages via email, or just read what other people have to say. Participants range from parents of newly diagnosed children to old hands who can provide excellent advice. There are also some doctors, nurses, teachers, psychopharmacologists, and psychiatric researchers who lend their expertise in online forums like BPParent.

You do have to be careful about online medical advice—it's no substitute for getting local medical care. But these groups can help parents learn as much as possible about these disorders, and about dealing with associated behaviors, school problems, and family issues.

A list of bipolar-related online support groups, discussion forums, and web sites is included in the appendix.

Wishful thinking

Parents who have experienced years of worry, fear, and pain due to a child's illness fear that hope will be lost somewhere along the way. Most parents know what kind of resources would be most useful for themselves and their child, but they despair of ever finding them. Their wishes can be powerful, though, because if enough families wish out loud (and then put their shoulders to the wheel) these resources might become a reality.

We asked several parents to complete the sentence, "If I could wave a magic wand to help families dealing with bipolar disorder, I would…" Here is what they said:

> …have a big building where parents can come and talk to other parents face to face about their child's illness, and where they can get an education on bipolar disorder, meds, etc. A place where kids could come and express themselves in creativity and art, feel safe, ask questions, and play with their peers. —Lynn, mother of 11-year-old Michael (diagnosed bipolar I disorder with mixed states and psychosis, OCD, tic disorder)

• • • • •

> …have free meds for people with mental disorders, or some kind of help we could access without worrying if we can afford to pay for it for the rest of our lives. That has happened to me when I had no insurance and ended up in the hospital. I fear that for my son. —Evelyn, mother of 14-year-old Robert (diagnosed bipolar I disorder and ADHD)

• • • • •

> …place them in a school/hospital setting until they are actually well. There are many schools and programs that can help these kids, but because of financial restraints, I know my son will never be one of the lucky ones unless something drastic happens (i.e., win the lottery, get help from Montel Williams, etc.). At this point, I have no hopes for him anymore. I just know that he will end up dead or in jail. —Cindy, mother of Nathan

• • • • •

> …educate, educate, educate. We need to educate pediatricians, family practice physicians, school nurses and teachers, and the public at large. I would provide respite for families coping with full-blown bipolar disorder, also restore an appropriate length of hospitalization for children who need an extensive work-up and stabilization on meds. I would educate pediatricians and family practice physicians in better differential diagnosis of ADHD and childhood depression, and encourage them to make more referrals to specialists before prescribing stimulants and SSRIs. Doctors need to provide earlier medication treatment of childhood bipolar disorder when needed and as long as the medication is appropriate. —Marlene, mother of 8-year-old Billy

What would you wish for?

CHAPTER 4

Medical Interventions

THERE IS A WIDE RANGE of medications available to treat bipolar disorders, and they work with varying degrees of effectiveness in adults. Perhaps the biggest problem that people with bipolar disorder have with medications is refusing to take them. Noncompliance isn't entirely the patient's fault. Some doctors, especially those who don't have a lot of experience in treating bipolar disorders, don't research medications very carefully. They forget to check for interactions with other medicine a patient might be taking for asthma or the flu. They start medications at doses that are far too high, causing side effects that the patient naturally refuses to tolerate. They don't explain enough about recognizing and preventing side effects.

Such is the state of medicine. It's a lucky patient who gets full information about a medication in the doctor's office and reliable follow-up while he continues to take it. The rest of us have to research and monitor efficiency and side effects on our own. Acting carefully increases compliance, and that can be crucial for your child's health.

In this chapter, we will cover all of the current options, with special attention given to the physiology and responses of children and adolescents. We will also look at some of the problems involved in treating patients who have epilepsy or other conditions in addition to bipolar disorders. We'll list and discuss all of the medications you may hear about, starting with lithium. Finally, we discuss hospitalization, including evaluating and working with inpatient and outpatient programs for bipolar youth.

Dosage details

Each person's body chemistry is different, and some people have unusual responses to certain medications. Selecting the correct dose is more of an art than a science, especially since most medications for bipolar adults have not been clinically tested in children. Doctors who are unfamiliar with a medication usually start with the manufacturer's guidelines, which set typical dosages based on the patient's weight and/or age. Differences in individual metabolism, and the use of other medications (including vitamins and herbal supplements) at the same time can make a lot of difference in what the optimal dose for your child should be.

When it comes to children, there is one dosage rule that should almost always be followed: start low, and go slow. If a patient is given too high a starting dose, or if medications are increased to the full therapeutic dose over just a few days, difficult side effects are far more likely to occur. Gradual titration (increase in dosage) over a period of weeks can make all the difference, even though patients are less likely to see dramatic, positive effects right away.

If possible, only one medication should be started, added, or increased in dose at a time. You shouldn't make major dietary changes or start taking an herbal remedy, vitamin, or supplement at the same time as starting a new medication. Otherwise, it's hard to tell what the culprit is, should a side effect occur.

> Nathan has taken Zyprexa and Remeron, and both caused extreme weight gain. He has been on lithium, Tenex, and risperidone at once, which was no help; Depakote and Dexedrine, no help; and clonidine, Prozac, Zyprexa, Dexedrine, Ambien (for sleeping) all at one time, which caused severe mania. —Cindy, mother of 16-year-old Nathan (diagnosed bipolar disorder, OCD, ADHD, post-traumatic stress disorder, chemical dependency, bulimia)

Sometimes the dose actually needs to be *lower*, not higher, when a medication doesn't seem to be working. This effect has occurred in many bipolar patients who take a mood stabilizer and an antidepressant, such as Prozac. In some cases a low dose of an antidepressant (sometimes very low) helps, while a higher dose (such as might be prescribed to someone with unipolar depression) can cause mania.

It doesn't help that drugs often come in one size only. Even the least powerful pill may be too much for some patients to start with. Surprisingly, many doctors are unaware of options that can help. These include:

- A number of psychiatric medications, including Prozac, Haldol, and Risperdol, are available in liquid form. Liquids can be measured out in tiny doses and increased very gradually. Incidentally, liquid medications can be easily administered to children who refuse pills. You may even be able to mix them with food or drinks (check with your pharmacist first).

- Some medications can be broken into fractions. Pill splitters are available at most pharmacies for just this purpose. Make sure that it's okay to split a medication before you go this route, however: time-release medications and some pills with special coatings will not work properly when broken. Generally speaking, if the pill is scored down the middle, you can split it. If it isn't, ask your pharmacist or call the manufacturer's customer hotline.

- Some pills that are too small or oddly shaped to split can be crushed and divided into equal parts. Again, ask your pharmacist before doing this, as it's difficult to get precise doses with crushed pills. Tiny mortar and pestle sets can be found at health food or cooking shops. You can buy empty gel caps to put the powder in, or you may be able to mix it into food or drink.

Some medications come in patch form. Tempting though it may be, don't try cutting these patches to get a smaller dose or to move up to a larger dose gradually. Doing so will keep the medication from being absorbed properly. Many patches need to be securely covered to deliver the full dose. If the patch comes with overlays that don't work well, as is the case with clonidine, try using the transparent, waterproof dressing Tegaderm or the large, decorated Nexcare "tattoo" bandages. You can guess which option younger kids would prefer. Patches should be placed on a padded, non-bony part of the body that doesn't flex too much. Many teens and adults prefer the upper arm area; children are more likely to leave them alone if you place them on an inaccessible area of the back.

Compounding pharmacies make medications to order in their own lab. For example, they can make a liquid version of a prescription normally available in tablet form only. These pharmacies are especially helpful to individuals with allergy problems. Many pills and syrups contain common allergens, including eggs, soy, corn, and dyes. If a hypoallergenic version isn't available from the manufacturer, seek out a compounding pharmacy. If there isn't one where you live, several allow patients with valid prescriptions to order over the Internet. Just use a search engine like AltaVista (*http://www.altavista.com/*) or Lycos (*http://www.lycos.com/*) to search for the term "compounding pharmacy." As always with Internet-based or mail-order businesses, check references before you pay for goods or services.

Follow any instructions about eating or drinking before, with, or after your medication. Also, avoid taking medications with grapefruit juice—it may sound nutty, but grapefruit juice can prevent the breakdown of certain medications.

Keep an eye out for unusual symptoms, and let your physician know about your concerns right away. Most people remember to do this when they first start taking a drug, but forget about it after they've had the same prescription for a long time. Vigilance is especially important when using newer medications. The FDA and similar government bodies in Canada and Europe require studies showing new medications are effective and safe in the short term. Long-term studies are expensive, and because they're not required, they are rarely done. In other words, with any medication introduced in the past ten or twenty years, real-life patients are the long-term study subjects.

Prescription notes

You may see some odd initials on your child's prescriptions or pill bottles. These stand for Latin words, so they are hard to figure out on your own. The following chart lists some of the most common abbreviations used by doctors and pharmacists:

Notation	Meaning
AC (*ante cibum*)	Take before meals
BID (*bis in die*)	Take twice a day
gtt (*guttae*)	Drops
PC (*post cibum*)	Take after meals
PO (*per os*)	Take by mouth
PRN (*pro re nata*)	Take as needed
QD (*quaque die*)	Take once a day
QH (*quaque hora*)	Take every hour
Q[number]H	Take every [number] of hours
QID (*quater in die*)	Take four times a day
TID (*ter in die*)	Take three times a day
ut dict. (*ut dictum*)	Take as directed

Discontinuing medication

Sometimes a doctor will ask that all medication be withdrawn for awhile to give her a baseline look at which symptoms are being caused by the disorder and which are due to over-, under-, or mismedication. This process can be exceptionally trying for patients and families if it is not managed well. There are very few medications that can be stopped cold without causing distress—and with some, such as clonidine, this can be life-threatening.

Ask your doctor if there are any symptoms you might expect during the withdrawal period. She might be able to recommend over-the-counter or dietary remedies for likely problems, such as diarrhea or nausea. Decide in advance on non-medication strategies for dealing with problem behaviors and bipolar symptoms that may occur as drugs are tapered off.

Gradually tapering off to a lower dose and then to none is almost always the best approach. Patients should be carefully monitored for signs of trouble. In some cases (such as for discontinuing benzodiazepine tranquilizer use after several years), medication withdrawal may need to take place in a hospital setting or under extra-careful home supervision.

Blood tests and EKGs

Blood levels will probably become a monthly routine for your child, because most of the mood stabilizers and many other drugs require them. These tests check physical functions, or make sure the medication has reached its therapeutic level.

These tests return a number indicating how much of the medication is found in the blood. Your doctor compares this level to a chart of therapeutic blood levels: amounts of the medication that have been found to be effective in patients of various sizes and ages. Be sure to find out where your child's therapeutic blood level and current blood level are. Often some other tests of body function are run at the same time as the lithium level is taken, such as thyroid function tests. A physician's assistant or nurse can help you understand what all of these test results mean. Try to learn how to read and understand these figures yourself—many times observant parents have caught mistakes that could have been dangerous. Typical problems include blood assessed with the wrong blood test, misinterpreted levels, and getting someone else's paperwork.

> In order to be really successful at living with the illness and the lithium, I've had to really become aware of my internal body. I always know roughly how much lithium is in me at any given time. I used to play a game and predict my level before getting a blood draw. I was almost

always right, and knew when I was at .5, .7, or .9. If I want to I can actually tweak my meds a little bit and get the number I want to. —Troy, age 30 (diagnosed bipolar I disorder)

Once a therapeutic level has been reached, your main job is to keep that level steady. Sometimes this requires raising the dose of medication over time. It's as if the body gets used to the drug, and requires more to get the same effect. This isn't the same as becoming addicted. Except for the benzodiazepine tranquilizers, most of the drugs used to treat manic depressive symptoms are not addictive when used as directed.

Good phlebotomists (blood-draw specialists) do not cause bruising or more than a twinge of pain when they do their job, unless the patient bruises very easily or has a low pain threshold. If this is the case, let the phlebotomist know—she may have a better way to obtain the sample. Numbing ointments can help.

Patients who do not have regular access to quality lab facilities, such as those living in remote areas, may have a very difficult time keeping up with this testing schedule. Talk to your healthcare provider about alternative ways to handle the need for monthly testing, such as having a visiting home-health nurse do the blood draw in your home and then mail the vial to a lab for testing.

In some cases, liver or heart function should be tested before your child starts taking a particular drug. Liver function is assessed with a blood test that checks the level of certain enzymes, while heart function is usually assayed with a regular blood-pressure test, a physical exam, and an electrocardiogram (EKG).

The EKG can be done in the doctor's office, and since it uses wires that stick on the chest with an adhesive patch or gooey substance, it doesn't hurt at all. You just have to lie still (not always an easy task for kids). The wires are attached to a mechanical device that looks something like a seismograph, or to a computer. The EKG machine will spit out a graph of the heart rate and any other cardiac activity it picks up. Your doctor can read this graph to find any changes in or problems with heart function.

Seizures and seizure-detection tests

Seizure disorders are believed to be more common in people with bipolar disorder than in the general population. A seizure-related phenomenon called kindling is theorized by some to be the cause for some sudden mood swings.

Seizures are caused by nerve cells that fire off abnormal electrical charges. They occur for many different reasons, and there is more than one type of seizure. There are three general types, two of which also have subcategories. These are:

- Generalized seizures, which affect the whole brain:
  - Absence seizures are sometimes called petit mal seizures, although this term may be applied to other types of mild seizures as well. These brief events are characterized by blank staring, and sometimes small, repetitive movements (automatisms).
  - Myoclonic seizures are jerking movements of muscles or muscle groups.
  - Atonic seizures, also called drop attacks, cause the person's body to have a sudden loss of muscle tone, preventing him from standing or sitting upright.
  - Tonic/clonic seizures, formerly called grand mal seizures, are the most obvious type of seizure. The person's body is rigid during the tonic phase, and jerks during the clonic phase. Tonic/clonic seizures are often followed by a foggy feeling, headaches, or sleep.

- Partial seizures, also called focal or local seizures, which affect only part of the brain.
  - Simple partial seizures cause one part of the body, or several body parts on one side only, to twitch uncontrollably. Alternatively, the person may see, hear, or smell things that are not there, or have a sudden flood of emotions. The person may feel confused and unsure of where she is. She will, however, be conscious.
  - Complex partial seizures are like a simple partial seizure, but with loss of consciousness. The person may walk, talk, or move around, but won't remember doing so afterward.

- Status epilepticus, a dangerous and possibly life-threatening condition in which multiple seizures occur one after another, without regained consciousness in between. Patients in the throes of status epilepticus need to be transported to the closest emergency room. Thankfully, this is a very rare condition.

Diagnosing seizure disorders

If seizures of any type are suspected, you should be referred to a neurologist. The primary test for seizure activity is the electroencephalogram (EEG), which records electrical activity in the brain. Electrodes are placed on the patient's scalp, picking up electrical impulses and carrying them to the EEG machine by wires. A printer attached to this device graphs this activity. Your physician or an EEG technician can compare the patterns that appear on the printout to expected patterns, thereby identifying abnormal activity.

Most EEGs take one or two hours. The EEG technician may try to get a reading while the patient is asleep, at rest, wide awake, during deep breathing exercises, and while a light is flashing. The test is not painful at all, and some little kids think it's cool, in a Frankenstein's lab kind of way. The doctor will use a gooey, glue-like substance to attach the electrodes. They don't penetrate into the skin.

If the regular EEG doesn't provide enough information, your doctor may order a sleep-deprived EEG. As the name indicates, the patient needs to be awake but bone-tired for this test. Parents can take turns keeping a child up all through the night, then bring him to the test site first thing in the morning. You can imagine how much fun this will be with a willful, cranky child! Movie marathons, midnight bowling, and shopping trips to the all-night convenience store are among the carrots that have kept some young ones (and many sleepy adults as well) awake through the night. The idea is for the exhausted patient to drop into a deep sleep right away, and it usually works.

But even this procedure may not show clear evidence of seizures. In cases where the doctor still suspects seizure activity, she may order 24-, 36-, or 48-hour EEG monitoring. This procedure can be done at home with a portable EEG unit, or in a hospital setting. The portable units are certainly more convenient, but they're rather cumbersome, and wires have a tendency to come loose. If they do, the test must be redone.

Other types of brain scans are available, but they are also much more expensive than EEGs. These include magnetic resonance imagery (MRI), single photon emission computed tomography (SPECT, or neuroSPECT), and positron emission tomography (PET) scans. An MRI can actually show physical changes that are associated with seizure activity. SPECT scans can show cerebral blood flow, which may be a helpful clue in identifying areas in which neural activity is abnormally high or low. PET images can show changes in cerebral metabolism.

Temporal lobe epilepsy, usually now called complex partial seizure disorder, is hard to diagnose. People with temporal lobe epilepsy experience odd states of mind rather than the easier-to-recognize physical seizures that result from activity in the parts of the brain that govern movement. During a temporal lobe seizure, the person's environment may suddenly seem unreal, for example. Objects and sounds may take on a hallucinatory quality. Strong emotions, such as fear or disgust, may come out of nowhere. Actual auditory and visual hallucinations may occur, often similar to the classic migraine aura or epileptic aura that brings visions of patterns and colors, or creating the sensation of smelling or tasting something that's not there. Some patients describe an internal sensation that flows up from their stomach to their head as a seizure begins.

Electrical malfunctions that occur deeper within the brain are even harder to ferret out. Physicians believe these occur in some people, but it would be surprising if one of these events just happened to occur while an expensive brain scan or EEG is taking place.

Coping with seizures

Seizures can occur in anyone as a result of fever or injury, so every parent and caregiver should know what to do. Here are the six basic steps:

1. Move the person to the floor and make sure anything nearby that could cause injury is moved.

2. Turn the person on her side to prevent choking. *Never* put an object in the person's mouth—there's no chance that she will swallow her tongue.

3. Loosen any tight clothing.

4. Stay with the person until the seizure ends.

5. Help the person get comfortable as she recovers from the seizure. If she needs help with cleaning up (for example, if she has soiled or wet clothing), offer assistance.

6. If a seizure lasts more than five minutes, or if seizures continue to follow each other during a ten-minute period, call for emergency medical care and wait with the person until it arrives.

Some medications and herbal supplements may lower the seizure threshold, causing seizures in patients who have not experienced them before, or worsening seizure activity in those who have epilepsy. Be sure to tell your doctor if seizures have happened before, or if they occur during medication or supplement use.

Panic attacks can have a seizure-like quality, including unusual body and eye movements, and cognitive disturbances. Telling the difference between a severe panic attack and a seizure can be a tough call, and may require inpatient hospitalization.

Many times doctors will insist that a seizure is psychosomatic (faked, or the result of a panic attack) unless the child wets his pants during the event. This is not necessarily correct. Since we have very poor tools for inexpensively and conveniently measuring seizure activity in the interior of the brain, it's likely that psychosomatic seizures occuring in people with bipolar disorder have been wrongfully labeled. If the person's function improves on antiseizure medication, that can be a form of diagnosis for these problems. Others may wish to pursue brain scans that could provide more information. These are expensive, and rarely covered by health insurance.

Important side effects

Many side effects associated with psychiatric medication are fairly minor, and can be handled with changes in diet or over-the-counter medications (always check with your doctor before trying to medicate away a side effect, of course—there is a danger of interactions between psychiatric meds and common home remedies, from Alka-Seltzer to cough syrup.)

Other side effects are signs of serious trouble, and a few are life-threatening. If your child experiences seizures, heart palpitations, blood in the urine or stool, or other symptoms that seem medically serious in nature, call your physician immediately. If your doctor is not available on short notice, report to an emergency room. These symptoms may be related to medication, or they may signify another serious health condition.

Serious side effects related specifically to psychiatric medications or other drugs that affect the nervous system include:

- **Akisthesia.** An intense internal sensation of physical restlessness, itchiness, and jumpiness—a need to move constantly. A person with akisthesia will look and feel uncomfortable if she tries to be still.

- **Bradyphrenia.** Slowed thought processes.

- **Dystonia.** Muscle rigidity and uncontrollable muscle spasms. It is associated primarily with the neuroleptics (also called antipsychotics).

- **Encephalopathic syndrome.** Symptoms are similar to those of neuroleptic malignant syndrome (see its description later), of which it may be a variant. Associated with lithium toxicity.

- **Extrapyramidal side effects (EPS).** Physical symptoms include tremor, slurred speech, akathesia, dystonia, anxiety, distress, paranoia, and bradyphrenia. Associated primarily with the neuroleptics.

- **Hyperkinesia.** Excessive motor activity, the physical expression of akisthesia. In children this can mimic common hyperactivity, but the movements may seem both driven and purposeless.

- **Neuroleptic malignant syndrome (NMS).** This potentially fatal condition is characterized by rigid muscle movements, fever, irregular pulse and heartbeat, rapid heartbeat, irregular blood pressure, heavy sweating, and strange states of mind. Discontinue the medication immediately and call your doctor if these symptoms occur. In extreme cases, the patient may need emergency care at a hospital. Physicians should report episodes of NMS to the Neuroleptic Malignant Syndrome Information Service (*http://www.nmsis.org/*), which has set up a registry to help researchers reduce the incidence of this problem. NMS is associated primarily with neuroleptics, although it may occur with tricyclic antidepressants or other medications.

- **Oculogyric crisis.** A patient in the throes of oculogyric crisis has a frozen upward gaze, often a very strange-looking facial expression and eye movements, and has contorted facial and neck muscles.

- **Orthostatic hypotension.** Dangerously low blood pressure caused by alpha-adrenergic blockade. Associated primarily with the neuroleptics.

- **Parkinsonian symptoms.** These mimic the neurological disorder Parkinson's disease, hence the name. They include a feeling of cognitive slowing, muscle and joint stiffness, tremor, and an unusually stiff and unstable gait. Associated primarily with the neuroleptics.

- **Serotonin syndrome.** When the brain has too much serotonin (for example, from combining two antidepressants), patients may experience shivers, headaches, diarrhea, profuse sweating, confusion, and akisthesia. If this happens, stop taking the antidepressant immediately and see your doctor without delay. In extreme cases, serotonin syndrome can be fatal. That's why patients taking SSRIs or other antidepressants should not also take natural antidepressants, such as St. John's Wort.

- **Tardive dyskinesia (TD).** This drug-induced movement disorder is characterized by twisting motions of the hands and feet, and smacking or chewing movements of the mouth. Rippling movements of the tongue muscles are considered an early warning sign. Discontinue the medication immediately and call your doctor if these symptoms occur. Between 20 percent and 30 percent of long-term users of the older neuroleptic drugs, such as Haldol and Thorazine, eventually develop this disorder. The new atypical neuroleptics are now preferred to these because they seem far less likely to cause TD. TD has also been associated with tricyclic antidepressants and some mood stabilizers. If TD is caught early, it may reverse itself once the medication is stopped. Entrenched TD is said to be irreversible. Some physicians recommend that people who take drugs that carry a risk for TD also take vitamin E supplements, which appear to stave off the disorder in some people.

  Tardive dyskensia is a worry for anyone who needs to take a neuroleptic on a long-term basis. Obviously, the atypical neuroleptics are greatly preferred due to their lower TD risk. Low doses are also preferable to high ones.

  For those who are already affected by TD, only one medication is currently known to help: Nitoman (tetrabenezine or TDZ), also marketed under the name Regulin. This drug depletes dopamine in nerve endings, and so it may interact with other drugs that affect dopamine production or use. Although Nitoman is available in Canada, Norway, Sweden, Japan, and the UK, in the US it can only be obtained through compassionate use programs (explained in the next section). Nitoman sometimes causes depression as a side effect, so bipolar patients should use it with caution.

These are serious and painful side effects, the kind that understandably make patients want to stop taking their medicine. Careful medication choice and dosage adjustment should reduce them, and complimentary adjustments to diet, vitamins, supplements, and relaxation techniques may also help.

Medications

Many people with bipolar disorders find relief from a single medication—usually lithium. Many others will need two or more medications, carefully balanced to address their individual symptoms without causing unbearable side effects. Medication types in current use for bipolar disorder and associated symptoms or conditions include mood stabilizers, including several that are also antiseizure medications; antidepressants, neuroleptics (also called antipsychotics), stimulants (for ADD/ADHD), drug and alcohol detox aids, and sometimes other medicines as recommended.

Most of these medications are available in the US and Canada, and are listed under their primary US brand name. Some are available in less-expensive generic forms, while others are not (although all have a generic chemical name). Brand names and formulations may vary in other countries, and some drugs may not be available elsewhere.

Of course, new medications are always under development. In fact, as this book went to press several drug companies were hard at work on new antidepressants and even a couple of new mood stabilizers. There may also be new medications approved for use in Asia or Europe that have not yet made it to North America. If you're curious about an unfamiliar medication, look it up by its generic name to find the names of non-US equivalents, or ask your doctor whether something similar is available where you live.

Sometimes medications that have not been formally approved by government regulators are available under compassionate use laws, including drugs that normally would only be available overseas. It is sometimes possible—if not absolutely legal—for a physician in one country to prescribe a medication available only overseas, and for patients to then have the prescription filled at an overseas pharmacy.

Some as-yet-unapproved drugs are made available to participants in human research trials. If you don't have success with any of the usual treatments for bipolar disorders, this may be an avenue to pursue. The US National Institutes of Mental Health (NIMH) runs many clinical trials each year, and may be aware of others being managed by other research centers or by pharmaceutical companies.

The National Alliance for the Mentally Ill is one of the best resources for information on new drugs for neurological disorders. Its web site (*http:// www.nami.org/*) often has reviews of new drugs, and previews of medications that are undergoing clinical trials.

Your nearest medical school or major research hospital may also have studies you could take part in.

Not all of the medications listed in this chapter are recommended—some, such as the old-line neuroleptics and the MAO inhibitors, are very much out of favor. That said, it's important to know as much as possible about drugs you are prescribed or that you hear about from other parents or patients.

We have listed commonly reported side effects and certain rare but especially dangerous side effects only. Less common and rare side effects may be associated with any medication, and you may experience side effects that no one else has ever had. If you experience unusual symptoms after taking medicine, or after combining more than one medication, call your doctor right away. You may also want to consult the drug reference sheet packaged with your medication by the pharmacy.

The information in this chapter was taken from the *Physician's Desk Reference*, pharmaceutical company literature, and other reputable sources. It should be accurate as of this writing, but new information may emerge. Be sure to personally check out any medications your child takes using a detailed medication reference, such as this book's appendix, *Resources*, to make you aware of all possible side effects and interactions.

Here are some more important things to consider:

- Do not allow your child to start or stop taking any prescription medication without her physician's advice.

- Make sure your child is careful to follow dosage, time, and other instructions ("take with food," etc.) specifically.

- If your teenage or adult child is pregnant or breastfeeding, or if she could become pregnant, ask the doctor or pharmacist about any side effects specifically related to female reproduction and nursing.

- If your teenage or adult child is actively trying to father a child, you may also want to ask about male reproductive side effects.

- Be sure to tell both the physician and pharmacist about all other medications your child takes, including over-the-counter drugs—even aspirin and cough syrup can cause dangerous side effects when mixed with the wrong medication.

- Inform the doctor about your child's use of alcohol, tobacco, any illegal drugs, and any vitamins or supplements (other than a regular daily multivitamin).

- If your child's physician is unsure of how a medication might interact with a supplement, you may need to help the doctor find more information about the chemical action of the supplement. Most doctors are not well informed about nutritional supplements or herbal medicines, but many are willing to work with you on these matters.

- If you suspect that your child has been given the wrong medication or the wrong dosage, call the pharmacist right away. Such errors do occur, and the pharmacist should be able to either reassure you or fix the problem.

Lithium

Lithium carbonate is still tops for treating bipolar disorders, and for many people it is indeed a miracle pill. More than likely it will be the first medication that a doctor prescribes for your child.

Lithium

Generic name: lithium (lithium carbonate, lithium citrate)

Also known as: Eskalith, Lithane, Lithobid, Lithonate, Lithotabs

Use: Bipolar disorders, mood regulation, manic psychosis, PMS, eating disorders, thyroid problems, aggression.

Action, if known: Regulates circuits within the brain, possibly by having an effect on the enzyme inositol monophosphatase. Phosphoinositide signals are believed to important for controlling the body's circadian rhythms.

Side effects: Hand tremor, excessive thirst and urination, nausea (this should pass), diarrhea, blurred vision. Any of these side effects occurring over a long period of time can be a sign of toxicity. Call your doctor if it persists.

Known interaction hazards: Potentiates neuroleptics, danger of encephalopathic syndrome. Counteracted by acetazolamide and by theophylline drugs, such as those used for allergy or asthma.

Tips: Before starting lithium, have kidney function, thyroid, blood salts, and blood cell counts checked. Lithium users must have heart function, kidney function, thyroid function, and therapeutic level monitored regularly. Lithium can be toxic in doses that are not much higher than the therapeutic dose. If you are allergic to tartrazine dyes, ask your pharmacist if these are used in your lithium product. If side effects are a problem, the slow-release Lithobid version may be more tolerable. People who have diabetes or a family history of diabetes should be very careful with lithium, which may affect the pancreas.

There are many good things that can be said about lithium. It's a naturally occurring salt, and has been in use for thousands—that's right, thousands— of years. Native Americans were well aware of the beneficial effect of drinking water from lithium springs, and sent their own mentally ill to take the cure at these bodies of water. You can spot several place names on a US map, such as Lithia Springs in Oregon, indicating that European settlers also quickly grasped the curative value of this water. Despite this long history of casual use as a remedy for emotional distress, lithium was not discovered by modern medicine until 1949. An Australian doctor was the first to figure out its usefulness for patients with manic depression. It was approved by the US Food and Drug Administration in 1969.

Now lithium is available in tablets, with carefully measured doses of pure lithium carbonate at various strengths. A time-release version is also available. Unlike drinking or soaking in lithium-rich water, this method of dosing is much more convenient, and more reliable. Because lithium has been in medical use for almost 40 years, there's plenty of information available about side effects. Most of these are minor. For a few patients, however, lithium can have dangerous effects on the body. This is the case for almost every medication used to treat the symptoms of bipolar disorders.

Things about lithium even your doctor may not know

Lithium and other mood stabilizers tend to take longer to begin working for adolescents than for adults. It may be several months before you see positive results.

Stopping lithium suddenly can bring on a manic episode in some patients, and it may not work again when you restart the medication after stopping. Always taper off your dose under a doctor's supervision, and don't expect to stop and start lithium more than once.

Lithium may have some antiviral effects, including the ability to suppress the herpes simplex virus (and possibly other herpatiform viruses).[1]

Calcium channel blockers can lower your lithium level.

Sodium bicarbonate (baking soda) counteracts lithium. People taking lithium probably don't need to worry about the minuscule amount of baking soda found in typical baked goods. Many common antacids are based on sodium bicarbonate, however, including Alka-Seltzer and Bromo Seltzer.

Mannitol, a sweet alcohol, is found in olives, beets, and celery, and is manufactured commercially from corn sugar and hydrogen. It counteracts lithium, although the amount found naturally in unprocessed foods may not cause problems. It is found in many sugarfree products, including gums, candies, powdered drink mixes, and manufactured sugarless foods. It may also be found in other powdered food products, chewable medicines and vitamins, and cereals. Mannitol is the main active ingredient of a few powdered laxatives. These laxatives are also commonly used by drug dealers to cut their product. Mannitol is believed to reduce pressure in the brain cavity, which may have something to do with its effects.

Some people find that they must avoid eating sweets (including fruit) until a couple hours have passed after taking lithium.

Urea counteracts lithium. Urea is a normal product of the body's ongoing internal detoxification efforts—this is an essential process, and there's no need to worry about the effect of this urea on lithium. Some very few people may be especially sensitive to urea from other sources, including animal milk and blood, urea-based fertilizers, and "outgassing" from products containing formaldehyde or other substances mixed with urea.

Inositol, a sugar present in organ meats, whole grains, vegetables, nuts, and beans, is also available in supplement form and in the health food staple lecithin. Inositol is also produced within the human body. People with bipolar disorders appear to better regulate this internal inositol level when taking lithium. So, taking inositol supplements might not be such a good idea when taking lithium—even though some small clinical studies have shown that inositol supplements taken alone can help stabilize some people with affective disorders, including bipolar disorders.

Ibuprofen (Advil, Motrin, Midol-IB, etc.) will raise the level of lithium in the blood.

Lithium causes the natural level of sodium (salt) in the body to decrease, which may cause cravings for salt or salty snacks.

Eating large quantities of salty foods (such as a big serving of potato chips) can raise the level of lithium in the blood.

Patient tips

Troy, a 30-year-old diagnosed with bipolar I disorder at age 17, has taken lithium successfully for almost 13 years. Here are his tips for young people:

> When I was an adolescent the main side effect that upset me was acne. I was taking a generic brand of lithium. I was eventually informed that the difference in capsule brands has to do with the filler (not lithium carbonate) that they put in them. Since more than 80 percent of the capsule is filler, this is important. I switched to Eskalith ("the Ferrari of lithium"), and most of my acne disappeared, along with my stomachaches. This wasn't a tough decision, since Eskalith cost me about four cents per capsule, rather than two.

> You should trust your body to know what the right dosage of lithium is for you. During the first few months I was taking lithium, my psychiatrist felt it was best to increase my dosage to 1200 mgs a day. On the second day of doing this I felt spaced out, so I went back to the 900 mg dose and soon felt "normal" again. I called up my psychiatrist and told him the situation, and that I was not going to take that extra 300 mgs.

Once you discover the right dosage for you, if you take the lithium on a regular basis and drink the right amount of water, it isn't too difficult to stay in a good range (.5 to 1.5). I take 900 mgs a day and drink about a gallon of bottled water a day. I drink most of the water in the afternoons and evenings after taking the lithium.

Without fail if my lithium level gets too high I get toxic and then I get diarrhea. This happened to me often when I was first taking lithium, but it rarely happens now. It would most commonly occur when I wasn't drinking enough water. I've become aware of my thirst enough to know now when that is happening so I can head it off by drinking more water to flush the lithium out of my body. I am most at risk for this when I go on a trip. There are times when travelling where I don't have access to enough water, or I don't want to drink a lot of water since a bathroom may not be available. I usually head this off by decreasing my lithium dosage during the trip. If you have a stable lithium level, small dosage changes over a couple of days won't really change anything.

When you take lithium for a long time, it becomes so habitual that you can actually take a capsule without remembering that you did so. A trick that's worked for me is to have my three capsules in a little container that I refill every day. Then when I'm not sure if I've taken it I just check the container.

One side effect lithium has given me is psoriasis of the scalp. I've been able to treat this with shampoo, so for me this is a very small price to pay for the mood balance I've been able to maintain.

When I first started taking lithium I had to have a blood draw every month to check my lithium level. For the past ten years, however, I've only had to see a psychiatrist twice a year for half an hour, and have a blood draw once a year to check my lithium level, and check on my kidneys and thyroid gland.

Other mood stabilizers

Many of these medications are also used to control seizure disorders. If you already take a seizure medication, your doctor will probably need to adjust your dosage of both drugs carefully. These drugs tend to have more side effects than lithium, but they are a better fit for some patients.

Like lithium, the other mood stabilizers may be part of a complex drug cocktail. This can increase the risk of side effects.

> *Depakote caused tremors, mainly in Lisa's hands, which the doctor was able to control with Propronolol. But Depakote also caused her to be hungry all the time and she could never get enough to eat. She put on about 150 pounds in one year. She was becoming so depressed because of her weight gain that we decided it was better to decrease the Depakote to help with that.*
>
> *In trying to help Lisa with her weight gain, the doctor first tried taking her off Risperdal. In one day's time that sent her into such terrible panic attacks that she temporarily lost her vision. The doctor put her back on it and doubled the dose to help her immediately.*
>
> *Since taking her off the Risperdal didn't work, the doctor started to gradually decrease her dosage of Depakote. She was on 2500 mg initially, then it was slowly decreased until last April she was taken off completely. Since then she has lost about 35 pounds, and is still working on it.*
> *—Donna, mother of 16-year-old Lisa (diagnosed bipolar II disorder, post-traumatic stress disorder, and anxiety disorder)*

Depakene

Generic name: valproic acid

Use: Seizure disorders, bipolar disorders, migraine, panic disorder, rages/aggression.

Action, if known: Antispasmodic—increases the levels of gamma-amino-butyric acid (GABA) in the brain, and increases its absorption. Also stabilizes brain membranes.

Side effects: Nausea, sedation, depression, psychosis, aggression, hyperactivity, changes in blood platelet function.

Known interaction hazards: Do not take with milk, and do not use charcoal tablets when taking Depakene. Be careful with alcohol, and with any medication that has a tranquilizing or depressant effect. Side effects may increase if you use anticoagulants (including aspirin), non-steroidal anti-inflammatory drugs, erythromycin, chlorpromazine, cimetidine, or felbamate.

Tips: Watch out for increased bruising or bleeding, an indicator of blood platelet problems. Regular liver tests are a must. Do not crush or chew tablets. Starting with a very small dose and titrating it up slowly can often help patients avoid even the common side effects. Depakene has recently been linked to polycystic ovaries in female patients. The symptoms of this problem include irregular periods and unexplained weight gain.

Depakote

Generic name: divalproex sodium (valproic acid plus sodium valproate)

Also known as: Depakote Sprinkles

Use: Seizure disorders, bipolar disorders, migraine, panic disorder, rages/aggression.

Action, if known: Antispasmodic—increases the levels of gamma-aminobutyric acid (GABA) in the brain, and increases its absorption. Also stabilizes brain membranes.

Side effects: Nausea, sedation (this usually passes after a few days), depression, psychosis, aggression, hyperactivity, changes in blood platelet function, hair loss.

Known interaction hazards: Do not take with milk, and do not use charcoal tablets when taking Depakote. Be careful with alcohol, and with any medication that has a tranquilizing or depressant effect. Side effects may increase if you use anticoagulants (including aspirin), non-steroidal anti-inflammatory drugs, erythromycin, chlorpromazine, cimetidine, or felbamate.

Tips: Watch out for increased bruising or bleeding, an indicator of blood platelet problems. Regular liver tests are a must. Therapeutic level tests can be misleading with Depakote: actual therapeutic levels may be higher (or perhaps lower) than published charts indicate. Do not crush or chew tablets. Starting with a very small dose and titrating it up slowly can often help patients avoid even the common side effects. Hair loss can be avoided by taking 50 mg of zinc daily; some patients also take .025 mg of selenium to boost zinc's effect.

Gabitril

Generic name: tiagibine HCL

Use: Seizure disorders, including partial seizure disorders.

Action, if known: Antispasmodic—enhances the activity of gamma-aminobutrytic acid (GABA), a chemical substance that inhibits electrical activity in the brain. May have other as yet unknown effects.

Side effects: Stomach problems, severe rash, weakness, possible eye effects. Can lower white blood cell and blood platelet count.

Known interaction hazards: Antacids. May interact with other anti-epileptic drugs, so monitor doses carefully.

Tips: This new medication has been approved for use in adolescents, but not for children under 12 years of age. Watch dosage increases closely to avoid toxic reactions.

Lamictal

Generic name: lamotrigine

Use: Seizure disorders, bipolar disorders, Lennox-Gastaut syndrome in children.

Action, if known: Binds to the hormone melanin. Stabilizes electrical currents in the brain and blocks the release of seizure-stimulating neurotransmitters.

Side effects: Headache, dizziness, nausea, general flu-like feeling, light sensitivity. If you develop a rash, call your doctor immediately as it may be a warning of a serious, even life-threatening, side effect. May make seizures worse in some people.

Known interaction hazards: Interacts with Depakote/Depakene, carbamazepine, and phenytoin—your doctor will have to monitor doses carefully. Potentiated by antifolate drugs. Phenobarbital and primidone may lessen its effects.

Tips: Not normally recommended for use by children. If you have heart, kidney, or liver disease, use only under careful supervision. Lamictal may act as an antidepressant when added to another mood stabilizer.

Neurontin

Generic name: gabapentin

Use: Seizure disorders, especially those that do not respond to other drugs, anxiety, panic, bipolar disorders, rage/aggression.

Action, if known: Antispasmodic—appears to act by binding a specific protein found only on neurons in the central nervous system. May increase the GABA content of some brain regions.

Side effects: Blurred vision, dizziness, clumsiness, drowsiness, swaying, eye-rolling.

Known interaction hazards: Alcohol and all other central nervous system depressants, including tranquilizers, over-the-counter medications for colds and allergies, over-the-counter sleep aids, anesthetics, and narcotics. Antacids may counteract the effects of Neurontin.

Tips: Titrate dose very slowly to avoid side effects. People with kidney disease should be carefully monitored while taking Neurontin. Corn is used as a filler in the usual formulation of this drug, causing allergic reactions in some people. Recent parent reports indicate that Neurontin can cause mania in some patients, especially younger patients. This can be offset by adding another medication, or by changing the dose of Neurontin or other medications used with it. Others report that Neurontin made their psoriasis worse. A new drug under development called Pregabolin is based on Neurontin, but with fewer side effects.

Tegretol

Generic name: carmazepine

Use: Seizure disorders, nerve pain, bipolar disorders, rage/aggression, aid to drug withdrawal, restless leg syndrome, Sydenham's chorea and similar disorders in children.

Action, if known: Antispasmodic—appears to work by reducing polysynaptic responses, and has other as yet unknown effects.

Side effects: Sleepiness, dizziness, nausea, unusual moods or behavior, headache, retention of water. May cause low white blood cell count. Call your doctor right away if you have flu-like symptoms or other unusual reactions while taking this drug.

Known interaction hazards: Never take with an MAOI (MAO or monoamine-oxidase inhibitor). Tegretol is often used in combination with other antispasmodics or lithium, but the dose of Tegretol and drugs used with it must be very carefully adjusted. Tegretol is potentiated by numerous prescription and over-the-counter medications, including many antibiotics, antidepressants, and cimetadine. It also counteracts or changes the effect of many drugs, including Haldol, theophyllin, and acetaminophen. Because these interactions can be very serious, discuss all medications you take—including all over-the-counter remedies—with your doctor before beginning to use Tegretol.

Tips: You should have a white blood cell count done before taking Tegretol, and be monitored thereafter. Do not take if you have a history of bone marrow depression. Tegretol can be fatal at fairly low doses, so all patients taking this drug should be carefully monitored, particularly since it interacts with so many other medications.

Topamax

Generic name: topiramate

Use: Seizure disorders, including as an adjunctive therapy for partial seizure disorders.

Action, if known: Antispasmodic—enhances the activity of gamma-aminobutrytic acid, a substance that inhibits electrical activity in the brain. Also acts as a calcium-channel blocker, and blocks the excitatory neurotransmitter glutamate. May have other, as yet unknown, effects.

Side effects: Sleepiness, dizziness, loss of coordination, slowed thinking and speech.

Known interaction hazards: Dosage must be adjusted carefully when used with other antispasmodics or any central nervous system depressant drug.

Tips: Topamax was recently approved for use in children with epilepsy, and is available in a "sprinkle" formulation that can be combined with soft food, such as applesauce or ice cream. Because of the side effects that can happen with this drug, it is recommended that patients start very low and titrate the dose upward very slowly.

SSRI antidepressants

The use of antidepressants alone to treat bipolar disorders is rarely a good idea, although there are some patients who do well. Most experienced clinicians will use antidepressants only in addition to a mood stabilizer. That's because SSRIs (and other types of antidepressants) can trigger a rapid swing into mania.

> *Kara got worse when she was put on just an antidepressant. She got very manic, agitated, and aggressive. For depression we tried Effexor, which caused stomach problems; Serzone, which caused a bad reaction—she got very psychotic and out of control; Wellbutrin, which did nothing for her; nortryptyline, which worked for awhile. On Prozac she couldn't sleep, and Luvox didn't work. Zoloft is working well for her, with Neurontin. —Cindy, mother of 19-year-old Kara (diagnosed bipolar disorder)*

· · · · ·

> *I have tried Prozac, and it was not good!!! Originally I was misdiagnosed as having depression. I was placed on Prozac, which caused a manic/hypomanic cycle. I was immediately taken off Prozac and rediagnosed as BP2. I was then placed on lithium, and I have been stable ever since.*

> *In addition to the lithium, I also take a small dose of Zoloft. This was done mainly because of the severity of my depressions. —Marcia, age 24 (diagnosed bipolar II disorder)*

Today's antidepressants are much more advanced than those used just a decade ago, but they're still a blunt instrument for attacking brain dysfunction. There are several different types, and within each group related medications may function quite differently. That's why you shouldn't write off a whole family of drugs just because one was a disaster. A slightly different medication may turn out to be infinitely preferable.

All of the antidepressants should be used with care. Check package inserts and pharmacy information sheets to avoid interactions with other medications. Be sure to tell your doctor about any over-the-counter drugs you use, even aspirin, herbal medicines, or supplements.

The brain is chock-full of serotonin receptors, tiny sites that bind with serotonin molecules to move chemical impulses through the brain. The selective serotonin reuptake inhibitors (SSRIs) block certain receptors from absorbing serotonin. Researchers believe this results in lowered or raised levels of serotonin in specific areas of the brain. Over time, SSRIs may cause changes in brain chemistry, hopefully in a positive direction. SSRIs may also cause actual changes in brain structure with prolonged use. There are also receptor sites elsewhere in the central and peripheral nervous systems, so SSRIs can have an impact on saliva production, appetite, digestion, skin sensitivity, and many other functions.

The SSRIs are not identical in either their chemical composition or their effects on the brain. Prozac and Zoloft tend to have an energizing and focusing effect as well as reducing depression, for example, while Paxil may calm anxious or agitated patients who are also depressed.

The following five drugs are currently considered part of the SSRI family.

Celexa

Generic name: citalopram

Use: Depression

Action, if known: SSRI—increases the amount of active serotonin in the brain. Has a calming effect.

Side effects: Dry mouth, insomnia or restless sleep, increased sweating, nausea, sexual dysfunction. Lowers the seizure threshold. Can cause mood swing in people with bipolar disorders.

Known interaction hazards: Alcohol. Never take with an MAOI, or soon after stopping an MAOI. Use with caution if you take a drug that affects the liver, such as ketoconazole or the macrolides.

Tips: People with liver or kidney disease should be monitored regularly while taking Celexa.

Luvox

Generic name: fluvoxamine

Use: Depression, OCD.

Action, if known: SSRI—increases the amount of active serotonin in the brain.

Side effects: Headache, insomnia, sleepiness, nervousness, nausea, dry mouth, diarrhea or constipation, sexual dysfunction. Lowers the seizure threshold. Can cause mood swing in people with bipolar disorders.

Known interaction hazards: Never take with an MAOI, or soon after stopping an MAOI. Potentiated by tricyclic antidepressants and lithium. Potentiates many medications, including clozapine, diltiazem, methadone, some beta blockers and antihistamines, Haldol and other neuroleptics.

Tips: Avoid taking this drug if you have liver disease. Cigarette smoking may make Luvox less effective. Luvox does not bind to protein in the body, unlike the other SSRIs, and may have a very different effect in some people.

Paxil

Generic name: paroxetine

Also known as: Seroxat

Use: Depression

Action, if known: SSRI—increases the amount of active serotonin in the brain. Has a calming effect.

Side effects: Headache, insomnia or restless sleep, dizziness, tremor, nausea, weakness, dizziness, sexual dysfunction, dry mouth. Lowers the seizure threshold. Can cause mood swing in people with bipolar disorders.

Known interaction hazards: Alcohol. Never take with an MAOI, or soon after stopping an MAOI. Potentiates warfarin, theophylline, paroxetine, procyclidine. Changes how digoxin and phenytoin act in the body.

Tips: People with liver or kidney disease should be monitored regularly while taking Paxil.

Prozac

Generic name: fluoxetine

Use: Depression, OCD, eating disorders, ADHD, narcolepsy, migraine/chronic headache, Tourette syndrome, social phobia.

Action, if known: SSRI—increases the amount of active serotonin in the brain. Usually has an energizing effect.

Side effects: Headache, insomnia or restless sleep, dizziness, tremor, nausea, weakness, dizziness, sexual dysfunction, dry mouth, itchy skin and/or rash. May cause change in appetite and weight. Lowers the seizure threshold. Can cause mood swing in people with bipolar disorders.

Known interaction hazards: Alcohol. Never take with an MAOI, or soon after stopping an MAOI. Do not take over-the-counter or prescription cold or allergy remedies containing cyproheptadine or dextromethorphan. Potentiated by tricyclic antidepressants. Potentiates lithium, phenytoin, neuroleptic drugs, carbamazepine, and cyclosporine. Reduces effectiveness of BuSpar.

Tips: Prozac has a long life in your body. People with liver or kidney disease should be monitored while taking Prozac.

Zoloft

Generic name: sertraline

Use: Depression, OCD, obsessive-compulsive behavior.

Action, if known: SSRI—increases the amount of active serotonin in the brain. Has an energizing quality.

Side effects: Dry mouth, headache, tremor, diarrhea, nausea, sexual dysfunction. May precipitate a manic episode in people with bipolar disorders. Lowers the seizure threshold.

Known interaction hazards: Alcohol and all other central nervous system depressants. Never take with an MAOI, or soon after stopping an MAOI. Potentiates benzodiazepine drugs and warfarin. Potentiated by cimetidine.

Tips: People with epilepsy, bipolar disorders, liver disease, or kidney disease should be carefully monitored if they take Zoloft. May affect therapeutic level of lithium.

Tricyclic antidepressants

Before Prozac became famous, the tricyclic antidepressants were the wonder drugs for depression and obsessive-compulsive disorder (OCD). Although they are rarely used in children these days, they are still the best choice for some patients. Most doctors will usually try an SSRI or two first. The tricyclic antidepressants work by inhibiting the uptake of various neurotransmitters at adrenergic nerve terminals, resulting in an increase of monoamine neurotransmission. Some doctors may add these to a mood stabilizer when treating bipolar disorders or patients with multiple psychiatric diagnoses, particularly if the patient has ADHD that does not respond well to stimulants, clonidine, or Tenex.

Along with treating depression and OCD, the tricyclics may help with bedwetting, appetite, sleep, alertness, anxiety, and hyperactivity.

These drugs require regular monitoring for heart problems and other potentially serious side effects. They can lower the seizure threshold. Of all the antidepressants, the tricyclics carry the highest risk of sending people with bipolar disorders into a manic phase. Some patients also complain of excessive weight gain. An overdose of these medications can be lethal.

There are several tricyclic antidepressants, many of which combine more than one active drug.

Anafranil

Generic name: clomipramine

Use: Depression, OCD, obsessive-compulsive behavior, panic disorder, chronic pain, eating disorders, severe PMS.

Action, if known: Tricyclic antidepressant—blocks norepinephrine and serotonin use, works against the hormone acetylcholine. Weak antihistamine properties.

Side effects: Sedation, tremor, seizures, dry mouth, light sensitivity, mood swing in people with diagnosed or undiagnosed bipolar disorders, weight gain. Lowers the seizure threshold.

Known interaction hazards: Alcohol, MAOIs, blood pressure medications (including clonidine and Tenex), thyroid medication. Potentiated by estrogen, bicarbonate of soda (as in Alka-Seltzer and other over-the-counter remedies), acetazolamide, procainamide, and quinidine. Cimetidine, methylphenidate, Thorazine and similar drugs, oral contraceptives, nicotine (including cigarettes), charcoal tablets, and estrogen may interfere with Anafranil's action in the body.

Tips: Take with food if stomach upset occurs. Take bulk of dose at bedtime to reduce sedation, if so directed.

Asendin

Generic name: amoxapine

Use: Depression, panic disorder, chronic pain, eating disorders, severe PMS.

Action, if known: Tricyclic antidepressant—blocks norepinephrine and serotonin use, works against the hormone acetylcholine.

Side effects: Sedation, tremor, seizures, dry mouth, light sensitivity, mood swing in people with diagnosed or undiagnosed bipolar disorders.

Known interaction hazards: Alcohol, MAOIs, blood pressure medications (including clonidine and Tenex), thyroid medication. Potentiated by estrogen, bicarbonate of soda (as in Alka-Seltzer and other over-the-counter remedies), acetazolamide, procainamide, and quinidine. Cimetidine, methylphenidate, Thorazine and similar drugs, oral contraceptives, nicotine (including cigarettes), charcoal tablets, and estrogen may interfere with Asendin's action in the body.

Tips: Take with food if stomach upset occurs. Take bulk of dose at bedtime to reduce sedation, if so directed.

Avenytl

Generic name: nortriptyline

Also known as: Pamelor

Use: Depression, panic disorder, chronic pain, eating disorders, severe PMS.

Action, if known: Tricyclic antidepressant—blocks norepinephrine and serotonin use, works against the hormone acetylcholine.

Side effects: Sedation, tremor, seizures, dry mouth, light sensitivity, mood swing in people with diagnosed or undiagnosed bipolar disorders.

Known interaction hazards: Alcohol, MAOIs, blood pressure medications (including clonidine and Tenex), thyroid medication. Potentiated by estrogen, bicarbonate of soda (as in Alka-Seltzer and other over-the-counter remedies), acetazolamide, procainamide, and quinidine. Cimetidine, methylphenidate, Thorazine and similar drugs, oral contraceptives, nicotine (including cigarettes), charcoal tablets, and estrogen may interfere with Aventyl's action in the body.

Tips: Take with food if stomach upset occurs.

Elavil

Generic name: amitriptyline

Use: Depression, panic disorder, chronic pain, eating disorders, severe PMS.

Action, if known: Tricyclic antidepressant—blocks norepinephrine and serotonin use, works against the hormone acetylcholine.

Side effects: Sedation, tremor, seizures, dry mouth, light sensitivity, mood swing in people with diagnosed or undiagnosed bipolar disorders.

Known interaction hazards: Alcohol, MAOIs, blood pressure medications (including clonidine and Tenex), thyroid medication. Potentiated by estrogen, bicarbonate of soda (as in Alka-Seltzer and other over-the-counter remedies), acetazolamide, procainamide, and quinidine. Cimetidine, methylphenidate, Thorazine and similar drugs, oral contraceptives, nicotine (including cigarettes), charcoal tablets, and estrogen may interfere with Elavil's action in the body.

Tips: Take with food if stomach upset occurs.

Limbitrol

Generic name: amitriptyline/chlordiazepoxide

Use: Depression, panic disorder, chronic pain, eating disorders, severe PMS.

Action, if known: Tricyclic antidepressant—blocks norepinephrine and serotonin use, works against the hormone acetylcholine.

Side effects: Sedation, tremor, seizures, dry mouth, light sensitivity, mood swing in people with diagnosed or undiagnosed bipolar disorders, weight gain. Lowers the seizure threshold.

Known interaction hazards: Alcohol, MAOIs, blood pressure medications (including clonidine and Tenex), thyroid medication. Potentiated by estrogen, bicarbonate of soda (as in Alka-Seltzer and other over-the-counter remedies), acetazolamide, procainamide, and quinidine. Cimetidine, methylphenidate, Thorazine and similar drugs, oral contraceptives, nicotine (including cigarettes), charcoal tablets, and estrogen may interfere with Limbitrol's action in the body.

Tips: Take with food if stomach upset occurs.

Norpramin

Generic name: desipramine

Use: Depression, panic disorder, chronic pain, eating disorders, severe PMS.

Action, if known: Tricyclic antidepressant—blocks norepinephrine and serotonin use, works against the hormone acetylcholine.

Side effects: Sedation, tremor, seizures, dry mouth, light sensitivity, mood swing in people with diagnosed or undiagnosed bipolar disorders, weight gain. Lowers the seizure threshold.

Known interaction hazards: Alcohol, MAOIs, blood pressure medications (including clonidine and Tenex), thyroid medication. Potentiated by estrogen, bicarbonate of soda (as in Alka-Seltzer and other over-the-counter remedies), acetazolamide, procainamide, and quinidine. Cimetidine, methylphenidate, Thorazine and similar drugs, oral contraceptives, nicotine (including cigarettes), charcoal tablets, and estrogen may interfere with Norpramin's action in the body.

Tips: Take with food if stomach upset occurs.

Sinequan

Generic name: doxepin

Use: Depression, panic disorder, chronic pain, eating disorders, severe PMS.

Action, if known: Tricyclic antidepressant—blocks norepinephrine and serotonin use, works against the hormone acetylcholine.

Side effects: Sedation, tremor, seizures, dry mouth, light sensitivity, mood swing in people with diagnosed or undiagnosed bipolar disorders, weight gain. Lowers the seizure threshold.

Known interaction hazards: Alcohol, MAOIs, blood pressure medications (including clonidine and Tenex), thyroid medication. Potentiated by estrogen, bicarbonate of soda (as in Alka-Seltzer and other over-the-counter remedies), acetazolamide, procainamide, and quinidine. Cimetidine, methylphenidate, Thorazine and similar drugs, oral contraceptives, nicotine (including cigarettes), charcoal tablets, and estrogen may interfere with Sinequan's action in the body.

Tips: Take with food if stomach upset occurs.

Surmontil

Generic name: trimipramine

Use: Depression, panic disorder, chronic pain, eating disorders, severe PMS.

Action, if known: Tricyclic antidepressant—blocks norepinephrine and serotonin use, works against the hormone acetylcholine.

Side effects: Sedation, tremor, seizures, dry mouth, light sensitivity, mood swing in people with diagnosed or undiagnosed bipolar disorders, weight gain. Lowers the seizure threshold.

Known interaction hazards: Alcohol, MAOIs, blood pressure medications (including clonidine and Tenex), thyroid medication. Potentiated by estrogen, bicarbonate of soda (as in Alka-Seltzer and other over-the-counter remedies), acetazolamide, procainamide, and quinidine. Cimetidine, methylphenidate, Thorazine and similar drugs, oral contraceptives, nicotine (including cigarettes), charcoal tablets, and estrogen may interfere with Surmontil's action in the body.

Tips: Take with food if stomach upset occurs.

Tofranil

Generic name: imipramine

Also known as: Janimine

Use: Depression, panic disorder, chronic pain, eating disorders, severe PMS.

Action, if known: Tricyclic antidepressant—blocks norepinephrine and serotonin use, works against the hormone acetylcholine.

Side effects: Sedation, tremor, seizures, dry mouth, light sensitivity, mood swing in people with diagnosed or undiagnosed bipolar disorders, weight gain. Lowers the seizure threshold.

Known interaction hazards: Alcohol, MAOIs, blood pressure medications (including clonidine and Tenex), thyroid medication. Potentiated by estrogen, bicarbonate of soda (as in Alka-Seltzer and other over-the-counter remedies), acetazolamide, procainamide, and quinidine. Cimetidine, methylphenidate, Thorazine and similar drugs, oral contraceptives, nicotine (including cigarettes), charcoal tablets, and estrogen may interfere with Tofranil's action in the body.

Tips: Take with food if stomach upset occurs.

Vivactil

Generic name: protriptyline

Use: Depression, panic disorder, chronic pain, eating disorders, severe PMS.

Action, if known: Tricyclic antidepressant—blocks norepinephrine and serotonin use, works against the hormone acetylcholine. More energizing than other tricyclics.

Side effects: Sedation, tremor, seizures, dry mouth, light sensitivity, mood swing in people with diagnosed or undiagnosed bipolar disorders, weight gain. Lowers the seizure threshold.

Known interaction hazards: Alcohol, MAOIs, blood pressure medications (including clonidine and Tenex), thyroid medication. Potentiated by estrogen, bicarbonate of soda (as in Alka-Seltzer and other over-the-counter remedies), acetazolamide, procainamide, and quinidine. Cimetidine, methylphenidate, Thorazine and similar drugs, oral contraceptives, nicotine (including cigarettes), charcoal tablets, and estrogen may interfere with Vivactil's action in the body.

Tips: Take with food if stomach upset occurs.

MAO inhibitors

Three monoamineoxidase inhibitors (MAOIs) are currently available in the US, but they are rarely used, especially in children or teens. These medications address depression by inhibiting the metabolization of the neurotransmitters serotonin, norepinephrine, and dopamine.

The MAOIs have unpleasant and even life-threatening interactions with many other drugs, including common over-the-counter medications. People taking MAOIs must also follow a special diet, because these medications interact with many foods. The list of proscribed foods includes chocolate, aged cheeses, beer, and many more.

If your child must take an MAOI, check for warning labels on everything, and familiarize yourself thoroughly with the dietary restrictions.

MAOIs can also produce hallucinations, and have been abused by some drug users to get this effect.

Aurorex

Generic name: moclobemide

Also known as: Manerix

Use: Depression, anxiety.

Action, if known: A so-called "reversible" MAO inhibitor, Aurorex increases levels of serotonin, norepinephrine, and dopamine in the brain.

Side effects: Headache, insomnia, dizziness, tremor, agitation, nervousness, sedation, anxiety, weakness. Said to be safer and to have fewer side effects than the older MAOIs.

Known interaction hazards: Tricyclic antidepressants, meperidine, cimetidine, other MAOIs, SSRIs, alcohol, anesthetics, amphetamines (including central nervous system stimulants like Ritalin and over-the-counter cold and allergy remedies containing ephedrine, ephedra, and similar stimulants.)

Tips: Not currently available in the US, Aurorex is still a relatively new drug in Canada and Europe. Although it appears to have fewer dangerous interactions with foods and medications than older MAOIs, caution, monitoring of medication doses and interactions, and careful eating are still recommended.

Nardil

Generic name: phenelzine

Use: Depression that does not respond to SSRIs or tricyclic antidepressants, eating disorders, migraine.

Action, if known: MAO inhibitor—interferes with the action of the enzyme monoamine oxidase (MAO), which normally breaks down neurotransmitters. This increases the amount of norepinephrine and other neurotransmitters stored throughout the central nervous system.

Side effects: Drowsiness, blurred vision, dizziness, tremor, agitation, uncontrolled muscle movements, loss of appetite, sexual dysfunction, insomnia. Can cause very high blood pressure in some. May aggravate stereotypic movements, palilalia, echolalia, tics.

Known interaction hazards: Never take with an SSRI, guanethidine, dextromethorphan (found in many over-the-counter drugs), another MAOI, or trancypromine sulfate. MAOIs change the affects of many other medications in potentially dangerous ways. Go over all drugs you take carefully with your doctor, including over-the-counter remedies. You will also need to strictly follow a special diet while taking Nardil, which you should discuss thoroughly with your doctor before starting this medication.

Tips: Do not take Nardil if you have high blood pressure; heart, liver, or kidney problems; headaches; or a history of minor or major strokes. Make sure you have exhausted your other antidepressant possibilities before taking an MAOI. Interactions between this drug, other medications, and even foods can be life-threatening. You must still avoid forbidden foods and medicines for two to four weeks after you stop taking Nardil.

Parnate

Generic name: tranylcypromine sulfate

Use: Depression that does not respond to SSRIs or tricyclic antidepressants, eating disorders, migraine.

Action, if known: MAO inhibitor—interferes with the action of the enzyme monoamine oxidase (MAO), which normally breaks down neurotransmitters. This increases the amount of norepinephrine and other neurotransmitters stored throughout the central nervous system.

Side effects: Drowsiness, blurred vision, dizziness, tremor, agitation, uncontrolled muscle movements, loss of appetite, sexual dysfunction, insomnia. Can cause mood swing in people with diagnosed or undiagnosed bipolar disorders. Can cause very high blood pressure in some people. May aggravate stereotypic movements, palilalia, echolalia, tics.

Known interaction hazards: Never take with an SSRI, guanethidine, dextromethorphan (found in many over-the-counter drugs), another MAOI, or trancypromine sulfate. MAOIs change the affects of many other medications in potentially dangerous ways. Carefully go over with your doctor all drugs you take, including over-the-counter remedies. You will also need to strictly follow a special diet while taking Parnate, which you should discuss thoroughly with your doctor before starting this medication.

Tips: Do not take Parnate if you have high blood pressure; heart, liver, or kidney problems; headaches; or a history of minor or major strokes. Make sure you have exhausted your other antidepressant possibilities before taking an MAOI. Interactions between this drug, other medications, and even foods, can be life-threatening. You must still avoid forbidden foods and medicines for two to four weeks after you stop taking Parnate.

Other antidepressants

Several antidepressants are now available that don't fit one of the three major categories.

Desyrel

Generic name: trazodone

Use: Depression, panic attacks and phobias, cocaine withdrawal.

Action, if known: Antidepressant

Side effects: Stomach distress, nausea, diarrhea, lightheadedness. May lower your blood pressure—be careful if using clonidine or other medications that affect blood pressure.

Known interaction hazards: Potentiates alcohol, tranquilizers (including over-the-counter sleep aids), and other central nervous system depressants.

Tips: Take with food.

> Cass had a terrible time sleeping, disturbed by horrid, graphic nightmares, usually involving my dismemberment. She started on 25 mgs of trazodone at bedtime, and slept well for the first time in her life. A few

months ago that was increased to 50 mgs, as she had started having the nightmares again.

Last month, she started wetting the bed. The doctor thinks it is because she is sleeping heavily due to the trazodone. She is so small that I was able to buy medium-sized Goodnights pants (pull-ups) for her to wear. I will take the trade-off of her having peaceful sleep and wearing a pull-up. — Stephanie, mother of 7-year-old Cassidy (diagnosed bipolar disorder, Tourette syndrome, OCD, ADHD)

Effexor, Effexor XR

Generic name: venlafaxine

Use: Depression, especially depression with anxiety.

Action, if known: Antidepressant—limits absorption of at least three neurotransmitters: serotonin, norepinephrine, and dopamine.

Side effects: Blurred vision, sedation, dry mouth, dizziness, tremor, nausea, sexual dysfunction, insomnia. Anecdotal evidence indicates it may cause mood swing in people with diagnosed or undiagnosed bipolar disorders.

Known interaction hazards: Do not take with MAOIs.

Tips: Take with food.

Reboxetine

Generic name: edronax

Use: Depression.

Action, if known: A non-tricyclic selective noradrenaline reuptake inhibitor (selective NRI), Reboxetine inhibits the reuptake of norepinephrine by cells, increasing noradrenaline availability in the synaptic cleft. Has an energizing effect.

Side effects: Dry mouth, constipation, insomnia, sweating, heart irregularities, dizziness, urine retention, sexual dysfunction.

Known interaction hazards: Alcohol and other central nervous system depressants. May interact with SSRIs, tricyclic antidepressants, and MAOIs. May change the way some antispasmodics work. If you take other medications, your doctor may need to adjust doses.

Tips: Reboxetine may counteract some of the interactions associated with MAOIs, and so it may be prescribed in concert with these. This combination should be monitored closely, of course. Not currently available in the US.

Remeron

Generic name: mirtazapine

Use: Depression, anxiety.

Action, if known: Noradrenergic and specific serotonergic antidepressant (NaSSA)—affects the neurotransmitter noradrenaline as well as some serotonin receptors. Has an energizing effect.

Side effects: Sleepiness, dry mouth, dizziness, weight gain, constipation. Lowers the seizure threshold. Can cause mood swing in people with diagnosed or undiagnosed bipolar disorders. Can depress the immune system, causing a lower white blood cell count.

Known interaction hazards: Never take with an MAOI, or soon after stopping an MAOI. Potentiates alcohol, tranquilizers (including over-the-counter sleep aids), and other central nervous system depressants.

Tips: If you experience fever, aches, sore throat, or infections, call your doctor. Take with food if stomach upset occurs. People with heart, liver, or kidney disease or hypothyroidism should be monitored while taking Remeron.

Serzone

Generic name: nefazodone

Use: Depression, especially if it occurs with agitation

Action, if known: Blocks the uptake of serotonin and norepinephrine in the brain, antagonizes some serotonin and noradrenaline receptors, increases the levels of two natural antihistamines in the bloodstream.

Side effects: Sleepiness, dizziness, confusion, dry mouth, nausea, visual disturbances, rash. Lowers the seizure threshold.

Known interaction hazards: Never take with an MAOI, astemizole, propranalol, terfenadine, alprazolam, or triazolam. Potentiates digoxin.

Tips: People with heart or liver trouble should be monitored while taking Serzone.

Wellbutrin

Generic name: buproprion

Also known as: Wellbutrin SR, Zyban.

Use: Depression, ADHD

Action, if known: Aminoketone antidepressant—appears to have mild effects on serotonin, dopamine, and norepinephrine; mild general central nervous system stimulant; affects hormonal system; suppresses appetite.

Side effects: Increases risk of seizures. Restlessness, anxiety, insomnia, heart palpitations, dry mouth, rapid heartbeat or heart palpitations, tremor, headache/migraine headache.

Known interaction hazards: Potentiated by L-Dopa, ritonavir. Effects decreased by carbamazepine. Interacts with MAOIs. Do not use with other drugs (or supplements) that lower the seizure threshold.

Tips: Take with food if stomach upset occurs. Be especially careful to start low, increase dose slowly, and limit dose size to reduce seizure risk. Compared to other antidepressants, Wellbutrin carries a lower risk of causing a bipolar patient to switch into the manic phase, according to some experienced clinicians.

Antiseizure medications

These antispasmodics are not normally used as mood stabilizers, although in some cases they may be prescribed for that reason. Their main function is prevention of epileptic seizures. Antispasmodics are often prescribed in combinations, as two can be more effective together than one. However, mixing drugs can increase the risk of side effects.

Phenobarbital can be addictive, and at too-high doses can produce an effect that looks like alcohol intoxication. For these reasons, it is rarely used anymore, except in low doses or as part of a combination that includes a newer antispasmodic.

Never stop taking an antispasmodic drug cold, unless you are directed to do so by your doctor. Many people experience an increase in the number or severity of seizures when they stop taking a medication.

Adolescent and adult patients with seizures can often make lifestyle changes that reduce the number or severity of episodes. One of the most important of these is becoming aware of environmental triggers. Avoiding discos with strobe lights, certain types of carnival rides, and uncontrolled stress, for example, can be helpful. Learning relaxation techniques, such as meditation or biofeedback, is another good step.

Some people with seizure disorders have reported beneficial effects from special diets and supplements, particularly from vitamin B6, and the supplements lecithin and DMG. These claims have been partially substantiated in small studies. One intervention that can definitely help in extreme cases is the ketogenic diet. This high-fat, low-protein, low-carbohydrate regimen has proved very useful for some young children with severe epilepsy that does not respond well to medication, although it's a less than pleasant experience for the patient and should *never* be undertaken without medical supervision.

In a very few cases, seizure disorders cannot be controlled with medication, diet, or other efforts. Surgery may be considered. A new procedure involves implanting a small device called a vagus nerve stimulator in the chest.

People with uncontrolled epilepsy must take steps to prevent harm during a seizure. They may need to wear a helmet, change their surroundings, or avoid driving a car.

Some forms of epilepsy may also be treated with a combination of steroids, such as prednisone, and antispasmodics. Steroids tend to cause weight gain and mood swings, and they suppress the immune system. Unless nothing else works, steroids should be avoided.

Cerebyx

Generic name: fosphenytoin

Use: Seizure disorders

Action, if known: Hydantoin antispasmodic—inhibits activity in the part of the brain where local-focal (grand mal) seizures begin.

Side effects: Gum growth, confusion, twitching, depression, irritability, and many more, some of which are very serious. Due to the many interaction problems with this drug, discuss its use thoroughly with your doctor and pharmacist.

Known interaction hazards: Potentiated by alcohol, aspirin, sulfa drugs, succinimide antiseizure medications, some neuroleptics and antidepressants, and many other drugs. Potentiates lithium, acetaminophen, and many other drugs. Effects are changed by use of calcium, antacids, charcoal tablets, and many prescription drugs.

Tips: Do not use if you have low blood pressure or heart trouble. Keep an eye out for skin rash or bruising, which can be serious warning signs. You may want to supplement with folic acid, which is depleted by Cerebyx. You will need to have regular blood tests while taking this drug. Take with food if stomach upset occurs—but not with high-calcium foods, such as dairy products, sesame seeds, or some nuts. Do not switch brands without telling your doctor.

Dilantin

Generic name: phenytoin

Use: Seizure disorders

Action, if known: Hydantoin antispasmodic—inhibits activity in the part of the brain where tonic-clonic seizures begin.

Side effects: Gum growth, confusion, twitching, depression, irritability, and many more, some of which are very serious. Due to the many interaction problems with this drug, discuss its use thoroughly with your doctor and pharmacist.

Known interaction hazards: Potentiated by alcohol, aspirin, sulfa drugs, succinimide antiseizure medications, some neuroleptics and antidepressants, and many other drugs. Potentiates lithium, acetaminophen, and many other drugs. Effects are changed by use of calcium, antacids, charcoal tablets, and many prescription drugs.

Tips: Do not use if you have low blood pressure or heart trouble. Keep an eye out for skin rash or bruising, which can be serious warning signs. You may want to supplement with folic acid, which is depleted by Dilantin. You will need to have regular blood tests while taking this drug. Take with food if stomach upset occurs—but not with high-calcium foods, such as dairy products, sesame seeds, or some nuts. Do not switch brands without telling your doctor.

Gabitril

Generic name: tiagabine hydrochloride

Use: Antispasmodic

Action, if known: Potentiates the action of GABA.

Side effects: Dizziness, drowsiness, nausea, irritability, tremor.

Known interaction hazards: Hepatic enzyme-inducing antispasmodics like carbamazepine may counteract Gabitril.

Tips: Gabitril is used mostly in addition to other antispasmodics. It is not yet recommended for use in children under the age of 12.

Klonopin

Generic name: clonazepam

Use: Seizure disorders, panic attacks, restless leg syndrome, manic psychosis, schizophrenia, chronic pain, speech problems from Parkinson's disease. Can also be used in acute mania to stop the manic episode, bringing on sleep and stabilizing the patient.

Action, if known: Benzodiazepine—depresses central nervous system activity.

Side effects: Drowsiness, unusual behavior, difficulty controlling muscles. Addictive—withdrawal may be difficult.

Known interaction hazards: Do not take with Depakene or Depakote. Avoid alcohol, narcotics, tranquilizers, central nervous system depressants, MAOIs, tricyclic antidepressants, and other antispasmodic drugs, or make sure your use of these is carefully monitored. Do not take with antacids. Potentiates digitoxin. Potentiated by cimetidine, ketoconozole, metoprolol, probenecid, propoxyphene, propranolol, rifampin. Works against the effects of L-Dopa.

Tips: You will need regular blood and liver function tests while taking Klonopin. Smoking may interfere with Klonopin's effectiveness. People tend to build up a tolerance to this drug quickly, so your dose may need to be changed frequently.

Luminol

Generic name: phenobarbital

Also known as: Solfoton

Use: Seizure disorder, insomnia.

Action, if known: Barbiturate—blocks or slows nerve impulses in the brain. Usually used in combination with another drug to control seizures.

Side effects: Drowsiness, slow reflexes, "stoned" feeling and actions, allergy-like symptoms, labored breathing. Call your doctor if any side effect becomes bothersome, or if you develop anemia or jaundice. Addiction risk—taper off dose carefully when stopping, and do so under medical supervision.

Known interaction hazards: Alcohol, MAOIs, and Depakote or Depakene all potentiate phenobarbital. Alcohol should be avoided. Neutralized by charcoal, chloramphenicol, and rifampin. Potentiates acetaminophen (Tylenol) and the anesthetic methoxyflurane. Changes how many other drugs act in the body, including anticoagulants, beta blockers, oral contraceptives, and corticosteroids. Be sure to go over all medicines you take with your doctor, as doses may need to be adjusted.

Tips: You may want to supplement with vitamin D when taking phenobarbital. People with liver or kidney disease should be monitored when taking this drug.

Mesantoin

Generic name: mephenytoin

Use: Seizure disorders

Action, if known: Hydantoin antispasmodic—inhibits activity in the part of the brain where local-focal (grand mal) seizures begin.

Side effects: Gum growth, confusion, twitching, depression, irritability, and many more, some of which are very serious. Due to the many interaction problems with this drug, discuss its use thoroughly with your doctor and pharmacist.

Known interaction hazards: Potentiated by alcohol, aspirin, sulfa drugs, succinimide antiseizure medications, some neuroleptics and antidepressants, and many other drugs. Potentiates lithium, acetaminophen, and many other drugs. Effects are changed by use of calcium, antacids, charcoal tablets, and many prescription drugs.

Tips: Do not use if you have low blood pressure or heart trouble. Keep an eye out for skin rash or bruising, which can be serious warning signs. You may want to supplement with folic acid, which is depleted by Mesantoin. You will need to have regular blood tests while taking this drug. Take with food if stomach upset occurs—but not with high-calcium foods, such as dairy products, sesame seeds, or some nuts. Do not switch brands without telling your doctor.

Mysoline

Generic name: primidone

Use: Seizure disorders

Action, if known: Antispasmodic—controls nerve impulses in the brain.

Side effects: Restlessness, especially in children. Dizziness, drowsiness, rash.

Known interaction hazards: Alcohol and all other central nervous system depressants, including tranquilizers, narcotics, and over-the-counter sleep aids, allergy drugs, and cold medications. May decrease the effects of corticosteroids, oral contraceptives, and blood-thinning medications. May interact with other antispasmodics, such as Depakote and Depakene. Do not take with MAOIs.

Tips: People with porphyria should not take Mysoline. If you have lung disease (including asthma), kidney disease, or liver disease, you will need to be carefully monitored while taking Mysoline.

Peganone

Generic name: ethotoin

Use: Seizure disorders

Action, if known: Hydantoin antispasmodic—inhibits activity in the part of the brain where local-focal (grand mal) seizures begin.

Side effects: Gum growth, confusion, twitching, depression, irritability, and many more, some of which are very serious. Due to the many interaction problems with this drug, discuss its use thoroughly with your doctor and pharmacist.

Known interaction hazards: Potentiated by alcohol, aspirin, sulfa drugs, succinimide antiseizure medications, some neuroleptics and antidepressants, and many other drugs. Potentiates lithium, acetaminophen, and many other drugs. Effects are changed by use of calcium, antacids, charcoal tablets, and many prescription drugs.

Tips: Do not use if you have low blood pressure or heart trouble. Keep an eye out for skin rash or bruising, which can be serious warning signs. You may want to supplement with folic acid, which is depleted by Peganone. You will need to have regular blood tests while taking this drug. Take with food if stomach upset occurs—but not with high-calcium foods, such as dairy products, sesame seeds, or some nuts. Do not switch brands without telling your doctor.

Topamax

Generic name: topiramate

Use: Seizure disorders

Action, if known: Antispasmodic—mode of action unknown.

Side effects: Slowed speech, thought, and action. Also, sleepiness, tingling in the extremities, nausea, tremor, depression, visual disturbances.

Known interaction hazards: Alcohol and other central nervous system depressants. Interacts with other antispasmodics, so your doctor may need to adjust dosages. Reduces effectiveness of digoxin and oral contraceptives.

Tips: People with kidney or liver problems should be monitored while taking Topamax.

Zarontin

Generic name: ethosuximide

Use: Absence (petit mal) seizure disorders.

Action, if known: Succinimide antispasmodic.

Side effects: Nausea, abdominal pain, changes in appetite, weight loss, drowsiness, headache, dizziness, irritability, insomnia. May lower the seizure threshold in some patients with mixed forms of epilepsy.

Known interaction hazards: Potentiates fosphenytoin, phenytoin, ethotoin.

Tips: You should have regular liver function and blood tests while taking this drug. May cause systemic lupus erythematosus (a medication-caused form of the autoimmune disorder lupus).

Neuroleptics: The old guard

The neuroleptics are also known as antipsychotics. These medications are used to treat a wide variety of serious mental illnesses, but they are certainly not limited to the treatment of outright psychosis. Most of these medications affect dopamine production or absorption; some also work on serotonin or other neurotransmitters.

The very first neuroleptics were discovered in the 1950s and 1960s, and represented the first major breakthrough in medical treatment for mental illness. However, the excitement was muted when the results of long-term use and overdose were discovered. Although for some patients they may be the only viable choice, knowledgeable physicians no longer use these older neuroleptics first. The atypical neuroleptics (see "Neuroleptics: The atypicals" later in this chapter) are infinitely preferable if something this strong is needed.

> Michael took Risperdal for psychosis, anger, and aggression. He stopped taking it because he had a rare side effect from it. He also put on a lot of weight with Risperdal. He then took Zyprexa. It did not work very well. Then he started taking Mellaril in place of the Risperdal, and it is working great. Cogentin is used in conjunction with the antipsychotics to control unwanted side effects. —Lynn, mother of 11-year-old Michael (diagnosed bipolar I disorder with mixed states and psychosis, OCD, tic disorder)

People involved in the care of institutionalized patients have noted that the older neuroleptics are used more often in these settings than one might think, possibly as a way to control patients in understaffed or poorly run facilities. Psychiatric nurses derisively refer to this approach as "using a chemical straitjacket." If your child is institutionalized, the potential for misuse or overuse of neuroleptics is something for which you should be on the lookout.

Side effects to watch out for with all neuroleptic drugs include agranulocytosis (a dramatic drop in white blood cell count), neuroleptic malignant syndrome, tardive dyskinesia, and extrapyramidal side effects (see "Important side effects," earlier in this chapter). Some patients also have withdrawal dyskinesias—temporary episodes that occur when the medication is stopped, and that have symptoms similar to tardive dyskinesia. Excessive weight gain is also a common problem.

Descriptions of the older neuroleptics follow:

Etrafon

Generic name: amitriptyline/perphenazine (Trilafon, however, includes only perphenezine)

Also known as: Trilafon, Triavil.

Use: Depression, panic disorder, chronic pain, eating disorders, severe PMS.

Action, if known: Neuroleptic with qualities similar to those of a tricyclic antidepressant—blocks norepinephrine and serotonin use, works against the hormone acetylcholine.

Side effects: Sedation, tremor, seizures, dry mouth, light sensitivity, mood swing in people with bipolar disorders. Danger of tardive dyskensia, extrapyramidal side effects, neuroleptic malignant syndrome.

Known interaction hazards: Alcohol, MAOIs, blood pressure medications (including clonidine and Tenex), thyroid medication. Potentiated by estrogen, bicarbonate of soda (as in Alka-Seltzer and other over-the-counter remedies), acetazolamide, procainamide, and quinidine. Cimetidine, methylphenidate, other neuroleptics, oral contraceptives, nicotine (including cigarettes), charcoal tablets, and estrogen may interfere with Etrafon's action in the body.

Tips: Avoid extreme heat when taking this drug. Not recommended for use in people with severe depression, lung disease, severe asthma, liver disease. Take with food if stomach upset occurs.

Haldol

Generic name: haloperidol

Also known as: Haldol Decanoate

Use: Psychosis, tics/Tourette syndrome, schizophrenia.

Action, if known: Affects the hypothalamus gland in the brain, which in turn affects metabolism, body temperature, alertness, muscle tone, and hormone production.

Side effects: Lowers seizure threshold. Sedation, jaundice (this should pass), anemia, changes in blood pressure or heartbeat, dizziness.

Known interaction hazards: Avoid alcohol and other central nervous system depressants, narcotics, and tranquilizers (including over-the-counter sleep aids). Potentiated by lithium, causing a greater risk of encepholopathic syndrome. Potentiates tricyclic antidepressants. Anticholinergic medications may make Haldol less effective. Risk of tardive dyskensia.

Tips: Do not take if you have low blood pressure, Parkinson's disease, or diseases of the blood, kidneys, or liver.

Loxipax

Generic name: loxapine

Also known as: Loxitane

Use: Psychosis

Action, if known: Blocks or changes the use of dopamine in several areas of the brain.

Side effects: May suppress the gag or cough reflex. Sedation, depression, light sensitivity, jaundice (this should pass), anemia, changes in blood pressure or heartbeat, dry mouth. Lowers the seizure threshold. Danger of tardive dyskensia.

Known interaction hazards: Alcohol, any tranquilizer or central nervous system depressant (including over-the-counter sleep aids), antacids, lithium, tricyclic antidepressants.

Tips: The drugs Motipress and Motival contain both loxapine and the anti-anxiety medication nortriptyline.

Mellaril

Generic name: thioridazine hydrochloride

Use: Psychosis, depression with anxiety, aggression.

Action, if known: Phenothiazine neuroleptic—affects the hypothalamus gland in the brain, which in turn affects metabolism, body temperature, alertness, muscle tone, and hormone production.

Side effects: May suppress the gag or cough reflex. Sedation, depression, light sensitivity, jaundice (this should pass), anemia, changes in blood pressure or heartbeat, dry mouth. Lowers the seizure threshold. Danger of tardive dyskensia.

Known interaction hazards: Alcohol, any tranquilizer or central nervous system depressant (including over-the-counter sleep aids), antacids, lithium, tricyclic antidepressants. Loses effectiveness when you eat or drink items containing caffeine.

Tips: Avoid extreme heat when taking Mellaril. Do not take if you have blood, liver, kidney, or heart disease, low blood pressure, or Parkinson's disease. Take with food or juice if stomach upset occurs.

Moban

Generic name: molindone

Use: Psychosis

Action, if known: Neuroleptic

Side effects: Drowsiness, sedation, depression, nausea, dry mouth. Risk of tardive dyskensia.

Known interaction hazards: Alcohol and all other central nervous system depressants, tranquilizers (including over-the-counter sleep aids), barbiturates, anesthetics, tricyclic antidepressants, lithium. Moban may have negative interactions with many other medications, including other antipsychotics, Asendin, and Cylert.

Tips: People with liver disease or Parkinson's disease should not take Moban.

Navane

Generic name: thiothixene

Use: Psychosis

Action, if known: Thiothixene neuroleptic—affects the hypothalamus gland in the brain, which in turn affects metabolism, body temperature, alertness, muscle tone, and hormone production.

Side effects: Sedation, depression, light sensitivity, jaundice (this should pass), anemia, changes in blood pressure or heartbeat. Danger of tardive dyskensia.

Known interaction hazards: Alcohol, any tranquilizer or central nervous system depressant (including over-the-counter sleep aids), antacids, lithium, tricyclic antidepressants. Do not combine with propranolol. Effect may be reduced by use of anticholinergic medications.

Tips: Avoid extreme heat when taking Navane. Do not take if you have blood, liver, kidney, or heart disease, low blood pressure, or Parkinson's disease. Take with food or juice if stomach upset occurs.

Orap

Generic name: diphenylbutylpiperdine

Also known as: Pimozide

Use: Psychosis, severe tics/Tourette syndrome, schizophrenia.

Action, if known: Neuroleptic—affects the amount and action of dopamine in the brain.

Side effects: Extrapyramidal side effects, such as restlessness and unusual movements. Risk of tardive dyskinesia, neuroleptic malignant syndrome (NMS).

Known interaction hazards: Do not take antihistamines (including over-the-counter cold and allergy remedies) or anticholinergic drugs. Alcohol, other central nervous system depressants, tranquilizers (including over-the-counter sleep aids.) Taking other neuroleptics increases your risk for tardive dyskensia, NMS, extrapyramidal side effects. Taking tricyclic antidepressants and many other medications with heart effects can increase your risk for heart problems with Orap. Your doctor may need to adjust dosages of other medications you take, especially antiseizure drugs.

Tips: You should have an EKG before starting Orap, and regular heart monitoring while taking it. Orap is considered more risky than some other old-line neuroleptics, not to mention the atypical neuroleptics. Make sure you have exhausted your other options first.

Prolixin

Generic name: fluphenazine

Also known as: Prolixin Decanoate

Use: Psychosis

Action, if known: Phenothiazine neuroleptic—affects the hypothalamus gland in the brain, which in turn affects metabolism, body temperature, alertness, muscle tone, and hormone production.

Side effects: May suppress the gag or cough reflex. Sedation, depression, light sensitivity, jaundice (this should pass), anemia, changes in blood pressure or heartbeat. Danger of tardive dyskensia.

Known interaction hazards: Alcohol, any tranquilizer or central nervous system depressant (including over-the-counter sleep aids), antacids, lithium, tricyclic antidepressants. Loses effectiveness when you eat or drink items containing caffeine.

Tips: Avoid extreme heat when taking Prolixin. Do not take if you have blood, liver, kidney, or heart disease, low blood pressure, or Parkinson's disease. Take with food or juice if stomach upset occurs.

Serentil

Generic name: mesoridazine

Use: Psychosis

Action, if known: Neuroleptic

Side effects: Drowsiness, dizziness, sedation, agitation, nausea, changes in appetite, weight gain or loss, sexual dysfunction. Lowers seizure threshold. Risk of tardive dyskensia and extrapyramidal side effects.

Known interaction hazards: Avoid alcohol and all central nervous system depressants, including tranquilizers, sedatives, over-the-counter sleep aids, narcotics. Potentiates atropine, phosphorus insecticides, quinidine.

Tips: Avoid extreme heat while taking this drug. You will need regular blood tests and eye exams while taking Serentil. Not recommended for people with severe depression, bone marrow depression, liver or heart disease. Those with high blood pressure should be carefully monitored while taking Serentil.

Stelazine

Generic name: trifluoperazine

Also known as: Vesprin

Action, if known: Phenothiazine neuroleptic—affects the hypothalamus gland in the brain, which in turn affects metabolism, body temperature, alertness, muscle tone, and hormone production. Blocks dopamine receptors in the mesolimbic system, increasing turnover of dopamine.

Side effects: May suppress the gag or cough reflex. Sedation, depression, light sensitivity, jaundice (this should pass), anemia, changes in blood pressure or heartbeat. Danger of tardive dyskensia.

Known interaction hazards: Alcohol, any tranquilizer or central nervous system depressant (including over-the-counter sleep aids), antacids, lithium, tricyclic antidepressants. Loses effectiveness when you eat or drink items containing caffeine.

Tips: Avoid extreme heat when taking Stelazine. Do not take if you have blood, liver, kidney, or heart disease, low blood pressure, or Parkinson's disease. If you have thyroid problems, use extreme caution. Take with food or juice if stomach upset occurs.

Thorazine

Generic name: chlorpromazine

Use: Psychosis, schizophrenia.

Action, if known: Phenothiazine neuroleptic—affects the hypothalamus gland in the brain, which in turn affects metabolism, body temperature, alertness, muscle tone, and hormone production. Interferes with the action of dopamine in the basal ganglia, mesolimbic area, and medulla. Anticholinergic.

Side effects: May suppress the gag or cough reflex. Sedation, depression, light sensitivity, jaundice (this should pass), anemia, changes in blood pressure or heartbeat, dry mouth. Lowers the seizure threshold. Danger of tardive dyskensia.

Known interaction hazards: Alcohol, any tranquilizer or central nervous system depressant (including over-the-counter sleep aids), antacids, lithium, tricyclic antidepressants. Loses effectiveness when you eat or drink items containing caffeine.

Tips: Avoid extreme heat when taking Thorazine. Do not take if you have blood, liver, kidney, or heart disease, low blood pressure, Reye's disease, or Parkinson's disease. Take with food or juice if stomach upset occurs.

Neuroleptics: The atypicals

The so-called atypical neuroleptics are recent discoveries. They blend functionality against schizophrenia, psychosis, self-injurious behavior, painful ticcing, and other major mental health symptoms, with far fewer side effects and dangers than their ancestors. That's not to say that these are safe, gentle drugs; risk is still there, and they do carry side effects that can be a problem (especially, for children, rapid weight gain). Patients currently taking older neuroleptics should definitely ask their physician about making a switch. The atypical neuroleptic family includes the following drugs:

Clozaril

Generic name: clozapine

Use: Schizophrenia

Action, if known: Atypical neuroleptic—works against the hormone acetylcholine, other actions unknown.

Side effects: Sedation, fever (this usually passes), changes in blood pressure or heartbeat, overproduction of saliva, tremor. Major dangers include agranulocytosis (a serious blood condition), seizures, neuroleptic malignant syndrome (NMS), tardive dyskensia.

Known interaction hazards: Alcohol, central nervous system depressants, drugs for high blood pressure, tricyclic antidepressants, and similar drugs should be avoided or used with caution. Danger of NMS increases when used with lithium.

Tips: Weekly blood tests are required. Women, people with low white blood cell counts, and some people of Ashkenazi Jewish descent have a higher risk of agranulocytosis when taking this drug. People with heart disease, glaucoma, prostate trouble, or liver or kidney disease should be monitored carefully. Smoking cigarettes can affect how quickly your body uses Clozaril.

Risperdal

Generic name: risperidone

Use: Psychosis, schizophrenia, rage/aggression.

Action, if known: Atypical neuroleptic—affects serotonin and dopamine, raises level of the hormone prolactin.

Side effects: Sedation, headache, runny nose, anxiety, insomnia. Weight gain, especially in children. Danger of neuroleptic malignant syndrome (NMS), tardive dyskensia.

Known interaction hazards: Decreases action of L-Dopa. Interacts with carbamazepine and clozapine. May potentiate, or be potentiated by, SSRIs.

Tips: You should have an EKG before starting Risperdal, and regular heart monitoring while taking it. In some patients, Risperdal (and possibly other atypical neuroleptics) may increase obsessive-compulsive symptoms.

Seroquel

Generic name: quetiapine

Use: Psychosis, rage/aggression.

Action, if known: Atypical neuroleptic—believed to increase availability of serotonin and dopamine at specific receptors in the brain.

Side effects: Drowsiness, dizziness, sedation, agitation, nausea, changes in appetite, weight gain or loss, sexual dysfunction. Lowers seizure threshold. Danger of neuroleptic malignant syndrome (NMS), extrapyramidal side effects, and tardive dyskensia.

Known interaction hazards: Avoid alcohol and all central nervous system depressants, including tranquilizers, sedatives, over-the-counter sleep aids, narcotics. Potentiated to a high degree by phenytoin. May interfere with the effects of drugs for high blood pressure. May be potentiated by other drugs, including ketoconazole, erythromycin, clarithromycin, diltiazam, verapamil, and nefazodone.

Tips: Avoid extreme heat while taking this drug. People with liver or kidney problems, heart disease, thyroid problems, or low blood pressure should be monitored while taking Seroquel.

Zeldox

Generic name: ziprasidone

Use: Psychosis, rage/aggression

Action, if known: Atypical neuroleptic

Side effects: Drowsiness, dizziness, nausea, lightheadedness.

Known interaction hazards: Not yet known, but probably similar to those of other atypical neuroleptics.

Tips: Regular heart monitoring is advised when taking Zeldox. This is a very new drug, not yet approved for use in the US. According to some doctors, this medication is less likely to cause rapid weight gain than the other atypical antipsychotics.

Zyprexa

Generic name: olanzapine

Use: Psychosis, rage/aggression, tics; also used in cases of hard-to-treat OCD, depression (usually with an antidepressant), or bipolar disorders (usually with a mood stabilizer).

Action, if known: Atypical neuroleptic—blocks uptake of dopamine and serotonin at certain receptors, may have other actions.

Side effects: Headache, agitation, dry mouth, hostility, disinhibition, insomnia, slurred speech, neuroleptic malignant syndrome (NMS), tardive dyskensia, dizziness, seizures.

Known interaction hazards: Alcohol. Potentiated by carbamazepine; potentiates medications for high blood pressure (such as clonidine and Tenex).

Tips: Avoid extreme heat. If you smoke, you may need to take Zyprexa more frequently.

Stimulants

Ritalin and other stimulant drugs are prescribed for ADD or ADHD, and sometimes to counteract the sluggish effects of neuroleptics or other medications. Stimulants affect the level of dopamine available at the synapse. Ritalin and Dexedrine block the dopamine reuptake mechanism as well as affecting some enzymes in the synapse that are dopamine antagonists. Other stimulants simply cause neurons to release dopamine directly. They are also believed to increase how much norepinephrine is released from the sympathetic nervous system, and to inhibit its reuptake by the caudate nucleus. In addition, stimulants increase the flow of blood to all parts of the brain.

The stimulants work similarly, but for different lengths of time and with varying danger of the dreaded rebound effect. This phenomenon's symptoms range from manic-like euphoria to depression or aggression.

The rebound effect can be addressed by careful dosing. Ritalin is the shortest-acting stimulant, and therefore the one with which the greatest amount of rebound trouble occurs. Doctors often ask that it be given at two-and-a-half to three-hour intervals, with half of a regular dose at bedtime to permit better sleep. A sustained-release version of Ritalin (Ritalin SR) is available, but gets low marks from patients when used alone. Dexedrine has a longer life (four to six hours), and the Dexedrine Spansule formulation can maintain its beneficial effects for up to eight hours.

Stimulants precipitate mania in some people with bipolar disorders.

BuSpar (see "Antianxiety medications") and clonidine or Tenex (see "Other medications") are alternatives for treating ADD and ADHD when stimulants are not well-tolerated or advisable.

Prescription stimulants

Adderall

Generic name: dextroamphetimine/amphetamine

Use: ADD/ADHD

Action, if known: Central nervous system stimulant.

Side effects: Loss of appetite, weight loss, headache, insomnia, dizziness, increased heart rate, agitation. May increase tic severity in people with an underlying tic disorder.

Known interaction hazards: Vitamin C supplements, citrus juices, citric acid, more than four cans per day of soda, or taking this medication with food can reduce its effectiveness.

Tips: Make sure you drink plenty of water, even if you're not thirsty. Adderall is not as well-known as Ritalin, but it may be a better choice for many patients. It time-releases different amphetamine compounds smoothly over several hours, resulting in less chance of rebound.

Cylert

Generic name: pemoline

Use: ADD/ADHD, narcolepsy.

Action, if known: Central nervous system stimulant.

Side effects: Irritability, insomnia, appetite changes, depression. Lowers the seizure threshold.

Known interaction hazards: Potentiates other central nervous system stimulants. May increase tic severity in people with an underlying tic disorder. Vitamin C supplements, citrus juices, citric acid, more than four cans per day of soda, or taking this medication with food can reduce its effectiveness.

Tips: You will need to have liver enzyme tests every six months—those with known liver problems may need to avoid Cylert. Not recommended for children with psychosis. Has the longest life of the stimulants commonly used for ADHD. You can take it with food if stomach upset occurs, but the dose may need to be adjusted. Make sure you drink plenty of water, even if you're not thirsty. Cylert has a long action period, but is rarely used unless other drugs have failed to have positive effects.

Das

Generic name: dextroamphetimine sulfate

Also known as: Dexampex, Dexedrine, Dexedrine Spansules, Dextrostat, Ferndex, Oxydess.

Use: ADD/ADHD

Action, if known: Central nervous system stimulant.

Side effects: Agitation, restlessness, aggressive behavior, dizziness, insomnia, headache, tremor, dry mouth, change in appetite, weight loss. May raise blood pressure. May increase tic severity in people with an underlying tic disorder.

Known interaction hazards: Do not use with MAOIs. Interacts with tricyclic antidepressants, meperidine, norepinephrine, phenobarbital, phenytoin, propoxyphene, acetazolamide, thiazides, and some medications for stomach distress. Vitamin C supplements, citrus juices, citric acid, more than four cans per day of soda, or taking this medication with food can reduce its effectiveness.

Tips: If you are diabetic, discuss your use of insulin and oral anti-diabetes drugs with your doctor, as Das may force a change in dosage. Not recommended for children with psychosis. Make sure you drink plenty of water, even if you're not thirsty.

Desoxyn

Generic name: methamphetamine (MTH)

Use: ADD/ADHD, narcolepsy.

Action, if known: Central nervous system stimulant.

Side effects: Agitation, restlessness, aggressive behavior, dizziness, insomnia, headache, tremor. May raise blood pressure. May increase tic severity in people with an underlying tic disorder.

Known interaction hazards: Never use with MAOIs. Effect of Desoxyn may be counteracted by barbiturates, tranquilizers (including over-the-counter sleep aids), and tricyclic antidepressants. Desoxyn may potentiate other central nervous system stimulants, including caffeine, over-the-counter cold and allergy medications. Potentiated by cetazolamide and sodium bicarbonate.

May interact with some GI medications. Vitamin C supplements, citrus juices, citric acid, more than four cans per day of soda, or taking this medication with food can reduce its effectiveness.

Tips: This is the most powerful and potentially addictive of the stimulants, and for that reason it is rarely used. If you are diabetic, discuss your use of insulin and oral anti-diabetes drugs with your doctor, as Desoxyn may force a change in dosage. Not recommended for children with psychosis. Make sure you drink plenty of water, even if you're not thirsty. Well-known as a drug of abuse, and therefore rarely prescribed in the US.

Ritalin

Generic name methylphenidate hydrochloride

Use: ADD/ADHD, narcolepsy, social phobia.

Action, if known: Central nervous system stimulant.

Side effects: Agitation, restlessness, aggressive behavior, dizziness, insomnia, headache, tremor. May raise blood pressure. May increase tic severity in people with an underlying tic disorder.

Known interaction hazards: Alcohol. Potentiated by MAOIs to a high degree. Potentiates tricyclic antidepressants. Reduces action of guanethidine. Vitamin C supplements, citrus juices, citric acid, more than four cans per day of soda, or taking this medication with food can reduce its effectiveness.

Tips: The rebound effect can be bad with Ritalin, which has the shortest life of the stimulants commonly used for ADHD. Some doctors combine Ritalin SR with regular Ritalin for the smoothest effect (SR's action is said to be erratic). Make sure you drink plenty of water, even if you're not thirsty. Some people, including quite a few doctors, swear that the brand-name Ritalin is superior to its generic counterpart. It may be worth trying the brand-name version if the generic didn't work well.

Over-the-counter stimulants

Many teenagers with bipolar disorders use and abuse over-the-counter stimulants, such as NoDoz, Vivarin, and similar drugs, diet pills, and preparations intended for colds and allergies that contain ephedrine, pseudoephedrine, caffeine, cyproheptadine, dextromethorphan, or other central nervous system stimulants. Others may use "legal speed" pills that mix caffeine, ephedrine, and other substances.

This is an extraordinarily dangerous practice, because it can throw the circadian clock out of whack. Many manic episodes have started off with an all-night cram session made possible by drugs such as NoDoz. Students with bipolar disorders need to develop study skills that make cramming into the wee hours unnecessary—they are literally survival skills. If your child is involved in an academic or after-school program that requires late-night hours, help her to find an alternative, change the program, reduce her involvement, or develop safe coping strategies. Athletic teams, theater and music departments, college-level architecture and design programs, and many otherwise excellent activities for teens and young adults can be unhealthy for those with manic depression. There's always a way to adjust the program to fit if you try.

Educate your child about reading the labels on all over-the-counter medications, and about recognizing the names of common stimulants that may wreak havoc with his mental state. Be especially sure to pound in the dangers of the stay-awake pills, herbal stimulants like Ma Huang or Happy Camper, and "legal speed." Used indiscriminately and/or in concert with other medication, illegal drugs, or alcohol, these concoctions can be deadly.

Drug and alcohol detox/ dependency aids

When a young person has a dual diagnosis of chemical dependency and a bipolar disorder, most doctors choose to treat both conditions at once. This can be difficult unless the patient is in a hospital or other residential situation, where presumably he will not have access to drugs or alcohol. Doctors must also be careful about possible conflicts between medications for bipolar symptoms and medications used for other purposes.

Drug and alcohol withdrawal can be a painful process. Several neural and hormonal systems are affected by substance abuse, and when it ends they are thrown into confusion. Effects can include noradrenergic hyperactivity, gamma-aminobutyric acid (GABA)-benzodiazepine receptor alteration, elevated hypothalamic-pituitary-adrenal axis, and changes in the N-methyl-

D-aspartate (NMDA) glutamate receptors. The patient's blood pressure may soar or become unstable, she may sweat profusely or develop tremors. Severe nausea and physical pain is also commonplace.[2]

For years, inpatient detox programs have prescribed the benzodiazepine tranquilizers as a way to blunt these difficulties. Unfortunately, these medications are also addictive—and may encourage patients to simply trade one addiction for another. They are still widely used to treat withdrawal from methamphetamine and cocaine, however, simply because there are few other medical options.

Methadone treatment is another option for heroin addicts. It involves swapping an illegal addiction for a legal one, which is controversial. However, methadone treatment has been shown to help keep drug addicts away from criminal behavior, and to help them become more productive members of society. When combined with counseling and other strategies, it may be a good first step on the road to actual detox. It certainly can improve the patient's health in many ways, as methadone is administered in a clinic, comes in a reliable dose to eliminate the risk of overdose, and is drunk rather than injected. It is the treatment of choice for pregnant addicts.

Cold turkey detox is always an option—and for some people, it works best despite the temporary discomfort. However, today's addiction specialists do have pharmacological tools at their disposal that can ease the pain and suffering of addicts in detox, and help prevent relapses. Intensive rehabilitation centers for people addicted to heroin and other opiates can use a one-day detox method that involves completely sedating the patient and administering ReVia or another opiate blocker intravenously. Follow-up care consists of continued use of oral opiate blockers and counseling. Some programs are also experimenting with implanted ReVia. Few teenagers can gain admission to these programs.

Some intensive detox programs claim a 75 to 80 percent success rate, although this cannot be confirmed. The cost of such treatment ranges to well over $7,000.

Currently there are no cocaine or methamphetamine antagonists available for those who are addicted to these drugs (which are, unfortunately, the drugs of choice for many people with bipolar disorders, probably because of their paradoxically—and temporary—calming effects on some BP individuals). Several potential cocaine antagonists are currently under development, but so far there have been many roadblocks in this research. Cocaine works by preventing certain nerve cells from accumulating the neurotransmitter dopamine, making dopamine widely available to the brain and causing a euphoric high. Blocking dopamine entirely produces many ill effects on the body, however.

Heavy methamphetamine and cocaine abusers often experience the symptoms of psychosis. Neuroleptics (see earlier in this chapter) are used to address these symptoms in some addiction treatment centers.

Supplementing with vitamin C, which can counteract the effects of prescription stimulants, may also help recovering methamphetamine addicts.

The tricyclic antidepressants, SSRIs, and BuSpar (all of which are listed earlier in this chapter) have shown some promise in helping recovering alcoholics stay sober. People with a bipolar disorder and substance dependency may find that recovery is easier if they use an antidepressant in addition to their regular mood stabilizer. Some doctors use clonidine or Tenex during drug or alcohol withdrawal. These, along with the nicotine antagonist Inversene and prescription nicotine, are listed later in this chapter under the heading "Other medications."

For obvious reasons, young people with drug and alcohol addiction should not be given unfettered access to these or any other prescription medications. Doses should be given individually, and drugs should be securely stored. Counseling support, including 12-step programs, can be helpful in preventing the development of prescription drug abuse in recovering addicts.

The following are medications that may be used to treat or prevent substance abuse. It should be noted that their use is rare in treating teenage patients.

Acamprosate

Generic name: calcium acetylhomotaurinate

Use: Prevention of alcohol abuse.

Action, if known: Acamprosate is a calcium channel blocker. It seems to stimulate inhibitory GABA receptors and to antagonize excitatory amino acids, such as glutamate. This should prevent some of the pleasurable, reinforcing effects of alcohol use.

Side effects: Diarrhea

Tips: Acamprosate is available in Australia and several European countries, but is still in clinical trials in the US.

Antabuse

Generic name: disulfiram

Use: Prevention of alcohol abuse.

Action, if known: Antabuse works by inhibiting the enzyme acetaldehyde dehydrogenase, which normally breaks down the toxic by-product acetaldehyde that forms when the body metabolizes alcohol. If you drink alcohol while taking Antabuse, acetaldehyde builds up immediately and you will become violently ill.

Side effects: Drowsiness, mood swings, unusual sensations in the hands or feet (tingling or pain). Antabuse can cause or exacerbate heart or liver problems. Drinking large quantities of alcohol while taking Antabuse can actually kill you.

Tips: Antabuse should be used only as part of a complete recovery program, including counseling and peer support. People taking Antabuse should be monitored for heart and liver problems. They must also be careful to avoid healthcare and skin products that contain alcohol, including many cough syrups. In addition, they should avoid contact with the fumes of chemicals that may contain alcohol, acetaldehyde, paraldehyde, or other related substances, including paint, paint thinner, varnish, and shellac. Most doctors feel that Antabuse is of little or no help in treating alcohol addiction—it is sometime used as a punitive, court-ordered deterrence measure rather than a legitimate medical treatment.

Calan

Generic name: verapamil

Also known as: Isoptin

Use: Angina, heart arrhythmia, high blood pressure, prevention of alcohol abuse.

Action, if known: Calcium ion influx inhibitor.

Side effects: Dizziness, constipation, nausea. Lowers blood pressure, can cause edema (water retention in the ankles and legs).

Known interaction hazards: Do not use with beta blockers. Calan may lower your lithium level. Potentiates digoxin. Be careful with Calan if you use any other medication that affects blood pressure. May counteract or interact negatively with verapamil, Quinidine, Disopyramide, flecainide, neuromuscular blocking agents, carbamazepine, cyclosporine, theophylline. Counteracted at least somewhat by rifampin, phenobarbital, and Sulfinpyrazone. May interact with inhaled agents used in anesthesia.

Tips: Blood pressure and liver function should be monitored while taking this drug, especially in patients with known liver damage. Take Calan with food.

Narcan

Generic name: naloxone hydrochloride

Use: Treatment of opiate and narcotic overdose or addiction, reversal of the effects of anesthetics.

Action, if known: Opiate antagonist. Unlike ReVex and ReVia, Narcan counteracts all of the effects of morphine.

Side effects: May raise blood pressure, may lower the seizure threshold.

Known interaction hazards: Do not use with bisulfate or alkaline solutions.

Tips: Naloxone has not been well-tested in treating chemical dependency.

ReVex

Generic name: nalmefene hydrochloride

Use: Treatment of opiate and narcotic addiction or overdose, reversal of the effects of anesthetics.

Action, if known: Opiate antagonist. Appears to activate the hypothalamic-pituitary-adrenal (HPA) axis more strongly than naloxone.

Side effects: Anxiety, nervousness, insomnia, abdominal discomfort, nausea, headache, muscle or joint pain. May lower the seizure threshold.

Known interaction hazards: Alcohol and all central nervous system depressants, including anesthetics, narcotics, and sedatives. ReVia may block the effects of these substances until they reach a critical, even deadly, level.

Tips: Other than the difference already noted, ReVex is essentially the same as ReVia—see the next entry.

ReVia

Generic name: naltrexone hydrochloride

Also known as: Trexan, NTX.

Use: Heroin/opiate and alcohol addiction withdrawal aid, treatment of narcotic overdose, self-injurious behavior (SIB), reversal of the effects of anesthetics.

Action, if known: Opiate antagonist—blocks opiate chemicals.

Side effects: Anxiety, nervousness, insomnia, abdominal discomfort, nausea, headache, muscle or joint pain. May lower the seizure threshold.

Known interaction hazards: Alcohol and all central nervous system depressants, including anesthetics, narcotics, and sedatives. ReVia may block the effects of these substances until they reach a critical, even deadly, level.

Tips: According to product literature, ReVia should not be used by people who are currently addicted to drugs or alcohol—it is used only after the detox process is over, to help the person stay sober. However, a number of intensive detox centers do rely on ReVia, and it does appear to help reduce cravings for drugs and alcohol. People with liver problems must be closely monitored while taking ReVia. Recent studies indicate that ReVia (and possibly other opiate blockers) can help stop the cycle of self-injurious behavior.

Antianxiety drugs

Most of the drugs prescribed for anxiety are in the benzodiazepine family of tranquilizers. Some of these medications may also help to prevent seizures and ease depression. Doctors try to avoid prescribing these for long-term use. Tranquilizers slow down central nervous system activity, they often don't mix well with other medications, and they can be addictive. However, for patients with severe anxiety, benzodiazepine tranquilizers can be very effective. Some people can take these on an as-needed basis, avoiding medication dependency. They include the following medications:

Ativan

Generic name: lorazepam

Use: Antianxiety, panic disorder, PMS, irritable bowel syndrome. May also be used in acute mania to bring on sleep and stabilize the patient—some doctors prefer Ativan to antipsychotics, which are commonly used for this purpose.

Action, if known: Benzodiazepine—slows central nervous system activity.

Side effects: Sleepiness (this usually passes after a week), lethargy, confusion, headache, slurred speech, tremor. Addictive—withdrawal may be difficult.

Known interaction hazards: Alcohol, all tranquilizers (including over-the-counter sleep aids), narcotics, MAOIs, antihistamines (including over-the-counter allergy and cold remedies), antidepressants. Potentiated by cimetidine, SSRIs, Depakene, disulfiram, isoniazid, ketoconazole, metoprolol, probenecid, propoxyphene, propranalol, rifampin, and oral contraceptives. Potentiates digoxin and phenytoin; decreases effect of L-Dopa.

Tips: If you smoke, take theophylline, or use antacids, Ativan may be less effective.

BuSpar

Generic name: buspirone

Use: Anxiety, decreasing emotional lability or mood swings, ADHD, PMS.

Action, if known: Non-benzodiazepine tranquilizer—enhances serotonin transmission, blocks dopamine receptors, increases metabolism of norepinephrine in the brain.

Side effects: Dizziness, nausea, headache, fatigue, jitteriness, tremor, sore muscles, heart palpitations, sweating, possible liver or kidney damage, tardive dyskensia-like movements or tics.

Known interaction hazards: Do not use with MAOIs. Potentiates Haldol and possibly other neuroleptics. Can cause liver inflammation when used with Desyrel. May have other side effects when used with antidepressants or similar drugs. Prolongs the effectiveness of SSRIs, and is sometimes prescribed for this specific purpose.

Tips: Side effects are a frequent problem with BuSpar, especially when taken in combination with other medications, including over-the-counter remedies. The BuSpar patch may be better tolerated and smoother-acting than the pill, especially for treatment of ADHD or mood swings. It has been tested with good results in children for treatment of ADHD without the same rebound effect as Ritalin, and for treating anxiety and irritability in children with neurological disorders. Many physicians like to prescribe BuSpar because it doesn't carry the addiction risk of the benzodiazepines.

Centrax

Generic name: prazepam

Use: Antianxiety, muscle spasm, seizures, panic disorder, irritable bowel syndrome.

Action, if known: Benzodiazepine, slows central nervous system activity.

Side effects: Sleepiness (this usually passes after a week), lethargy, confusion, headache, slurred speech, tremor. Addictive—withdrawal may be difficult.

Known interaction hazards: Alcohol, all tranquilizers (including over-the-counter sleep aids), narcotics, MAOIs, antidepressants, antihistamines (including over-the-counter allergy and cold remedies). Potentiated by cimetidine, disulfiram, SSRIs, Depakene, disulfiram, isoniazid, ketoconazole, metoprolol, probenecid, propoxyphene, propranalol, rifampin, and oral contraceptives. Potentiates digoxin and phenytoin; decreases effect of L-Dopa.

Tips: Many people should not take Centrax, including people with severe depression, lung disease, liver or kidney disease, sleep apnea, alcoholism, or psychosis. Intended for short-term use. If you smoke, take theophylline, or use antacids, Centrax may be less effective.

Librium

Generic name: chlordiazepoxide

Use: Anxiety, panic attacks, irritable bowel syndrome.

Action, if known: Benzodiazepine, depresses central nervous system activity.

Side effects: Sedation (this should pass), depression, stupor, headache, tremor, dry mouth, sexual dysfunction. Addictive—withdrawal may be difficult.

Known interaction hazards: Avoid other central nervous system depressants, including alcohol, narcotics, tranquilizers (including over-the-counter sleep aids), MAOIs, antidepressants, and both prescription and over-the-counter antihistamines. Do not take with antacids. Potentiates digoxin and phenytoin; reduces potency of L-Dopa.

Tips: Many people should not take Librium, including people with severe depression, lung disease, liver or kidney disease, sleep apnea, alcoholism, or psychosis. Intended for short-term use. Smoking may reduce the effectiveness of Librium.

Serax

Generic name: oxazepam

Use: Anxiety, muscle spasm, seizures, panic disorder, irritable bowel syndrome.

Action, if known: Benzodiazepine, slows central nervous system activity.

Side effects: Sleepiness (this usually passes after a week), lethargy, confusion, headache, slurred speech, tremor. Addictive, withdrawal may be difficult.

Known interaction hazards: Alcohol, all tranquilizers (including over-the-counter sleep aids), narcotics, MAOIs, antidepressants, antihistamines (including over-the-counter allergy and cold remedies). Potentiated by cimetidine, disulfiram, SSRIs, Depakene, isoniazid, ketoconazole, metoprolol, probenecid, propoxyphene, propranalol, rifampin, and oral contraceptives. Potentiates digoxin and phenytoin; decreases effect of L-Dopa.

Tips: Many people should not take Serax, including people with severe depression, lung disease, liver or kidney disease, sleep apnea, alcoholism, or psychosis. Intended for short-term use. If you smoke, take theophylline, or use antacids, Serax may be less effective.

Tranxene

Generic name: clorazepate

Use: Anxiety, panic disorder, irritable bowel syndrome.

Action, if known: Benzodiazepine—slows central nervous system activity.

Side effects: Drowsiness (this should pass), confusion, tremor, dizziness, depression. Addiction danger, withdrawal may be uncomfortable.

Known interaction hazards: Do not take with antacids. Alcohol and other central nervous system depressants, tranquilizers (including over-the-counter sleep aids), narcotics, barbiturates, MAOIs, antihistamines (including cold and allergy medications), and antidepressants all interact negatively with Tranxene. This drug potentiates digoxin and phenytoin. Potentiated by cometidine, disulfiram, fluoxetine, isoniazid, ketoconazole, metoprolol, probenecid, propoxyphene, propranolol, rifamin, and Depakote/Depakene.

Tips: You should not take Tranxene if you have lung, liver, or kidney disease, psychosis, or depression. Intended for short-term use. Smoking may interfere with the action of Tranxene.

Valium

Generic name: diazepam

Use: Anxiety, muscle spasm, seizures, panic disorder, irritable bowel syndrome.

Action, if known: Benzodiazepine, slows central nervous system activity.

Side effects: Sleepiness (this usually passes after a week), lethargy, confusion, headache, slurred speech, tremor. Addictive, withdrawal may be difficult.

Known interaction hazards: Alcohol, all tranquilizers (including over-the-counter sleep aids), narcotics, MAOIs, antidepressants, antihistamines (including over-the-counter allergy and cold remedies). Potentiated by cimetidine, disulfiram, SSRIs, Depakote/Depakene, disulfiram, isoniazid, ketoconazole, metoprolol, probenecid, propoxyphene, propranolol, rifampin, and oral contraceptives. Potentiates digoxin and phenytoin; decreases the effect of L-Dopa.

Tips: Many people should not take Valium, including people with severe depression, lung disease, liver or kidney disease, sleep apnea, alcoholism, or psychosis. Intended for short-term use. If you smoke, take theophylline, or use antacids, Valium may be less effective.

Xanax

Generic name: alprazolam

Use: Anti-anxiety, panic disorder, PMS, irritable bowel syndrome.

Action, if known: Benzodiazepine, slows central nervous system activity.

Side effects: Sleepiness (this usually passes after a week), lethargy, confusion, headache, slurred speech, tremor. Addictive, withdrawal may be difficult.

Known interaction hazards: Do not use with alcohol, tranquilizers of any kind (including over-the-counter sleep aids), MAOIs, antihistamines (including over-the-counter allergy and cold medicines), or antidepressants, unless under strict medical supervision.

Tips: Many people should not take Xanax, including people with severe depression, sleep apnea, liver or kidney disease, lung disease, alcoholism, or psychosis.

Other medications

Several other medications may be prescribed to your child to treat specific symptoms. One group of these, estrogen and related hormones used to treat menstrual irregularities, are discussed in more detail in Chapter 6, *Other Interventions*. Other drugs for bipolar-related symptoms that don't fit in the earlier categories follow:

Catapres

Generic name: clonidine

Use: High blood pressure, ADD/ADHD, tics/Tourette syndrome, extreme impulsivity, migraine, drug and alcohol withdrawal aid, ulcerative colitis, childhood growth delay.

Action, if known: Stimulates alpha-adrenergic receptors in brain to widen blood vessels, stimulates similar receptors throughout the body.

Side effects: Dry mouth, dizziness, constipation, sedation, unusually vivid or disturbing dreams, weight gain.

Known interaction hazards: Could interact with other medications for blood pressure.

Tips: Do not use if you have heart trouble, disease of the blood vessels in the brain, or chronic kidney failure. The time-release clonidine patch is far less sedating than the pills. You can become tolerant of clonidine, requiring a higher dose. You should have regular eye exams, as clonidine can affect the retina.

Habitrol

Generic name: nicotine

Also known as: Nicoderm, Nicotrol, ProStep.

Use: Aid to stopping smoking; may be prescribed to potentiate neuroleptics or atypical neuroleptics without increasing the actual dose.

Action, if known: Affects many central nervous system functions—not all actions known. May reduce tics and anxiety in some people.

Side effects: Diarrhea, insomnia, nervousness. Addiction possible.

Known interaction hazards: Caffeine interferes with absorption.

Tips: People with insulin-dependent diabetes, heart problems, liver or kidney disease, high blood pressure, or pheochromocytoma should be carefully monitored when using nicotine in any form (including cigarettes).

Inversine

Generic name: mecamylamine HCl

Use: High blood pressure, rage/aggression, aid to stopping smoking.

Action, if known: This older drug, now rarely used for hypertension, blocks nicotine receptors in the brain and relaxes blood vessels.

Side effects: Dizziness, blurred vision, nausea, dry mouth, constipation.

Known interaction hazards: Interacts with sulfa drugs and antibiotics. Potentiated by antacids, bicarbonate of soda, acetazolamide, potassium or sodium citrate, citric acid. Decreases the effects of ambenonium, neostigmine, and pyridostigmine.

Tips: The use of Inversine for rage and aggression is still experimental, although early research looks promising. Those with bladder, kidney, prostate, or bowel problems will require regular monitoring while taking Inversine. May make glaucoma and heart problems worse.

Tenex

Generic name: guanfacine

Use: High blood pressure, migraines, extreme nausea, heroin withdrawal aid, ADHD/ADD, tic disorders/Tourette syndrome.

Action, if known: Stimulates central nervous system to widen blood vessels, and has other as yet unknown effects.

Side effects: Sleepiness, changes in blood pressure or heart rate, nausea.

Known interaction hazards: Alcohol and other central nervous system depressants. May be counteracted by stimulants such as Ritalin and many over-the-counter drugs; by estrogen and oral contraceptives; and by indomethacin, ibuprofen, and non-steroidal anti-inflammatory drugs.

Tips: If you take another medication that lowers blood pressure, your doctor will need to adjust your Tenex dose accordingly to prevent problems. Most people take Tenex at bedtime due to its sedating effect.

Thyroid hormone replacements

Generic name: levothyroxine, liothyronine, T3, T4.

Also known as: Euthroid, Armour, S-P-T, Thyroid Strong, Thyrar, Cytomel, and many more.

Use: Treatment of thyroid disorders, mood disorders that do not respond to conventional treatment, or as an adjunct to antidepressants.

Action, if known: Potentiates effects on noradrenergic receptor sensitivity, increases the efficiency of noradrenergic neurotransmission, corrects thyroid abnormalities by replacing deficient natural hormones.

Side effects: May negatively affect your body's natural production of thyroid hormone, as do other forms of hormone replacement therapy. Overdose symptoms include headache, irritability, nervousness, sweating, and irregular heartbeat—call your doctor if these continue over a period of time. Can cause hair loss in children at the beginning of therapy, although this usually reverses.

Known interaction hazards: Potentiates antidepressants (and is sometimes used for this specific effect). Do not use with maprotiline. May be potentiated by aspirin and other salicytates. Dosage needed will be affected by the use of other hormones, including estrogen and insulin. Reduces the effectiveness of some beta blockers, may potentiate theophylline drugs.

Tips: Thyroid status must be monitored via regular blood tests. A few people have an allergic skin reaction to thyroid hormone, and should not take it. T3 is usually more effective than T4.

The meds merry-go-round

This merry-go-round is not all that merry. Your child may try many different medications over the years before one or more are found that work for him. As he gets older and larger, medications may become less effective.

> *For depression, Prozac worked a little but not really well, and Well-butrin did nothing for Craig. Zoloft he's still taking, and it works great. For mood swings, Tegretol was starting to work, but he broke out in a rash, Depakote was not working, Lithium worked somewhat, but he had problems with diarrhea. Neurontin works really well along with the Depakote.* —Cindy, mother of 16-year-old Craig and 19-year-old Kara

Puberty is a typical time for what once worked to become ineffective. The transition period between the teen years and adulthood is another. Girls may also find that effectiveness of their medications waxes and wanes according to their menstrual cycle.

Your best protection is to arm yourself with hard information and solid medical support when managing your child's medications. Keep careful records of all medication trails and their results, and involve your child as much as possible in self-reporting efficiency and side effects as he grows older.

Alternative medicine

Many people see alternative medical practitioners instead of, or in addition to, a traditional MD or GP. These specialists, including naturopaths, homeopathic physicians, chiropractors, practitioners of Asian and Ayurvedic medicine, and acupuncturists, may have different ideas about treating bipolar disorders than those presented in this chapter. Most experts agree that no one should rely entirely on herbal remedies,

Be sure to check the credentials of your alternative practitioners, and use the same cautions with herbal and homeopathic remedies, vitamins, acupuncture, and other treatments that they may suggest, as you would with Western medicine. Look for hard evidence that a treatment is effective for the symptom you want to treat before trying it. There may be much of value in these approaches for some patients, but not all alternative therapies are appropriate for all patients.

If you use alternative medicine as well as Western approaches, be sure that all of your healthcare practitioners know what you're doing. If you can, get them to talk to each other. It's certainly not universal, but many Western doctors are gaining a great deal of respect for alternative modalities.

Be careful about the herbal remedies you try, too. In the US, supplements are not regulated for content or potency. For example, the *Los Angeles Times* commissioned an independent lab analysis of ten major brands of St. John's Wort in 1998. Three proved to be less than half as potent as their labels claimed, and four others were less than 90 percent potent.[3] Until there are firm standards, either voluntary or government-imposed, consumers must educate themselves well.

Chapter 6 discusses a number of specific alternative therapies that have been used by some people with bipolar disorders.

Hospitalization

There are several situations that may cause a bipolar child to need hospitalization. They include:

- When the child is a danger to himself, either through suicide threats or attempts, or through serious self-injurious behavior.

- When the child is a danger to others because of aggressive, assaultive behavior or serious threats.

- When the child is in an acute manic, depressed, or mixed state and cannot be safely managed at home with the addition of medication and support services.

- When the child is suffering from severe medication reactions or unusual symptoms that are too difficult medically to handle at home.

- When a child with a seizure disorder in addition to a bipolar disorder is experiencing severe and medication-resistant seizures.

- When a child with a bipolar disorder also has an eating disorder that is not responding to traditional treatment.

- When a child with a bipolar disorder complicated by substance abuse or dependency needs intense medical supervision.

Of course, children with bipolar disorders may also fall victim to disease or injury that's not psychiatric in nature. When these problems require hospitalization, parents should confer with the staff to ensure that their child's diagnosis and current medical treatments are thoroughly understood, and that his needs for medication management, therapy, and special education services can be met in the hospital while he recovers.

If your child is injured due to a suicide attempt, self-injury, medication or drug overdose, or a reckless bipolar-related accident and needs immediate medical care, go directly to the nearest emergency room. Call your psychiatrist to let him know what's going on, and then stay with your child. Her behaviors may be puzzling to workers in the emergency room. Sometimes patients who come in with self-inflicted injuries are denigrated or forced to wait longer than others by poorly educated medical personnel. The presence of a parent who can advocate for proper care should help.

You may have to wait a long time to see someone in the emergency room, especially if it's a busy weekend night or most personnel are attending to car accident victims and other life or death emergencies. Probably the first person you'll see is an intake worker, who will get your child's identifying and health insurance information. If you need help to control your child in the ER, tell the intake worker or the first security guard you see. Should your child need to be restrained, stay with her to let her know that you'll be there to ensure her safety.

After intake, you should next see a triage nurse, who's specially trained to assess the severity of cases presenting at the ER. Let this person know what your greatest concerns are, especially if you feel your child could be a danger to herself or others. At this point a decision will be made about whether to admit your child immediately.

When you go to the emergency room, bring any medications, supplements, and herbal remedies your child uses. If you know or suspect that your child has recently used any illegal drugs or alcohol, let the emergency room personnel know it right away. These things affect what medical intervention they can safely use. You may also want to bring a book your child enjoys, a Walkman with tapes of soothing music, some toys, and a change of clothes in case your child needs to be admitted overnight (or longer). If there's no time to collect these items, don't worry—you can have someone else deliver them to you later at the hospital when the situation stabilizes.

Once your child has been admitted to the ER, you'll see a doctor and/or nurses. They may take your child's blood pressure, check her heartbeat, take blood or urine samples to test for drugs, alcohol, lithium toxicity, infection, or other issues, and give emergency medical treatment including drugs. Make sure you understand what drugs are given, especially if your child is released into your care immediately after treatment rather than being held for observation.

For other mental health crises, such as serious episodes of mania or depression, it helps to have a plan worked out in advance. The best place to start is, of course, your child's psychiatrist. Call and ask for an emergency evaluation. If it is after hours or your doctor is unavailable, call your primary care provider, general practitioner, or HMO and ask for an immediate referral. In some cases you may need to take your child to the emergency room for safety's sake until a doctor can arrive to evaluate your child.

If you reach your doctor, she should cancel routine appointments to see your child immediately if the situation warrants it. If you think you'll need help getting your child to his office, say so—she may be able to send a mental health aide or other staff member to your assistance. If this kind of help is not available through her office, ask your spouse, other relatives, friends, neighbors, or even the police for help. In some areas your county or provincial mental health department may be able to send someone out. If your child is physically difficult to control or at risk for self-harm, the momentary embarrassment you may feel from asking for help will rapidly be overshadowed by the need to ensure her safety.

Some larger cities have a separate "ER alternative" for mental health emergencies—the mental health triage center. This is a type of facility that really should be available to all people with mental illness everywhere. The regular ER's parade of accident victims, gruesome injuries, screams, and high drama can be a real horror show for someone suffering from mental distress.

In a mental health triage center, trained personnel are on staff 24 hours a day to deal with crisis situations. Psychiatrists, appropriate medications, and security measures are on hand to meet your needs. Whenever possible, the environment is carefully constructed to be as peaceful, quiet and non-threatening as possible—just the kind of place you would want to be if you were in emotional pain. There may be a play area for younger children.

Usually a triage specialist will meet with you within just a few minutes. As in the emergency room, the triage nurse will assess your child's condition and start the process of obtaining emergency treatment. Vital signs checks, blood and urine samples, and interviews with the patient are often performed quickly. You may also be interviewed, with your child or separately.

Whether you take your child to your psychiatrist's office, the ER, or a mental health triage center, the criteria for hospital admission will be largely the same. If the patient can be stabilized right there, he may be sent home with you. He may be held for overnight observation, or he may be admitted for short- or long-term treatment.

Parents with HMOs or managed care plans may be required to jump through some hoops to get their child admitted. You will probably need to emphasize, and perhaps even exaggerate, the problems that have culminated in the current emergency. Many parents have reported that it's extremely hard to get their child admitted even when he is a suicide risk or when the family is in danger from his violent actions. Others note that some facilities release their children far too early, often due to less than positive treatment outcomes than to negative news from the family's insurance company.

Nathan has been hospitalized three times. The last time we were beginning to see some results after three months at this one particular hospital, but our insurance benefits were used for the year and he had to leave. So it did not work out when he came home because he was not ready. We can get no mental health benefits for my son at the Army Hospital, which is supposed to be a major medical facility. —Cindy, mother of 16-year-old Nathan

Hospitals: The good stuff

There are many different types of hospitals for psychiatric care. Most young patients will be admitted to a special psychiatric wing of a local hospital. These adolescent mental health units are usually locked wards, to both protect the patients themselves and to prevent escape. They are designed mostly for short-term care, holding patients for observation for a few days or weeks.

Lisa had been having her medications changed frequently, trying to find the right dose. Things were not going well for her. She was more belligerent than ever and was having a hard time coping at school and with friends. She was only going to school part of the day, usually calling me halfway through to pick her up because it was too hard to concentrate, and she was getting into fights with teachers and students. Finally, she asked to be put in the hospital. She knew she couldn't keep on the way she was, and she had tried committing suicide.

We put her in the Richard Young Mental Facility in Omaha for a one week inpatient stay and one-week outpatient stay. It mainly helped to get her medications straightened out, but she was also given a lot of therapy and was taught coping skills. She still uses these skills today. —Donna, *mother of 16-year-old Lisa*

Patients in need of long-term hospitalization are usually sent to a standalone mental facility. This may be a private facility, a therapeutic residential care facility that specializes in treating mentally ill or emotionally disturbed youth, or a public mental hospital. Generally speaking, public mental hospitals in the US get only the most difficult-to-treat cases, along with uninsured patients. This is not necessarily the case elsewhere in the world, where publicly funded mental health care is available to all citizens.

The type of facility matters far less than the appropriateness of its program for your child. Facilities for children and teens need to have a strong education program to prevent patients from slipping too far behind in school. They should be medically savvy, knowledgeable about the latest advances in treatment, and have therapy options that are appropriate for your child's age and needs. For example, facilities that accept very young children should have play therapists on staff, and programs for older children and teens should have considerable resources for treating drug and alcohol abuse and addiction along with psychiatric problems. They should be ready and willing to work closely with parents and other outside helpers. Cleanliness and basic safety are important issues too, as are human decency and kindness.

A lot of the time, you have to go with your gut instinct. If the staff members you meet appear to be well-trained, competent, and gentle with the young people in their care, that's a good sign, as is the presence of a sense of humor and a genuine caring for their patients.

If you have time, talk to your local NAMI chapter or another advocacy group to get other people's opinions about facilities you are considering. If your child is difficult to treat with the usual medications and therapies, you may want to consider a research-oriented hospital, up to and including the special bipolar disorders unit at NIMH in Bethesda, Maryland.

As mentioned in Chapter 3, *Living with Bipolar Disorders*, parents are strongly urged to personally evaluate child and adolescent inpatient psychiatric facilities before their child is in crisis. Programs vary greatly, as does their expertise with bipolar disorders. Talk to the head of the program about their typical treatment program for children with your son or daughter's specific diagnosis. Also ask about how you can be part of their program, and how they will involve your child's regular psychiatrist, therapist, other outside mental health providers such as a county social worker, and school personnel.

When your child is being cared for in a high-quality hospital or residential care facility, you should feel reasonably comfortable with the care she receives. The environment should be not unlike any other kind of hospital. It'll probably be less sterile and featureless than some, in fact. The food may be a drag, as hospital food usually is. Your child will probably chafe at some of the rules, too. Many children's psychiatric units have very strict regulations about appearance, smoking, language, and activities. They may be enforced punitively (not a good thing) or with an effective reward system. Many use a token economy to reinforce positive behavior on the ward. Teens are very likely to resent being told that they can't wear their favorite heavy metal T-shirt, or that they must remove jewelry from various body parts. Let them know that these appearance issues are the hospital's thing, not yours, and that they're usually there to protect more sensitive patients from being offended or frightened.

> Lili hated her stay in the hospital. They took away her clothes, jewelry, cigarettes, and makeup, and she complained constantly about the rules, the staff, and the food. Only certain types of innocuous pop music were allowed, and she felt far too much time was occupied with art therapy and craft projects.

> She had some learning experiences there too. The youngest child was a psychotic boy about 12 years old who had set someone on fire. Another girl had never come down from an acid trip and walked around asking everyone strange questions. I think one thing that convinced her to try medication was not wanting to be as ill as these kids. Other teens were very much like her. One of the girls has remained a friend, which of course the hospital discouraged. They have both made a good recovery, and I think the bond they forged in the hospital may have helped.

From my point of view, the only benefit was that she was safe when we had been worried about suicide. She was misdiagnosed, mismedicated, and released before this could be discovered because our insurance company refused to pay. It ended up costing us over $7,000 for six days. We are still paying it off three years later. —Sarah, mother of 17-year-old Lili

When your child is first admitted you may not be able to see her for a period of time, possibly based on her behavior on the ward. You should be able to meet with the staff during this period, however, and start planning her treatment and after-care program. Once you do get to visit, be prepared for some ugly words, especially if she was admitted against her will. Don't let yourself get upset. This oppositional behavior seems to be a part of the adjustment process, and it should pass.

Alternatively, you may be shocked to see your child looking drugged up. Be sure that you discuss your concerns with the staff, and that any medications given are to treat the condition, not to simply control the patient's behavior. If your child still seems to be in a haze after the first few days, he may be overmedicated. This should be addressed.

If your child is in the hospital for a long time or has been admitted before, she will probably adjust to the routine quite well. You may even find that your visits are less of a special treat than they were at first, as your child eagerly waits to go back to playing or chatting with the other kids on the ward. This can be disconcerting for parents, but be assured that regular visits from you are essential to your child's well-being, even if she doesn't act like it.

One thing that isn't a great idea is visits from your child's friends. Most mental health facilities do not allow these for underage patients, but if yours does, make sure they are supervised and that you have control over which friends are allowed in. Supportive friends are the best thing in the world for a child suffering from mental illness. Friends who encourage your child to blame you for his problems, leave the facility, or refuse medication are not. "Friends" who try to sneak in drugs or alcohol for your child are even worse. If you suspect this may be happening, contact the staff immediately.

Your child may be disturbed or frightened by the behavior of some other patients. Most children's psychiatric facilities care for patients with a wide variety of conditions, ranging from eating disorders to active psychosis to neurological problems like autism or Tourette syndrome. Some children will probably be very, very ill. Others will be well on their way to recovery. When you visit, talk to your child about anything he may have seen or heard that bothers him. He may feel uncomfortable bringing up these concerns in group or individual therapy sessions. Information about other mental illnesses or neurological disorders should be able to help him better understand what his fellow patients may be experiencing.

A good hospital is probably the safest possible place for your child to be while in a mental or medical health crisis. Medication reactions can be carefully observed, therapy can be delivered on a daily basis, and families can be helped to rally around their child's treatment and recovery plan by concerned professionals.

> Michael had been out of control for a long time and I just dealt with it, it never sunk in my head that this was more than normal tantrums. He got to the point of wanting to commit suicide so we had him hospitalized, and it was the best thing we could ever do. He was diagnosed, put on the correct meds, and safe. He was hospitalized the second time for suicide attempts; they changed some of his meds and he was better. The third time he was hospitalized it was for suicide watch. Again they changed meds and made sure he was stable before he came home. —Lynn, mother of 11-year-old Michael

Hospitals: The scary stuff

For many of us, our image of a mental hospital comes from old movies like *The Snake Pit*, depictions of past horrors in films like *Frances* (the story of actress Frances Farmer), or books by people who suffered in horrid institutions. Today, there are many good hospital programs, but there are still a few that verge on the criminal. Danger signs include frequent use of physical restraints and isolation rooms to control "dangerous" patients, a reliance on psychoanalysis as the primary cure for major mental illnesses, lack of knowledge about the most current medications, and poor relationships with family members, schools, and other outside care providers.

> I would avoid state institutions at any cost. I was watched by a male nurse when I showered. The nurses locked themselves in a glass room, and talked and played cards. The only interaction between them and us was when they handed out meds. I was afraid of being killed by a fellow patient (I almost said inmate!). After almost two days of no sleep due to that fear, a guy I made friends with sat outside my room watching so I

could sleep safely. This was not deranged paranoia—this was a very, very scary place.

My parents were out of options, due to our lovely insurance system. [Psychiatric care] was covered only partially, and had a limit that they were way over, so I was not able to be admitted to the hospital I was usually in. Maybe that was good, as it removed the desire to go into the hospital again. —Stephanie, age 32

It appears that many facilities working with young patients still blame parents for their child's mental illness. This attitude can prevent patients from getting proper treatment, and it drives patients away from the people they need most—those charged with the responsibility to care for them when they leave the hospital.

There's no reason for parents to tolerate hostility from administrators or staff. Of course, none of us is perfect in how we've raised our children, and there are many things we can learn and do to help them more. But these suggestions can only be listened to in an atmosphere of mutual assistance, in which parents are seen as the greatest source of information about their child, and as the greatest resource for helping their child continue his recovery outside of residential care.

If the facility your child is in can't seem to change its attitude, do what you can to change his location.

Certain treatments used in mental hospitals have gained notoriety. These include electroshock therapy, insulin shock therapy, wet sheet packs, aversives, restraints, and isolation. Any program that relies on these is substandard and to be avoided at all costs. In certain cases, these treatments may be well-advised, however.

Electroconvulsive therapy (ECT)

Also called electroshock therapy, this intervention is what many patients fear most when admitted to a hospital for treatment of a mental illness. Scenes from *One Flew Over the Cuckoo's Nest* come to mind—and at the time that book and film were written, those scenes were a grim reality in many mental hospitals. Until the mid-1970s, ECT was used indiscriminately and even punitively in many mental hospitals.

I was hospitalized five or six times in a four-and-a-half year period. I was given everything, none of which worked very well. I also received two series of ECT therapy, in two rounds, for a total of 32 treatments.

I have managed unmedicated for thirteen years now. However, I do not recommend this approach to others. —Stephanie, age 32 (diagnosed with bipolar disorder at age 15 and now the mother of a bipolar child)

ECT is still in use today, still controversial and probably sometimes misused, and still an option that helps many bipolar patients who have drug-resistant mania or severe, delusional depression. In fact, ECT is a very effective and safe treatment for depression in adults. For children and adolescents, however, it is rarely used, and only in very controlled conditions (as in research facilities, and for cases that do not respond to conventional treatments).

ECT induces a seizure through application of a low-level electric shock to the head. The patient is given a relaxing medication, so the seizure should not cause pain. Retrograde amnesia almost always prevents memory of the actual ECT and seizure. It occasionally wipes out some other memories, however.

NAMI has been involved for many years in encouraging further study and regulation of ECT. You can learn more about its efforts at *http://www.nami. org/helpline/ect.htm.*

Insulin shock

Early in this century, physicians discovered that giving schizophrenic or psychotic patients massive doses of the pancreatic hormone insulin—enough to cause convulsions or even coma—seemed to "cure" some of them. This therapy has not been used in the US or Europe for many years, but was done into the 1970s and may still be current in other countries. It did work for some patients, but its use was long ago eclipsed by advances in medical care.

Hydrotherapy

Hydrotherapy, the use of water in some form to ease mental distress, is probably one of the oldest remedies around. The efficacy of lithium springs was probably enhanced by the beneficial effects of a long, relaxing soak. Hydrotherapy is still a mainstay of treatment in many Russian, eastern European, and Asian mental hospitals, particularly where modern pharmaceuticals are hard to obtain. It is also widely used by naturopathic doctors and other alternative practitioners, and many patients give warm soaks, some types of wet wraps or compresses, and steam baths high marks as gentle adjuncts to medications or other treatments.

A particular type of hydrotherapy called wet sheet packs is still used in some US and Canadian facilities to calm manic patients. It involves wrapping the patient tightly in cold, wet sheets. Most patients describe this practice as uncomfortable and invasive. It is no longer considered proper medical practice.

Aversives

Many mental health facilities use behavior modification techniques to control and improve patient behavior. Token economies and reward programs are examples of positive behavior modification techniques. Some facilities do use aversives, however, which can range from a squirt or removal of privileges on up to mild electric shocks. For obvious reasons, no aversive technique with the capacity to cause physical harm or more than momentary emotional distress in a young patient should be employed. If this is not the case in a particular facility, most experts would agree that patients are being abused.

Restraints

Restraints are sometimes a necessary part of mental health care when a patient is truly dangerous to himself or others. They are also potentially deadly: every year about 50 mental patients die while restrained, often as a result of suffocation, strangulation, or deliberate self-harm using the restraint mechanism.

If your child needs to be restrained temporarily, he should in no circumstances be left alone and unobserved. Nor should restraints be used as a method of "treatment" (they do nothing to treat mental illness), as punishment, or as a substitute for supervision.

Isolation

Most mental health facilities do have isolation facilities that can be used to temporarily contain violent or suicidal patients. This should be their sole function, and no child should ever be left unobserved in isolation. The "rubber room" or padded cell should never be used as a threat, punishment, or routine behavior-control device.

After the hospital

What happens after a patient leaves a hospital or residential care center is almost as important as what happened inside. Without follow-up care, failure is far more likely. The hospital begins to look preferable to suffering through life on the outside.

> I liked the hospital.... I would do things to get sent back: cut my wrists, act up in school, etc. I was so miserable inside, but at the hospital, there were people around all the time so I did not feel so lonely. If I could not sleep, I could play cards or shoot pool with a night nurse. It was my safe haven, and I would act out just enough while I was in there to avoid being discharged. —Stephanie, age 32

Before your child leaves the hospital you should have a schedule of appointments set up to manage her needs. These will include monthly visits with a psychiatrist, psychopharmacologist, or other doctor to manage her medication, and therapy appointments as needed. If family therapy or other interventions have been recommended, these should also be in place—and perhaps already started, if practical.

While your child is in the hospital, talk to the program's staff about ways to handle discipline and guidance for your child at home.

Parents need to understand how medications should be given, how often, and why. Compliance issues are paramount, and if they're handled badly at home it can be a real problem. Discuss ways to ensure that your child takes her medication with the hospital staff at length before her release.

Also be sure you know how to spot dangerous side effects, and what to do if they emerge.

One of the most difficult issues for young patients is integrating back into a school setting. We'll talk more about specific ways to ease this transition in Chapter 8, *School*, but parents should begin working with the hospital's education team right after admission to develop a transition plan and to get ideas for setting up a school program that works. If your child has not had special education services before, these will be needed. The hospital team should be able to provide concrete suggestions to your Individual Education Plan team—and to back them up with a medical diagnosis and prescription. The latter can make a major difference in ensuring these recommendations are followed at school.

Most children will go from the hospital to their home, but some will have an intermediate stay in a halfway house, supported living community, therapeutic foster care home, or other residential center. You may need legal help to handle tricky questions of custody and support at this point.

> *Vanessa was in a locked residential center for several months for bipolar disorder, before being placed in a therapeutic group home. The residential center had on-ground school; she now attends a public high school. — Sue, mother of 16-year-old Vanessa (diagnosed bipolar disorder, OCD, borderline personality disorder, passive-aggressive personality disorder)*

Some older children may be of an age to move from the hospital to adult life. Transition services (see Chapter 9, *Transitions*) need to be brought to bear on the difficult issues involved when this happens.

Another option is moving from an inpatient unit into a day treatment facility. Day treatment patients live at home, but spend their days in a therapeutic center where they can be carefully monitored and cared for. Some day treatment centers are strongly medical in nature, and may be located inside a hospital. Others are standalone facilities that are more like special schools. Your child may be mixed in with others who have garden-variety emotional problems, or with children who are victims of physical or sexual abuse. As long as the facility is carefully administrated and uses individualized techniques for working with its clients, this does not have to be a problem.

Newly released kids may need a lot of extra reassurance, and cling to familiar places, people, and activities. Put yourself in their shoes; no one enjoys a hospital stay. It's disruptive and uncomfortable under the best of circumstances, and your child is probably burdened by not knowing what to say to her friends or how people at school will react. She may feel embarrassed or frightened. Remember the importance of scheduling in this difficult period—and especially of scheduling plenty of down time and stress reduction activities.

CHAPTER 5

Therapeutic Interventions

MEDICATION ALONE CAN HELP reduce the symptoms of bipolar disorder, but it can't cure the illness entirely. Nor can it help a child or teenager cope with the stress, alienation, and residual symptoms that remain. That's where therapy—the process of exploring feelings, motivations, strategies for change, and personal goals with a trained professional—comes in.

Therapy is also not a cure, but when it's done well, it contributes greatly to better personal functioning and happiness.[1]

> Lisa sees a wonderful therapist who uses mainly traditional psycho-
> analysis. The symptoms the therapist concentrates on are whatever Lisa
> bring in for that particular meeting. If she's had a particular problem in
> some area, like when her boyfriend broke up with her, or just in dealing
> with her bipolar symptoms at times, the therapist gives her hints, such as
> the coping skills Lisa learned while in the hospital, to help her get through
> a particular situation. —Donna, mother of 16-year-old Lisa (diagnosed
> bipolar II disorder, post-traumatic stress disorder, and anxiety disorder)

This chapter will describe the various types of therapy available, with special attention to the needs of children, adolescents, and their families. First, we'll look at what therapy is, what kind of professionals work in the field, and who can benefit from it. Then we'll look at various styles of therapy, including some that do not rely on conversation. Finally, we'll look at ways to integrate therapeutic principles into everyday life.

What is therapy?

From time immemorial, people have known about the healing power of a listening ear, a shoulder to cry on, and wise advice. These resources have always been prized, whether they came from family members, friends, or religious advisors.

The industrial revolution of the late nineteenth century changed the way people relate to each other, and also made life more stressful and complex. Many people began looking for professional advisors, and often the person they turned to was a trusted physician. Some physicians did have a high level of expertise at helping people handle everyday emotional problems, and did so as a matter of course while they also treated physical troubles. Some, like Austrian neurologist Sigmund Freud, became fascinated with the serious life difficulties faced by people with major mental illness.

When Freud and his circle of European colleagues founded the modern practice of psychoanalysis in the late 1800s, not much was known about mental illness, and no effective treatments existed. Freud himself believed that bipolar disorder, schizophrenia, and some other major mental illnesses were biological in nature, largely because he found that long-term psychoanalysis didn't seem to help these patients very much. To benefit from psychoanalysis, it seemed to him, the patient had to have a great deal of insight into the roots of unusual thoughts or behaviors, not just a desire to change.

The Freudians identified many emotional disorders (most are like what today's psychiatrists call personality disorders) that he believed were based on unresolved sexual conflicts, ensuing life experiences, and other factors. The psychoanalytic process relied on conversations between patients and therapists about childhood memories and experiences, dreams, and current experiences to uncover the causes of problems and find avenues for healing. Because the thoughts and behaviors associated with major mental illnesses actually come from chemical imbalances, efforts at ferreting out their roots in childhood traumas were fruitless.

That's not to say that no one tried. Psychoanalysis was indeed touted as a treatment for major mental illness until very recently, and still is suggested by some doctors. Until very recently, some people with bipolar disorders who could afford it submitted to years of intense psychoanalysis. The process was sometimes enlightening on a personal level, but rarely afforded any reduction in troublesome symptoms. In fact, for some patients, analysis itself was so stressful that it exacerbated their symptoms! But until the advent of psychiatric medication in the 1950s and '60s, and the first glimmerings of other types of psychological therapy around the same time, psychoanalysis was simply the only treatment available.

The goal of psychoanalysis is deep personal understanding that eventually leads to positive behavior changes. The patient gains this understanding by forging a strong, trusting relationship with his psychiatrist, which allows him to bring buried feelings to the surface in their discussions. It's a very intensive process involving weekly or even more frequent visits with a trained psychotherapist. The therapist helps the patient look at how his life experiences, starting as early as the emotional trauma that some people believe is associated with the birth process, have created roadblocks to optimal personal development.

Today, it's a rare patient with bipolar disorder who would look at psychoanalysis as a first-line intervention...or even at all. There are other therapeutic approaches that are more useful. These include:

- Cognitive therapy
- Play therapy
- Family therapy
- Group therapy
- Peer support groups
- Milieu therapy
- Counseling
- Behavior modification

All of these approaches share one basic characteristic with psychoanalysis: they rely on forging a strong relationship between the patient (who may be called a client) and a therapeutic professional to lay the groundwork for change. Unlike psychoanalysis, however, these methods rarely delve into the metaphysical or unconscious aspects of thought patterns or behavior. Instead, therapists in these disciplines address specific symptoms with targeted intervention techniques. Clients may even have homework assignments that involve applying the lessons learned in therapy to real life. In most cases, intervention is seen as a short-term process, although because of the chronic and fluctuating nature of their illness, many people with manic depression will need ongoing therapeutic help.

Some therapists are specialists in a particular method. Jungian therapists use psychoanalysis-like techniques based on the theories of Freud's contemporary, Carl Jung. Gestalt therapists specialize in helping people uncover and meet hidden needs (encounter groups and sensitivity training are two Gestalt-related ideas that were popular in the '60s and '70s), and fall into the general category of humanistic or experiential therapy. Holistic psychologists or therapists suggest diet changes, meditation, and other interventions, and will be discussed in Chapter 6, *Other Interventions*. There are other specialized therapy styles. Most of these methods, while interesting, have not shown any particular usefulness for bipolar disorders.

Many therapists use an eclectic approach: they take the best ideas from each school of thought, and employ whatever methods and concepts seem most likely to work with each patient.

The goals of therapy are usually set by the client in concert with her therapist and, in the case of children, with the child's parents or other caretakers. Goals are as varied as individuals with bipolar disorders are.

> *Kara used to see a psychologist who worked with her on her self-esteem, and on coping techniques.* —Cindy, mother of 19-year-old Kara (diagnosed bipolar disorder)

· · · · ·

> *Vanessa sees a therapist, and the concentration is on anger management. Work is done in both group and family therapy.* —Sue, mother of 16-year-old Vanessa (diagnosed bipolar disorder, OCD, borderline personality disorder, passive-aggressive personality disorder)

· · · · ·

> *Billy sees a psychologist for a combination of cognitive-behavioral therapy and play therapy. The primary focus has been on coping with frustration.* —Marlene, mother of 8-year-old Billy (diagnosed cyclothymic disorder)

Your child's therapeutic goals might include:

- Discussing the nature of her illness and how it can be treated
- Identifying personal mood-swing triggers
- Identifying ways to prevent or shorten mood swings
- Identifying and stopping detrimental thought patterns
- Coping with problem symptoms and medication side effects
- Improving behavior at home, at school, or in the community

- Obtaining support for making positive lifestyle changes, such as maintaining sobriety

- Developing personal strengths, resiliency, and self-esteem to counter the detrimental social and personal effects of manic depression

If you don't think a therapeutic relationship is working well for your child, or if a therapist tells you something about your child that doesn't seem right, don't be afraid to seek a second opinion.

> I saw a counselor when I was about 10. I was smart enough to out-smart him, but not smart enough to know that it was not in my best interest to do so. He told my parents I just had a bad attitude. For years after that, school personnel and family friends tried to get my parents to seek help for me, but they always relied on what that first guy said, and declined further evaluations. —Stephanie, age 32 (diagnosed with bipolar disorder at age 15 and now the mother of a bipolar child)

Who does therapy?

Many different professionals deliver therapeutic services. Because there are many approaches to therapy, be sure to ask any therapist you are considering about her orientation. Some approaches are not as effective for children as for adults, and vice versa. Others don't have much to offer for people with bipolar disorders.

The best indicators of a good therapist are personal rapport with your child, training (and preferably board certification) for working with children and/ or adolescents, experience working with bipolar patients, and an appropriate level of expertise in handling any co-morbid disorders, such as substance abuse or dependency. You'll also want to make sure your therapist is properly credentialed, both for your own peace of mind and for insurance billing purposes.

Note for readers outside the US: The following information about credentials applies mostly to therapists practicing in the US. Contact your national, regional, or provincial government's mental health authority for information about choosing a qualified, credentialed professional in your area. Those in Canada may wish to contact the Canadian Mental Health Association (416-484-7750) for additional information.

Psychiatrists

Psychiatrists are medical doctors (MDs) whose special area of expertise is psychiatric disorders. As doctors, they must be licensed by their state medical board (for a complete list of state medical licensing boards, see *http://www.psych.org/*). Psychiatrists may also be certified by the American Board of Psychiatry and Neurology (847-945-7900, *http://www.abpn.com/*) in one of several specialties.

Today, psychiatrists are usually busy with evaluating patients, diagnosing mental disorders, and prescribing and managing psychiatric drugs. In small towns and in some special circumstances, however, your child's psychiatrist might also be his therapist.

Some adult patients say they prefer to see a single psychiatrist for both their medication and therapy needs. Others note that because therapy can bring up strong emotions, it's best to have medications handled by someone other than their therapists—just in case they get mad enough to quit therapy.

Psychiatrists usually (but not always) charge more than other mental health professionals.

Psychiatric nurses

Some clinics and hospitals employ psychiatric mental health nurse practitioners (PMHNP). A psychiatric nurse practitioner is a registered nurse (RN) who has completed several additional years of training and supervised practice in this specialty.

Psychiatric nurse practitioners can diagnose patients, and they can prescribe and manage psychiatric drugs. Most do not have specific training in therapy techniques, and they are unlikely to provide therapy services. As with psychiatrists, however, some psychiatric nurse practitioners may play a dual role.

Other psychiatric nurses are simply RNs who work with psychiatric patients. Most will have had at least some specialized training, although due to periodic nurse shortages, it's not rare for this training to be done on the job. That means that while most psychiatric nurses are experienced and knowledgeable, some newer hires may have little information about mental illness.

Psychologists

Psychologists in private practice have a doctorate in philosophy (PhD), doctorate in psychology (PsyD), or doctorate in education (DEd) degree. They have completed a program of instruction that allows them to diagnose mental illness and to treat it with therapeutic interventions—but not with medication—and they have practiced under supervision as a clinical intern.

Licensed psychologists have passed a national examination to receive credentials from the states where they work. Limited licensed psychologists have an MA, have done some doctoral work, and operate under supervision only. Licensed psychologists may go on to become certified in a specialty by the American Board of Professional Psychology (573-875-1267, *http://www. abpp.org/*) or the American Board of Clinical Neuropsychology (734-936-8269, *http://www.med.umich.edu/abcn/*). In the latter case, they may use the title clinical neuropsychologist. Those who have achieved the top level of board certification are called diplomates. Others will add the initials FAClinP (Fellow in the Academy of Clinical Psychology) to their list of titles.

The Certificate of Professional Qualification in Psychology (CPQ) is issued by the Association of State and Provincial Psychology Boards, and is an international credential accepted by many US states and Canadian provinces.

School psychologists often have an MA only, and work primarily with psychological screening, conduct disorders, emerging personality disorders, and emotional distress or mental illness that is secondary to life events. Some school psychologists do have expertise at working with bipolar children; others do not.

The best psychologists to choose are those who combine expert knowledge of bipolar disorders and a willingness to work closely with your child's psychiatrist and/or medical doctor.

Social workers

Social workers are usually employed by public or private programs that help people or families in distress. Some social workers have job assignments that are investigative in nature; for example, they might be assigned to check out cases of suspected child abuse. Others help families access community resources. Many provide interpersonal services that are very much like therapy, or make therapy a specific part of the services they offer their clients. This is especially true of social workers in private practice.

Social workers may have a BA (Bachelor of Arts degree) in social work, or an MSW (Master of Social Work). Certified social workers (CSW or ASCW) have an MSW degree, have passed an examination by the National Association of Social Workers (202-408-8600, *http://www.socialworkers.org/*), and have practiced under supervision for two years. The National Association of Social Workers also offers the school social work specialist (SSWS), qualified clinical social worker (QCSW), and diplomate in clinical social work (DCSW) credentials. Diplomates of the Academy of Certified Social Workers are at the highest level of professionalism.

Licensed clinical social workers (LCSW) have received a license from their state board. Consult the American Association of State Social Work Boards (*http://www.aasswb.org/*) for a list of state boards from all 50 states, several US possessions, and the Canadian province of Alberta.

Therapists and counselors

Depending on where you live, there may or may not be legal restrictions on who can use the professional titles "therapist" and "counselor." In some US states and in many other countries, these terms are not regulated in any way—anyone who wishes to can hang out a shingle and start seeing clients. Ask any therapist or counselor you are considering taking your child to about his training, and make sure he keeps up with current developments and has all of the other qualities of a good therapist mentioned earlier in this chapter.

Most US states offer a licensed professional counselor (LPC) or certified professional counselor (CPC) credential. Each state's requirements are different, but most include an MA or a master's degree in education (MEd) with a major in counseling, a period of supervised practice, and passing an exam. The American Association of State Counseling Boards (*http://pweb.netcom. com/~aascb/aascb.html*) maintains a complete list of these boards.

Other counselors may practice with a licensed marriage and family counselor (LMFC), licensed marriage and family therapist (LMFT), or marriage, family, and child counseling (MFCC) credential. In most states, these require a specific program of college courses in a BA and/or MA program, passing a state exam, and practicing under supervision for several years. Counselors-in-training may use the initials MFCI (marriage, family and child intern) or MFTI (marriage and family therapy intern).

Counselors may go on to become nationally board-certified by meeting requirements set by the National Board for Certified Counselors (336-547-0607, *http://www.nbcc.org/*). This board offers the national certified counselor (NCC) credential as well as subsequent specialty credentials, including the certified clinical mental health counselor (CCMHC) and the national certified school counselor (NCSC) certificates. Another board, the Commission on Rehabilitation Counselor Certification offers the certified rehabilitation counselor (CRC) credential and some specialty credentials as well.

Group therapy is a special technique, and so there is a specific credential for that, too. Ask your group therapist if she is certified by the National Registry of Certified Group Psychotherapists. Its CGP credential requires specific training in group therapy techniques and membership in the American Group Psychotherapy Association.

In the US, some counselors are associated with particular religious denominations, and may advertise themselves as "Christian counselors" or other similar titles. If your religious beliefs are very important to you, finding a qualified therapist who also shares or supports these views can add an extra dimension to the healing process. However, parent reports indicate that a few Christian counselors reject modern knowledge of mental disorders in favor of ancient "demon possession" theories, and have attempted to treat their child with exorcism or prayer only. Others have accused families of causing mental illness due to lack of proper religious practice, or have made false and painful accusations of Satanic activity and/or child abuse. Obviously, these are not mainstream beliefs among well-educated counselors, Christian or otherwise, and any counselor with these biases should be avoided by people seeking help for someone with a bipolar disorder.

The governing body of your religious denomination should be able to help you locate a qualified mental health practitioner who can also take your spiritual needs into account. Alternatively, your pastor, rabbi, or other spiritual advisor may be able to work with your therapist to create a personal therapeutic plan that incorporates both spirituality and science.

Behavior therapists use behavior modification techniques, which are described later in this chapter. Behavior therapists can come from a number of different educational backgrounds. Some design or oversee behavior modification programs to be carried out by parents, teachers, or others. Others provide direct services to children at home, or in classroom, clinic, or hospital situations.

Two other sets of initials you may see after a practitioner's name are QMHA (qualified mental health associate) and QMHP (qualified mental health professional). These are basically hiring credentials used by mental health agencies, indicating a basic level of education and experience.

Your state or provincial licensing board can let you know whether a practitioner's credentials are legitimate, and may be able to tell you if she has ever been reprimanded or censured by the board. Your local chapter of NAMI or another advocacy group should have information about therapists who have worked effectively with bipolar patients.

Finally, always pay attention to your personal intuition, and your child's. Because the personal relationship that grows between the therapist and client is at the heart of producing results, your child's therapist must be someone he feels comfortable with.

Who benefits from therapy?

Generally speaking, therapy cannot produce changes in people with bipolar disorders unless their most troubling symptoms are intermittent or starting to recede. A person who is actively psychotic, extremely manic, or depressed to the point of needing hospitalization usually cannot benefit from therapy, although they may seek out and greatly appreciate their therapist's support while weathering these storms. Once medication is starting to help or the state is receding on its own, there is a window of opportunity for therapeutic work.[2]

Over a period of time, a bipolar patient in therapy should expect to develop better strategies for handling his mood swings and other symptoms. As these strategies begin to work, he will become even more able to benefit from therapy.

Even preschoolers can make gains in certain types of therapy. Play therapy was developed especially for the youngest children, and can be very effective. In fact, recent studies have shown that therapy may actually have long-term effects not just on how we feel, but in how our brains work physically, including which neurotransmitters are produced in what quantity. When therapy is undertaken in early childhood, it may change for the better how the brain develops.

Therapy styles

This section describes the types of therapy that appear to be most useful for people with bipolar disorders, and mentions which kinds of patients are most likely to benefit from each. As mentioned previously in this chapter, many good therapists use techniques and concepts from several of these disciplines.

Cognitive therapy

Insurance companies love cognitive therapy (also called cognitive-behavioral therapy), because it sometimes produces relief from troubling symptoms within a defined, limited period of time. Patients like that too, especially those who are strongly motivated to help themselves.

The cognitive therapist begins by helping the patient identify which negative behavior patterns he would like to work on. Together, they identify what kinds of thoughts and feelings precipitate these behaviors.

Next, the therapist helps the patient figure out strategies for replacing thoughts that have negative consequences with new thoughts that have positive consequences. In other words, the cognitive therapist helps you "think yourself well."

> In addition to bimonthly visits with her neurologist and psychiatrist, Cass sees a therapist weekly for an hour. His focus is behavior modification, and he is her friend. She loves to see him. I have a distrust of therapists, but am very comfortable with him. He has helped me to work with specific goals in mind for her. —Stephanie, mother of 7-year-old Cassidy (diagnosed bipolar disorder, Tourette syndrome, OCD, ADHD)

Cognitive therapy works best for handling specific "thought errors" and behaviors. For example, if a teenager with bipolar disorder tends to catastrophize when depressed, seeing only the negative side of everything and then becoming further depressed as a result, cognitive therapy can help him find strategies for breaking this negative thought spiral. These strategies might include the use of affirmations, consulting with the therapist or another trusted adult to double-check negative thoughts, or mentally substituting positive thoughts for the negative ones.

Does it work? Not always, but more often than one might think. Cognitive therapy has helped many people identify and combat errors in thinking, and has even proved useful for stopping thoughts that can lead to troubling behaviors, including self-injurious behavior. It has a good track record for helping people with compulsive behaviors, those in recovery from substance abuse or dependency, and patients suffering from anxiety, panic, and other out-of-proportion reactions to daily events. Evidence is mounting that cognitive therapy produces actual physical effects, such as changes in the production and absorption of neurotransmitters.

In the hands of a professional who has strong rapport with young children, cognitive therapy can be a powerful tool, even for preschoolers. Not every therapist has the ability to work well with this age group, however. It has been well-tested for use with adolescents and teens.

Cognitive-behavioral therapy has also shown effectiveness for educating bipolar patients about monitoring their mood cycles and symptoms, and for encouraging treatment compliance.

Play therapy

Young children express their fears, desires, and emotions in play, and they can often be reached and helped through the medium of play when conversation with an adult is impractical. Play therapists are specialists in this kind of therapy, which can work powerful magic when done with skill and caring.

Play therapists can work with children as early as infancy to build and improve skills in the areas of attention, interpersonal relationships, perception, and mood. They can also help young children who have been victimized by abuse or who have experienced other kinds of life traumas, such as the death of a parent.

> *Michael's therapist does play therapy, which is what works best with my son. At the beginning she concentrated on his sexual abuse issues. When that got better, the focus was whatever was going on at the time. If he was paranoid, they would talk about that. Self-esteem is always an issue. They discuss bipolar disorder and what it means for him.* —Lynn, *mother of 11-year-old Michael (diagnosed BPI with mixed states and psychosis, OCD, tic disorder)*

There are many tools for play therapy, and many schools of thought. One of the most interesting types for use with young children is called floor-time play therapy, and is championed by Dr. Stanley Greenspan. (Dr. Greenspan's books are listed in the appendix, *Resources*.) The techniques of floor-time play involve creating structured play sessions with a client—or with your own child, because this is one kind of therapy that parents can deliver with ease—that help him overcome deficits in attention and relatedness. Filial therapy is another type of play therapy that uses similar ideas, and involves parents or other caregivers taking turns at initiating structured interactions.

Most play therapists work in a clinic or school setting, and use toys, games, and art supplies in their practice. For example, they might employ dolls or stuffed animals to help a young child talk about conflicts in the home, or they might use animal figures and a sand table to model desirable behaviors. With older children, art-based activities may be more interesting and a better communication tool. Communication, of course, is the goal. Parents might or might not be part of the play therapy session.

Because it's play-based, this type of therapy is best suited for preschool or grade school children. Activity choices should be based on the child's developmental level.

Be sure that your child is comfortable with the play therapist, or not much will get done in their sessions together. Talk to the therapist in advance about your child's diagnosis and what areas you hope can be worked on. Many play therapists are highly experienced at working with traumatized children, but may not know how to work with a child whose problems are neurological in nature.

Incorporating some floor-time play therapy techniques into your daily activities with a young child is a great idea. If your child's therapist uses this method, ask if she can train you as part of her work with your child. If not, see if training is available from a parent education group, or consult Dr. Greenspan's books for ideas.

Family therapy

A family is a group formed by individuals for their mutual benefit, with each member having his or her own personality, needs, and desires. Whenever one member of the group is ill or in emotional distress, it affects all the other members.

Family therapists work with the entire family together, although they may also see some members individually. They see the family as a system; probably not a perfect one (whose is?), but a system that at least *tries* to meet everyone's needs. The therapist helps each member express his or her fears, angers, and wishes, and then helps the family restructure itself in healthier ways.

You don't have to be the classic dysfunctional family to benefit from family therapy. Meeting as a group with a therapist can help a lot, even if only one person's behavior is seriously disordered. In fact, this approach is strongly recommended for the families of children with bipolar disorders, even if the child is seeing an individual therapist. In family therapy sessions, you'll have a safe place to talk about your frustrations, and to develop strategies for helping your child without neglecting the needs of parents and siblings. Without this opportunity, family members can undergo severe stress.

> My mother said she almost had a nervous breakdown watching me disintegrate from a 4.0 student-body president to someone who couldn't finish a single verbal sentence, choose something to eat, or really do much at all except stay in bed and complain a lot. I think I was putting a lot of pressure on her by constantly turning to her for help that she could never give. Our relationship went through the toughest time when I was hospitalized. It took years to heal the wound that occurred from this. It wasn't until years later that I found out they weren't at all accurate with the information they were giving her. —Troy, age 30 (diagnosed bipolar I disorder at age 17)

Manic depression is very hard for families to handle, and yet a strong support system is essential for bipolar children. Clinical experience has shown that the more patients, their parents, and even their siblings know about bipolar disorders, the better their prognosis is. That should mean fewer hospitalizations, better medication compliance, and fewer serious legal and educational problems.[3]

A good family therapist will be someone who is supportive and who is also knowledgeable about the biological nature of bipolar disorders and any comorbid conditions. The last thing you need is a therapist who blames your child for her own difficulties. You also don't need to see someone who blames your parenting skills.

That said, some parenting styles and behaviors are especially detrimental to bipolar kids. Physical, sexual, and emotional abuse are just the most obvious examples. Children with bipolar disorders are emotionally fragile, and may be affected more strongly by family stresses such as financial difficulties, marital discord, and divorce. Family therapy can provide a venue for putting these issues on the table, for healing the pain caused by errors and misunderstanding and, perhaps most importantly, for setting family ground rules that ensure they don't happen again.

Another area where family therapy can help is identifying other family members who may have undiagnosed bipolar disorder or another related condition. Because of the genetic nature of manic depression and the low rate of appropriate diagnosis, it is fairly common for a parent to be diagnosed after their child. The thought styles and symptoms associated with bipolar disorder can then become a focus of family therapy, helping all family members understand each other better, improve how they relate to each other, and become a more cohesive and supportive unit.

As in any type of interpersonal treatment, there are a few common pitfalls to family therapy. Misplaced assumptions are one. Although piles of self-help books have been written about family relationships, the truth is that every family is a unique blend. Although knowledge of common personal behavior patterns and family structures can certainly be useful, watch out for a therapist who instantly labels your family as having typical adult children of alcoholics (ACOA) problems or who uses some other quick pop psychology explanation. The assumptions that accompany labels can prevent appropriate therapeutic work, and may lead the therapist away from concentrating on those of your family's needs that are specifically related to bipolar disorder. See the section "Teens in therapy" later in this chapter for some other cautions.

Families also need to know that therapy is not a cure-all, although it will sometimes be presented that way by well-meaning professionals. If your child's difficulties are such that medications, therapy, and even hospitalization do not help much—and although these cases are the minority, they do exist—the goals of family therapy will need to be identifying survival strategies for coping with unmanageable symptoms, or it will probably be a useless exercise.

We went to family therapy religiously, to no avail. I do know that when Nathan was hospitalized, we were a happy family with him out of the picture. (Doesn't that sound awful?) When he is here, he is the cause of the turmoil, and if he does not want the help, then it does not make any difference what approach they use or how much family therapy you attend. —Cindy, *mother of 16-year-old Nathan (diagnosed bipolar disorder, OCD, ADHD, post-traumatic stress disorder, chemical dependency, bulimia)*

Group therapy

Group therapy brings together several people who are dealing with the same or similar problems, placing them under the guidance of a professional therapist. Within the group meetings, they can help themselves and each other.

Like family therapy, group therapy can be a very positive experience. Your child can form supportive relationships with peers as well as with her therapist, and will get the benefit of the other participants' real-life experiences and insight. Group therapy also tends to be less expensive than individual therapy sessions.

You may be able to take part in therapy groups for parents of bipolar children, or your child may be able to be in a group for bipolar kids around the same age. As long as the therapist in charge is knowledgeable and supportive, group therapy can be very useful for almost any patient and family. It is especially powerful with adolescents, who are often more likely to listen to their peers than to an adult therapist. Most residential centers, day treatment facilities, and hospitals use some form of group therapy with their young patients.

Some people never feel comfortable being open in a group situation, however. For these very introverted types, individual therapy is a better fit—although ability to function in a group may be one of the goals of that therapy, leading to group therapy later on.

Peer support groups

Peer support groups are a little like group therapy—but without the therapist. These range from ad hoc support groups formed by parents to professionally mediated support groups that may be available through a mental health clinic or public agency. Usually peer support groups do not charge participants, although a collection for snacks or meeting-room expenses might be taken up. Clinic-run groups, of course, may carry a fee.

Alcoholics Anonymous, Narcotics Anonymous, and other programs that use the 12-step model or a similar self-help approach are a particularly advanced kind of peer support group. These well-known programs bring together people with a common problem, and use methods for effecting personal change and supporting all members of the group that can be very effective. If substance abuse or dependency, eating disorders, or compulsive behavior disorders are additional problems for your bipolar child, you may want to look into the resources available along these lines.

The support experienced and friendships made in a peer support group can be very helpful for almost any family. Peer support groups for patients themselves can also be great—but without adult supervision, they can also be dangerous for bipolar teens. Before your child joins a support group, find out more about the program and the other participants. Some support groups provide a wonderful healing environment where young people with bipolar disorders can share their experiences with others who have been there. In a few strictly patient-run support groups for youth, however, solid information can go missing and misinformation can be spread. That can turn support group meetings into parent-bashing sessions, or lead participants to stop taking their medications due to peer pressure.

Local support and advocacy organizations, such as the National Alliance for the Mentally Ill (NAMI) and the National Depressive and Manic-Depressive Association (NDMDA), are often involved in setting up, sponsoring, and helping parents find peer support groups for bipolar children.

Milieu therapy

If your child is in a day treatment center, residential center, or hospital, milieu therapy is probably one of the program's underlying concepts. "Milieu" is a French word for site and setting. Milieu therapy endeavors to make the site and setting of everyday activities in a school, hospital, or living center therapeutic. This requires paying close attention to physical characteristics, such as making sure that the classrooms and dorms are not dingy and depressing, and ensuring that toys, games, and activities are available that build positive experiences and help to eliminate negative behaviors.

Of course, careful structuring of interpersonal relations in the milieu is of prime importance. Every interaction between a patient and a staff member has therapeutic potential, whether that staffer is the cafeteria cook or an actual therapist.

This is obviously a thoughtful, intelligent premise for constructing a program to support and enhance the lives of young people with mental illness. If a program promises to follow the precepts of milieu therapy, that's usually a good sign. Parents may also be able to take some ideas from milieu therapy and use them at home; see "The therapeutic home," later in this chapter.

Counseling

The most common place for children to see a counselor is at school. School counselors usually have a dual role: they advise students on academic issues and guide them through the college admissions process, and they also help them with personal problems. In the latter role, their focus is on maintaining wellness rather than on treating psychiatric disorders.

Accordingly, most school counselors are not equipped to provide regular therapeutic help to a child with a bipolar disorder—but they can be a key part of your child's therapeutic team. The counselor's office may be your child's designated safe place at school, a place where he can go if the stress is building up too high and he feels a crisis coming on. The counselor (or a school nurse) may be able to control as-needed medication for symptom exacerbations at school. She can be the person the student or his teacher comes to in case of immediate problems. She may also be able to act as a sort of resource broker, helping the student and family get hooked into more intensive help through the school district or through community-based programs.

Outside of schools, other professionals may provide counseling services in private practice or in a clinic. As discussed earlier in this chapter, the title of counselor may or may not have a legal meaning in your state or province.

Behavior modification

Behavior modification, also called behavior therapy, focuses on identifying problem behaviors, finding out what causes them, and eliminating them. That's far less simple than it sounds on paper.

You are most likely to encounter "behavior mod" experts, also called behaviorists, in more restrictive settings, such as day treatment centers, hospitals, and youth corrections facilities. The quality of their training and expertise varies widely. Their role in your child's treatment might include analyzing behavior and its antecedents and helping to develop a behavior plan to address problem areas (in a school setting, this is called a Functional Behavior Analysis plan, and will be discussed further in Chapter 8, *School*). Some behavior therapists work one on one with bipolar youths, using techniques that are very similar to the related practice of cognitive-behavioral therapy.

One area where behavior therapy has proved particularly effective is the reduction of compulsive behavior, including self-injurious behavior. Another is the reduction of anxiety and panic. The exposure-reduction approach to phobias is an example that many people are familiar with. A child who has a severe school phobia, for example, would begin treatment by meeting with the therapist to discuss her fear. Then the therapist and patient would devise and carry out a plan to gradually and safely expose the child to the fearful situation or place, increasing the exposure over time.

Unfortunately, some behavior therapists are purists who feel that all human activity is based on conditioned responses to environmental stimuli. It's important to find a professional in this discipline who understands, accepts, and works with the role of neurochemistry in the origin and treatment of bipolar symptoms. In the case of school phobia, for instance, medication can play a role in both causing the problem and in solving it.

Teens in therapy

Even without the added difficulty of mental illness, teenage behavior problems often bring families into a therapist's office. Parents may drag their teen to a professional in hopes of tackling oppositional and defiant behavior, or stopping their child's drug or alcohol abuse, for example.

When the family therapist starts with healing the wounds in the family system as his goal, there's a reasonable chance that these objectives can be met. However, therapists are human, and sometimes they take sides. If they take the parental side, the teen may become so alienated that therapy sessions are a waste of time. If they take the teen's side, parent and child may find themselves turned against each other by the therapist.

When Lili got out of the hospital, we were totally broke because of the bills. A social services agency set up family therapy with a young therapist in training as her after-care program. Oh, it was awful... every session started with bickering, quickly moved on to screaming, and ended in tears. Frankly, we had experienced plenty of that over the past few years and we did not need more now. Lili cursed at us and blamed us, and then the therapist managed to get my husband and me fighting as well. When we got to our car after the third session I turned around and asked the whole family, "Does anyone actually feel better after seeing this lady?" We all agreed that we felt worse, and we never went back. —Sarah, mother of 17-year-old Lili (diagnosed bipolar II disorder, OCD)

Back in the days of Freudian analysis, parents took almost all of the blame for mental illness. If anything, this attitude intensified in the 1960s and '70s, even as Freud's concepts were losing ground to modern science. Although the anti-parent speculations of discredited theorists like Bruno Bettleheim should have been relegated to the trash heap years ago, they have not disappeared from the training or the mind-set of some therapeutic professionals. Indeed, the culture of blaming the family is still with us, as today's news coverage of youth crime, substance abuse, and social pathology shows. Our society's reaction to teenage crime is increasingly skewed toward incarcerating the child, throwing away the key, and then blaming (or even fining or jailing) the parents. Many clinical treatment programs for disorders such as bulimia, anorexia, self-injurious behavior, and even depression still encourage patients to blame their families for their troubles, which adds to the heavy burden of parental guilt.

The verbal skills of bipolar teenagers can make them master manipulators of therapists. False claims of abuse may be used as a sympathy ploy, and actual parental shortcomings may be magnified beyond recognition. Experienced therapists usually know how to spot a fib, and know to look for hard documentation if they do have concerns about abuse. They also know that even imperfect parents are better than none at all.

There is no place for blame in family therapy. All parties need to own up honestly to their personal failings, of course, but with the understanding that not everything done wrong is a calculated effort to harm or annoy. The message should be that we all have shortcomings to work on, we all make mistakes, and we all can move on to have better lives together. Even though it's tough to stick with it for the long haul, compliance with medical treatment and ongoing work on personal issues in therapy can make those better lives a reality for all family members.

Non-talk therapies

Chapter 6, *Other Interventions*, will discuss a variety of approaches to bipolar disorders that are therapeutic but that do not rely on talk as the primary principle. These include bodywork, light therapy, and other interventions that you may hear about. Most of these are considered alternative medicine by psychiatrists and psychologists—although many professionals support or even recommend trying them.

For bipolar children, certain other interventions that use the word "therapy" may also be recommended, based on individual symptoms and needs. These have been used for many years to help children with other neurological problems, and have been effective for some people with bipolar disorders as well. They include:

- Auditory integration training
- Occupational therapy
- Sensory integration
- Speech therapy

Auditory integration training

Some children with unusual sensitivity—or lack of sensitivity—to sounds or types of sounds have found relief with auditory integration training (AIT) or auditory processing stimulation, both relatively new approaches.

Although it's rarely addressed in the medical literature, extreme auditory sensitivity is actually fairly common in people with bipolar disorders. These patients will describe many normal sounds as affecting them like fingernails scraping a blackboard. Naturally, this distortion can increase a child's level of anxiety and discomfort, make school more difficult, and encourage him to withdraw from social contact.

Many audiologists (hearing specialists) and other professionals can test for auditory sensitivity and offer therapeutic treatment. Based on principles first developed by French audiologist Guy Bérard, AIT involves listening to particular sounds through earphones. The process is believed to retrain the hearing mechanism, and there is some evidence that it is effective for many patients. A similar therapy is called the Tomatis method.

The most dramatic results from AIT have been in people with autism or related disorders. You can learn more from the Society for Auditory Integration Training (*http://www.teleport.com/~sait/*) or through the Autism Society of America (*http://www.autism-society.org/packages/auditory.html*).

Strides are also being made in auditory processing stimulation and other auditory therapies for those who seem to have problems in differentiating and processing sounds.

Dance, music, or art therapy

There is no proof that dance, music, or art therapy has curative value for people with bipolar disorders, but these activities often draw out hidden talents, bring a sense of joy and accomplishment, and help young children communicate nonverbally. They may be a part of a play therapy program, especially for older children. Sometimes dance, music, or art therapy is integrated into hospital or day-treatment programs.

Occupational therapy

Occupational therapy (OT) is intended to help people with fine motor skill problems or other impediments improve their ability to perform daily activities, ranging from walking to writing. Because young children with bipolar disorders sometimes have an erratic pattern of development due to their illness, occupational therapy may be recommended to address specific problem areas.

If the focus of OT is on school-related skills, such as handwriting, it should be available at no charge through your Early Intervention program or school district. OT services can be delivered via consultation with the child's teacher, or directly to the child within the classroom or in an office.

Another type of OT focuses on self-care skills, vocational skills, esteem-building activities such as arts and crafts, and therapeutic exercise. Your child may have this kind of program in day treatment or in a hospital, or you might ask that it be added to her school program. This form of OT can be especially useful as part of transition planning in the teen years.

Sensory integration

Sensory integration (SI) is a specific type of occupational therapy that can be invaluable for people whose sensory systems are unbalanced. Like the auditory processing problems described earlier in this chapter, sensory integration difficulties seem to be more common in people with bipolar disorders than the literature would indicate. These can include over- or undersensitivity to smell, taste, texture, types of touch, and even the forces of gravity.

Sensory integration therapy can help reduce or enhance sensitivity levels as needed. It is used with increasing frequency for children with other neurological problems, including cerebral palsy, autism, and ADHD, but has rarely been offered to bipolar children. If your child has symptoms of sensory dysfunction, ask about SI.

In bipolar disorders, sensory disturbances can be cyclical. A person in a manic phase may find that she has a heightened response to certain types of sensation. This increased sensitivity may be perceived as pleasurable, but in some cases it can be painful. Bipolar children seem to be especially sensitive to sensory input when they are in a depressed-irritable state, sometimes to the point of being unable to wear their usual clothes (jeans and socks are suddenly too scratchy), eat their regular diet (everything smells gross, tastes weird, and makes them feel like retching), or handle a normal level of sensory input (the sounds and smells of school or the shopping mall become rapidly overwhelming).

Occupational therapists who know about SI use simple techniques to retrain the body's sensory apparatus. These can include brushing and joint compression, exercises that improve and strengthen the sensory part of the nervous system, and targeted work on specific sensory difficulties. Much SI work does not require any special devices, or employs inexpensive items like stretchy strips of rubber for arm exercises or weighted vests for calming. Many SI specialists do use occupational therapy equipment, such as scooter boards, huge therapy balls for improving balance, and prone-position swings.

One area in which SI techniques really shine is helping children with eating problems. If your child limits her food choices to a very few items, sensory problems can be at the root of this potentially unhealthy behavior. Certain textures and tastes may simply be unbearable. It is possible to desensitize the nerve endings in the mouth and throat enough to permit eating more types of food, and even desensitizing the taste buds a bit can be done.

SI specialists recommend making a sensory diet part of the classroom and home environment for children with difficulties. This means building experiences with different types of textures, tastes, smells, and physical sensations into daily activities. *The Out-of-Sync Child,* by Carol Stock Kranowitz, which is listed in the appendix, can provide some suggestions for home exercises.

SI therapists can also teach patients how to use self-calming activities and devices when they are reaching the point of sensory overload. Parents can be trained on the signs of sensory difficulties and on how to initiate these activities.

Speech therapy

Speech defects such as apraxia, dyspraxia, stuttering, or cluttering occur slightly more often in people with bipolar disorder. However, as far as medical science knows, these are a separate problem.

If your child has problems with producing understandable speech, he should be evaluated as early as possible. Speech therapy can be tremendously helpful. Provide his speech therapist with information about bipolar disorders in children so that his behavior will be better understood, and provide suggestions for structuring speech sessions to minimize behavior problems and maximize compliance. Token economies and other reward systems are widely used by speech therapists, and can help a lot. Short, frequent sessions may be more effective than long, infrequent ones. Your child may perform better in one-on-one sessions than in a speech group. Also, as at home and in the classroom, the rules for speech time should be clearly delineated.

Problems with prosody (speech flow and conversational skills) and volume are seen rather often in bipolar children. Children with these difficulties are less likely to be referred to a speech and language specialist than are children who cannot produce certain sounds or who stutter, but they can benefit nonetheless from speech therapy. Make sure the evaluator or therapist your child sees for these difficulties knows these topics well—not all speech specialists have expertise in these areas.

Prosody problems lend themselves best to group work. If your child's speech is consistently too loud or too soft, one-on-one work seems to be most effective, often using a tape recorder and other tools in order to encourage self-observation and to build skills for assessing and using proper speech volume.

The therapeutic home

Parents of bipolar children often change their home environment to make their child's life—and the whole family's life—easier. It's one of those things that moms and dads do without really thinking about it. Just as you look at your home in a new light when an infant begins crawling and exploring, the emergence of bipolar symptoms in a child warrants some revisions. You might think of it as making your home a therapeutic environment.

Families can take many cues from hospitals—not from the typical sterile hospital room, but from the better sort of psychiatric ward for adolescents. Warm, soft colors are chosen for their soothing nature. Lighting is bright where it is needed for reading and studying, soft where the mood should be restful. Furniture is comfortable and too heavy to throw in anger. Knick-knacks and valuables are safely stowed out of reach. Accident and suicide hazards are eliminated. There is a designated place to go when rage and anxiety take over—not a "rubber room" for punishment, but a time-out area for cocooning and regrouping. There are activities available that the child can master and enjoy, such as puzzles, board games, art supplies, and developmentally appropriate toys.

Your home has many advantages over even the best hospital ward, of course. At the top of the list is the presence of people who not only care, but who truly love your child deeply. No professional can substitute for you in this department.

Today, most US families feel they need two incomes to achieve a middle-class standard of living. Your child's health is going to challenge that standard, if it hasn't done so already. You may find that having a parent, grandparent, or other permanent adult at home with your child is the most important therapy there is. Depending on your family's financial situation, this can mean doing without some of the trappings of middle-class success, or even without a great deal more. If one parent—and it doesn't have to be Mom—can move to a part-time schedule to provide firm guidance and limits after your child's school hours, it may make more of a difference than anything else you do. Numerous studies have shown that children and teens who are unsupervised between school and their parents' return from work are more likely to abuse drugs and alcohol, have sex at an earlier age, and engage in other self-destructive behavior. And these studies were looking at all adolescent latch-key kids, not just those with the additional risk factor of a bipolar disorder.

Families of bipolar children have made all sorts of creative arrangements to balance their child's needs with the family's financial needs. These include staggering work schedules (one parent works nights, one works days; one parent works part-time and weekends only while the other works full-time), two parents working part-time so that one is always home, exploring options for working at home and/or self-employment, and making permanent childcare arrangements with grandparents or other family members.

> Because I homeschool, I have the flexibility to work with Cass's moods. On good days, we may cover all kinds of materials. When she is "off" the school day may consist of my reading to her snuggled on the couch. —Stephanie, mother of Cassidy

Single parents have the most difficult time with this, of course, and public assistance has unfortunately become less of an option. Some single parents whose extended families or former partners have not been willing or able to help have banded together to share childcare chores, sometimes even sharing a home with another single mom or dad. Others have found ways to ensure reliable, safe after-school care through school-based programs or community resources.

It's not going to be easy, but bipolar kids need the extra supervision, and the feeling that their parents are going to be there for them no matter what. They need to know that they are more important to you than a swank wardrobe, new cars, or a larger house. Your love and your time are really the only thing that can give your child the inner feeling of security that eludes so many people with bipolar disorders.

Drop-in centers

Some older teens, especially those who are finished with high school but not yet ready for adulthood, can access drop-in centers for the mentally ill. These can combine access to therapists, peer support groups, and socialization help. Well-run drop-in centers have esteem-building activities, opportunities to learn new job skills, and an atmosphere of camaraderie. They may also be able to place regulars in supportive housing and work.

Liberty Place Clubhouse Downtown in Pennsylvania's Allegheny County, for example, provides hang-out space for people with mental illness. They meet their peers in a structured, supervised environment, and can gradually reintegrate into society. The staff (most of whom are also clients) provides transitional employment leads, housing help, and personal advice.[4]

Don't call it therapy

Everyday life with a bipolar disorder is stressful, and yet it's in everyday life that children have the experiences that form their adult personalities. Parents can help build affirmative, life-enhancing, joyful and, yes, therapeutic experiences into the rhythms of our children's daily experiences. When we do so, we become their protectors, guides, and friends as they journey toward adulthood.

Here are just a few activities that build important skills and self-esteem. Whatever you do, don't call these activities therapy (even though they are):

- Keeping a personal journal or diary
- Taking personal time to play or listen to music, read, or work out for stress reduction
- Playing card games and board games
- Enjoying swimming or sports
- Playing on the playground, at the park, or in your yard
- Playing less-competitive group games like London Bridge and freeze tag (see books on "New Games" for some cooperative play possibilities for groups)
- Using costumes and props for imaginative play
- Starting and maintaining collections of rocks, stamps, cards, or toys
- Turning off the television and video games in favor of relating to one another
- Gaining mastery of lifelong activities like cooking, mechanical work, or the arts
- Caring for a pet or a garden
- Helping others in need, whether it's by participating in a charity marathon, volunteering in a homeless center, or choosing an important cause to which you will donate money

Finally, while therapy, medical appointments, and taking pills are going to be part of your child's life for a long time, maybe even forever, they shouldn't be the totality of it. Therapies are intended to enhance life, not turn it into an endless grind of appointments and to-do lists. Make time for relaxation, play, hugs, Saturday morning cartoons, and just watching the clouds go by. Treasure the times when your child is well, and store up energy then to deal with the inevitability of future problem episodes. Find therapeutic professionals whose work can buttress what you can accomplish at home, and then take it one day at a time.

CHAPTER 6

Other Interventions

BECAUSE BIPOLAR DISORDERS are illnesses of the nervous system, they have physical roots and repercussions. This chapter will describe various ways to address bipolar symptoms other than talk therapy and psychiatric drugs, with special attention to the needs of children and adolescents.

We'll begin by looking at several types of alternative practitioners and what they do. Next we'll provide information on light therapy, addressing sleep problems, essential fatty acids, special diets, allergy treatments, hormonal treatments, and antiviral and immune-system treatments. We'll discuss vitamins, minerals, herbal remedies, and dietary supplements that appear to help some people with bipolar disorders. Finally, we'll talk about social skills training, stress reduction, and other ways to improve resiliency in bipolar children.

Careful choices

In the US, most people have tried at least one form of alternative medical treatment for one ailment or another, such as saw palmetto extract for prostate problems or avoiding wheat products to ease the pain of celiac disease. Many of these non-pharmaceutical interventions are widely accepted, even by doctors. In fact, medical studies are proving that quite a few of the vitamins, supplements, tonics, exercises, and diets long touted for various illnesses can be effective, and they often do not carry the same risks and side effects as prescription drugs.

But before you leave your psychiatrist for the nearest health food store or alternative healthcare provider, there are two things you should know.

First, it is very unwise to rely solely on alternative measures to treat bipolar disorders, with the possible exception of mild cyclothymia or seasonal affective disorder. The risks of going without medical treatment include death by suicide or accident, and the terrible personal consequences of self-injurious behavior, manic spending sprees, hypersexuality, and all the rest. Parents must be especially careful to ensure proper medical care for bipolar children and adolescents, as minds and bodies cannot develop properly when a child is in the throes of depression, mania, or psychosis.

Second, there is much misinformation—some of it deliberate—abroad in alternative healthcare. Botanical formulas can differ wildly in their potency, both from manufacturer to manufacturer, and from vial to vial. There is also a potentially dangerous lack of scientific and regulatory oversight in this field, and sometimes a blatantly anti-science attitude. Some alternative practitioners are well-trained and highly competent, while others are charlatans.

Accordingly, you must be wary of the claims you read in advertisements, in magazine and newspaper articles, or on the Internet. Check the credentials of alternative practitioners before you heed their advice, especially if it involves expensive tests or remedies. And be doubly doubtful if an alternative practitioner encourages you or your child to forego prescription medications. None of the herbal remedies or other alternative treatments available today is known to cure bipolar disorders; in fact, if you see or hear such claims, you should be highly suspicious right away.

Note for non-US readers: Your experience may differ from that of US patients, depending on where you live. In Germany, for example, standardized herbal remedies are available by prescription and are widely used. There have also been more clinical trials of herbal formulas in Europe. However, parents must still research carefully and proceed with caution, especially if they are planning to use an herbal remedy at the same time as a prescription drug.

Despite the ease with which adults demand the latest prescription pill for everything from premature balding to weight loss, many people are very much against giving psychiatric medications to children. Well-meaning friends and relatives may approach you with information about natural cures for childhood behavior problems or mental illness, and get angry if you say you're not interested. Often these people either don't know your child's actual diagnosis, or have no idea what a serious illness it is. Just as you have a right to consider alternative medical treatments, you also have a right to stick with your doctor's regimen—especially if it's working.

I haven't tried anything alternative yet. I have read about these treat-
ments, but he is stable on prescribed meds, and I don't want to play with
that. —Lynn, mother of 11-year-old Michael (diagnosed BPI with mixed
states and psychosis, OCD, tic disorder)

The role of alternative treatments

A holistic approach to health takes into account all aspects of physical, emotional, and spiritual well-being. That's important when treating bipolar disorders because of their far-reaching impact on personal functioning. You can
complement pharmaceuticals with some alternative treatments, often reducing the dose and thereby eliminating some of the dangers and side effects
carried by many psychiatric medications. This combination approach is
called complementary medicine: using the best of what medical science has
to offer, and complementing it with less invasive techniques.

Many alternative treatments have a preventive focus, rather than merely
treating symptoms of illness after they emerge. Alternative practitioners also
stress empowering the patient, making him responsible for self-care measures. Even if all that does is make patients feel better because they're putting out more effort on their own behalf, the effects can be powerful.

Finally, a few people with bipolar disorders never find full relief from any
medication, especially those who are rapid cyclers. Don't give up on finding
a better medication or combination of medications, but if your child has
seemingly tried it all for an adequate amount of time without benefit, you
may find at least partial relief with a different approach.

Occasionally a patient will have very valid health reasons for giving up pharmaceutical treatments that are actually working. For example, almost all of
the medications used to treat bipolar disorders are believed to cause birth
defects, so pregnant girls and women who are bipolar can find themselves
faced with a terrible choice. Temporary reliance on alternative methods
under careful supervision, with a return to the use of effective medication as
soon as possible, can protect both the developing fetus and the mother's
health. Should your child develop another serious health condition, such as
cancer, conflicting medications might have to be temporarily discontinued
during chemotherapy, preparation for surgery, or certain types of medical
treatment. So even if alternative treatments are not right for your child now,
they might be useful someday.

Alternative treatments rarely produce dramatic changes. When they work, they usually assist your body's own self-righting mechanisms, promoting better sleep, fewer and less severe mood swings, improved general health, and a better frame of mind.

Evaluating alternative interventions

To get the clearest picture possible of any alternative interventions, you must introduce them independently of each other, and independent of pharmaceuticals or therapeutic interventions. Obviously, this will often be impractical—you wouldn't stop lithium just to see if B vitamins might be useful.

Barring the one-thing-at-a-time scenario, keep careful, daily records of supplements and dietary changes you introduce, when they are given and in what amounts, what brands you used, and any visible effects that you observe. If after four to six weeks you have not seen improvements with a supplement, it's unlikely that it will be of benefit. Dietary changes, bodywork, and other interventions may take much longer to bear fruit.

Remember that many parents report initial problems with supplements and dietary changes, and some children may be resistant to bodywork at first as well. Don't gloss over dangerous side effects, but expect to weather some behavior problems for a couple of weeks.

If you can convince your physician to make alternative therapies part of his prescription, you're in luck. Some actively oppose them, and that may force you to find a new doctor. Whatever you do, don't operate behind your doctor's back in any significant way. If you're philosophically incompatible, you should simply part ways—but you need a medical expert on your team.

Alternative practitioners

Alternative treatments may be suggested by your family doctor or psychiatrist, or by a specialist in a particular type of treatment. The most common types of alternative medical practices are explained in the following sections:

Acupuncture

Developed in China, acupuncture is based on the idea that an energy force called *ch'i* flows through the human body. If your *ch'i* is blocked, as acupuncture theory states, illness results. Modern acupuncturists use tiny, sterile, disposable needles inserted into the skin to undo these blockages. Some also employ heat, (noninvasive) lasers, magnetic devices, or electrical stimulation.

You don't have to believe in the *ch'i* concept to enjoy the benefits of acupuncture. Even the alternative medicine skeptics at the National Institutes of Health admit that it has value for treating chronic pain, and as an adjunct to other methods in the treatment of drug addiction (in fact, NIH is currently funding several studies on acupuncture). Some Western doctors think that acupuncture may work by influencing the body's production of natural opioid chemicals and neurotransmitters.

Reputable research indicates that properly applied acupuncture treatments may help heal nerve damage, which may in turn reduce anxiety and mood swings. There have been anecdotal reports from bipolar adults about acupuncture as an effective treatment for manic episodes (actress Margot Kidder, who has bipolar I disorder, claimed to have been successfully treated by an acupuncturist after a much-publicized manic/psychotic episode a few years ago). If you can find a good acupuncturist, it might be a worthwhile adjunct to other types of medical care.

Ayurvedic and other traditional medicine

Before the advent of modern medicine, people everywhere relied on herbal remedies. India's Ayurveda and traditional Chinese medicine (which also includes acupuncture) are two herbal systems that have been studied to a great extent. The Ayurvedic medicine concept revolves around a life-force called *prana*, which is comparable to the Chinese *ch'i* mentioned previously.

Ayurvedic practitioners will give you a thorough exam and tell you which "type" you are in their diagnostic system. Then they'll suggest an appropriate diet, lifestyle adjustments, and probably meditation. They may also have various suggestions about cleaning out your digestive tract, and may prescribe herbal remedies.

Chinese traditional medicine practitioners take a very similar approach, although their dietary recommendations tend to be less strict than a typical Ayurvedic plan. They may recommend physical and breathing exercises as well as herbs.

There is a vast array of Ayurvedic and Chinese herbal remedies available, most of which have not been tested by Western researchers. Some of these concoctions are probably quite effective, while others could be dangerous to your health. Try to find out exactly which herbs are in a remedy, and then check out their known effects in a reference book on herbs. For example, the popular Chinese herb Ma Huang (ephedra) is a common ingredient in traditional "nerve tonics." It is also a powerful central nervous system stimulant, and should be taken with caution.

Chiropractic

Chiropractors use their hands or special equipment to make "adjustments" to the spine and related body structures. This is useful for some people with back pain, and sometimes appears to help with other disorders.

There is no scientific reason for chiropractic adjustments to alleviate the symptoms of bipolar disorders, but some people have reported symptom reduction. There could be something about chiropractic and the nervous system that's yet to be discovered.

Massage and bodywork

"Bodywork" is a general term that covers a wide variety of therapeutic practices. Most of them involve massaging, manipulating, or moving the muscles and body parts in specific ways. These practices differ in style, intensity, and intent, and include:

- **Acupressure.** Similar to acupuncture, it employs firm or light pressure applied to specific sites on the body rather than needles. Acupressure does have a track record in helping with chronic pain and some physical disorders. Its efficacy for bipolar symptoms is unknown.

- **Massage.** There are many forms, including Swedish, Shiatsu (which resembles acupressure), and more. It can promote relaxation, physical comfort, and body awareness. It may also help decrease sensory defensiveness. Its efficacy for other bipolar symptoms is unknown.

- **The Feldenkrais Method.** Developed by Moshe Feldenkrais, this concentrates on rebuilding sensory and movement systems, particularly through unlearning poor movement patterns. A number of Feldenkrais practitioners work with children who have neurological problems. The therapy is gentle, and some children have experienced gross-motor, fine-motor, sensory, and relational improvements. A variant called Feldenkrais for Children with Neurological Disorders (FCND) is specially geared toward this population. The efficiency of Feldenkrais for bipolar symptoms is unknown. For more information on FCND, see the Movement Educators web site (*http://www.movement-educators.com/children.html*).

- **Craniosacral therapy.** Involves delicately manipulating the plates of the skull and the "cranial tides" of the body. Some may question the scientific basis of craniosacral work, but it is gentle, noninvasive, and parents of many children with neurological problems say it has been helpful. Most craniosacral therapists employ a certain amount of talk therapy along with the bodywork, which may or may not appeal to your child. Its efficacy for bipolar symptoms is unknown. Although it was developed by osteopath John Upledger, craniosacral therapy is practiced by trained members of other professions, including some occupational therapists and physical therapists. Upledger includes some accounts of beneficial use of this therapy for people with mental illness in his book *Your Inner Physician and You: Craniosacral Therapy and Somatoemotional Release* (1997, North Atlantic Books). For more information, see the Craniosacral Therapy web site (*http://www.craniosacral.co.uk/*).

- **The Alexander Technique.** Used to help patients streamline and increase the gracefulness of their movements. Practitioners teach patients new, more balanced movement patterns. Since self-awareness is an important part of this approach, the Alexander Technique is probably more applicable to teenagers and adults than to children. Its efficacy for bipolar symptoms is unknown. For more information, see the Alexander Technique web site (*http://www.alexandertechnique.com/*).

Some bodywork believers make extravagant claims. For any bodywork method, including those not mentioned here, check the practitioner's credentials, and make sure you feel comfortable with both the person and the methodology.

All of the modalities listed here have accrediting bodies in most Western countries. Generally speaking, accredited, well-trained practitioners are more likely to do beneficial work than self-trained or non-accredited practitioners.

If you happen to be near a massage school or a training center for another bodywork method, inexpensive classes may be available. Some schools also operate free or low-cost clinics that allow students to practice on patients under close supervision.

Naturopathy

Naturopaths are licensed to practice medicine in some countries, and also in some US states and Canadian provinces. They use the designation ND rather than MD. Their focus is on preventive and holistic healthcare.

Naturopaths vary in their personal philosophy about Western medicine. Some will refer patients to an MD for ailments they feel are out of their league, others prefer to rely only on nutritional and natural medicine.

> When Lili was 13, she saw a naturopath a few times who tried to treat her with B-vitamin injections and a better diet. It seemed to clear up her constant bronchial symptoms a bit and brighten her mood, but the effects wore off quickly. On the other hand, the herbal remedy he gave her for a urinary tract infection worked as well as any pharmaceutical I've ever seen. —Sarah, mother of 17-year-old Lili (diagnosed bipolar II disorder, OCD)

Be careful when you choose an ND. In the US, some people calling themselves naturopaths have not completed an accredited program. Properly licensed naturopaths receive medical training that is roughly comparable to traditional medical school, but with a different emphasis.

For information about finding a licensed naturopath in the US or Canada, contact the American Association of Naturopathic Physicians (http://www. naturopathic.org/) or the Canadian Naturopathic Association (http://www. naturopathic.org/canada/Canada.Assoc.List.html).

Holistic psychology

Technically, a holistic psychologist should have the same credentials as a regular psychologist (see Chapter 5, *Therapeutic Interventions*), plus training in holistic health-promotion practices. In practice, this may not be the case, so be sure to ask. Depending on the practitioner, holistic psychology would appear to be of significant value to people with bipolar disorders who would like to combine talk therapy with alternative healthcare practices.

A holistic psychologist might recommend a combination of dietary changes, nutritional supplements, exercise, biofeedback, and mood control techniques, such as meditation or self-hypnosis. Helping the patient build an effective support system should also be part of the plan. These interventions would have the overall goal of helping to normalize physical health, improve mental stability, and help the patient have a more enjoyable and productive life.

Homeopathy

Homeopathy is based on the principle that remedies containing infinitesimal amounts of substances that could cause the medical condition being treated can instead prod the immune system into action against the condition. Homeopathy is considered to be fairly mainstream in the UK.

In the US and Canada, homeopathic physicians are not licensed to practice medicine. However, some MDs and NDs do recommend homeopathic treatments, and a few homeopaths are also fully licensed medical or naturopathic doctors. For information about homeopaths in North America, see the National Center for Homeopathy web site (*http://www.homeopathic.org/*).

Homeopathy does not seem to have a good track record as an intervention for bipolar disorders, although some patients report that certain homeopathic remedies can occasionally provide relief from anxiety and physical distress associated with mood swings. Most mainstream physicians believe that homeopathic remedies contain too little of the active ingredient to have any medical effect. That said, homeopathic remedies are also too diluted to cause any harm, and it's a well-known fact that if you believe a placebo will help, you may actually experience a reduction in symptoms.

Nutrition-based therapies

Nutritionists are experts in how food intake affects health. Some are employed by hospitals, clinics, and long-term care facilities to improve patient care through appropriate diet. Others work in private practice. Some nutritionists have very traditional views about diet, while others may recommend what seem like radical changes. Be sure to check the credentials and training of any nutritionist you consult, and pay attention to your intuition if her suggestions seem unreasonable or potentially unhealthy.

If your child has an eating disorder in addition to a bipolar disorder, a nutritionist with background in dietary interventions for these disorders should definitely be part of your treatment team. You may also want to consult a nutritionist about dietary changes that could be beneficial, such as the special diets mentioned later in this chapter.

Orthomolecular medicine

The most famous proponent of orthomolecular medicine was its late founder, Dr. Linus Pauling. Better known for receiving the 1954 Nobel Prize for Chemistry and the 1962 Nobel Prize for Peace, Pauling spent most of his later life studying and publicizing the effects of megadoses of vitamins, particularly vitamin C. Many of Dr. Pauling's more extravagant claims have not been substantiated by research, but his reputation forced the medical establishment to take his ideas seriously.

Some MDs, NDs, nutritionists, and other practitioners are firm believers in orthomolecular medicine, and Pauling's principles underlie many of the megadose vitamin concoctions on health food store shelves. Since large doses of vitamins can have side effects as well as potential benefits, be sure to talk with your doctor about what to watch out for and how any benefits will be assessed. You definitely shouldn't do megadose vitamin therapy without consulting a competent professional first.

Osteopathy

Osteopaths operate somewhat like chiropractors, adjusting the musculoskeletal system to effect improvement. In the UK, licensed osteopaths participate in the National Health scheme. Osteopaths are licensed to practice medicine in all US states, and use the initials DO (Doctor of Osteopathy) instead of MD.

One area of osteopathy-related treatment, craniosacral therapy, is often recommended for children with neurological challenges (see "Craniosacral therapy," earlier in this chapter).

Light therapy

Light therapy for seasonal mood swings is actually a rather mainstream intervention. If your child's depression and mania is clearly tied to the seasons (a fact that can best be determined by keeping a careful mood diary), the use of full-spectrum light bulbs, a special light box, or so-called dawn simulation techniques may be recommended by your physician or psychiatrist.

The good news is that these devices are very likely to help! Numerous scientific studies have shown that light therapy is effective for the reduction of seasonal mood swings. Light therapy also seems to be effective for people with seasonal eating disorders.[1]

Why does it work? Recent medical research indicates that people with seasonal affective depression and other seasonal mood swings have a built-in lower sensitivity to light at the retinal level.[2] The presence of light suppresses the production of melatonin, the sleep hormone. It appears that bright light also has an effect on how the body produces and uses serotonin. Specific types and frequencies of light may have other as yet unknown effects.

The most frequently studied type of light therapy requires exposure to 2500-lux cool-white fluorescent light (filtered for UV rays) via a light box for two hours per day. The light box can be installed in any room where the patient is likely to be for two hours: the bedroom, the kitchen, or a child's playroom.

Other studies have indicated that 30 minutes of daily exposure to a more intense 10,000-lux light source can be just as effective, and considerably easier to build into your day.

Although light boxes are the most common devices used in light therapy, inventors have also developed various head-mounted devices and light visors that are said to deliver the same effect while allowing the patient to move about freely.

Dawn simulation is a newer and more complex technique that involves exposure to increasingly bright light in the early morning hours, simulating a summer dawn. It has not been well studied, but could be as effective as the older forms of light therapy.

A new technology tested so far only on patients with the autoimmune disorder lupus uses the A-1 ultraviolet wavelength. This is not the same UV wavelength used in tanning-salon beds, which can be quite dangerous for people with lupus. One of the most prominent features of lupus is severe mood swings, and patients in the NIH-sponsored study did find some relief in the areas of mood, energy levels, and skin rash.

Further resources for starting a light therapy program, including companies that sell light boxes, are listed in the appendix, *Resources*. Also see the section on vitamins later in this chapter for related information.

Another light-related strategy is increasing your child's exposure to natural sunlight. If your child tends to spend most of his day indoors, see if you can add 30 minutes to an hour of outdoor activity to his daily schedule. It is unlikely to be as effective as using a light box, but it costs nothing and could help support other interventions.

Fixing sleep problems

If the heart of bipolar disorders is a built-in problem with the body's circadian clock, as many researchers believe, it naturally follows that readjusting that clock is a possible treatment. Light therapy is one approach that follows this reasoning. Sleep-related changes are another—and one that patients and researchers both report can be highly effective. If you can control your sleep pattern, you can reduce the number of mood swings, and also reduce their severity and length.

Sleep deprivation can definitely set off hypomanic and manic episodes, and one of the earliest visible signs of impending depression is a desire to sleep much more than usual (hypersomnia). Strict scheduling can be the key here. That means setting a bedtime and a wake-up time and sticking to them, even if there's a big test tomorrow or a rock concert tonight, and even if it's Saturday morning and you want to sleep in. Obviously, this is not going to be a popular point with teenagers, who want to share in the nightlife of their peers, and who delight in lazy weekend mornings.

Light therapy, as discussed earlier, can be used to improve the duration and quality of sleep in people who are in or about to be in a hypomanic or manic phase. It appears that exposure to bright light at midday increases the amount of melatonin naturally produced during night hours. This should encourage more restful and regular sleep. Using light therapy in the morning as is usually done for depression, however, appears to increase cycling among manic or hypomanic patients.[3] Light therapy times and amounts can be changed to fit where your child's mood cycle is each day. That gives it a certain advantage over medications that usually must be taken daily to be effective.

Some clinical studies have used controlled, supervised sleep deprivation to break a depressive downswing. Please don't try this without your doctor's help in setting up a plan.

Other researchers have found that sleep schedules can be reset during manic episodes by inducing sleep, either through the use of medication, or by high levels of activity that eventually wear the person out and bring on sleep. Again, this isn't something to attempt without help—although you can probably safely encourage hypomanic teenagers to add extra strenuous activity to their schedule in an effort to bring on sleep and stave off full-blown mania. Most of the sleep-promotion strategies outlined in the rest of this section are also safe during hypomanic episodes.

Other advice for improving the quality, duration, and regularity of sleep applies to anyone who experiences occasional insomnia or oversleeping. This generic advice includes:

- Avoid unnecessary artificial stimulants and depressants, such as coffee, tea, or alcohol.

- Avoid over-the-counter medications with a stimulating or depressive effect, such as OTC allergy preparations, aspirin with caffeine, No-Doz and other OTC stimulants, and most commercial cough syrups.

- Avoid hyper-exciting television programs, music, or games right before bed. Parents can decide when the activity level should start to wind down slowly.

- Use your bed for sleeping only, not for reading, watching television, or playing. This helps associate the concepts of bed and sleep in your mind.

- If you can't get to sleep at the proper time, don't just lie there tossing and turning. Get out of bed, and do something really, really boring—like housework, or putting together an old jigsaw puzzle.

- Make a relaxing ritual part of bedtime. For young children, this could be a story with mom and some warm milk. Teens might prefer using a computer or reading for 20 minutes at a certain time, followed by brushing teeth, donning pajamas, laying out tomorrow's school clothes, or other end-of-the-day chores. A nice, long bath is another great way to end the day.

- Some people find certain scents very soporific and have added aroma-therapy to their relaxation plan. These can be added to massage oil and rubbed into the skin for a doubly relaxing effect.

Melatonin

Melatonin is produced by the pineal gland, and is responsible for helping the body maintain sleep and other biochemical rhythms. Melatonin supplements given about half an hour before bed may be useful for addressing these problems. The effect may not be lasting, however.

Melatonin's effects may also differ for people with bipolar disorders. Some studies have found that taking a melatonin supplement on a regular basis can actually make depression worse. Supplementing directly with any kind of hormone can be problematic in the long run, as in some cases the patient's body may respond by producing less of the natural substance.

> *Katie is very interested in trying anything natural she hears about. We've said no to St. John's wort and some other herbal medications, but last month she started taking melatonin when she can't sleep. It does seem to help. —George, father of 18-year-old Katie (diagnosed bipolar I disorder, anxiety disorder)*

If you do decide to try melatonin, talk about it with your doctor or psychiatrist, and set up a dosage plan and observation schedule first. Most bipolar adults who have reported good results from melatonin use it only when their sleep cycle first begins to get out of kilter, and then only until it is back on track. This evidence is strictly anecdotal, though, and it's best to consult with your physician before trying melatonin.

Other sleep supplements

You may be tempted to try natural sleep aids. Of the options mentioned here, chamomile is probably the safest and mildest. Be extremely careful to avoid using other central nervous system depressants, including alcohol, at the same time as these substances. Other depressants may potentiate the active ingredients in some of these substances, with possibly dangerous effects.

Indeed, although these herbal potions are not as dangerous as prescription sleeping pills, they are also not inconsequential. It's never a good thing to be dependent on a pill to sleep, and little is known about the long-term effects of herbal sleep aids, or of their over-the-counter counterparts (Ny-Tol, etc.).

Simply taking a good multivitamin may also help regulate sleep. Vitamins implicated in insomnia and/or hypersomnia include the B vitamins (especially B2 and niacin), potassium, and magnesium.

Vitamin B2 may be of extreme importance in regulating sleep. Scientists at the University of North Carolina discovered in 1998 that B2 binds to cryptochrome, a light-absorbing pigment found in the retina of the eye. UNC researcher Dr. Aziz Sancar believes that a B2 deficiency may be implicated in some cases of SAD and related disorders. Others with SAD may have a deficiency in one of the two varieties of cryptochrome itself.[4]

Supplements believed to affect sleep include:

- **Valerian (Valeriana officinalis).** A strong herbal sedative (and one of the secret ingredients in the soporific liqueur Jagermeister). It should not be given to young children, but can help teens and adults fight episodic insomnia.

- **Kava-kava (Piper methysticum).** A mild sedative herb used for centuries in the South Pacific. It has a slight potential for abuse, although such misuse is rare.

- **Chamomile (Anthemis nobilis).** A mild but effective sedative traditionally used to treat sleep disorders or stomach upsets. It is a member of the daisy family, so avoid this herb if you are allergic to its cousin, ragweed.

- **Passion flower (Passiflora incarnata).** Has sedative, antispasmodic, and anti-inflammatory qualities.

- **Skullcap (Scutellaria lateriflora).** A medium-strength sedative with anticonvulsive properties as well. Traditional uses also include menstrual irregularity and breast pain, indicating that it probably has hormonal effects.

- **Hops (Humulus lupulus).** The herb used to flavor beer, and the reason beer makes many people sleepy. It's available in capsules or as a dried herb for use in tea, and works as a gentle sleep aid.

- **Tryptophan.** An amino acid that raises the levels of serotonin in the brain. It's not currently available in the US due to a badly contaminated batch several years ago, but it is sold over-the-counter in Europe and by prescription in Canada. It appears to help regulate sleep, and to have an antidepressant effect not unlike that of an SSRI. For that reason, people with bipolar disorders should be wary of possible manic effects from taking tryptophan. In any case, do not take this substance with any pharmaceutical antidepressant. If you can purchase tryptophan, buy it from a trustworthy source. Take it at bedtime with sweetened milk, fruit juice, and vitamin B-6 for maximum effect. A 1997 study of light therapy found that SAD patients who were initially poor responders benefited more when they also took L-tryptophan, the type of tryptophan that is most easily absorbed.

- **5-HTP (5-hydroxytryptophan).** Synthesized from tryptophan and an even more direct precursor to serotonin. It is available in the US. It appears to help regulate sleep, and to have an antidepressant effect not unlike that of an SSRI. For that reason, people with bipolar disorders should be wary of possible manic effects from taking 5-HTP. Do not take this substance with any pharmaceutical antidepressant.

- **Taurine.** Another amino acid that can counteract insomnia. It works by slowing down nerve impulses.

Essential fatty acids

More exciting alternative treatment news for people with bipolar disorders also came in 1998, when Dr. Andrew L. Stoll and his colleagues at McLean Hospital announced that Omega-3 fatty acids appear to act as a mood stabilizer for some people with bipolar disorders.[5]

Omega-3 fatty acids are a type of essential fatty acids (EFAs) that are found almost exclusively in fish oils. As the "essential" in their name implies, these fatty acids are needed to build cells, and also to support the body's anti-inflammatory response. They are the good polyunsaturated fats that improve cardiovascular health when substituted for the bad saturated fats.

Two Omega-3 fatty acids are found in oily, cold-water fish: eicosapentaenoic acid (EPA) and docosahexanoic acid (DHA). Another Omega-3 fatty acid, alpha-linoleic acid, is found in flax-seed and perilla oils, among other sources.

Omega-6 fatty acids are also important for optimal health. The Omega-6 family includes linoleic acid and its derivatives, including gammalinolenic acid (GLA), dihomogamma-linolenic acid (DGLA), and arachidonic acid (AA). These substances also come from animal fats and some plants, such as evening primrose oil, which is a good source of GLA, flax-seed oil, black-currant seed oil, hemp-seed oil, and borage oil, which contains both GLA and very long chain fatty acids (VLCFAs).

Unfortunately, the high levels of arachidonic acid found in evening primrose oil have been reported to lower the threshold for frontal-lobe seizures, so people who have seizures should exercise caution. Also, the VLCFAs found in borage oil can be irritating to the liver and central nervous system, and are therefore not heartily recommended for use by children and people with nervous system disorders. Other oils with a high VLCFA content are canola oil, peanut oil (including the oil in peanut butter), and mustard seed oil.

When oils are heated, most will convert at least part of their fatty acids into trans-fatty acids, which are substances to be avoided. Hemp oil is one of the few that can resist this heat-driven conversion progress, but it isn't readily available for cooking or medicinal use in the US.

Researchers believe that achieving a dietary balance between Omega-3 and Omega-6 fatty acids provides the most benefits. The ratios usually recommended are 3:1 or 4:1 Omega-6 to Omega-3.

EFA basics

Now that you know the good news about EFAs, here's the not-so-good news: to get the mood stabilizing benefits reported in the McLean Hospital study, patients took 9.6 grams per day of concentrated fish oil. Think about that for a moment; 9.6 grams is a lot of oil to drink from a spoon, much less take in capsule form (that's almost 30 capsules per day). Many patients who have tried to duplicate this experiment at home have found it difficult, both for the sheer amount they had to use, and for the side effects that can ensue.

> We tried the fish oil, but only for about a week because it caused diarrhea. She wasn't on it long enough for us to know if it worked.
> —Donna, mother of 16-year-old Lisa (diagnosed BPII, post-traumatic stress disorder, and anxiety disorder)

Since announcing his initial results, Dr. Stoll has produced an "Omega-3 Fatty Acid User Guide" that is highly recommended.[6] He notes that 5 grams of Omega-3 fatty acids may be sufficient to stabilize mood in adults (of course, the dose for children should be reduced according to body weight). Although he recommends fish oil because it has been studied the most, Dr.

Stoll notes that the concentration of Omega-3 EFAs in flax-seed and perilla oils is actually higher, and the taste of these oils is far more palatable. Two to three teaspoons per day of these oils in their liquid form should be sufficient for an adult, he says, although dosage will need to be adjusted according to body size and individual chemistry. The maximum effective dose Dr. Stoll reports using is 15 grams of oil per day.

Other sources have suggested trying much lower doses, in the range of 1 to 3 grams per day. This might be a safe place to start for a child.

EFA tips

The following tips for using EFAs as mood stabilizers have been collected from a variety of sources, including researchers at NIH and US mood disorder clinics whose patients are trying this approach, and patients themselves:

- Take antioxidant supplements during treatment with EFAs to prevent your body from simply oxidizing the extra oil. One mood disorder clinic recommends 1200 IUs (international units) of natural vitamin E and 2000 mg of vitamin C for adults weighing approximately 150 pounds, with doses for children reduced according to body weight.

- If you choose fish oil, fishy burps are the most commonly reported side effect—and they are most unpleasant. Patients have recommended swallowing a whole clove of garlic or a garlic tablet with the fish oil as a breath deodorant. You know these burps are not nice if garlic is recommended as a cover-up! Taking the fish oil at night or with orange juice also seems to help.

- In Iceland and Scandinavia, flavored fish oils have long been available as an old-fashioned health tonic (mint is a favorite). If demand rises, these may be seen on North American shelves soon. If you're curious about these, see *http://www.lysi.is/wpp/lysi/lysi.nsf/pages/contents*.

- Stomach troubles are reported from EFA use, as is excessive flatulence. Garlic or a garlic pill might help with these problems. Some patients report trying acidopholous capsules or other probiotics, yogurt with live cultures, or over-the-counter stomach or gas remedies. If you try OTC medications, do be careful. Many of these can interact with or counteract psychiatric medications, and they just might affect the action of EFAs as well. Perilla oil seems to be better tolerated by the stomach than fish oil or flax-seed oil.

- Diarrhea or oily stools can be another unpleasant side effect, especially if the dose is over 10 grams per day. In fact, flax seeds are well known for promoting regularity—and when you ingest a lot, you may be a little too regular. Taking several small doses of oil rather than one large one should help.

It's great if you can get at least some of your EFAs in food. Low-fat diets are part of the reason some people, especially those who are trying to lose weight, may not get enough. Many cold-pressed salad oils, including olive, safflower, sunflower, corn, peanut, and canola oils, do contain EFAs, as do coconut oil and coconut butter. When these oils are processed with heat, however, the fatty acids may be changed or destroyed. Corn and soybean oils are both rather high in Omega-6 fatty acids. Olive oil is probably your best EFA choice for oil-based dressings and marinades.

Oily, cold-water fish themselves are another great EFA source, although again, cooking may be a problem (and not everyone is a sushi fan).

It is possible to have lab tests done to discern EFA levels, although few doctors know much about them. You might have to send a sample to a specialty lab.

Diabetics may experience adverse effects from too much EFAs, and should talk to their physician before supplementing with EFA products. If excess weight is already a problem for your child, you should probably consult a nutritionist about how to substitute these good fats for bad, while cutting calories in other areas.

Commercial EFA preparations that you may hear about include:

- **Efalex.** A brand-name EFA supplement made by Efamol Neutriceuticals Inc., Efalex is widely touted as a supplement for people with ADD/ADHD. It contains a mix of Omega-3 fish oil, Omega-6 evening primrose oil and thyme oil, and vitamin E.

- **Efamol.** Another product from the same firm, Efamol is marketed as a treatment for PMS. It combines evening primrose oil, vitamins B-6, C, and E, niacin, zinc, and magnesium. Both products are now available in the US, Canada, and the UK, and can be purchased by mail order. Unlike many supplements manufacturers, Efamol adheres to strict standards and also sponsors reputable research.

- **EicoPro**. Made by Eicotec Inc., it combines Omega-3 fish oils and Omega-6 linoleic acid. Eicotech is another supplements manufacturer known for its high manufacturing standards.

- **Monolaurin**. Made by the body from lauric acid, another medium-chain fatty acid that is found in abundance in coconuts and some other foods, including human breast milk. It is known to have antibacterial and antiviral properties. Monolaurin may be the active ingredient in colostrum, the pre-milk all mammals produce to jumpstart a newborn's immune system. Cow colostrum is available in supplement form in some areas.

- **NutriVene-D**. A supplement created especially for people with Down syndrome that mixes EFAs, vitamins, and other substances.

- **Essential Balance/Essential Balance Jr**. Made from sesame, sunflower, flaxseed, pumpkin-seed, and borage oils. The adult formulation is a capsule, while the children's version is available as a liquid.

Several other suppliers of EFA supplements are listed in the appendix.

Diet

Some basic dietary advice applies to anyone who suffers from mood swings: eat a variety of healthy foods at regular intervals, do not skip meals, and avoid an excess of sugar and junk food. Unfortunately, this advice goes against the grain with many children and teens.

Many bipolar children are extremely picky eaters, and bipolar teens may have coined the term "junk food junkie." As discussed in Chapter 5, limited food choices are sometimes the result of sensory dysfunction, a cause that can be addressed. In other cases, they're simply the result of personal rigidity, perhaps an effort to control one of the few areas of life where children can exercise a choice.

The problem with poor diet is that is does not promote general health. Taken to the extreme, self-restricted diets can turn into full-blown eating disorders. Both anorexia nervosa and bulimia are more common in people with bipolar disorders, and probably have similar neurological triggers.

As the section on essential fatty acids earlier in this chapter indicated, one dietary change that may help with mood regulation is eliminating hydrogenated (trans) fats. Experts in fatty acid metabolization note that hydrogenated fats short-circuit the body's ability to metabolize the good fatty acids needed to, among other things, produce normal amounts of neurotransmitters and other hormones.

Simply raising the level of (good) fat in the diet could also help. In 1996, Dr. Keith Ablow published some intriguing musings on the relationship between fat intake and mental disturbances in the article "Fat Chance" (*http://www.mhsource.com/exclusive/psychandsoc0796.html*). His observations on fat intake and mood are echoed by many anecdotal reports on the calming effects of high-fat foods from parents of bipolar teens.

Whatever science may say about the subject, parents also know that certain foods seem to set their kids off. Finding out just what the culprit for off-the-wall behavior might be can require some sleuthing. Parents of bipolar children report trying all sorts of diets, fad and otherwise, to improve their child's behavior. In most cases, there is little to no effect.

> We cut out all sugar, as well as red and yellow dyes, with no results.
> —Cindy, mother of 16-year-old Nathan (diagnosed bipolar disorder, OCD, ADHD, post-traumatic stress disorder, chemical dependency, bulimia)

Whether dietary changes are as effective as their proponents claim, one thing is certain: eating healthier never hurt anyone. Besides, changing your child's diet is relatively easy, inexpensive, and noninvasive.

The Feingold diet

Dr. Ben Feingold, creator of the well-known Feingold diet for treating hyperactivity and other childhood behavior disorders, recommended avoiding synthetic flavorings and food colors, certain preservatives, and sometimes other additives.

The Feingold Association formed to support families using his diet plan. Its useful Pure Facts newsletter lists commercial foods that meet (or do not meet) the restrictions. There is a membership charge to join this group, which can provide meal plans, food lists, information about doctors and nutritionists who support the diet, and contacts with other parents using the diet.

Clinical testing has not proven Dr. Feingold's claims true, but some parents have reported improvements in behavior, attention, and other symptoms. If you want to know more about the Feingold diets, see the Feingold Association web site (*http://www.feingold.org/indexx.html*).

The ketogenic diet for seizure disorders

This diet plan is a nutritionist's nightmare: it includes almost no starches or sugars. Instead, you consume one gram of protein for every four grams of fat. The body is then forced to burn fat for energy rather than carbohydrates, causing it to produce an abundance of waste products called ketones. These ketones somehow suppress seizure activity in about 30 percent of people with epilepsy that does not respond to medication. Patients may have to stay on the ketogenic diet for life.

Under no circumstances should this diet be tried on your own, without medical supervision. Not only is it potentially dangerous, it's pretty hard to make it appetizing. Each food portion must be carefully weighed, and foods must be given in specific combinations. It is very high in fats, and weight gain may be an unavoidable side effect. However, for those with intractable seizure disorders, it may be worth that comparatively minor risk. A medical center that specializes in epilepsy treatment should be able to provide guidance and expert nutritional advice if this option is recommended for you or your child.

If your child has a medication-resistant seizure disorder in addition to manic depression, you may want to investigate this difficult (but potentially lifesaving) diet. The Johns Hopkins Epilepsy Center (*http://hopkins.med.jhu.edu/HealthcarePros/neuro/epilepsy/keto.html*) has been at the forefront of this research.

The amino acid carnitine will minimize ketone buildup, so carnitine (and its precursors lysine and methionine) should not be taken by people on the ketogenic diet unless you are so directed by your physician.

Some nutritionists recommend that people with seizure disorders also avoid the protein-based artificial sweetener aspartame (Equal).

Casein-free and gluten-free diets

Quite a few children with autism or related neurological conditions seem to have problems metabolizing casein (milk protein) and/or gluten (the protein found in wheat and several other grains). Eliminating one or both of these proteins from the diet has been reported to result in noticeable improvements in behavior, including a reduction in aggressive or raging behaviors, increased attempts to relate to other people, and better overall health. These benefits do not apply to all autistic-spectrum children, and their applicability to bipolar disorders has never been tested.

Lisa Lewis has written an excellent book on the topic of casein- and gluten-free diets, *Special Diets for Special Kids* (1998, Future Horizons). She also maintains two web sites (*http://members.aol.com/lisas156/index.htm* and *http://www.autismNDI.com/*). There is more information about casein-free and gluten-free diets in books written for people with celiac disease. These individuals must also avoid gluten, and many eschew dairy foods as well.

Two other sites of interest are maintained by Don Wiss: the Gluten-Free Page (*http://www.panix.com/~donwiss/*) and the No Milk Page (*http://www.panix.com/~nomilk/*).

Anti-Candida diets

Some people suffer from an over-abundance of Candida albicans yeast in the digestive tract, especially those with autoimmune disorders, such as AIDS. Although it's a controversial topic with some mainstream medical professionals, some researchers believe that Candida can also cause or exacerbate mental problems. These are the same yeasts that can cause raised, red diaper rash in infants, the itchy white throat coating called thrush, and unpleasant gastrointestinal systems after a course of antibiotics.

Anti-Candida diets are gluten-free, and many people avoid dairy foods as well. For more information, see the many books available on Candida albicans or the Candida web site (*http://www.panix.com/~candida/*).

Elimination/re-introduction diet
for food allergies

About 5 percent of all children have food allergies, but the rate of both food allergies and food sensitivities among people with bipolar disorders appears to be higher.

Diets to detect and eliminate actual food allergies should be carried out under the aegis of an allergist or other knowledgeable physician. Most start patients out with an elimination diet, taking out all of the most common allergens: dairy products, eggs, all gluten-containing grains, corn, citrus fruits, bananas, nuts (especially peanuts), soy, and vegetables from the night-shade family (tomatoes, eggplant, potatoes, and peppers). Obviously, if you already know of or suspect an allergy to another food, this item should be eliminated as well. Most people stay on this very restricted diet for at least four weeks—some doctors recommend an elimination diet for as long as six months.

Next comes the re-introduction process: add back the foods you eliminated, one at a time. Have your child eat the re-introduced food at every meal. If she suffers no ill effects, she isn't allergic to that food, and it can be added back to her regular diet.

If your child does seem to have an allergic reaction to a food, eliminate it again for several weeks and then re-introduce it again. You may need to fol-low this last step several times to make sure you know which food is caus-ing the possible allergic reaction.

Rotation diet for food allergies

If you find definite food allergies or food sensitivities, allergists usually rec-ommend following a rotation diet. This plan requires that you eat different foods each day in a four-day period to decrease the likelihood of developing new allergies. People with mild food sensitivities may find that they can eventually tolerate foods that once caused them distress when they follow a rotation diet, but re-introducing these foods should be done very carefully.

Other allergy tests and treatments

Other than diet, the most common allergy tests are the skin-prick test and the radioallergosorbent test (RAST). Of the two, the RAST is preferred for young children or anyone with eczema. It is also more specific and reliable, although the skin test may actually be more sensitive. The RAST is a blood test that measures the level of immunoglobulin E (IgE) antibodies to specific foods or substances. If there are no IgE antibodies present in the blood, the person does not have an allergy to that item.

Tell the allergist what medications your child takes before the RAST is administered. Antihistamines, steroids, and some other medicines can skew results by inhibiting the inflammatory response.

The only sure treatment for food allergies is food avoidance. There are desensitization shots available for other types of allergens, such as pollens, but this therapy is only in its formative stages for food allergies. Some allergists are willing to try so-called neutralization shots or sublingual drops, also called low-dose immunotherapy. The efficacy of these is not proven, although some clinical trials have been very promising.

Severe allergic reactions are rare, but those at risk must be extra-careful about reading labels and should always carry an emergency kit. Your allergist can help you put this together. People who have both asthma and allergies have a higher risk of dangerous allergic reactions. Food sensitivity reactions can sometimes be cut short with a simple dose of baking soda, or commercial preparations containing bicarbonate of soda, such as Alka-Seltzer. (Before using these, double check to make sure they won't have a harmful interaction with any drug your child is taking.)

Although proper treatment for allergies promotes better health, it may have little to no impact on bipolar symptoms, despite what some alternative health practitioners say.

> *We tried allergy therapy for one and a half years... it was no help.*
> *—Evelyn, mother of 14-year-old Robert (diagnosed bipolar I disorder and ADHD)*

· · · · ·

> *Billy's asthma and allergy medications, as well as measures we've taken to reduce his exposure to allergens, have not impacted his psychiatric diagnoses. —Marlene, mother of 8-year-old Billy (diagnosed cyclothymic disorder)*

Hormonal treatments

Many bipolar girls and women have noticed that taking birth control pills, estrogen supplements such as Premarin (synthetic estrogen), or other hormonal medications, such as the birth-control shot Depo-Provera (medroxyprogesterone, a synthetic cousin of the hormone progesterone) can have a profound effect on their mood swings. Sometimes the effect is not a beneficial one, but many young patients report gaining increased control over their emotions and moods while taking these medications.

Considering the importance of the endocrine system in mood, it's entirely reasonable to believe these patients are telling the truth—and yet very few psychiatrists use these medications to treat bipolar symptoms or to augment other treatments.

It may be worthwhile for parents of bipolar daughters to explore these possibilities with their physician. Early puberty seems to be more common in bipolar girls, and may cause both physical and emotional distress. Older bipolar girls and women tend to report menstrual irregularities and premenstrual mood problems. Leveling out their production of hormones may help.

For the parents of girls who may be sexually promiscuous when manic, birth control obviously has other attractions.

Because the hormonal cycles of men are less obvious than those of women, there has been little research into hormone-based treatments for physically healthy men. It seems likely that at least some males with bipolar disorders also suffer from hormonal imbalances that could be treated. Unfortunately, there isn't much information available at this time, anecdotal or otherwise.

You might also consider looking at natural alternatives to hormone supplementation. Soy isoflavones, yams, vitamin E, essential fatty acids, and other substances that affect estrogen or progesterone production could be beneficial—or could disrupt hormonal cycles that are functioning normally.

If you're interested in pursuing the hormonal angle, be sure to work with a competent endocrinologist, even if you plan to use natural supplements only. Hormones are not something to mess around with on your own.

Antiviral treatments and immunotherapy

These therapies may soon be moving from the alternative health world into the mainstream. There is ample reason to believe that for at least some people with bipolar disorders, viral infections of the central nervous system are part of the problem. Possible culprits include enteroviruses, various human herpes viruses, including varicella zoster (the virus that causes chicken pox) and the Epstein-Barr virus (EBV); paramyxoviruses (the family that includes measles, mumps, and some types of influenza-like viruses), retroviruses, cytomegaloviruses, or something completely new.

In the years before psychoanalytic theory, physical illness was often assumed to be the cause of mental illness, since it was well-known that syphilis, influenza, and other diseases could also cause dementia. It's only recently that medical researchers have taken up the quest for infectious agents again. Some alternative practitioners, however, have long encouraged their mentally ill patients to pursue antiviral therapies, sometimes with encouraging results.

Among the recent findings that give credence to viral infection theories are lymphocyte abnormalities (lymphocytes are white blood cells involved in immune system response), protein abnormalities, antibodies to the patient's own tissues (autoantibodies) including antibodies to brain tissue, and increased levels of the immune-system regulators, called cytokines, in some people with bipolar disorder or schizophrenia. Some researchers have also found viruses or antibodies to viruses in the blood or brain tissue of people with mental illnesses. The discovery that lithium and some other psychiatric medications have antiviral properties has also intrigued researchers.

Viral infection could result in brain lesions or structural changes in the brain that cause bipolar symptoms, or it could have other effects on the nervous system. A virus may affect the use or production of certain neurotransmitters, for example, or it might impact the immune system in ways that cause psychiatric symptoms. The actual infection may occur before birth, which would help to explain the slightly higher number of minor birth defects seen in people with mental illnesses. Many viruses can lay dormant in the human brain or other tissue for years, emerging only when some other insult to the immune system (such as extreme stress or infection with another illness) sets them off.[7]

The re-emergence of viral theories of bipolar disorders doesn't mean that researchers are throwing out their genetic theories—the two ideas are actually complementary. It's now known that susceptibility to damage from viruses, and particular types of unusual immune responses to infection, are very much genetically linked.

Some of the most interesting work on viruses and bipolar disorders is being done at the Stanley Foundation Neurovirology Laboratory (*http://www.med.jhu.edu/stanleylab/*) at Johns Hopkins University's School of Medicine. Using cells from the brains of deceased people with either schizophrenia or bipolar disorders, researchers at this lab have identified the telltale signs of infection with a virus that seems to be from the paramyxovirus family. They've also found evidence of retroviral activity.[8]

So how can you find out if a virus is part of your child's problems, and what can be done to help? Few psychiatrists treating bipolar patients are aware of potential viral angles. Your best bet may be an alternative practitioner who has a strong understanding of how to support and enhance the immune system with vitamins, supplements, diet, and in some cases prescription medications. If you don't have an actual neuroimmunity specialist in your area, you might ask around for an alternative practitioner who works with some patients who have AIDS, multiple sclerosis, or other conditions that combine viral activity with neurological symptoms. He should be familiar with the major therapies, and hopefully will be able to tailor a program for your child's specific case.

There are medical tests available that can help to identify immune system impairments and/or viral activity. These include:

- **Blood count.** A low white blood cell count can indicate that there is a virus or other infection active somewhere in the body.

- **Sedimentation rate.** This test measures how quickly the red cells separate from the serum in a test tube. In most inflammatory or autoimmune diseases, they separate quickly, although unusually slow separation could also indicate trouble.

- **Immune panel test.** This general screen may include a search for antibodies, mitogen, antigen, and lymphocyte surface markers, and blood tests for various specific immune-dysfunction markers.

- **Antineuronal antibody (ANA) screen.** The ANA looks for antibodies to brain tissue in the bloodstream. Their presence is a general indicator for a variety of autoimmune disorders, such as lupus. Note that the antinuclear antibody test, also abbreviated as ANA, may also be ordered. This test is part of the screening procedure for several autoimmune inflammatory diseases.

- **Specific viral antibodies tests.** There are tests that look for unusual levels of specific viral antibodies, such as those associated with the Epstein-Barr virus, other human herpes viruses (HHV6, HHV7, HHV8, HSV-1, HSV-2), chronic mononucleosis syndrome (CMS), cytomegalovirus (CMV), or rubella (German measles).

- **Immunoglobulin G (IgG) subclass abnormalities tests.** There are tests to check for IgG subclass abnormalities (IgG1, IgG2, IgG3, IgG4), which are found in patients with increased susceptibility to viral or bacterial infections due to a compromised immune system, autoimmune diseases, or immune-mediated neurological disorders. It's possible to plot the distributions of IgG subtypes against patterns associated with specific viruses or conditions.

- **Amino acid profile.** Markers for an impaired immune system include low amounts of the amino acids lysine and arginine.

- NeuroSPECT. This brain scan shows the diffusion of blood through the brain, indicating areas of low and high activity.

A multifaceted immune panel can turn up many small pieces of evidence that, taken together, indicate a compromised immune system.

If you find viral activity or immune system problems, there are many possible treatments. Many alternative practitioners rely on vitamins and supplements that are believed to boost the immune system.

AIDS research has resulted in new medications that could be called immune system stimulants or immune system modulators. The majority of these drugs have side effects that make them undesirable for use except for patients faced with a life-threatening immune deficiency. Others may deserve a trial for treating immune-system-linked bipolar disorders. As the saying goes, "your mileage may vary" with these medications and supplements.

A few of the immune modulators are:

- **Kutapressin.** A porcine liver extract comprised of very small proteins or polypeptides. Kutapressin inhibits human herpes viruses (its best-known use is as a medication for herpes zoster, or shingles) and reduces inflammation. It is given in intramuscular injections, can be rather expensive since the supply is currently limited, and may not be a long-term solution for herpes infection.

- **Dimethylglycine (DMG).** A vitamin-like supplement that appears to give a mild boost to the immune system, possibly by boosting the number of natural killer (NK) cells.

- **Inosine pranobex (Isoprinosine).** An older antiviral that is also active against human herpes virus and other infections. It is a relatively weak immune modulator.

- **Acyclovir (Zovirax).** A potent antiviral that works against several human herpes viruses, Epstein-Barr virus, herpes zoster, varicella (chicken pox), cytomegalovirus, and other viruses.

- **Foscarnet.** Another anti-herpes drug (unfortunately, rather toxic).

- **Ampligen.** A nucleic acid compound that apparently heightens production of the body's own immunological and antiviral agents, such as interferon. It is expensive, administered via intravenous infusion, and not available to all patients or in all countries.

- SSRIs. May affect neurotransmitters in ways that not only address depression and other neurological disorders, but that directly or indirectly regulate the immune system. When used for this purpose, they are often given at very low doses. Lithium also appears to have antiviral action.

For some kinds of virulent infections, intravenous immunoglobulin G (IVIG) or plasmapheresis may even be suggested. These invasive procedures involve cleansing and replacing blood components.

Evaluating supplements

Once upon a time, only the health nuts crowed about the virtues of herbs from the Peruvian rain forest or multivitamin bars. Now soft drinks are spiked with St. John's wort and gingko biloba, and One-a-Day vitamins share a shelf with a One-a-Day herbal mood supporter.

> *My mom is always sending me articles she clips out of magazines about herbal remedies and how vitamins can cure everything. I'm curious, but nervous. I actually bought some grapeseed oil, but I still haven't opened it. I make sure [my daughter] takes her vitamins and that's about it. Maybe someday I'll try the grapeseed oil and see if it helps. At least it should be safer than some of the things she has been given by her doctor!*
> —Estella, mother of 8-year-old Selena (diagnosed bipolar II disorder)

Although the glossy, new veneer of today's supplements may make them look attractive, it's just as important to be a smart consumer in this area as it is with traditional medicine. Being well-informed can be more difficult, however. Medications with approval from the FDA or similar government bodies undergo rigorous testing. Study results and detailed information about these compounds are available in numerous books, online, or directly from the manufacturers.

With supplements, that's not always the case. It seems like every week another paperback book appears making wild claims for a new antioxidant compound or herbal medication. These books—not to mention magazine articles, web sites, and semi-informed friends—sometimes wrap conjecture up in a thin veneer of science. They may reference studies that are misinterpreted, that appeared in disreputable journals, or that were so poorly designed or biased that no journal would publish them.

Supplement salespeople, and particularly those who take part in multilevel marketing schemes, seem to have taken lessons from their predecessors in the days of the traveling medicine show. They have little to lose by making outrageous claims for their products, and much to gain financially. Here are just a few of the unsupported claims found in a single five-minute sweep of supplement-sales sites on the Internet:

- "Glutathione slows the aging clock, prevents disease and increases life."
- "Pycogenol...dramatically relieves ADD/ADHD, improves skin smoothness and elasticity, reduces prostate inflammation and other inflammatory conditions, reduces diabetic retinopathy and neuropathy, improves circulation and enhances cell vitality..." [and, according to this site, cures almost anything else that might ail you!]
- "Sage and bee pollen nourish the brain."
- "Soybean lecithin has been found to clean out veins and arteries—dissolve the gooey sludge cholesterol—and thus increase circulation, relieve heart, vein and artery problems. It has cured many diabetics—cured brain clots, strokes, paralyzed legs, hands and arms!"

Take the time to browse your local store's shelves, and you'll probably spot a number of dubious products. Some companies try to deceive you with sound-alike names, packaging that mimics other products, or suggestive names that hint at cures. Other colorful bottles of pills contain substances that can't actually be absorbed by the body in oral form—for example, "DNA" (deoxyribonucleic acid, the building block of human genetic material) graces the shelves of some shops. One manufacturer of this useless "supplement" claims that "it is the key element in the reprogramming and stimulation of lazy cells to avoid, improve, or correct problems in the respiratory, digestive, nervous, or glandular systems." This company notes that its "DNA" is extracted from fetal cells; other brands are apparently nothing but capsules of brewer's yeast.

Some other supplements provide end products of internal procedures, such as glutathione, instead of the precursors needed for the body to make a sufficient supply on its own, such as vitamin E. This approach may not work. When in doubt, consult with your doctor or a competent nutritionist.

How can you assess supplement claims? Start by relying primarily on reputable reference books for your basic information, rather than on advertisements or the popular press. Watch out for any product whose salespeople claim it will cure anything. Supplements and vitamins may enhance health and promote wellness, but they rarely effect cures. Be wary of universal usefulness claims. The worst offenders in supplement advertising tout their wares as cure-alls for a multitude of unrelated conditions.

There are a few other sales pitches that should make you wary. If a product's literature references the myth of the long-lived Hunzas, someone's trying to pull the wool over your eyes. This tale of hardy Russian mountain folk who supposedly all live to be well over one hundred years old was refuted long ago by reputable researchers. If it's a natural substance but a particular company claims to be the only one to know the secret of its usefulness, that really doesn't make much sense. Be especially cautious when sales pitches are written in pseudoscientific language that doesn't hold up under close examination with a dictionary. This is a popular ploy. For example, one supplement sold by multilevel marketers claims to "support cellular communication through a dietary supplement of monosaccharides needed for glycoconjugate synthesis." Translated into plain English, this product is a sugar pill.

Even when you have seen the science behind a vitamin or supplement treatment, there's still the problem of quality and purity. It's almost impossible for consumers to know for sure that a tablet or powder contains the substances advertised at the strength and purity promised. Whenever possible, do business with reputable manufacturers that back up their products with potency guarantees or standards. In many European countries, potency is governed by government standards; in the US, it's a matter of corporate choice.

Natural does not mean harmless. Whenever a vitamin or supplement is powerful enough to heal, it also has the power to harm if misused. Be sure to work closely with your physician or a nutritionist if your child will be taking anything more complex than a daily multivitamin.

Herbal remedies

Many herbs have been used to treat neurological disorders through the ages. Herbalists call these substances nervines, and some may prove useful for treating specific symptoms of bipolar disorders.

Of all the herbal remedies, this group of plant extracts are among the strongest, and the most likely to cause serious side effects. Along with the herbal sleep aids mentioned earlier in this chapter, nervines that have been tried by people with bipolar disorders or related conditions include:

- Black cohosh (Cimicifuga racemosa). A nervous system depressant and sedative, sometimes used by people with autoimmune conditions for its anti-inflammatory effects. Its active ingredient appears to bind to estrogen receptor sites, so it may cause hormonal activity.

- Damiana (Turnera aphrodisiaca). A traditional remedy for depression. As its Latin name indicates, it is also believed to have aphrodisiac properties. Whatever the case may be there, it does seem to act on the hormonal system. Its energizing quality might be dangerous for bipolar patients.

- Gingko biloba. An extract of the gingko tree, advertised as an herb that can improve your memory. There is some clinical evidence for this claim. It is an antioxidant, and is prescribed in Germany for treatment of dementia. It is believed to increase blood flow to the brain.

- Ginseng (Panax quinquefolium). Has an energizing effect that may be helpful to people whose depression is accompanied by extreme fatigue and lethargy.

- Grapeseed oil and pycogenol. Both are extra-powerful antioxidants. (Pycogenol is derived from marine pine trees.)

- Gotu kola (Centella asiatica, Hydrocotyl asiatica). An Ayurvedic herbal stimulant sometimes recommended for depression and anxiety.

- Licorice (Glycyrrhiza glabra, Liquiritia officinalis). Boosts hormone production, including hormones active in the digestive tract and brain.

- Sarsaparilla (Hemidesmus indicus). Like licorice, it seems to affect hormone production as well as settling the stomach and calming the nerves.

- St. John's wort (Hypericum perforatum). Has gained popularity as an herbal antidepressant. It has the backing of a decent amount of research, but as noted in Chapter 4, *Medical Interventions*, those choosing to use this remedy should follow the same precautions as with SSRIs and

MAOIs, two families of pharmaceutical antidepressants. It can also cause increased sensitivity to light. It is available by prescription in Germany, where it is the most widely used antidepressant. It is potentially dangerous to use St. John's wort with prescription antidepressants or any other medication that could affect serotonin.

The only herbal remedy I tried was St. Johns wort, and I saw no improvement in my mood. —Stephanie, age 32 (diagnosed with bipolar disorder at age 15 and now the mother of a bipolar child)

Vitamins

A varied, healthy diet is your best source of vitamins. Some researchers believe that people with bipolar disorders may metabolize certain vitamins differently, and therefore require either careful intake via food or supplementation.

If you plan to pursue vitamin therapies, purchase a basic guide to vitamins and minerals that includes information about toxicity symptoms. Some people metabolize vitamins and minerals differently, and may be more or less susceptible to potential toxic effects. Along with your doctor's guidance, a good reference book can help you avoid problems.

Also, take vitamin company sales pitches and dosage recommendations with a grain of salt. The testimonials these companies produce are intended to sell their products, not to help you develop a treatment plan. Consult a physician or a professional nutritionist who does not sell supplements for unbiased, individualized advice.

Vitamins often cited as important in mood regulation include the B vitamins. If you are deficient in any of the Bs, depression, anxiety, and fatigue can result. The B vitamins work together, so it's best to take a B-complex supplement that mixes them in proper proportions along with folic acid. The Bs have a generally energizing effect and help build up the immune system. Some alternative practitioners recommend vitamin B-12 shots for depressed patients. They don't always work, but sometimes they can have surprisingly quick mood-elevating effects. Because of that energizing effect, however, they may not be a good idea for those who are hypomanic or manic. B vitamins are used up more quickly when the body or mind is stressed, so supplementing during these times could have a preventive effect. A list of B vitamins follows:

- **Vitamin B-1 (Thiamin).** Alone, or in addition to a regular B-complex pill, B-1 might be a good idea for bipolar patients who suffer from circulation problems, tingling in the extremities, anxiety, irritability, night terrors, and similar symptoms.

- **Vitamin B-6 (Pyridoxine).** In addition to a regular B-complex pill, B-6 might be indicated for bipolar patients who present with a great deal of irritability, and for those with marked premenstrual symptoms and/or motion sickness. If you start to experience tingling in your hands or feet, reduce or discontinue the B-6.

- **Vitamin B-12.** Helps your body turn food into energy, and without enough of it you are likely to feel listless and fatigued. Vegetarians may also be deficient in B-12, as it's found mostly in meat.

- **Vitamin E.** An antioxidant that also seems to reduce the frequency of seizures in some people who have epilepsy. It's especially important to take vitamin E if you take Depakote, Depakene, or another anticonvulsant, as these drugs deplete vitamin E. If you have high blood pressure, monitor it carefully after starting vitamin E, and reduce the dose if your blood pressure rises.

Vitamins A and D are fat-soluble, so they are stored in the body's fat cells for later use. Having a little socked away for a rainy day is probably okay, but if you take too much, hypervitaminosis may develop.

Symptoms of hypervitaminosis A include orangeish, itchy skin; loss of appetite; increased fatigue; and hard, painful swellings on the arms, legs, or back of the head. Symptoms of hypervitaminosis D include hypercalcemia, osteoporosis, and kidney problems.

Don't overdo it with any fat-soluble vitamin, and also be careful with fish-oil supplements (and cod liver oil), which are high in both vitamins A and D.

Folic acid can counteract the effects of Depakote, Depakene, and some other anticonvulsants if taken in large amounts. It may also cause manic mood swings.

Minerals

Minerals are naturally occurring substances that are basic building blocks for cells and chemical processes in the body. Most of them are needed in relatively small amounts, amounts that are covered through the combination of a reasonably decent diet and a regular multivitamin with minerals.

Supplementing with specific minerals can be helpful for alleviating bipolar symptoms, however. Minerals that are sometimes suggested include:

- **Calcium.** Important for the regulation of impulses in the nervous system and for neurotransmitter production. If you supplement with magnesium, you should also take twice that amount of calcium—these two minerals need each other to work. However, excessive levels of calcium (hypocalcinuria) can result in stupor.

- **Chromium picolinate.** May help control the sugar and carbohydrate cravings that many patients experience while taking Depakote or Depakene. Chromium picolinate can act like a stimulant, however, so keep an eye out for this side effect.

- **Magnesium.** Lowers blood pressure, and is also important for the regulation of impulses in the nervous system and neurotransmitter production. Magnesium deficiency can cause anxiety and insomnia, and it can also lower your seizure threshold. This mineral is rapidly depleted during periods of stress, hard work, hot weather, or fever, and that's probably one of the reasons that these conditions can precipitate a seizure. If you are supplementing with vitamin B-6, you will need to add magnesium as well.

- **Manganese.** Deficiency is marked by fatigue, irritability, memory problems, and ringing or other noises in the ears. It is needed in trace amounts only, but some people's diets do not include enough.

- **Zinc.** Another trace mineral that's often absent from the diet. Symptoms of deficiency can include mental disturbance.

Nutritional supplements

If it's not an herb, vitamin, or mineral, you can simply call it a nutritional supplement. That means the manufacturer agrees not to market it as a drug, and the FDA agrees to consider it a food. Meanwhile, consumers are left unsure about whether these supplements provide nutrients (they usually don't), cure disease (rarely, if ever), or simply promote health.

The supplements category includes amino acids. There are 22 of these simple compounds, which combine to create all of the body's proteins. Most amino acids are produced by the body itself, but some people do report benefits from taking amino acid supplements. These may combine several amino acids, or include just one.

Along with the amino acids listed in the section "Other sleep supplements" earlier in this chapter, supplements that may be suggested for symptoms of bipolar disorders include:

- **Lecithin (phosphatidyl choline).** A phospholipid found mostly in high-fat foods. It is said to have the ability to improve memory and brain processes. Lecithin is necessary for normal brain development; however, double-blind studies of patients with Alzheimer's disease did not substantiate claims that it can help people recover lost brain function. The ketogenic diet increases the amount of lecithin in the body, which may be one of the reasons for its success in some cases of hard-to-treat epilepsy. Some people with epilepsy have also reported reducing their number and severity of seizures from taking lecithin alone.

  Some studies of lecithin-use by people with bipolar disorder indicate that it can stabilize mood, while others indicate that it tends to depress mood (and might therefore be more useful to a person who is manic or hypomanic). It does not appear to cause harm, and there are some logical reasons to think it might help—especially for patients who also have seizures. Lecithin capsules are available, but many people prefer the soft lecithin granules. These are a nice addition to fruit juice smoothies, adding a thicker texture. Lecithin is oil-based, and it gets rancid easily. It should be refrigerated.

- **Choline.** One of the active ingredients in lecithin. It is needed by the brain for processes related to memory, learning, and mental alertness, as well as for the manufacture of cell membranes and the neurotransmitter acetylcholine. Acetylcholine is involved in emotional control and other regulatory functions. Its effectiveness for bipolar symptoms is unknown.

- **Inosital.** Another active ingredient in lecithin. It is required by the neurotransmitters serotonin and acetylcholine, and may repair some types of nerve damage. Clinical studies indicate that inositol supplements may be helpful for some people with obsessive-compulsive disorder, depression, and panic disorder. Its effectiveness for bipolar symptoms is unknown.

- **Taurine.** An amino acid that appears to have antiseizure capabilities, and has gotten good reviews from some adults with bipolar disorders. It inhibits abnormal electrical activity in the brain, and is often found to be deficient in brain tissue where seizures have been occurring. Interestingly, rapid cyclers report the best results. Recommendations range from 500 to 1000 mg per day, divided into as many as three doses. Experts recommend buying only pharmaceutical-quality L-taurine from reputable manufacturers. Unusual EEG activity has been reported in patients using doses over 1000 mg per day.

- **GABA (gaba-amino butyric acid).** An amino acid-like compound that acts like a neurotransmitter by inhibiting other neurotransmitters. A number of medications are under development that would affect GABA production or usage; some existing drugs that affect GABA, such as Gabapentin and Depakote, are used to treat manic depression. You should not take these medications with GABA supplements unless your physician recommends it and oversees the process. Supplementation with over-the-counter GABA is sometimes recommended for anxiety, nervous tension, and insomnia, especially insomnia associated with racing thoughts. If you experience shortness of breath, or tingling or numbness in your hands or feet when taking GABA, lower or discontinue this supplement.

- **Tyrosine.** An amino acid that serves as a precursor to the neurotransmitters norepinephrine and dopamine. It may help the body form more of these neurotransmitters, and is also believed to provide support for optimal thyroid gland function. Tyrosine can raise blood pressure, so talk to your child's doctor about using it if your child takes other medications that affect blood pressure.

- **Phenylalanine.** An essential amino acid, as well as the precursor of tyrosine. It has an indirect effect of boosting production of norepinephrine and dopamine. Like tyrosine, phenylalanine can raise blood pressure.

- **Methionine.** An antioxidant amino acid that has been shown to be helpful for some individuals suffering from depression. It has an energizing effect—and as with SAMe, below, that could precipitate mania in bipolar patients.

- **SAMe (S-adenosyl-methionine).** A metabolite of methionine that is used to treat depression and arthritis in Europe. It became available in the US in early 1999. It is believed to affect dopamine and serotonin, and to have anti-inflammatory effects. However, it is not recommended for people with bipolar disorder, as it may cause mania.

Stress-busters

Being bipolar always brings with it the unwanted baggage of stress. When you're manic, your body and mind are being pushed to their very limits. When you're depressed, just going through the motions can be intensely stressful. And even when you're well there's the stress of dealing with the mess you made during your last episode of illness, and of worrying about what will happen next.

Every young person with bipolar disorder can benefit from knowing many ways to beat back stress. What works will depend on the individual, his state of mind, and the situation. It's not enough to say "just relax." If your child is totally stressed out, he needs to have a plan to follow or it will seem like a hopeless task.

Perhaps the oldest stress-busters are meditation, prayer, and breathing exercises. These simple activities, either alone or in various combinations, relax the body and the mind simultaneously. To some young people, they seem hopelessly hokey, of course.

There are many different schools of meditation, and types of prayer or contemplative thought have been developed over the centuries that can fit any individual, of any religion (or none), in any situation. For example, yoga offers many relaxation techniques that combine physical movements, special breathing patterns, and mental exercises. Working with a well-trained instructor can help your child master whichever technique interests him most.

Breathing exercises can actually reduce the sensation of pain, gradually help agitation to subside, and even lower a racing heartbeat, as any woman who has tried Lamaze breathing during childbirth can tell you. One technique that works during anxiety or panic is sometimes called candle breathing. You breathe in through your nose in short bursts, and breathe out forcefully, as if blowing out a stubborn candle a couple of feet away. Done repeatedly, this usually has a calming effect.

Hyperventilation is a common side effect of extreme mania, anxiety, and panic. It increases all the most unpleasant aspects of those states, can make a person pass out, and can even mimic the physical sensation of a mild heart attack if you are unaware that you are hyperventilating.

A hyperventilating person takes sharp, short, ragged breaths uncontrollably. Her whole body may seem to be wracked by the effort of this forced breathing. To stop the process, have her breathe into a small paper bag. As less oxygen comes in, her breathing process will slow down and become more regular until the episode of hyperventilation ends.

Sensory integration techniques (see Chapter 5, *Therapeutic Interventions*) can be very effective as well, especially for young children and for people who are too agitated to exercise much self-control. Parents report that slow, deliberate pressure on the head and joint compression are calming activities for some bipolar children. Others may respond better to more traditional massage.

Of course, hugging and holding your child can reduce his stress. Some children do well in a tight hug. They may struggle a bit, and then relax with obvious relief. For others, being unable to get away would be intensely uncomfortable and only increase their stress. You know your child best, and can decide whether hug therapy is likely to be effective.

Especially for older children and teenagers, exercise is a great stress-fighter. Help your child find a type of exercise that seems to meet his needs when he's overstressed or feeling the first twinges of mania. Running, which produces certain endorphins and depletes others, is a favorite strategy for many bipolar adults. You may have to run along with your child to ensure his safety, however. Bicycling, aerobics, racquet sports, and jumping on a trampoline are other high-energy activities that may help take the edge off.

> It was the day before I had two final exams to take at the university I was attending, when I felt a manic episode coming on. I was very irritable and unable to concentrate on my studying. I took my basketball and went down to a local park that had some courts. I started shooting baskets, and then some people showed up and I ended up playing basketball until dusk. When I got home I was a little tired and able to study each subject for an hour or two. I took the exams the next day and ended up getting As on both of them.

The best therapy for me when I'm really depressed is to take a long walk and then write in my journal. —Troy, age 30 (diagnosed bipolar I disorder at age 17)

If you're stuck indoors, calisthenics, stair climbing, or using a stationary bicycle or treadmill can also work well.

Social skills instruction

Social skills instruction is needed by every child, although direct lessons are rarely given. Most children pick up the rules by osmosis: they observe what others do, and respond to the praise and social responses they get for appropriate behavior by repeating that behavior. That's how skills are built during early childhood and beyond.

But what about the child whose behavior is sometimes beyond his control due to mania or depression? Important social skills may be missed while he is unwell or unable to socialize due to absences from school or hospitalization, or he may learn only some of what he needs to know. These children find that they are not sure how to make friends or how to act in a variety of social situations. Although they may be able to cover up their faux pas with verbal skills, every misstep can be another blow to their self-esteem.

Social skills work may actually be harder today than it was 50 years ago, despite everything we've learned about behavior and human development. The rules of society are in flux everywhere, and children may not see the lessons of the home or classroom reinforced in everyday life. Interestingly, school district officials often comment that the most well-behaved children they meet when visiting schools are in the special education classes, where standards are explicitly spelled out and enforced for all students.

Parents of young bipolar children can take a page from the special education teacher's rulebook. That means rehearsing social interactions in advance, deliberately pointing out social skills lessons in children's books and movies (and seeking out materials that reinforce these lessons), and being as explicit as possible about appropriate social behavior.

Do your best to keep it positive. Bipolar kids seem to enjoy butting heads with the rules, but when they see the advantage of compliance, they can be motivated.

Social stories

A tactic called "social stories" can help young children handle potentially stressful social situations. Originally developed by educator Carol Gray, social stories are a written way to rehearse expected or desired social behavior. They provide the child with a narrative about events that are going to happen, or that should happen. They are short, easy to remember, and can be told over and over to help the child internalize what's expected. Here's a sample of a social story:

James Is a Good Bus Rider

When James gets ready for school in the morning, he has his coat and backpack nearby before the school bus arrives.

When the bus comes, he gives his mom a hug and gets on the bus right away.

James sits in the seat right behind the driver as soon as he gets on the bus. He puts on his seat belt. Then he puts his backpack on his lap.

Sometimes James talks to his friends when he is riding the bus. They talk quietly.

Sometimes James draws pictures or looks at a book when he is riding the bus. He makes sure that his paper, crayons, and books are in his backpack when the bus gets to school.

If someone bothers James on the bus, he can ask the bus driver for help.

When the bus gets to school, James is the first to get off the bus. He waits with Mr. Smith until all of the children have gotten off the bus, and then they walk to class in a line.

You'll notice that this story is about all the good things that James does, or should do, on the bus. It isn't a list of don'ts, no matter how tempting it might be to add a line like "James doesn't hit or bite the other children on the bus."

Some parents and teachers like to set social stories to music, which can make them more fun and easier to remember. Others have made them into picture books with illustrations or photographs. For example, James might be asked to act out his bus social story while a teacher or parent takes some instant photos. Then the book can be written out with one line and one photo per page.

Thick paper and lamination can be used to protect social stories that children want to carry with them.

Social skills groups

Some schools and mental health clinics are starting to sponsor social skills training groups. This potentially powerful strategy brings together several children in a friendship club under the direction of an adult. Each session is structured with different types of social interactions—all of them as fun as possible. The activities are intended to teach and model specific social skills.

A one-hour group might start with a brief circle time for introductions and passing out the day's agenda, then move on to a cooperative game or a craft activity. Then the participants could serve each other a snack, clean up, and enjoy another activity. At the end, they could discuss how everything went, and perhaps choose the next week's activity and snack. It's not unlike a Scout meeting, except that the adult in charge has some special training and purposes in mind.

Some social skills groups are for students with social skills deficits only, while others mix them in with peers whose skills are more developed.

The healing power of humor

As the movie *Patch Adams* reiterated, humor can be a powerful healing force. It lifts the spirits of people who are depressed, and can gently show those whose thinking has become disordered how to get back on track.

> The best thing I've found for defusing [violent] obsessions has been humor. When the thoughts got terrifically gory, Bobby and I would imagine adding humorous bits to the scenes. Together we have designed weapons of mass destruction, such as a slingshot loaded with peanut-butter coated marshmallows. It helped to take the edge off the obsession, and allowed it to wither away. —Tracy, mother of 11-year-old Bobby (diagnosed bipolar I disorder and Tourette syndrome)

Humor sloughs off the cruel remarks and taunts of other children, and makes possible an offbeat perspective on things that could otherwise be overwhelming, like hospitalization and having to take psychiatric medication. With an intact sense of humor, your child can better withstand what his health and the world throw at him without giving in to despair.

CHAPTER 7

Insurance

MENTAL HEALTH CARE can be difficult to get and manage, not to mention expensive. Many medical insurance plans don't cover anything more than prescription medication, while others give mental health care second-class status or make it hard to access.

You don't have to have health insurance for this chapter to be useful. We'll cover private insurance, including health maintenance organizations (HMOs) and other forms of managed care, public health insurance plans, and alternatives to health insurance as well. We'll describe typical insurance roadblocks, and show you how to get around them. We'll begin by talking about health insurance in the US, but the systems of other English-speaking countries are also addressed.

And because public assistance in the US and some other countries is closely tied to eligibility for public health benefits, we'll also cover SSI disability income and other welfare benefits that may be available to families with disabled children.

Private insurance: The American way

In the US and other countries where private medical insurance is the norm, the system can be hard to deal with under the best of circumstances. Each insurance company offers multiple plans with various rates and benefits, and there's no central oversight. As a result, a child's mental health diagnosis can come with an unpleasant surprise: the healthcare services she needs aren't covered, even though you have paid your insurance premiums. Some insurance plans specifically refuse to cover any mental or neurological disorder, and in many cases it's legal for insurers to make that choice.

Other companies cover mental health care in a substandard way. For example, the company may cover only short-term therapy programs; it may have no qualified in-plan practitioners but refuse to make outside referrals; or it may limit your child to a certain number of outpatient visits or inpatient hospital days each year, regardless of what he actually needs.

Making insurance choices

Whenever you are in the position of choosing a new insurance plan, try to find out in advance what its attitude is about treatment for mental illness. You may be surprised at what you learn.

Your best bet is a plan that has an out-of-network clause. These plans allow you choose your own providers if you can't find the right professional on its list of preferred providers or HMO members. You will generally pay more for out-of-plan visits, but you also won't have to run the referral gauntlet as often. The cost of using these providers regularly, such as for weekly therapy visits, may be more than your budget will bear.

> We have Tricare [the federal insurance plan for US military personnel], formerly known as Champus. Anyone who thinks the military is great obviously is not in it. We can get no mental health benefits for my son at the Army hospital, which is supposed to be a major medical facility, and it costs us a $20 co-pay for every visit on the outside. If inpatient is allowed, we have to pay $20 a day. That may not sound like a lot to some people, but for someone on a very limited budget as we are, the money is just not there. — Cindy, mother of 16-year-old Nathan (diagnosed bipolar I disorder, OCD, ADHD, post-traumatic stress disorder, chemical dependency, bulimia)

The most difficult companies to deal with are usually those that contract with a so-called carve-out for mental health care. These plans do not provide any mental health care themselves, but instead refer patients to outside providers. Sometimes these outside programs are very good. Unfortunately, patients can end up feeling like a ping-pong ball as they are bounced between their major medical carrier and the mental health program, substance abuse program, and other cut-outs. Your insurer or HMO, your medical care facility, and your outside provider may argue with each other about what kind of treatment is needed, who should deliver it, and who will pay for it. Meanwhile, your child may go without appropriate care.

One would think that integrated HMOs would do a better job. These are companies that provide both mental and physical care in the same plan, and sometimes at the same site. Some do, but not all. Even within a single company there can be turf wars, payment disputes, and outright denial of services.

If your employer does not offer insurance that covers mental health care, out-of-network providers, or other needed services, take up the issue with the human resources department (or, in small companies, the boss). When the cost is spread over a group, these additional benefits may not be very expensive. You can also make a very persuasive case that providing mental health benefits will keep employees on the job more days, because they will be less likely to need hospitalization or long periods off work for their own mental health issues, nor will they be as likely to take time off to care for a mentally ill child.

Insurance for families or individuals affected by any long-term disability is very hard to get in the private market (i.e., without going through an employer). It's available, but premium costs can be extraordinarily high. If you are leaving a job that provides you with health insurance for one that does not, pursue a COBRA plan. These plans allow you to continue your coverage after leaving employment. You will pay the full rate, including the contribution previously made by your employer, but it will still be less than what you'd pay as an individual customer.

Maintaining continuous health insurance coverage is critical to prevent being locked out of healthcare by preexisting conditions. If a COBRA plan is not available, other lower-cost possibilities include group plans offered by trade associations, unions, clubs, and other organizations. You may also want to look into public health insurance options, which are discussed later in this chapter.

The appendix, *Resources*, lists several books and publications that can help you in your quest to secure insurance coverage and appropriate healthcare services for a person with a disability. For managed care issues, the National Coalition of Mental Health Professionals and Consumers maintains a useful (if opinionated) web site (*http://www.NoManagedCare.org/*).

Managing managed care

Managed care, the dominant trend in today's medical world, ought to be consumer-friendly. In most HMOs and other managed care entities, providers and provider groups earn more if their patients stay healthy. An emphasis on preventive care and timely intervention can definitely benefit the greatest number patients. Patients with long-term disabilities, however, may be perceived as obstacles in the way of profits.

There are four basic rules for managing your insurance affairs, whether you're dealing with an HMO, another type of managed care organization, an old-style fee for service arrangement, or a public health agency. Following these steps can help you be more secure when dealing with care providers and insurers:

- Make yourself knowledgeable
- Document everything
- Make your providers into allies
- Appeal

Make yourself knowledgeable

Informed insurance consumers are a rarity. Most people look at the glossy plan brochure and the provider list, but unless something goes wrong, that's about as much as they want to know. For parents of bipolar children, that's not going to be enough. You'll need a copy of the firm's master policy, which specifies what is and isn't covered.

To get this hefty document, call your employer's human resources office (for employer-provided insurance or COBRA plans administered by a former employer) or the insurance company's customer relations office (for health insurance that you buy directly from the insurer). Read it. It will be tough going, but the results will be worthwhile.

If you need help interpreting this document, disability advocacy organizations and related sites on the Web can help.

Find out in detail what the chain of command is for your provider group and insurer. You'll need to know exactly whom to call and what to do if your child needs a referral to a specialist, partial or full hospitalization, or emergency services during a mental health crisis.

Document everything

You will want to keep copies of all your bills, reports, evaluations, test results, and other medical records. You'll also want to keep records of when and how your insurance payments were made. This information will be essential if you have a dispute with your healthcare provider or insurer.

You'll also need to document personal conversations and phone calls. You needn't tape-record these, although if a dispute has already begun this can be a good idea (make sure to let the other party know that you are recording, of course). Simply note the date and time of your call or conversation, whom you spoke with, and what was said or decided. If a service or treatment is promised in a phone conversation, it can be a good idea to send a letter documenting the conversation. For example:

> *Dear Dr. Lawrence:*
>
> *When we spoke on Tuesday, you promised to authorize a referral to Dr. Martin at the Child Neurology Center for Jenny's sleep-deprived EEG and neurological exam. Please fax a copy of the referral form to me at xxx-xxxx when it is finished. Thanks again for your help.*

Referral forms are especially important. Most managed care firms send a copy to both the patient and the provider. This document usually has a referral number on it. Be sure to bring your referral form when you first see a new provider. If the provider has not received his or her copy of the form, your copy and the referral number can ensure that you'll still be seen, and that payment can be processed. Without it, you may be turned away.

Make your providers into allies

Money is a motivator for doctors and other healthcare providers, but most of them also care about helping their patients. Your providers are the most powerful allies you have. Give them additional information about bipolar disorders if they need it, and make sure they know you and your child's case well. Let them know how important their help is. They have the power to write referrals, to recommend and approve treatments, and to advocate on your behalf within the managed care organization.

> *Thank God for our insurance coverage! I pay ten dollars a visit for up to twenty visits without precertification. Beyond that she will have to be precertified. Our doctors think that will be no problem, as she would likely end up inpatient if she was not seeing them regularly. They think the insurance company will pay for many weekly visits to avoid paying for a day treatment or inpatient program. — Stephanie, mother of 7-year-old Cassidy (diagnosed bipolar disorder, Tourette syndrome, OCD, ADHD)*

Don't rely on your providers completely, however. They have many patients, some of whose needs will likely take precedence over yours. A life-or-death emergency or a large caseload may cause paperwork or meetings on your behalf to be overlooked temporarily or even forgotten.

Another staff member, such as a nurse or office assistant, may be able to keep your provider on track, but you will have to be persistently involved as well. Make sure that you return calls, provide accurate information, and keep the provider's needs in mind. For example, if you have information you want to give to your doctor about a new treatment, summarize it on one page, and attach the relevant studies or journal articles. The doctor can then quickly scan the basics in her office, and read the rest when time permits.

Appeal

Would you believe that 70 percent of insurance coverage and claims denials are never appealed? It's true. Most healthcare consumers are so discouraged by the initial denial that they don't pursue it further.

However, all insurance companies and managed care entities have an internal appeals process, and it is worth your while to be part of the persistent 30 percent. The appeals process should be explained in the master plan. If it is not, call the insurance company's customer service office or your employer's human resources department for information.

A grievance or appeal is not the same thing as a complaint. Companies can ignore complaints at their leisure, as they do not require a legal response. Grievances and appeals do have legal status, and healthcare consumers are entitled to have matters presented in this way addressed. Grievances should be made in writing, and clearly marked "grievance" at the top of the document.

When you file a formal grievance, the managed care entity will convene a grievance committee made up of people not involved in your problem. This committee will meet to consider the matter, usually within 30 days of receiving your written complaint. Particularly in HMOs, where the committee is usually made up mostly of physicians, your medical arguments may fall upon receptive ears.

It's unlikely that you will be personally present at an insurance company or HMO appeal. You can send written material to support your appeal, such as medical studies that support your position. It's best if your physician or care provider will also write a letter of support, explaining why they support your request for a specific service.

Some companies have more than one level of grievance resolution, so if you are denied at first, ask if you can appeal the committee's decision to a higher body. You may have the right to appear in person at this higher-level hearing, to bring an outside representative (such as a disability advocate, outside medical expert, or healthcare lawyer), and to question the medical practitioners involved. In other words, if a second-level procedure is available, it will be more like a trial or arbitration hearing than an informal discussion.

If you are still denied, you may be able to pursue the matter with your state's Department of Health or Insurance Commission. If your managed care plan is part of a public insurance program (for example, if you receive state medical benefits and have been required to join an HMO to receive care), you may also have an appeals avenue through a state agency, such as your county AFDC office.

Semi-sneaky tips

Some people are better at managing managed care than others. The following suggestions may be a little shady, but they have worked for certain managed care customers:

- Subvert voicemail and phone queues. If you are continually routed into a voicemail system and your calls are never returned, or if you are left on hold forever, don't passively accept it. Start punching buttons when you are stuck in voicemail or on hold, in hope of reaching a real person. If you get an operator, ask for administration (claims and marketing never seem to have enough people to answer the phone). Nicely ask the operator to transfer you directly to an appropriate person who can help, not to the department in general. The old "gosh, I just keep getting lost and cut off in your phone system" ploy may do the trick.

- Whenever you speak to someone at your HMO, especially if it's a claims representative, ask for her full name and direct phone number. It will make her feel more accountable for resolving your problem, because she knows you'll call her back directly if she doesn't.

- If you can't get help from a claims or customer service representative, ask for his supervisor. If you're told that he isn't available, get the supervisor's full name, direct phone line, and mailing address. Simply asking for this information sometimes makes missing supervisors magically appear.

- Use humor when you can. It defuses situations that are starting to get ugly, and humanizes you to distant healthcare company employees.

- Be ready to explain why your request is urgent, and to do so in terms that non-doctors can understand. For example, if receiving a certain treatment now could mean avoiding expensive hospitalization later, that's an argument that even junior assistant accountants can comprehend.

- Whatever you do, stay calm. If you yell at managed care people, they'll dismiss you as a loony. That doesn't mean being unemotional. Sometimes you can successfully make a personal appeal. You can act confused instead of angry when you are denied assistance for no good reason. You may also want to make it clear that you're gathering information in a way that indicates legal action—for instance, asking how to spell names, and asking where official documents should be sent.

One bright spot in insurance company practice is a move toward integrated case management. PacifiCare, for example, is instituting a new program called the Assertive Case Management model that the company says will coordinate care with child protective services, social welfare agencies, the school system, parents, clergy, social workers, and others. This model will include weekly contact between patient or parent and a permanent case manager.

If this kind of case-management system is implemented by many insurers, it should help families obtain more consistent care. That will prevent relapses and reduce the number of mental health crises and hospitalizations, saving both insurers and families a great deal of money.

Fighting denial of care

Refusal of appropriate mental health care is the top insurance complaint voiced by parents of bipolar children. You can fight denial of care, but it isn't easy. Begin by asking the insurance company's claims department for a written copy of the denial of coverage or services. Make sure that the reason you were given verbally is also the reason given in this document.

Your next stop is the insurance company's own documents. Somewhere in the fine print of the master policy that you should already have in your files, you will probably find a provision stating that if any of the company's policies are unenforceable based on state law, they cannot be asserted. Most insurance company claims adjusters know very little about state insurance law. Your job is to educate yourself, and then educate them.

Now you need to find out what your state says about coverage for mental illness in general, and about bipolar disorders in particular. The answer may be found in actual legislation. For example, California's state legislature has specifically declared that as illnesses with organic causes, bipolar disorder, schizophrenia, and many other mental illnesses are to be considered medical conditions under the law. Your state may have similar laws or public policies on the books. State mental health parity laws and laws protecting the disabled against discrimination may also have bearing.

Your state's insurance commission—every state has its own, there's no federal insurance commission—will also have policies about mental health coverage. Remember, actual state law trumps state policy statements every time. State laws may be more restrictive than federal regulations, in which case the state prevails. If state laws are less restrictive than federal mandates, the federal government prevails.

Your state's National Alliance for the Mentally Ill (NAMI) chapter will probably already have the information you need on hand, and the national NAMI office also collects information on state insurance laws. If no one seems to know the status of insurance law and bipolar disorders in your state, you'll have to start researching on your own. If you have Internet access, state laws, some public policies, and possibly insurance commission decisions may be available online. You could also call your state representative's office and ask a staff member to research this issue for you. Insurance commission staff members should also be able to help you.

If you can show your insurance company that it is trying to assert a provision that violates a state or federal law, it should back down and provide treatment. Legal arguments of the sort needed to secure coverage can be hard for a layperson to craft. Advocacy groups may be able to help you write a well-written and persuasive letter of appeal on legal grounds. Some families have even gotten their state representative or a member of Congress to intervene on their behalf, especially if the problem involves a public insurance program or facility.

Formal arbitration is another possibility, although experienced advocates warn that since arbitrators are paid by the healthcare plans, it's a tough arena for consumers. Consumers can't recover their legal costs in arbitration, which can range upwards of $50,000. Most consumer-law cases in the courts are taken by lawyers who work on contingency, so it's hard to secure legal help for an arbitration.

Which brings us to the issue of taking your insurance company to court. This is something that you should consider only as a last resort. It's expensive, and it takes so long for a decision to come down and then be implemented that your child is likely to reach adulthood before the process is over. If you have the means and the gumption, don't be dissuaded from making things better for the rest of us. Just don't pin all your hopes on a quick resolution by a judge. If only it was that easy!

Your best bet is to research the reason your insurance company or provider is denying care, and find persuasive evidence that can change its mind. The next sections cover three of the most typical reasons for refusal, and offer some suggestions.

Denial for plan limits

If your insurance company only provides treatment for bipolar disorders as part of a limited mental health or nervous disorders benefit, you can challenge that limitation. It's easy to show that bipolar disorders are biologically based, so you may be able to get out from under the mental health limit altogether.

> When Lili was admitted to the hospital, we just naturally assumed that it would be paid for. It wasn't. The very day that the hospital found out our insurance company was refusing to pay because it excluded all mental and neurological care, she was suddenly well enough to go home. Because our state permits these kinds of exclusions in individual insurance plans, we were left holding the bill. We refinanced our house to pay the majority of it off, but almost five years later we still owe $175 to a psychiatrist she saw for perhaps ten minutes. You can bet that our next insurance company's literature got a closer inspection. —Sarah, mother of 17-year-old Lili (diagnosed bipolar II disorder, OCD)

One piece of information to gather in advance is how the company treats acquired nervous-system disorders, such as stroke, brain tumors, or traumatic brain injuries. If your insurance covers long-term care for these conditions, most states mandate equal benefits for patients with biologically based brain disorders.

Incidentally, a neurologist may be your best witness. Many people with bipolar disorders have concrete signs of neurological dysfunction, which can't be written off as simply psychological.

Your child's psychiatrist can also help plead your case by showing the importance of the treatment he has recommended. He can explain its cost-effectiveness by showing the insurance company what the financial risk is of going without the treatment. Hospitalization, for example, is far more expensive than adequate therapy, medication, and case management.

And as noted previously, some states have laws that specifically exempt bipolar disorders from mental health limits.

Denial for educational services

After blanket denial of coverage or strict limits on mental health care, the second most frequent insurance roadblock is the educational services exclusion. This usually comes into play for services that may also be delivered by school districts, such as speech therapy, but many insurers try to force schools into paying for day treatment and residential programs for mentally ill children as well.

In all honesty, when the services provided are medical services, the school district should be able to bill your insurance for them. That's what you paid your premiums for! School districts, state healthcare programs, and the federal government are logical allies in the fight to force insurers to do their share. As long as insurers shirk their duty, families are forced to turn to overworked, underfunded taxpayer programs like Social Security disability, Medicaid, and the schools.

However, school districts only started to try billing parents' insurance for medical services provided in school settings at the end of the 1990s. Many parents rightfully fear that denial of payment will lead to denial of services by the school district—it is illegal, but lack of funds is one of the most frequent excuses given for refusal of needed special education services. Parents who have been persistent enough to get therapeutic services from both the school district and their insurance company are afraid that their services will be cut in half, not augmented. And since schools and medical facilities generally have very different approaches to therapeutic interventions, this could be detrimental in other ways. For example, the services of an MA-level school psychologist may or may not be equal to those of a psychologist your child could see through your HMO.

You can sometimes challenge denial of therapeutic services by explaining that speech or other therapeutic goals are essential activities of everyday life, useful not only in school but for functioning in the larger world. This "essential activities of everyday life" rationale is what people with orthopedic disabilities use to get the therapies they need covered by insurance.

It's important to note that schools can be required by special education law to provide certain types of medical and therapeutic services that make it possible for your child to learn. This will be discussed in Chapter 8, *School*. However, schools are not always the best or most knowledgeable of healthcare providers—after all, it's not their primary purpose. If you can get your child's school and his healthcare professionals to work together as a team, that will give him the best of both worlds.

Getting coverage for new treatments

All insurance plans bar coverage for experimental treatments. Some do have a "compassionate care" exception, which comes into play when regular treatments have been tried unsuccessfully and the plan's medical advisors agree that the experimental treatment could be workable. This exception is generally available only to people with life-threatening illnesses.

So what do you do to pay for promising new treatments for bipolar disorders, such as newly developed medications that aren't on your insurance company's approval list? You either pay out of pocket, or you work closely with your physician to get around the experimental treatment exclusion.

"Creative coding" is the term doctors use to describe billing the insurer or managed care entity for something that's not quite what was actually delivered. For example, a therapist might bill participation in a social skills training group, which the insurance company probably would not pay for, as something else that the insurer will pay for, such as an individual therapy session.

Creative coding is not exactly ethical, and it may not be desirable, either. Providers who do it take tremendous risks, and parents or patients for whom it is done must remember that they can't discuss these services with the rest of their healthcare team for fear of exposing the deception. That said, the practice seems to be increasingly common.

Another option is appealing to your insurer or HMO for special treatment. Your physician may have to prepare a letter of medical necessity to support your request—or this task may fall to you. This letter must include:

- The diagnosis for which the service, equipment, or medication is needed
- The specific symptom or function that the service, equipment, or medication will treat or help with
- A full description of the service, equipment, or medication and how it will help the patient
- If the service, equipment, or medication is new or experimental, evidence (medical studies, journal articles, etc.) to support your request
- If there are less expensive or traditionally used alternatives to the new or experimental service, equipment, or medication, well-supported reasons that these alternatives are not appropriate for this patient

Public healthcare in the US

Some US families have an extremely serious health insurance problem: they just can't get any. If this ever-growing group includes you, the main publicly funded option is Medicaid, with or without a Katie Beckett waiver (see the section "The Katie Beckett waiver," later in this chapter). The federal government also has the Tricare plan for those in current military service and their dependents and, through the Veterans Administration, coverage for former military personnel.

Medicaid

Medicaid is the federal health insurance program for those who are not senior citizens. It will pay for doctor and hospital bills; six prescription medications per month; physical, occupational, or speech therapy; and adaptive equipment. If you are old enough to receive regular Social Security, or if you receive Social Security survivor's benefits, your child should already be eligible for Medicaid. Otherwise you can get Medicaid coverage for your child by becoming eligible for SSI (see below) or, in some cases, by qualifying for state health plans for children that are based on Medicaid.

> I am on Social Security, and my daughter's care is court-ordered.
> Therefore, the state of Arizona pays for her care. —Sue, mother of 16-

year-old Vanessa (diagnosed bipolar I disorder, OCD, borderline person-
ality disorder, passive-aggressive personality disorder)

There is one more, drastic, way to get Medicaid: making your child a ward of the state by giving him up to the foster care system. Unfortunately, every year hundreds of families whose children are mentally ill must make this agonizing choice simply to ensure that their children can be admitted into a publicly funded residential facility, or even just to get them medical and mental health care. This means not only losing physical custody of your child in most cases, but also losing the right to be involved in decisions about his healthcare, education, and living conditions. In almost every case you will retain visitation rights and some role in treatment decisions—after all, you have not had your parental rights terminated by a judge due to abuse or neglect. You may be treated as if you did, however. Transferring parental rights is done in family court.

Medicaid is one of the few insurance plans that will pay for in-home ther-apy services, therapeutic foster care, partial hospitalization or day treatment, crisis services, and long-term hospitalization or residential care for people with mental illnesses. Although it is excessively bureaucratic, it is in many ways superior to private insurance coverage for people who have serious problems with mental illness.

SSI

Supplemental Security Income (SSI) is a related benefit. Disabled adults and children who qualify for SSI automatically qualify for healthcare coverage via Medicaid. SSI provides a small monthly stipend for people with serious health impairments and either low family income (for children or adults), or limited ability to earn a living (for adults). Benefits range from around $300 to $500 per month for children or for adults living in another person's household, to over $600 per month for teenagers or adults living indepen-dently. This money is only to be used for the direct needs of the disabled individual: it is not family income per se. You will need to keep receipts for all your child-related expenditures.

To remain eligible for SSI, your assets and income from other sources usu-ally must be limited. This can force parents desperate for Medicaid coverage for their children to spend down any savings and let their careers slide. It's a particularly unfair situation, since a stable home situation often depends on having enough money saved to permit flexibility during periods of crisis. Current SSI and AFDC regulations make it very hard for parents to provide a safety net for their families today, or to provide for their child's adult security later on (see Chapter 9, *Transitions*, for more on this topic).

To apply for SSI and/or Medicaid, go to your nearest Social Security office or call the Social Security hotline at (800) 772-1213 for a eligibility pre-screening. If you are given a green light by the eligibility screener, your next step is making an initial interview appointment and filling out a disability report (Form SSA-3820-BK) for your child. This eleven-page form asks dozens of difficult questions, including information about every physician or clinic that might have medical records or test results for your child, information about his school performance and academic testing, and information about your previous contacts with public health agencies. You'll want to provide copies of as many of your child's mental health records as you can.

If you need help in completing this form (and many families do), a county or school social worker may be able to assist you. Disability advocacy groups may also have staff members or volunteers who can assist you.

Make sure this form and all of your records are complete when your initial interview takes place. You can be interviewed in person or over the phone. Most experienced applicants say in-person interviews are best, but they aren't always possible. Careful record-keeping and having phone numbers and addresses for your doctors and school personnel handy are extra important if you choose a phone interview.

At the interview, the Social Security representative will go over the disability report with you. She may ask extra questions. Some of them may seem rather prying to people who have never applied for any type of government assistance.

In fact, the SSI application process has become increasingly adversarial over the past two decades. You may get the distinct impression that the people interviewing you think that you and your child are trying to con them—and your impression may be right. The Social Security department will order an Individualized Functional Assessment (IFA), which may mean a review of your medical documentation by Social Security representatives and/or interviews and observations of your child by a psychiatrist working for Social Security. You have the right to be present for this interview, although parents report that some doctors seem to want to exclude them from the process.

Most applicants for SSI are rejected on their first try. You do have the right to appeal SSI denial, however—and you should, because a high percentage of appeals succeed. In addition, successful appellants get a lump sum equal to the payments they should have received had their original application been properly approved. This sum can be several thousand dollars, and has helped many families fund things like more secure housing, special tutoring, and expert psychiatric care.

If your application for SSI is denied, contact a disability advocacy agency through the National Association of Protection and Advocacy Systems, listed later in this chapter. These publicly funded agencies can help you through the application process, and most can provide legal assistance if you need to appeal.

Additional information about the SSI program for children with disabilities is available online at *http://www.ssas.com/ssikids.html*.

The Katie Beckett waiver

SSI is usually an income-dependent program. If you are working and earn more than the regulations allow, your child will not be eligible for SSI. In some cases, family income will reduce the amount of SSI received to as low as one dollar per month, but the beneficiary will get full medical coverage. Other families must apply for a special income-limit waiver called the Katie Beckett waiver.

The waiver program is named for Katie Beckett, a severely handicapped child whose parents wanted to care for her at home. Government regulations would only cover Katie's care in an expensive hospital setting. Her family, which could not bear the full cost of at-home care but had an income too high to qualify for SSI, successfully lobbied for a program that would allow seriously handicapped children to qualify for Medicaid coverage.

The waiver program is administered at a state level. Some states have severely limited the number of Katie Beckett waivers they will allow. You must apply for SSI and be turned down to qualify. When you are denied SSI, ask for a written proof of denial. Next, contact your county Child and Family Services (CFS) department and ask for a Medicaid worker. Schedule an appointment with this person to apply for a Katie Beckett waiver.

This appointment will be long, and the questions will be intrusive, so be prepared. You will need copious documentation, including:

- Your SSI rejection letter

- Your child's birth certificate and Social Security number

- Proof of income (check stubs or a CFS form filled out and signed by your employer, and possibly income tax forms)

- Names, addresses, and phone numbers of all physicians who have examined your child

- Bank account and safety deposit box numbers, and amounts in these accounts

- List of other assets and their value, including your house and car

- A DMA6 medical report and a physician referral form signed by the doctor who knows your child best (CFS will provide you with these forms)

If you have a caseworker with your county's Mental Health offices, or if you regularly work with someone at a Regional Center or in an Early Intervention program, this person may be able to help you navigate the SSI, Medicaid, and Katie Beckett waiver process.

If you have specific problems with accessing appropriate medical benefits under Medicaid, state health plans, or other public healthcare plans, your caseworker or an advocate from NAMI or similar groups may be able to help. If your problems are of a legal nature, such as outright refusal of services or discrimination, call your state Bar Association and ask for its pro bono (free legal help) referral service, or contact the National Association of Protection and Advocacy Systems in Washington, DC, (202) 408-9514.

You can also consult the Health Law Project at (800) 274-3258.

State and local public health plans

As of this printing, twelve states have their own children's health insurance plan, and seventeen more have applied to the federal Department of Health and Human Services (DHHS) to start one. These plans are called State Children's Insurance Plans (SCHIP), and may offer uninsured children the same or similar benefits as Medicaid does.

Most state plans make innovative use of state funding combined with federal Medicaid payments. They are intended to cover low-income residents, residents with disabilities, and people who have been refused coverage due to preexisting conditions.

For updated information about state programs, see NAMI's special SCHIP site at *http://www.nami.org/youth/schip.htm*.

In some areas, city or county health programs are available that include access to mental health services.

> *During the first few years after my diagnosis, I used county mental health services. Given my low level of income, I didn't have to pay much money for these services and they were very good. I was able to see the same therapist every month to talk about everything I was going through while coping with the illness, and then a psychiatrist would come into the session for about five minutes to prescribe lithium to me and discuss anything related strictly to the medication. —Troy, age 30 (diagnosed bipolar I disorder at age 17)*

The problem with public health plans

Coverage is a fine thing, but what happens when no one will accept you as a patient? This is the situation faced by millions of Americans who have government-provided healthcare. You may find yourself limited to using county health clinics or public hospitals, and to those private providers who are willing to work for cut-rate fees. Medicaid and its cousins pay healthcare providers less than private insurers do, and there's no law that says a given provider must take patients with public insurance.

This means that facilities may be run-down, understaffed, and hectic. In fact, the emergency rooms of some public hospitals are downright frightening on weekend nights! Familiarize yourself with all of the options covered by your public healthcare plan. You may have more choices than you are initially led to believe. In some cases you may have the option to join one or more HMO plans, receiving the same benefits as non-subsidized HMO members. Check with other recipients or local advocacy groups if you are offered this choice—some of these plans do a good job of caring for disabled clients, while others are not preferable to plain old Medicaid or state healthcare.

Sadly, there is also an "anti-welfare" attitude abroad amongst some healthcare workers, who may not know or care what financial and medical troubles drove your family to need public healthcare or income help. You shouldn't have to tolerate substandard or unbusinesslike treatment from providers. If it happens, ask your caseworker about complaint options.

Other public assistance for disabled children

While Canada, all Western European nations, and many other countries provide family support allowances to encourage one parent to stay home with young children, the US government has cut support even to single parents, and provides extraordinarily low allowances when they are available. This policy affects the parents of children with disabilities particularly harshly.

> I had to stop work and go on welfare to get medications for Robert and myself because the cost is too high for a single parent. —Evelyn, mother of 14-year-old Robert (diagnosed bipolar I disorder and ADHD)

Between the 1950s and the 1980s, single, low-income parents of children with disabilities tended to receive Aid to Families with Dependent Children (AFDC, or "welfare") and SSI. When put together, income from these two programs permitted them to eke out a living. While they remained well below the poverty line, they could generally obtain housing and adequate food. For many of these families, the most important benefit of receiving public assistance was access to Medicaid, which came with AFDC as well as with SSI.

Welfare reform has changed this picture drastically. AFDC has been replaced by the Temporary Assistance for Needy Families (TANF) program, a system of short-term emergency supports. All states have now imposed stringent rules, such as limiting assistance to once in a lifetime, insisting that parents work for their grants, or forcing parents into job-training schemes geared toward a rapid transition to low-wage employment. Although most states have also added childcare services to their offerings to help parents receiving TANF grants transition to the workplace, affordable childcare slots for children and teens with mental illness are almost nonexistent. This leaves even the most determined low-income parent at a severe disadvantage.

Federal law permits exceptions to TANF regulations be made for some—but not all—parents caring for disabled children, and for parents who are themselves mentally ill. However, caseworkers are responsible for holding down the number of exemptions to 20 percent or less of their clients, even though as many as a third of families on welfare include either a mother or a child with a serious disability (see "Recent Studies of AFDC Recipients Estimate Need for Specialized Child Care" at http://www.welfare-policy.org/childdis.htm if you'd like to know more).

If you have a bipolar disorder or other handicap yourself and are parenting, TANF may work for you or against you. Some parents who have let their caseworker know about a personal mental problem have been exempted from certain regulations. Others have lost their children to the state. You should see a welfare rights organization or sympathetic social worker before making the decision to tell. They can help you ensure your children's security by approaching the issue correctly.

You can apply for TANF at your county's Child and Family Services department. The program is primarily for single parents, but two-parent families are eligible in some areas and under some circumstances. The amount of the monthly grant varies. It is determined by the county government, which administers TANF programs at the local level. Grants range from around $150 per month in some rural Southern counties to about $650 per month in expensive cities like San Francisco, where a small supplemental housing benefit is factored into the grant

You'll need to provide very complete documentation to get and retain benefits on the basis of needing to provide full-time home care for a child. You can expect to have an eligibility review at least every three months, during which all of your documents will be reviewed and you will be re-interviewed. Generally speaking, you cannot have savings or possessions worth over $1,000, although you may own a modest home and car. You may be forced to sell a late-model car and other valuables before you can receive benefits. Your AFDC grant may be reduced by the amount of other financial assistance you receive. If you find part-time work, your grant will also be reduced by this amount or a portion thereof—some states do have work incentive programs, however. Court-ordered child-support payments to AFDC recipients are paid to the county rather than directly to the parent, and your grant will be debited for these as well.

You may be eligible for food stamps, "commodities" (free food), and other benefits, such as job training, if you receive TANF. People leaving TANF programs may be eligible for certain short-term benefits, such as subsidized child care and continued health insurance.

If you need help in obtaining public assistance, contact a local welfare rights organization or advocacy group. For national information and referrals, contact the National Welfare Monitoring and Advocacy Partnership at *info@nwmap.org* or on the Web at *http://www.nwmap.org/index.htm*.

Indirect financial help for your family

In the US, tax deductions have replaced direct financial assistance to the poor in many cases. Since these benefits are provided but once a year, they are less convenient, but families coping with the high cost of caring for a mentally ill child should take advantage of them.

One of the most important tax benefits is the federal income tax medical deduction. You can write off not only the direct cost of doctor's visits not covered by health insurance, but also health insurance co-pays and deductibles, out-of-pocket expenses for medications, travel costs related to medical care, and at least some expenses related to attending medical or disability conferences and classes. Self-employed people can deduct most of their health-insurance premiums.

Because medical deductions limit your federal tax liability, they will also reduce your state income taxes, if any (state taxes are usually based on taxable income figures taken from your federal form). Some states have additional tax benefits for the disabled. In Oregon, for example, each disabled child counts as two dependents.

Another important federal tax benefit is the Earned Income Credit (EIC) program. This benefit for the working poor can actually supplement your earnings with a tax rebate, not just a deduction. You can file for EIC on your federal 1040 tax form.

Mortgage interest is also tax-deductible, as most people are aware. Since your home is usually not considered an asset when determining eligibility for direct financial assistance, such as SSI, this makes home ownership particularly attractive to families who are providing care for a bipolar child, especially if the child's condition is severe enough that they can expect to continue this role into adulthood. Some banks and credit unions have special mortgage programs for low- and moderate-income families. Given the strong financial benefits of home ownership, including the opportunity to keep your housing costs from going up in the future, purchasing a house is very advisable.

Very low income families, including young adults with bipolar disorders who rely on SSI or fixed-income trusts, may be able to get additional help in reaching the goal of home ownership from organizations like Habitat for Humanity or Franciscan Enterprises. Mental health advocacy and service organizations have recently begun to push to increase the level of home ownership among mentally ill adults. In some cases the home can be part of a special trust that provides professional management services, preventing the adult from being conned out of it, selling it, or seriously damaging it during a period of more severe symptoms.

Health Canada

In Canada, the Canada Health Act ensures coverage for all Canadian citizens and for non-citizens who need emergency care. Healthcare regulations are the same nationwide, although providers can be hard to find in the less-populated northern provinces.

To initiate an evaluation for bipolar disorders, parents might go through the school system or talk to their child's pediatrician. Adults would first see their primary care physician. The pediatrician or family doctor would then make a referral to an appropriate specialist.

> The disorder might manifest itself in such ways that you become aware of it when the child enters school, for example, if the child is disrupting class, not sitting still, or has difficulty with doing some of the work. If this is the case, as it was for our son, then the school might suggest an assessment and this would be done by the school district psychologist. Or you might go via the medical route. We did this too. D'Arcy started talking about killing himself, so we started in what to me is the most obvious place and would probably be for most Canadians—the family pediatrician or family physician.

> Our family doctor referred us to a specialist pediatrician who specialized in emotional problems in children. She assessed D'Arcy carefully and then referred us on to the area Mental Health Clinic, where D'Arcy was seen by (and still sees) a psychiatrist. The psychiatrist arranged for necessary tests (EEG, CAT scan, MRI) and arranged for D'Arcy to meet regularly for about a year with a counseling psychologist. —Rae, mother of 13-year-old D'Arcy (diagnosis in progress, includes fetal alcohol effect, tic disorder, and depression)

A wide variety of specialists are available through the Canadian health system, which is called Health Canada/Santé Canada. Many of the best are affiliated with university hospitals. Waiting lists are a reality, but parents report that calls and letters (especially if they come from the pediatrician or family doctor as well as the patient or patient's family) can often open up opportunities quicker than usual.

If no qualified providers are available in rural areas, public assistance programs may be available to help a patient get expert care in the closest city. This help may include covering transportation costs, housing the child and parent during evaluation and treatment, and providing regular consultations later on with a pediatrician or family doctor who's closer to home. In practice, however, families in rural Canada sometimes have great difficulty in obtaining adequate care for children with mental illness.

Therapeutic services may be delivered in a medical or school setting. There isn't much coordination between the school and healthcare systems, according to Canadian parents.

Parents also report that privatization and other changes are starting to limit their access to healthcare. Some families are now carrying private insurance to ensure timely and frequent access to care providers.

Canadians in border areas may wish to consult with specialists in the US. Except for rare and pre-approved cases, these visits will not be covered by Canada Health.

Disability income in Canada

Welfare is available in Canada for people with disabilities, single parents, and unemployed adults with or without children. The amount of the monthly payment is set at the provincial level. The disability payment varies from a low of about $580 per month in poor provinces like New Brunswick to around $800 per month in more expensive Ontario and British Columbia. Under the Canadian system, payments to parents caring for children, single or otherwise, are higher than those for disabled adults.

To apply for state welfare benefits, visit your nearest Ministry or Department of Social Services. For disability benefits, regulations vary by state. Generally speaking, however, you must be 18 years of age or older and require, as a direct result of a severe mental or physical impairment, one of the following:

- Extensive assistance or supervision in order to perform daily living tasks within a reasonable time

- Unusual and continuous monthly expenditures for transportation or for special diets or for other unusual but essential and continuous needs

In addition, you must also have confirmation from a medical practitioner that the impairment exists and will likely continue for at least two years or longer, or that it is likely to continue for at least one year and then reoccur.

There are limits on the amount and kinds of savings and other property that a person or family receiving benefits can have.

As in the US, welfare reform is a growing trend in Canada. Some states have introduced mandatory workfare programs for single adults and for some parents on welfare. These provisions generally do not apply to people receiving disability benefits, and parents caring for disabled children may be able to have welfare-to-work requirements waived or deferred.

Canadians who are denied benefits or who have other problems with the benefits agency can appeal its decisions to an independent tribunal.

Some assistance for people with disabilities may also be available at the federal level, or from First Nations (Native Canadian) agencies.

Indirect financial help in Canada

Other direct and indirect income assistance is available to Canadians, such as subsidized travel and tax benefits. For example, college students with permanent disabilities can have their student loans forgiven, and are also eligible for special grants to pay for hiring a note-taker, paying for transportation, and other education-related expenses.

You can get help with medical and disability issues from the support and advocacy organizations listed in the appendix, *Resources*.

National Health in the UK

The National Health system in Britain and Scotland has undergone tremendous upheaval over the past three decades. All services were once free to UK citizens, while private-pay physicians were strictly for the wealthy. Public services have since been sharply curtailed, and co-pays have been introduced. Nevertheless, services for people with mental illness are probably better now than they were in the past, when institutionalization was the norm.

Parents who want to have a child assessed for bipolar symptoms may begin with their health visitor, pediatrician, a psychiatrist or psychologist, a Child

Development Centre, or a local or specialist Child and Family Guidance Clinic. Adult patients will probably want to access a specialist through their general practitioner. Referrals to specialists are notoriously difficult to obtain, even for private-pay patients.

Since healthcare practitioners are an important part of the Statement of Special Needs ("statementing") procedure for getting Early Intervention and special education services, it may be quite practical to pursue both a medical diagnosis and statementing at the same time.

You can get advice and help from MIND (the National Association for Mental Health, 0181 519 2122), as well as from support and advocacy organizations listed in the appendix.

Disability income in the UK

In the UK, people with disabilities have access to three major types of direct state benefits. You can apply for these programs at your local Benefits Agency Office.

The Disability Living Allowance (DLA) is for adults or children with a disability. Parents or carers can apply on behalf of a child. Payment ranges from £15 to £35 per week. The DLA forms are relatively complex, so find an experienced disability advocate to help you fill them out if possible. MIND and other mental health advocacy groups may have DLA experts on staff, as may your local council.

Parents and others caring for a child who receives DLA can apply for the Attendants Allowance (also called the Carers Allowance) program as well.

Any person over five years old who receives DLA can also get a Mobility Allowance, a small sum of money to help them get to appointments, and meet general transportation needs.

Your local council may also have its own benefits scheme. These may be direct payments, such as a supplemental housing benefit, or tax offsets.

Indirect financial help in the UK

A number of supported work schemes are available for people with disabilities and adults receiving other forms of public assistance. In some cases, these programs are mandatory. Your teenage child should start learning about these programs before school-leaving age.

Teens and young adults attending college or trade school may find them-selves in a Catch-22 situation: on some occasions benefits officers have decided that if they are well enough to go to college, they're well enough to work, and canceled their benefits. You can appeal these and other unfavor-able decisions to a Social Security Appeals Tribunal.

Help with disability benefit issues is available from most of the UK groups listed in the appendix.

Disability benefits in the Republic of Ireland

Disability Allowance and Disability Benefit are available in Ireland, but are far from generous. Both are administered via the Department of Social Welfare. Disabled students can continue to receive these benefits while attending third level courses, although they may lose other types of public assistance, such as Rent Allowance.

Maintenance Grant (a general benefit for poor families) is not affected by these benefits.

Supported work schemes are available, although your earnings may make you lose your disability benefits. The exception is work that the local wel-fare officer agrees is "rehabilitative" in nature.

A number of scholarship and grant programs are available to assist students with disabilities in Northern Ireland. An online report at *http://www.ahead.ie/ grants/grants.html#toc* offers more information.

Some direct mental health care is available from public or charitable hospi-tals and clinics in Ireland at low or no cost.

Medicare in Australia

Medicare, the Australian health plan, pays 85 percent of all doctor's fees. It also qualifies Australian citizens for free treatment in any public hospital. Many general practitioners and pediatricians bulk-bill: they charge the gov-ernment directly for all of their patient visits and let the 15 percent co-pay-ment slide. Specialists usually won't bulk-bill. Once a certain cost level has been reached, Medicare pays 100 percent of the bill.

Patients can see the physician of their choice without getting a preliminary referral, but many specialists have long waiting lists.

A number of programs have been set up to identify and help Australian children with disabilities at an early age. Parents say that medical professionals are sometimes less than savvy about neurological disorders in general, but if you can make contact with one who is, services are available.

> In the past, the government used to provide a free screening for all children at age four, and again at around age six. This would be conducted in kindergartens, some day-care centres, and in schools. This was mainly a medical screening, but basic developmental and behavioural differences were sometimes picked up at this stage. Nowadays the screening is no longer universal... either the parent or teacher/child-care worker has to request it. Many children who would benefit from intervention thus slip through the net.
>
> In Australia, some paediatricians specialise in behavioural issues (the specialty of "ambulatory paediatrics"), and at the present time children with neurological issues end up being sent to one of these. Neurologists and psychiatrists are not involved in the care of children, except in cases of clear physical signs (e.g., epilepsy) or adolescent depression.
>
> Psychologists and non-medical providers are generally not covered by Medicare. However, the school system provides limited services of this sort (free) and the public hospital system is also involved.....but overcrowded and underfunded. —Kerry, mother of 12-year-old Kim

Services may be delivered in the child's home, in a school, or in a clinical setting. Parents in rural areas may find access to qualified practitioners difficult, although the emergency healthcare system for rural Australia is enviable. In some situations, parents or patients in very rural areas may be able to access professionals for advice or virtual consultations over the Internet, telephone, or even radio.

Some prescription medications are not covered by Medicaid, and there is a sliding-scale co-payment for those that are.

Disability benefits in Australia

A variety of income support programs are available to Australian citizens, including direct financial assistance for adults with disabilities, parents caring for children with disabilities, single parents, unemployed single adults, youth, and students. Programs related specifically to disabled citizens and their families include:

- Disability Support Pension
- Related Wife Pension
- Sickness Allowance
- Mobility Allowance
- Carer Payment
- Child Disability Allowance

Indirect financial help in Australia

Employment programs for people with disabilities are many and varied, including the Supported Wage System (SWS), which brings the earnings of disabled workers in sheltered workshops or other types of supported or low-wage employment closer to the livability range.

Indirect benefits may also be available under the Disability Services Act in the areas of education, work, recreation, and more.

You can find online information about all of Australia's benefit schemes at the Centrelink web site (*http://www.centrelink.gov.au/*). To apply for benefits or disability services, contact your local Department of Family and Community Services.

You can get help with disability income and health benefit issues from the support and advocacy organizations listed in the appendix.

New Zealand

About 75 percent of all healthcare in New Zealand is publicly funded. Care is delivered through private physicians who accept payment from the public health system. Treatment at public hospitals is fully covered for all New Zealand citizens, and also for Australian and UK citizens living and working in New Zealand.

Healthcare and disability services are both provided through a central Health Authority, which has for the past few years been making special efforts to improve the delivery of mental health, child health, and minority-group care. To start an assessment for bipolar disorder, parents or adult patients should first talk to their pediatrician or family physician about a specialist referral. Self-referral is also possible.

Urban patients may have access to group practices centered around Crown (public) hospitals, which often have excellent specialists. Maori patients may access healthcare and assessments through medical clinics centered around traditional iwi (tribal) structures if they prefer.

About 40 percent of the population in New Zealand carries private insurance, primarily for hospitalization or long-term geriatric care only. This insurance is helpful when you need elective surgery and want to avoid waiting lists at public hospitals. It is not needed to access speech therapy, occupational therapy, physical therapy, psychiatric care, or other direct health or disability services.

New Zealanders complain that waiting lists for assessments and major medical treatments can be excessive. Until recently, patients on waiting lists were not given a firm date for their visits, and were expected to be available immediately should an opening occur. A booking system was instituted in 1998 that is said to be more reliable.

Private care options

For patients in need of temporary or permanent residential care, volunteer organizations (particularly churches) are heavily involved in running long-term care facilities in New Zealand. These facilities are usually free of charge to the patient or family, although some are reimbursed by public health.

Privatization is a growing trend in New Zealand. Public hospitals and their allied clinics have been recreated as public-private corporations. However, the government still provides most of the funding and regulations for healthcare.

Disability income in New Zealand

Direct benefits in New Zealand are similar to those provided in Australia, although the payments have historically been much lower. Domestic Purposes Benefit is for single parents, including those with disabled children. There are also a number of additional services available to the disabled and their carers, including training schemes, supported employment, and recreational assistance. The social safety net in New Zealand is currently being revamped, but services for people with disabilities are actually expected to expand.

To apply for benefits or services, contact your local Ministry of Social Welfare office, which runs the Income Support program. If you need help with paperwork or appeals, Beneficiary Advisory Services (*http://canterbury.cyberplace.org.nz/community/bas.html*) in Christchurch provides assistance and advocacy, as do a number of disability advocacy groups, particularly the information clearinghouse Disability Information Service (*http://canterbury.cyberplace.co.nz/community/dis.html*).

Alternatives to insurance

No matter where you live, there are alternatives to expensive medical care. Those who don't have insurance, or whose insurance is inadequate, will want to investigate these resources.

In some cases, creative private-pay arrangements may be possible with psychiatrists and other providers. Parents have traded services or products for care, and others have arranged payment plans or reduced fees based on financial need. The larger the provider, the more likely it is to have a system in place for providing income-based fees. The smaller the provider, the more receptive she is likely to be to informal arrangements, including barter.

> *My insurance coverage is very good: Blue Cross/Blue Shield. We've had no problems with having them cover the doctor and hospital and drugs. The only thing they don't cover is Lisa's therapist, because their definition of a clinical social worker is a social worker who has a master's or doctorate degree, has at least two years of clinical social work practice, and a license if required by the state. Our therapist doesn't have a master's, but has a license and over 15 years experience. Lisa has formed a very tight attachment to our therapist and neither of us want to change. To make it affordable to us, her therapist is only charging us half price to keep Lisa from having to go somewhere else. —Donna, mother of 16-year-old Lisa (diagnosed bipolar II disorder, post-traumatic stress disorder, and anxiety disorder)*

Hospitals and major clinics usually have social workers on staff who can help you make financial arrangements.

Sources of free or low-cost healthcare or therapeutic services may include:

- Public health clinics, including school-based health clinics
- Public hospitals

- Medical schools, and associated teaching hospitals and clinics

- College special education programs (for learning disabilities and cognitive testing, and sometimes for direct help with educational planning and techniques)

- Hospitals and clinics run by religious or charitable orders, such as Lutheran Family Services clinics

- Charitable institutions associated with religious denominations, such as Catholic Charities, the Jewish Aid Society, and the Salvation Army

- The Urban League, which provides counseling services for troubled teens in some cities and can sometimes refer clients for psychiatric care

- United Way, an umbrella fund-raising organization for many programs that can often provide referrals

- Children's Home Society, the Boys and Girls Aid Society, and similar local children's aid associations

- Grant programs, both public and private

In the UK, special resources outside of National Health include:

- MIND

- The Mental Health Foundation (*http://www.mentalhealth.org.uk/*)

- Community Trust associations, particularly the Zito Trust (0171 240 8422)—see the Mental Health Foundation web site and *CharitiesDirect* at *http://www.caritasdata.co.uk/* for lists of many UK trusts related to mental illness, substance abuse, and related issues, including many that focus on particular ethnic or religious communities

- The New Masonic Samaritan Fund (for members and families of Masons)

- Samaritans (0345 909090)

Medical savings accounts

This is a new healthcare payment option in the US that may have benefits for some children and adults with bipolar disorders. A medical savings account (MSA) allows families to put away a certain amount of money specifically for healthcare costs. This income will then be exempted from federal (and in some cases state) income taxes. Unused funds continue to gain tax-free interest. These accounts can be used to pay for insurance deductibles, co-payments, prescriptions, and medical services not covered by insurance.

Families faced with paying out-of-pocket for an expensive residential program or experimental medication might be able to use an MSA to reduce their costs by an impressive percentage. You'll need to check the regulations of the specific MSA plan to see what expenses will qualify.

Help with medications

Low-income patients may be able to get their medications for free by providing documentation to charitable programs run by pharmaceutical companies. In the US, the Pharmaceutical Manufacturers Association publishes a directory of medication assistance programs. Doctors can get a copy of the PMA's official guide by calling (800) PMA-INFO. Alternatively, you or your doctor can call the company that makes your medication directly to find out about its indigent patient program:

Pharmaceutical Company	Phone Number
3M Pharmaceuticals	(800) 328-0255
Allergan Prescription	(800) 347-4500
Alza Pharmaceuticals	(415) 962-4243
Amgen	(800) 272-9376
Astra USA	(800) 488-3247
Berlex	(800) 423-7539
Boehringer Ingleheim	(203) 798-4131
Bristol Myers Squibb	(800) 736-0003
Burroughs-Wellcome	(800) 722-9294
Ciba-Geigy Patient Support Program	(800) 257-3273 or (908) 277-5849
Eli-Lilly	(317) 276-2950
Genetech	(800) 879-4747
Glaxo	(800) 452-7677
Hoechst-Roussel	(800) 776-5463
Hoffman-Larouche	(800) 526-6367
Ici-Stuart	(302) 886-2231
Immunex Corp.	(800) 321-4669
Janssen	(800) 253-3682
Johnson & Johnson	(800) 447-3437
Knoll	(800) 526-0710
Lederle	(800) 526-7870
Lilly Cares Program	(800) 545-6962

Pharmaceutical Company	Phone Number
Marion Merrel Dow	(800) 362-7466
McNeil Pharmaceuticals	(800) 682-6532
Merck Human Health	(800) 672-6372
Miles	(800) 998-9180
Ortho Pharmaceuticals	(800) 682-6532
Parke-Davis	(202) 540-2000
Pfizer Indigent Patient Program	(800) 646-4455
Pharmacia	(800) 795-9759
Proctor & Gamble	(800) 448-4878
Rhone-Poulenc Rorer	(610) 454-8298
Roche Labs	(800) 285-4484
Roxane Labs	(800) 274-8651
Sandoz	(800) 937-6673
Sanofi Winthrop	(800) 446-6267
Schering Labs	(800) 521-7157
Searle	(800) 542-2526
Serono	(617) 982-9000
SmithKline Access to Care Program	(800) 546-0420 (patient requests) or (215) 751-5722 (physician requests)
Solvay Patient Assistance Program	(800) 788-9277
Survanta Lifeline	(800) 922-3255
Syntex Labs	(800) 822-8255
UpJohn Co.	(800) 242-7014
Wyeth-Ayerst	(703) 706-5933
Zeneca Pharmaceuticals	(800) 424-372

An organization called the Medicine Program can help you and your doctor apply to indigent patient programs. Call them at (573) 778-1118, email at *help@themedicineprogram.com*, or see their web site at *http://www.themedicineprogram.com/*.

Most of these programs require that you have no insurance coverage for outpatient prescription drugs, that purchasing the medication at its retail price would be a hardship for you due to your income and/or expenses, and that you do not qualify for a government or third-party program that can pay for the prescription.

Doctor's samples

Another source for free medications is your physician's sample cabinet. All you have to do is ask, and hope that the pharmaceutical rep has paid a recent visit. Samples can help tide you over rough financial patches, but you can't rely on getting them monthly.

Mail-order medications

In some cases, you can reduce the cost of your monthly medication bill by using a mail-order or online pharmacy. These pharmacies can fill your prescription and mail it to you, sometimes at a substantial savings. Medications may be available by mail-order within your country or from overseas. The latter option can be surprisingly inexpensive, and may provide you with access to medications that normally would not be available where you live.

Your doctor may have to fill out some paperwork before you can use these mail-order services. As with any other transaction by mail or over the Internet, you'll want to do as much as you can to check out the company's reputation and quality of service before sending money or using your credit card.

Communicating via fax, email, or telephone generally works best with these firms, which can usually send you a three-month supply in each order. If you are doing business with an overseas pharmacy, check customs regulations that might prohibit you from importing medication before ordering, especially if the drug is not approved for use in your country.

Some mail-order and online pharmacies were initially created to serve the market for AIDS medications, but have since expanded to cover a wide selection. Many will accept health insurance if you have a drug benefit— some will actually cover your medication co-payment as part of the deal.

If you are stationed overseas with the US military, contact your Tricare health benefits representative about mail-order arrangements.

The appendix, *Resources*, contains contact information for mail-order pharmacies that some families have worked with successfully.

Clinical trials

Some patients have received excellent medical care by taking part in clinical trials of new medications or treatments. Others have suffered unpleasant side effects or felt that they were treated like guinea pigs. Before enrolling your child in a clinical trial, make sure that you feel comfortable with the procedure or medication being tested, the professionals conducting the study, and the facility where it will take place. Be as fully informed as possible.

CenterWatch, Inc., is an international listing service for current clinical trials, and is available on the Web at *http://www.centerwatch.com/*. If you don't have Web access, contact CenterWatch in Boston at (617) 247-2327.

Miscellaneous discounts

Don't forget, children with bipolar disorders and sometimes, by extension, their families may be eligible for a variety of discounts and special access programs for the disabled. For example, the US National Parks Service offers a lifelong pass that gives disabled individuals free entry to all national parks, as well as half-price camping privileges. If the recipient is a child, her family also gets the discount. Disneyland, Disney World, and many other theme parks offer special privileges to people with disabilities, such as not having to wait in line for attractions.

There are a number of programs around the world that help disabled people get access to computers and the Internet. One that offers *free* computers is Minneapolis-based DRAGnet; call (612) 378-9796, fax (612) 378-9794, or email *gille027@tc.umn.edu*.

If your child needs medical care in a location far from home, but you can't afford the cost of a flight or hotel, following are some resources that may be able to help in the US or Canada:

- AirCare Alliance: (800) 296-1217 (referrals for TWA Operations Liftoff and AirLifeLine)

- AirLifeLine: (916) 429-2166 or (800) 446-1231

- Corporate Angel: (914) 328-1313 (arranges flights on corporate jets for patients)

- Miles for Kids in Need: (817) 963-8118

- Continental Care Force: (713) 261-6626

- Wings of Freedom: (504) 857-0727 (negotiates with commercial airlines for low-cost tickets)

- National Association of Hospitality Houses: (800) 524-9730

Similar corporate programs may be available in Europe, Australia, and New Zealand; contact the public relations office of your national airline to find out more. You may also be eligible for an emergency travel grant from a social services agency to cover these needs.

Changing the rules

Advocating for changes in the insurance system or your national healthcare system is a big job. Unless you want to make it your life mission, it's probably too big for any one patient or parent. But by working together, individuals can accomplish a lot.

Advocacy organizations can be the point of contact between healthcare consumers, insurers, HMOs, and public health. NAMI has been at the forefront of efforts to protect patients and their families by mandating insurance coverage and treatment, but it's an uphill battle.

The federal Mental Health Parity Act was passed with much fanfare in 1996, and went into effect at the beginning of 1998. Many people now believe that all insurance plans in the US must cover mental health care at the same level as they do physical healthcare. This is a misconception. This law affects only employer-sponsored group insurance plans that wish to offer mental health coverage. They are not required to do so. Additionally, if such coverage raises the company's premium cost by more than 1 percent, they need not comply with the law. Companies with fewer than 50 employees are also exempted.

The Mental Health Parity Act raises the annual or lifetime cap on mental health care in the plans that it covers, but it does not prevent insurance companies from limiting access or recovering costs in other ways. They may, for example, legally restrict the number of visits you can make to a mental health provider, raise the co-payment required for such visits, or raise your deductible for mental health care.

At the time of this edition, many states have passed their own, more restrictive, mental health parity laws. As noted previously, these laws supersede the federal regulations. Eleven other states have parity laws that are equal to the federal act, and others have less-restrictive parity laws. Of the twelve with tighter restrictions, all of the laws are written in ways that should require coverage for bipolar disorders. Colorado, Connecticut, Maine, New Hampshire, Rhode Island, and Texas specifically require coverage for "biologically based" mental illnesses. For parents and patients living in these states, this is a step in the right direction, although it remains to be seen how these laws will be enforced and what steps some insurers may take to evade responsibility.

The University of South Florida maintains an informational web site on state and federal mental health parity research, laws, and proposed laws at *http://www.fmhi.usf.edu/parity/parityhome.html.*

At press time, the Mental Health Equitable Treatment Act of 1999 had just been introduced in Congress. This law would force insurers to cover major mental illnesses, including bipolar disorders, at the same rate as physical disorders. It would also prevent them from limiting outpatient visits and hospital stays when they are needed for effective treatment.

However, because insurance regulation is mostly at the state level, that's probably where the most effective parity action will take place. There's a need for education, for public advocacy, for legislative action, and in some cases for legal action. Parents and patients can and should be involved in these efforts.

Parents and patients can make common cause with healthcare providers, many of whom are angry at how their patients with mental illnesses are being mistreated. For example, the Washington, DC-based American Psychological Association (APA) has filed suit against Aetna US Healthcare Inc. and related managed care entities in California, alleging that the company engaged in false advertising when it claimed to offer "prompt, accessible mental health treatment services." The APA has further alleged that Aetna put hidden caps on its already limited mental health benefits, disregarded what practitioners had to say about medical treatment of their patients, and deliberately delayed referrals.

> *Despite the managed care industry's argument to the contrary, it's typically the managed care company that determines and controls the treatment of patients, not the doctor, and the financial bottom-line, not patient need, is usually the controlling factor.* —Russ Newman, PhD, JD, *executive director for professional practice for the American Psychological Association (1998 APA press release)*

Of course, parity laws will do little for the increasing number of children and families who are uninsured. That's both an economic issue and a public policy problem, and it will take movement on both of those fronts to effect real change.

All of us—parents, patients, and practitioners—want to see improvements in healthcare and in how it's delivered. By working closely with our allies in the public, private, and volunteer sectors, we can make it happen. Even insurance companies and managed care entities can be brought on board if they're shown the positive benefit of better-functioning patients, who require much less emergency care, fewer hospitalizations, and less expensive medications. Alternative models for delivery of care are evolving, and with hard work these new systems can be both more humane and more cost-efficient.

Other insurance issues

Parents of bipolar children in the US and other areas where litigation is common may want to consider carrying other types of insurance. For example, you might want to bolster your homeowners or renters insurance to cover damages to property that could be caused by your child, and ensure that your insurance includes liability coverage in case your child injures someone. You may also want to add additional liability coverage to your automotive insurance. If your child is severely affected, long-term disability insurance (if you can find a policy that covers mental illness) could help him live more independently as an adult.

CHAPTER 8

School

CHILDHOOD BIPOLAR DISORDER can have profound effects on your child's education. This chapter will cover working with your child's school, navigating the special education system, writing and using a 504 plan or IEP to help your child achieve in school, and school-related problems, including the issue of school violence and mental illness. We'll begin by talking mostly about the US education system and appropriate laws, but education in other English-speaking countries will also be covered. Parents of very young children will want to consult the "Early Intervention" section near the end of this chapter first.

Deliberate ignorance?

Most school officials know next to nothing about mental illness. They assume it's rare, and that it's simply an issue they'll never be faced with. Or they assume that a mentally ill child would not be able to attend school, and should probably be institutionalized. You may be told that your child is the first and only person with a bipolar disorder who has ever graced this school's halls.

Since you now know how prevalent bipolar disorders are, you also know that this can't possibly be true.

And since mental illness in children isn't exactly a taboo topic these days, you have to wonder if school officials are deliberately going about their business with blinders on. In any school with 500 students, it's likely that ten or more will have a serious mental illness, such as clinical depression, a bipolar disorder, or schizophrenia. That's at least ten students out of every group of 500 that moves through the school over a period of years—not an insignificant number at all.

According to 1997 statistics from the Centers for Disease Control and Prevention, 20 percent of high school students will be emotionally upset enough in any given year to consider suicide, and almost 8 percent have made one or more suicide attempts. Some of these troubled youth have a mental illness, others are reacting (or overreacting) to difficult life events.[1]

Put together the number of children with mental illness and the number of children who are experiencing severe, if transient, emotional distress, and you get a figure that makes you wonder how this population could be overlooked.

Ignorance of mental illness goes beyond the issue of missing its presence in schools. It also prevents children from receiving an adequate education. It causes teachers to punish students for symptoms of their illness, makes kids feel like failures when they can't perform, and creates a rift between schools and parents at a time when they should be uniting to help a child.

> *The schools really need to be educated about mental illness. They were not very understanding at all. They just could not understand why he wasn't doing his work. I kept telling them it is because he is so depressed. They said he needed to "snap out of it!" —Cindy, mother of 16-year-old Craig (diagnosed bipolar disorder)*

Along with ignorance, there is a pervasive fear of mental illness in our society that extends past the schoolroom door. You've probably felt it yourself, and you've no doubt seen it in the reactions of some friends and relatives when they learned of your child's diagnosis. This fear causes many schools to push out affected children by denying them special education services, denigrating them and their families, refusing to create support systems that might make education easier, and doing anything within their power to move them into another setting, *any* other setting, even sitting at home on the couch without a diploma and with little hope of decent employment.

Indeed, the results of fear and ignorance are tragic. In 1999, the US Department of Education released its annual report on special education. This document trumpeted the excellent news that thanks to new laws, parental efforts, and better teaching methods, 31 percent more students with disabilities are now receiving high school diplomas. Buried in this report was the sad news that the trend does not yet extend to children with "emotional disturbances," the special education category that includes major mental illnesses. According to the DOE, an outrageous 55 percent of emotionally disturbed children leave school without earning a diploma. They also fail more courses, earn lower GPAs, miss more school, and are held back more often than students with other types of disabilities.[2]

That's a shameful record, one that must be changed. Children with mental retardation, children whose physical disabilities confine them to wheelchairs, and those with other health problems are making great strides in accessing an education. This wasn't always the case. These changes have only come about through the efforts of dedicated parents and educational researchers, working in concert with teachers, school administrators, and lawmakers to revamp school programs for the disabled. A similar effort is now underway for students with mental health and neurological problems, and parents and caring professionals are duty-bound to be a part of it.

As a parent, you can do three things to dispel ignorance and fear of bipolar disorders in schools. You can:

- Communicate with your child's school about his diagnosis. The potential stigma of labeling your child as having a bipolar disorder is far less serious than what will happen if the school labels your child as a bad kid, a behavior problem, or a juvenile delinquent.

- Use the special education laws to put supports into place for your child at school.

- Educate the educators: provide reading material about bipolar disorders, and be available to teachers, counselors, and administrators who want to know more.

Legal help for bipolar students

Discriminating against the disabled is illegal in the US in almost every setting, including schools. Federal law also specifically mandates that all children receive a free and appropriate education, regardless of disability. That means providing, free of charge, special education programs, speech therapy, occupational therapy, physical therapy, psychiatric services, and other interventions as needed to help the child learn.

There are several laws that should protect your child. These include:

- Section 504 of the Rehabilitation Act of 1973
- The Individuals with Disabilities Education Act (IDEA)
- The Americans with Disabilities Act (ADA)
- Other state and federal laws concerning disability rights and special education

504 plans

At the very least, your child should have a 504 plan in place—an agreement between the child's family and the school about accommodations the child needs. Section 504 of the Rehabilitation Act of 1973, one of the very first laws mandating educational help for students with disabilities, lays out the regulations for such plans, hence the name.

Unlike special education eligibility, Section 504 eligibility is not based on having a certain type of disability. Instead, it is based on:

1. Having a physical or mental impairment that substantially limits a major life activity, such as learning. Note that in contrast to IDEA regulations, learning is not the only activity that applies: 504 plans can cover other major life activities, such as breathing, walking, and socialization.

2. Having a record of such an impairment, such as a medical diagnosis.

3. Being regarded as having such an impairment.

A 504 plan is a good idea even if your child has never had an academic or behavior problem in school. The nature of bipolar disorders dictates that symptoms could emerge at any time, and have unexpected effects on school performance, or even the child's safety. Your child's 504 plan can be used to put procedures into place regarding issues such as who will give out medication and where it will be stored, communication between home and school, requiring certain organization systems for homework and books, exemption from timed tests, the provision of a classroom aide, or what to do if your child has a difficult behavior episode at school.

Bipolar children and teens are prone to the occasional meltdown, and this is one area where a 504 plan shines. Episodes of anxiety, rage, or unusual behavior may occur in response to stress, fear, teasing, illness, missed medications, or simply out of the blue. You can develop a response in advance and put it in place via a 504 plan. It can include procedures for giving emergency medication, calling for outside help, and keeping the child and others safe until that help arrives. Without advance planning, it's easy for a bad day to turn into a crisis.

If you apply for 504 status and are still denied services, appeal this decision to your state's Office of Civil Rights. If your child has been diagnosed with a bipolar disorder, he should not be denied this limited protection under any circumstances—a 504 plan is the very least that any child with a health impairment qualifies for. Even students with mild ADHD or occasional asthma attacks qualify for services under a 504 plan.

Some special education advocates recommend that parents request a 504 evaluation at the same time they start the Individualized Education Plan (IEP) process. This can mean asking the 504 coordinator to attend your IEP meetings. It may confuse your district, because it isn't a common practice, but it will save time in obtaining some services and accommodations if services are denied under IDEA and the parents have to appeal. (See the section "Your child's IEP," later in this chapter.)

Because most 504 plans are fairly uncomplicated documents, you may be tempted to simply set up an informal agreement with your child's school instead. Don't do it. Informal agreements only work as long as the people involved stay the same, and as long as everyone chooses to honor them. If your school gets a new principal or your child's teacher decides to change plans in midstream, you'll be right back where you started.

IDEA and special education

Special education has been revolutionized by the Individuals with Disabilities Education Act (IDEA), a set of comprehensive rules and regulations that was most recently revised and expanded in 1997. IDEA's mission is to ensure that all children get an adequate education, regardless of disabilities or special needs. This includes children with bipolar disorders or other mental illnesses.

The special education process starts with evaluation. In most areas, eligibility is determined by a committee of specialists, which might be called the multidisciplinary team (M-team), eligibility committee, child study team, or a similar name. As the parent, you should have input during this eligibility process. You may be asked to fill out forms, and you can also request a personal interview with the team and submit information to help it make its decision.

The eligibility team will decide if your child has a condition that qualifies him for special education services. Exact language differs between states, but typical qualifying categories include:

- Autistic
- Hearing impaired (deaf)
- Visually impaired

- Both hearing impaired and visually impaired (deaf-blind)
- Speech and language impaired
- Mentally retarded/developmentally delayed
- Multihandicapped
- Severely orthopedically impaired
- Other health impaired (OHI)
- Seriously emotionally disturbed (SED)
- Severely and profoundly disabled
- Specific learning disability
- Traumatic brain injury

Check your state's special education regulations for the list of labels used in your state.

The condition that causes the most impairment in school-related activities will usually be called the primary handicapping condition, and any others that coexist with it will be called secondary handicapping conditions. For example, a child might be considered eligible for special education under the primary condition deaf/blind, with SED as a secondary label. In this case, the child would also qualify as multihandicapped.

Most children and teens with bipolar disorder who receive special education services are classified under the OHI or SED labels. An SED designation is often required to access day treatment or residential slots; on the other hand, it may prevent your child from being admitted to some alternative school programs without a fight.

Although the eligibility committee will take your child's medical diagnosis and the opinions of Early Intervention evaluators into account when they make their determination, these categories are defined by the school district or state Department of Education in terms of education, not medicine. If your child has a bipolar disorder diagnosis from a psychiatrist, neurologist, or other physician, the committee can still decide that your child does not meet the educational definition of SED or another label. This may mean that the committee feels your child does not need special services to take advan-tage of educational opportunities. On the other hand, it may mean that the team is denying your child needed services. Technically, a medical diagnosis of a bipolar disorder should automatically qualify a child for the label OHI, even if his illness is currently controlled via medication or his symptoms are not prominent.

You have a right to appeal the eligibility team's decision your child's educational label or any other issue. If its decision prevents your child from receiving special education eligibility or needed services, you should do so. It is helpful to prepare a detailed list of ways your child's problems impact his ability to be educated without the added help of special education services.

Your child's IEP

The special education evaluation forms the basis of a document that will soon become your close companion: your child's Individualized Education Plan (IEP). The IEP describes your child's strengths and weaknesses, sets out goals and objectives, and details how these can be met within the context of the school system. Unlike the IFSP, a similar kind of plan used in Early Intervention programs for preschool children (see the section "Early Intervention" later in this chapter), the IEP is almost entirely about what will happen within school walls. Unless the IEP team agrees to include it, there will be little information about services from outside programs, services provided by parents, or services provided to parents.

The IEP team

The IEP is created during one or more meetings of your child's IEP team, which has a minimum of three members: a representative of the school district, a teacher, and a parent. The district may send more than one representative. If your child has more than one teacher, or if direct service providers such as her therapist would like to attend, they can all be present. If it is your child's first IEP and first assessment, one team member is required by federal law to have experience with and knowledge of the child's suspected or known disabilities. You may want to check this person's credentials in advance. "Specialists" employed by some school districts can have as little as one college psychology course, or even no qualifications other than the title itself.

Both parents should participate in the IEP process if possible, even if they do not live together. Parents can also bring anyone else they would like: grandparents or other relatives, a friend, an after-school caretaker, a mental health advocate, or a lawyer, for example.

The child himself can also be at the IEP meeting if the parents would like—however, it's a good idea to bring a sitter with a young child to avoid disruptions. You want to be able to give the IEP process your full attention, and that's hard if you're also trying to keep a child out of trouble. Most young children find IEP meetings rather boring.

Districts are trying to involve middle school and high school students in the IEP process more often, and this is probably a good trend. You may want to discuss the meeting with your child and elicit her suggestions in advance. Some adolescents prefer to write up their suggestions rather than (or in addition to) attending the meeting. As with young children, bring someone to take care of your child if she tends to be disruptive, and bring a book or game in case the meeting gets boring. It's not beneficial to force an unwilling child to take part in the meeting.

Recently parents of older teens in special education have reported a disturbing new trend: school districts that try to circumvent IDEA by making teens "self-advocates" at the age of 18, regardless of their ability to make wise choices, and regardless of their parents' wishes. If parents agree—and only if parents agree—any child in special education who has reached age 18 can take full control of all further contacts with the school district. Needless to say, this is a very unwise thing to agree to with a bipolar child. In most cases, the outcome has been that the child immediately leaves school and loses all services.

If your district tries this ploy, there is a way back in. As an adult self-advocate, your child can appoint another person to advocate for her. That person can (and should) be you, or if you prefer, a professional advocate.

Remember that unless you permit it, special education services continue until at least the age of 21 or the attainment of a regular high school diploma (not a GED or IEP diploma).

The IEP meeting

Usually the IEP meeting is held at a school or a district office. However, you can request another location for the meeting if it is necessary—for example, if your child is on homebound instruction, or has severe behavior problems that make caring for him impossible away from the controlled environment of home at this time. The meeting date and time must be convenient to you (and, of course, to the other team members).

Your first IEP meeting should begin with a presentation of your child's strengths and weaknesses. This may be merely a form listing test scores and milestones, or it can include verbal reports of observations by team members—including you. You can use this time to tell the team a little more about your child, her likes and dislikes, her abilities, and the worries that have brought you all together for this meeting. Even if you're repeating information that the team members already know, this kind of storytelling humanizes your child and yourself. You'll want to keep it brief, though, so you may want to use a short outline and even practice in advance. Five or ten minutes seems about right, although you may find that you need more time. If you can keep your written description to one or two pages, that would be good.

This kind of information may also be entered on an evaluation or record summary form.

The IEP has two important parts: the cover sheet, usually called the accommodations page (see Figure 8-1), and the goals and objectives pages (see Figure 8-2). Your district may have its own bureaucratic names for these pages, such as a "G3" or an "eval sheet." If team members start throwing around terms you don't understand, be sure to speak up! If the wrong forms are filled out, or if important paperwork is left undone, you may not have an acceptable IEP at the end of the meeting.

Accommodations

Parents tend to focus on the goals and objectives pages, and often overlook the accommodations page. That's a mistake. The goals and objectives are all about what your child will do, and if they are not accomplished, there's no one who can be truly held accountable but your child. The accommodations page, however, is about what the school district will do to help make your child able to meet those goals: what services it will provide or pay for, what kind of classroom setting your child will be in, and any other special education help that the district promises to provide.

The accommodations page is where the district's promises are made, so watch out: saying your *child* will do something costs the district nothing, but promising the *district* will do something has a price tag attached. Be prepared to hear phrases like "I don't want to commit the district to that" over and over—and to methodically show that the accommodations you're asking for are the only way the goals and objectives the team wants to set can be met.

Student's Name: _____ Birthdate: _____ Grade: _____ PPS ID#: _____

Home School: _____ Attending School: _____ IEP Meeting Date: _____

IEP Manager: _____ Position: _____ Projected Review Date: _____

Specially Designed Instruction

Regular PE ☐ Yes ☐ No

Attends Home School ☐ Yes ☐ No
If no, explain: _____

	Service Time	Date of Initiation	Anticipated Duration
☐ Adapted PE	____	____	____
☐ Independent Living	____	____	____
☐ Language Arts	____	____	____
☐ Mathematics	____	____	____
☐ Motor	____	____	____
☐ Recreation/Leisure	____	____	____
☐ Self Management	____	____	____
☐ Social/Behavioral	____	____	____
☐ Speech/Language	____	____	____
☐ Vocational/Career Ed	____	____	____

Extent of participation in general education classes/activities: _____

Modifications and/or supplementary aids and services: _____

High School Students Only

Projected Diploma: ☐ Standard
☐ Modified ☐ Certificate

Credits earned to date: _____

Passed PALT/GST:

Math ☐ Yes ☐ No

Reading ☐ Yes ☐ No

Pre-Requirement Completed ☐ Yes ☐ No

Individual Transition Plan Completed/Updated ☐ Yes ☐ No

Social Security Number: _____

Related Services Necessary

	Service Time	Date of Initiation	Anticipated Duration
☐ Audiology	____	____	____
☐ Counseling/Interv.	____	____	____
☐ Health Care	____	____	____
☐ Occ. Therapy	____	____	____
☐ Physical Therapy	____	____	____
☐ Transportation	____	____	____
☐ _____	____	____	____
☐ _____	____	____	____
☐ _____	____	____	____
☐ _____	____	____	____
☐ _____	____	____	____

Participants in Individualized Education Program

Parent/Guardian/Surrogate: _____

_____

Teacher: _____

District Representative: _____

Student: _____

Other: _____

Other: _____

Figure 8-1. A sample accommodations page

Individualized Education Program Goals and Objectives

Page: _____ of: _____

Student's Name: _____ ID Number: _____ Date: _____

Home School: _____ Attending School: _____ Grade: _____ Birthdate: ____

Skill Area: _____

Present Level of Educational Performance (including test data, remedial areas, etc.): _____

_____

_____

Annual Goal: _____

√ If Objective Carried Over	Short-Term Objectives	Criteria	Evaluation Procedure(s)	Schedules

Figure 8-2. A sample IEP goals and objectives page

Most district representatives see their role in the IEP meeting as being the gatekeeper. This role may be interpreted as spending as little money as possible, or ensuring that children are matched with services that meet their needs, depending on the person, the district, and the situation. Most district representatives struggle to balance these two goals. As your child's advocate, your job is to persuade the representative to tip the scales in your child's favor.

Accommodations your child may need include:

- A specific type of classroom.

- Provision of other types of environments, such as a resource room setting for certain subjects, mainstreaming for other subjects, or an area for time-outs or self-calming.

- A set procedure for allowing the child to take a "self time-out" when overwhelmed, angry, or especially symptomatic. For example, your child might quietly show a green card to the teacher, who could send him on his way to a quiet area (the school nurse's office or the school library, for example) for a predetermined length of time with a nod of her head.

- A reduced number of required courses for graduation.

- Class schedules adapted to the child's ability to concentrate and stay alert, especially during times of acute stress (such as just after release from the hospital) and during medication changes.

- Specific learning materials or methods.

- Accommodations for testing, such as untimed tests, extended test-taking times, oral exams (this is an especially good idea for those students who have hand tremors), or exemption from certain types of tests.

- Grade arrangements that take into account assignments and school days missed due to symptoms or to hospitalization. These might include estimating semester grades based only on the work that was completed; offering the option of an "incomplete" grade to allow the student to finish the course when well; or basing grades on some combination of class participation when present, work completed, and a special oral exam.

- A personal educational assistant, aide, or "shadow"—either a monitoring aide who simply helps with behavior control, or an inclusion or instructional aide.

- Other classroom equipment needed to help your child learn if he has auditory processing or learning disabilities, such as a microphone or sound field system, a slanted work surface, or pencils with an orthopedic grip.

The cover page should also summarize any therapeutic services your child will receive, including who will deliver them, where they will be delivered, and how frequent they will be.

The accommodations page should not already be filled out when the IEP meeting begins, as your child's individual goals and objectives should dictate what accommodations will be needed.

Goals and objectives

Goals and objectives in the IEP should be as specific as possible. Often each team member will come to the IEP meeting with a list, hopefully with each goal already broken down into steps. This saves a lot of time, and allows everyone to concentrate on the pros and cons of their ideas rather than having to actually come up with the ideas themselves at the meeting. You may choose to meet one on one with these team members to talk over IEP ideas before the big meeting.

There is a tendency for a bipolar child's IEP to look more like a behavior plan than an education plan. Goals like "Ian will comply with his teacher's instructions nine times out of ten" are fairly typical—and almost useless. They specify that the student—and the student alone—will do something that has obviously been difficult in the past. For behavior improvements to occur, teachers and parents need to know why misbehavior has happened in the past. This is where a well-researched, well-written behavior plan (see "School behavior and school violence," later in this chapter) should come into play.

Appropriate behavior goals for the IEP can be tied to what you've learned from analyzing the child's problem behaviors, and how the behavior plan addresses them. These two documents can work together. For example, if Ian has often been noncompliant in the past due to having little knowledge of how to get appropriate attention from his teacher or his peers, a better set of goals might be "Ian will identify three appropriate ways to get his teacher's attention" and "Ian will be able to identify appropriate and inappropriate times to seek his peers' attention." Other behavior goals might include "Ian will find three unobtrusive activities he can do in the classroom when he feels like fidgeting," "Ian will take a self time-out for five to ten minutes when he is feeling overwhelmed," and "Ian will learn to use two stress-reduction strategies when he is becoming irritated or angry at school."

Although these behavior goals still seem to be all about what the student will do, fulfilling these goals will really require the active participation of teachers and other professionals. Ian is not going to learn these strategies for improving his behavior by osmosis—someone is going to have to teach him, work with him to improve his skills, and reinforce him when he gets it right. To as great an extent as possible, you want to spell out just how that will be done, and by whom, in the IEP and/or the behavior plan.

Academic goals on IEPs are controversial. Schools do not want to guarantee that a student will learn certain material; they usually don't even want to promise that they'll try to teach it. And if most of your child's academic skills are age-appropriate or even superior, it is very hard to have anything written into the IEP about maintaining or developing these skills further. Special education services are about addressing deficits, say the educators. (One exception to this rule is the state of Massachusetts, which has regulations requiring school districts to "maximize the potential" of disabled students.)

In reality, the student's achievement is not to be compared against the average or that of other students, but against his own ability as measured by past performance or ability testing. If there is a measurable and significant discrepancy between ability and achievement, you have room to ask for academic goals on the IEP.

Parents also know from experience that any gifts or islands of competence their child has are essential to his emotional well-being and educational success. Parents and experienced, caring teachers can often show the rest of the team why IEP goals based on strengths can be as important as those based on deficits or discrepancies. For example, your daughter may excel in reading and music. Just as schools often claim that sports programs keep certain at-risk kids in school, enhanced opportunities to pursue her special interests may motivate your daughter to attend classes regularly and keep up her GPA—especially if you can take a page from the football team's book and tie allowing her to participate in a desired activity, such as band or chorus, to maintaining passing grades. As every parent knows, the carrot is often mightier than the stick!

Generally speaking, children in special education programs should be educated to the same standards as all other students whenever that is possible. They should work with the same curriculum and objectives, although specific requirements can be adjusted to fit the child. For example, if third graders in your district are normally required to present a ten-minute oral report about state history, a child with medication-induced fatigue might be allowed to present a shorter oral report, to have her written report read out loud by a helper, or to present her report in two parts.

As a parent, you'll want to talk to your child's teacher about the academic curriculum in use in your child's school and in the district itself. Make sure that your child is being instructed in the skills, concepts, and facts needed to proceed in school.

Many bipolar children are quite bright and thrive in a challenging academic environment. You won't want the IEP to dumb down their classes or take away the joy of achieving something difficult. You do want the IEP to provide flexibility: for example, permitting your child to audit some courses before taking them for credit, and arranging in advance for using correspondence courses, distance learning (courses taken over the Internet), or independent study to fill in gaps created by hospitalization or relapse.[3] Being a special education student does not imply being unintelligent. In fact, many children in gifted and talented programs have IEPs.

In some states, children are required to meet certain benchmark standards to move on to the next grade level, to complete high school, or to earn a type of diploma that qualifies them to attend state colleges. You may be able to include a provision in your child's IEP regarding how any standardized achievement tests of this type will be handled. This may range from exempting the child from the testing requirement to insisting that the school provide extra academic help and/or test-taking accommodations to allow the student an equal chance of doing well on the test.

Another important area for IEP goals is socialization. Again, you may be told that this is not part of special education. However, all the book learning in the world will not enable your child to function in the real world if he has not also mastered the give and take of social interaction.

The best place for children to learn appropriate social skills is in supervised activities with peers, and most schools make a plethora of these available to their students. This makes school an especially appropriate area for children to develop socialization skills.

Socialization opportunities may be provided through school activities, such as student clubs or arts groups, in targeted classroom exercises on social skills, or via non-affiliated community programs. You can write supports into the IEP that will let your child succeed in these activities despite her illness.

Some schools have introduced social skills groups or peer mentoring programs for students who need extra help in socialization. Often these pair younger students with older students, under the guidance and supervision of adults. The older student can show younger kids the ropes, help integrate them into school and after-school activities, and encourage them to feel like they belong at the school. For children entering a new school, returning to school after a long period of hospitalization or homebound tutoring, or whose social deficits have been very severe for some time, peer mentoring and social skills groups can be fabulous.

Signing the IEP… or not

When the IEP is complete, the accommodations page will include a list of each promise, information about where and when it will be met, and the name of the person responsible for delivering or ensuring delivery. If the complete IEP is acceptable to everyone present, this is probably also where all team members will sign on the dotted line.

You do not have to sign the IEP if it is not acceptable. This fact can't be emphasized enough. If the meeting has ended and you don't feel comfortable with the IEP as it is, you have the right to take home the current document and think about it (or discuss it with your spouse or an advocate) before you sign. You also have the right to set another IEP meeting, and another, and another, until it is truly complete. Don't hinder the process unnecessarily, of course, but also don't let yourself be steamrolled by the district. The IEP is about your child's needs, not the district's needs.

Needless to say, you should never sign a blank or unfinished IEP: it's a bit like signing a blank check. Certain school districts ask IEP meeting participants to sign an approval sheet before even talking about the IEP. Others are in the habit of taking notes for a prospective IEP and asking parents to sign an approval form at the end of the meeting, even though the goals, objectives, and accommodations have not been entered on an actual IEP form. This is not okay. If they insist that you sign a piece of paper, make sure to add next to your name that you are signing because you were present, but that you have not agreed to a final document.

If your child already has an IEP in place from the previous year, this IEP will stay in place until the new one is finalized and signed. If your child does not, you may need to come to a partial agreement with the district while the IEP is worked out.

If the process has become contentious, be sure to bring an advocate to the next meeting. A good advocate can help smooth out the bumps in the IEP process while preserving your child's access to a free and appropriate education.

Placement decisions

Two factors govern the choice of school for your child: the most appropriate educational program and the least restrictive environment. For most children with bipolar disorders, the least restrictive environment is their neighborhood school, or one very much like it that happens to have an especially good teacher or support services.

This is called inclusion, full integration, or mainstreaming. Inclusion is usually the best strategy for children and teenagers with bipolar disorders, as long as an IEP is in place and the school is willing to accommodate your child's special needs.

Over and over, parents interviewed for this book stressed the importance of teacher and classroom flexibility in the face of this unpredictable illness.

> Billy attends a regular public elementary school. He goes to the resource room each day to work on his dyslexia and dysgraphia, and this has reduced his frustration level. A teacher who is flexible and likes to work with individual differences is helpful. —Marlene, mother of 8-year-old Billy (diagnosed cyclothymic disorder)

· · · · ·

> Michael is in the local school system in our town, in special education and with an IEP. The teacher has to be flexible. If they are rigid and unbending, it will be a fight all the way. If they are flexible and understanding, it can be no problem. —Lynn, mother of 11-year-old Michael (diagnosed BPI with mixed states and psychosis, OCD, tic disorder)

Many bipolar children do very well in school, to the extent that school officials may be completely unaware that they have a mental illness. Often these same children let it all hang out at home, saving angry outbursts and other obvious symptoms for their parents. The rigid scheduling, reliable feedback, and daily routine of school is appreciated by these kids, who are often able to use their excellent verbal skills and quick minds to excel academically, despite inner turmoil.

Characteristics of successful inclusive classrooms include:

- Caring, informed personnel
- Adequate ratio of children to classroom personnel
- Frequent and productive communication between classroom personnel, specialists, and parents
- Availability of appropriate teaching materials
- Individualized educational programming for each child with a disability
- Encouragement of interaction between children with disabilities and their nondisabled peers
- Consistent expectations regarding behavior and academic work, with flexibility built in to allow for changes in the child's psychiatric symptoms and needs

Full inclusion is not a magical solution to school problems. Too often schools use it as a way to deny special education services to the students who need them. That's why many classroom teachers dread having children with mental or physical disabilities in their classes—it's not that they're callous or think these kids don't deserve an equal education, it's that they are not given any additional resources to work with them. Imagine yourself teaching a class of thirty junior high students in which two or three have ADHD, one has autism, and another has a bipolar disorder. Without help from classroom aides and specialists, administrative support, well-written IEPs, and the resources to help each child meet his goals, your job would be a nightmare.

Parents are often the key to making sure their children are properly served in an inclusive setting. Most of the time, the teacher will be sympathetic if she knows you will go to bat with the administration or district to get the help she needs to do a good job.

Then again, some schools are barely capable of meeting the needs of average students, much less those with special needs.

Nathan is enrolled in high school, but they cannot even keep track of where he is on any given day, when he does get out of bed. There are no truant officers in this school district, and because I live on a military installation, I have no police back-up to get him to go to school.

I have not found anything that works, other than a total locked-in facility for living and attending school. Otherwise, he just will not do any work. He has spent two years in ninth grade, and next year will be his third. —Cindy, mother of 16-year-old Nathan (diagnosed bipolar disorder, OCD, ADHD, post-traumatic stress disorder, chemical dependency, bulimia)

Special classrooms

Some children will not be able to handle the noise, confusion, and demands of a traditional school program. For each of these children there should be a range of placements, ranging from staying in the neighborhood school but spending part or all of the day in a resource room or special education classroom, to learning at home with one-on-one instruction, to residential placement.

There are many types of self-contained special classrooms. Children with bipolar disorder are most likely to be sent to a behavioral classroom, where their classmates will be other children with mental illness, oppositional defiant disorder or conduct disorder, severe ADHD, and other disabilities that impact behavior.

Most of these classrooms use some variation of the behavior modification approach. Many use a levels system, where children start with no privileges at all and earn each privilege by meeting behavior goals. As their behavior improves (or declines) they work their way through levels that might be numbered or given the name of a color. A child on green level, for instance, would be performing optimally and able to have recess time, eat lunch with peers, and perhaps have a special treat at the end of the week. A child on blue level would be performing badly, confined to the classroom for recess and lunch, and unable to have cookies with the green level guys on Friday.

Levels systems and behavior mod techniques work very well with children who are deliberately misbehaving, perhaps as a result of learning poor behavior at home. Level systems do not work well with children whose behaviors are due to neurological dysfunction. These kids may simply feel humiliated when symptom exacerbations prevent them from reaching behavior goals. Their teachers may also be mystified when techniques that worked so well when the child's illness was well-controlled on medication suddenly become useless as the medication no longer works.

Despite the drawbacks of the level system/behavior mod approach, some behavioral classrooms are excellent learning environments for kids with bipolar disorders. They are usually small (no more than fifteen children, sometimes as few as six), they often have aides and support staff in place to meet the children's needs, and they are headed by teachers with training and, hopefully, expertise in working with kids who have special needs.

The curriculum in a behavioral class should be identical to that used in regular classrooms, with adaptations as needed for each student. Many of these classes mix students who are in several grades, however, and it takes a skilled teacher to ensure that each child learns what he needs to know.

In most school districts, behavioral classes are seen as a short-term placement—sort of like boot camp class for kids who behave badly. For children with bipolar disorders whose symptoms are severe, this view is neither realistic nor wise. If a particular behavioral class is working well for your child, see what you can do to hold on to that placement.

Some school districts do have special classes for seriously emotionally disturbed students. Unfortunately, many of these also use level system/ behavior mod techniques exclusively, without the level of therapeutic support that most of the kids they serve really need. If your child is offered placement in a classroom that *does* have a good therapeutic support program, grab it!

Most districts have special classes for children with moderate to severe developmental delays (mental retardation, autism, and so on). In small districts, this may be the only special education classroom available. Such a placement might seem like a terrible idea for your child—and it might well be a mistake. However, if the classroom happens to have a very good teacher and will make other needed supports available to your child, it could be worth considering. There may a be a stigma attached for your child, of course—especially if the class is in his neighborhood school and neighbor kids will know that he has been put in the "retarded kids class." Many of these classes are actually quite good, with a caring and individualized approach that some of the behavioral classes would do well to emulate. For some bipolar kids, especially the very youngest students, there will be times that being the smart kid in a DD class is a great solution to a difficult education problem.

Some children will only need a special classroom for part of the day. Perhaps they need special help with math or reading, or perhaps their behavior seems to get drastically worse as the day wears on. A resource room can be part of the solution. This is a space in the school where kids can get help from a special education teacher to meet their individual needs.

If you walk into a typical resource room, you'll usually see several activities going on. At one table a group of children are working together on reading skills, in another corner of the room a student with Tourette syndrome whose tics are flaring up is taking a time-out from his regular classroom, and at a third table a speech therapist is doing one-on-one work with a child who stutters. A child whose medication makes him sleepy might be napping, while another group of kids works with special math software on the room's computers.

Each of these children is in the resource room for only part of the day, either for a scheduled visit with a specialist (such as the speech therapist) or on an as-needed basis due to symptoms. When children use a resource room for certain types of work, that's called a "pull-out." The rest of the day these kids are in either a regular class or a special education class. Well-run resource rooms act as a safe haven within a busy school.

The law mandates that children be educated in the most inclusive environment possible, and that's an important value. However, recognizing that the best environment for an individual child may not always be fully inclusive is of equal importance.

Parents must also remember that the school's classrooms, computers, and books are often of secondary importance when compared to the value of caring teachers and administrators. If your child has an ally in his school—a favorite teacher, a super counselor, a teacher's aide who bends over backwards to help her—that person can often do more to help her get through school than the best-designed special education program. Parents should try to identify and develop allies for their children within their school, wherever they are placed.

*I went to public grade school and made As and Bs, went to a private
Christian school for three years and got the same grades, and then went
back to public for high school. I had home-based instruction for a semester during my sophomore year when I was in the hospital.*

*I was intelligent enough to be able to do well academically with little
to no effort. The only class I ever worked hard in was debate, which I
enjoyed. I was on the debate team, and I trophied at every tournament I
was in. My teacher/coach was one that pushed just enough... brought out
my strengths while not trivializing my challenges. He was the only
teacher I ever had that I liked or that I felt liked me.*

*I dropped out the beginning of my junior year, as I was unable to
handle the stress of just going to school. I left with a cumulative 3.6 GPA.
—Stephanie, 32 years old (diagnosed with bipolar disorder at age 15,
and now the mother of a bipolar child)*

Alternative school

For some bipolar students, alternative schools (including the charter schools
that are springing up in some parts of the country) offer the best mix of high
academic expectations, strong behavioral supports, and flexibility. Of course,
that depends on the alternative school program itself. Large urban districts
may offer all sorts of public alternative schools, ranging from special schools
for at-risk/gang-affected youth to arts magnet schools. Small, rural districts
may have no choices at all. Suburban areas may have only alternative
schools that emphasize behavior modification rather than academics, and
they often use them as a dumping ground for problem students with little
regard for these children's actual needs or abilities.

If your district does offer alternative programs, be sure to look before you
leap. Visit the site with your child, and ask for a guided tour. If your child
can get a chance to talk to other kids about the school, that usually helps
(assuming that these peers don't hate their school). Sit in on a typical class. If
you can, talk to other parents whose children attend the school, and meet the
actual teachers your child would be working with. Make sure you feel comfortable with the alternative school's philosophy, methods, and objectives.

Take your time—if your child has had difficulty handling school in the past,
you don't want to set him up for additional failure by making a hasty decision. Finding the right fit will make school success more likely.

Once Craig became ill, he was placed on homebound instruction. He tried returning to school this fall, and it was a disaster. He is now enrolled in an alternative school, and it is going well. —Cindy, mother of 16-year-old Craig

Alternative schools and, in most cases, charter schools will still need to abide by your child's IEP. Often these schools are much more flexible, but occasionally they have been set up with a very specific program in mind, such as a levels-based behavior modification system or an arts-centered program designed for self-directed learners. If you sense that the alternative school is rigid in its format, make sure that format is already a good fit for your child. Like a regular public school that has a one-size-fits-all mentality, alternative schools with a specific mission are unlikely to change their approach, even to meet your child's IEP objectives.

Diagnostic classroom

If your child's diagnosis is still not set in stone, your district might suggest placement in a diagnostic classroom. This classroom might be a joint project of the school district and a regional medical center or medical school.

Diagnostic classrooms are used for long-term medical or psychiatric observation and evaluation of children whose behavior and abilities don't seem to fit the profile of any typical diagnosis. This is not a permanent placement, but if your child's case is especially unusual she may stay in the diagnostic classroom for quite some time.

A well-run diagnostic classroom offers your family a unique opportunity to have your child seen at length by experts, and to try new medications, therapies, and other treatments in a medically savvy setting. Make sure that the classroom staff and doctors involve your whole family in the diagnostic and treatment process. Parents report that some diagnostic classrooms are so patient-centered that they forget to talk to parents after the initial interview process.

Special schools

There are very few special public schools for children with mental illness. Some private schools do exist that serve "emotionally troubled" youth, who may or may not have an actual clinical diagnosis. Some special schools are excellent.

If your child is unable to attend a regular school, either in an inclusive situation or in a special education classroom, she may be able to go to a special school. If it's public, it will be very much like going to alternative school.

Many districts contract with private schools that work with certain types of students. For example, they might contract with a private school that uses the Orton-Gillingham method to teach students with dyslexia, or with a private school that specializes in educating deaf and blind students.

One would expect a special school for mentally ill children to have a psychiatrist and therapists on staff, and to do some form of milieu therapy (see Chapter 5, *Therapeutic Interventions*) in addition to academic work. For children with mental illnesses, most contract programs involve day treatment centers. If the district sends your child to a special school or day treatment center, it will pay the full costs. You will not be required to pay tuition or additional fees.

Day treatment centers for children are for those with very difficult behaviors, such as self-injurious or aggressive behavior, that make even a self-contained special education classroom inappropriate. They may be attached to or affiliated with a residential school or hospital. At the end of the school day, children in day treatment go home to their families.

Good day treatment centers provide medical and psychiatric support, specially trained staff, a very secure environment, and intensive intervention. However, many specialize in the treatment of behavior disorders (such as behavior problems that occur as a result of child abuse), and may not have a full understanding of bipolar disorders.

The other problem with many current day treatment programs is that they tend to be conceived as short-term interventions. Slots may be limited to one school year, or even to as little as three months. Students cycle in and out, and staff turnover may also be high. Since most bipolar children do not deal well with constant upheaval, this can present a problem. Your child may also be in class with children whose behaviors are even more unmanageable than her own.

As with any other placement, be sure to tour the facility, meet the staff, and ask lots of questions before you say yes to a day treatment placement.

Residential schools

In some cases, residential programs are your only option. If you live in a small, rural school district, there may simply be no appropriate placement available—assuming that homebound instruction would not be appropriate for your child or your family situation. If your child is dangerously aggressive or actively suicidal, residential settings offer the safest setting—and unlike hospital inpatient programs, they usually have a strong educational component, not just psychiatric treatment, as a focus.

Residential schools offer educational programming and 24-hour care for the child. If your school district asks to send your child to a residential program, the district will pay her tuition and all associated costs. Of course, you also have the option to choose a residential program for your child and pay for it yourself, if you have the financial means.

The best residential programs have staff with a strong medical/psychiatric background, a high level of employee retention, and a commitment to communicating with and working with students' families. As with any other type of school program, you'll want to proceed with caution. Visit the campus, observe a classroom, see the living quarters, talk to staff and (if possible) students, and try to talk to other parents whose children have attended the school. No place is perfect, but some residential schools have deservedly bad reputations.

If your child needs a residential setting, security is probably a major concern. Make sure security measures are more than adequate to prevent students from self-harm, assault, and running away. Also find out how they manage difficult behaviors. Schools that rely on isolation rooms, restraints, or chemical straitjacketing should be avoided at all costs.

You'll also want to know about how the residential program handles transitioning, whether it's preparing your child for a return to his former school after he stabilizes, or simply moving him into a less-restrictive residential setting.

> *Vanessa's residential center had an on-ground school; she now lives in a therapeutic group home and attends a public high school. —Sue, mother of 16-year-old Vanessa (diagnosed bipolar disorder, OCD, borderline personality disorder, passive-aggressive personality disorder)*

Hospital-based education

If your child needs to be an inpatient in a psychiatric hospital (or in a regular hospital, if he has a medical problem in addition to a bipolar disorder) for more than a week or so, he'll still need to get an education. Most child and adolescent psychiatric wards don't exactly excel in this department, though. With the trend toward short hospitalizations in crises only, there's barely time to find out what the student should be working on, much less to devise a program of instruction.

Instead, adolescents who have spent time as inpatients report that much of their daily schoolwork consisted of art projects, lessons copied out of workbooks, and perhaps current affairs discussions. Often that's all a kid in psychiatric crisis can handle, of course.

If your child is going to have a planned hospitalization, contact the hospital program and find out who's in charge of communicating with patients' schools. There may be a formal school-hospital liaison. Make sure this person is in contact with your child's teacher (or in the case of a high school student who has many teachers, a school counselor, homeroom teacher, or other person who is willing to act as a go-between) before your child's scheduled entry date, and that they have set up an educational program in advance. This might include providing lesson plans and reading lists, sending your child's homework assignments to the hospital, and returning graded papers to you, for example.

If the hospitalization is sudden, you will probably need to act as the go-between yourself. Call your child's teacher or teachers and make arrangements for what they feel would be appropriate work to complete during her illness. Before her release, make plans for what she should be doing at home while she recuperates, or how to segue her back into school. You can then make arrangements with hospital staff to ensure that she has the tools and time she needs to do the work. Staff can also let you know if the her teacher's plans are too ambitious, and can provide medical documentation for reducing or even eliminating schoolwork for awhile if needed.

Homebound instruction

Homebound instruction is considered the most restrictive school environment, because it involves sending someone to teach your child individually. However, children may prefer homebound instruction to attending a special school or entering a residential program because it keeps them in the company of their parents and siblings, even though it does restrict their ability to interact with same-age peers.

The most successful experience Lili had in high school was being placed on homebound instruction while we waited for her special education evaluation to be completed. "Homebound" is actually the wrong term to use: the only time her teacher met her at home was to talk about what topics they needed to cover, and so she could meet all of us together.

She worked with an older, experienced teacher who had a sympathetic attitude. She understood that Lili had been through a lot with her recent hospitalization, medication trials, and leaving school. She still challenged her intellectually, helping her to see that she was still the same bright girl she has always been.

They met three days a week at the public library, where plenty of books and an Internet connection were readily available. She gave Lili homework at each session, including a research paper, several short writing assignments, and math handouts.

Of course, the district didn't want to keep paying for this arrangement. In fact, they denied her special education services when her formal evaluation finally happened. The only option they were willing to offer without special education status was placement in a transitional behavioral classroom at her former high school, where she would have spent the day in the company of recently suspended students with violent behaviors. There was little academic work done in this class, and what there was could charitably be called remedial.

We then pursued a second special education evaluation, and started looking at alternative schools. The evaluation gave us the information we needed to force the district into giving Lili special education status. But she was still on the wrong medication, and the uncertain school situation was causing a lot of unneeded stress. She continued to have mood swings, and they now included some violent behavior.

If only she could have stayed on homebound instruction, at least until the second evaluation was done, I think she might have remained stable enough to return to high school—perhaps in a small, alternative-school classroom. As it was, she ended up just getting a GED. That has worked out okay too, but I worry that it may limit her as an adult. —Sarah, mother of 17-year-old Lili

Homebound instruction can be delivered in person, as Sarah describes above, via correspondence courses or distance learning (classes by Internet) arrangements, or with any combination of these methods. If your child is in high school, you'll probably need to make sure his homebound program will help him meet the requirements for graduation. This may mean having the instructor follow specific lesson plans, use certain textbooks, or help your child complete required projects.

You'll want to meet with the homebound instructor privately to explain your child's symptoms and go over his IEP. Grading arrangements should also be worked out in advance.

Homeschooling

Educating your children at home is legal in most US states. Each state has its own regulations about who can homeschool, what (if anything) must be taught, and how (or if) children's educational achievements will be tested. If your state mandates standardized testing for homeschooled students, exceptions to the testing requirements for disabled children are usually not written into the law. You will want to be very careful about doing baseline testing, and about documenting any reasons that your child may not do well on required standardized tests, or may have regressed due to his illness or medication.

Eligible homeschooled children are entitled to Early Intervention and special education services. These services may be delivered in the child's home, at a neutral site, or in a nearby school or clinic. This means that even if you choose to teach your child at home, you can still have an IEP with the school district that provides your child with speech therapy, counseling, and other needed services. Homeschoolers can choose to take part in extracurricular activities at their neighborhood public school, and may even be able to take some classes at school (advanced math, for example) while doing the bulk of their schoolwork at home.

Some districts have programs to help homeschooling parents create good programs for children with disabilities, while others go out of their way to make it difficult.

When home learning opportunities are well-planned, it isn't necessary for children to spend an eight-hour day doing schoolwork. Consider how much of a typical school day is taken up with lunch, recess, waiting for the teacher's help, filling out ditto sheets, and other relatively nonproductive activities. It's easy to see that just a couple hours each day of structured learning activities with one-on-one attention could provide equal educational benefits. Add in unstructured learning opportunities, like impromptu math lessons while measuring ingredients in the kitchen, and the school day at home looks rather inviting. For bipolar kids whose attention problems or uncontrolled symptoms make attending school for long periods too difficult, homeschooling offers an especially flexible option.

It's important to set up socialization opportunities if you are homeschooling. Many homeschooling families share teaching duties with other parents, bringing several children together for certain lessons or activities.

If you are forced to homeschool your child because your district cannot or will not provide a free and appropriate educational placement, you may be eligible to be paid to teach your child. This option has worked for parents in very rural areas, as well as for some in districts that could not provide a safe setting for a child with assaultive behaviors.

> We homeschool, and Cass tests three to five grade levels above in every area except spelling and listening, both areas she struggles with— and even with those, she tests at her grade level. She loves homeschooling and participates in many outside activities, including art, musical theater, and judo. She is not always able to participate in those classes, as sometimes she just is too "off" to handle them. She loves to ride horses in the summer, but is as happy walking a horse in a field as she is actually riding them. We hope to move next year so we can have our own horses for her.

> We make life learning, so to us, school is our world, not always a sit-down lesson at the table. Even her therapist, who was very wary of homeschooling when we first met him, has told me he would never want her schooling changed, that she does better than she could possibly do anywhere else and is very happy. I have found that her homeschooling friends are much nicer to her than their traditionally schooled counterparts.
> —Stephanie, mother of 8-year-old Cassidy (diagnosed bipolar disorder, Tourette syndrome, OCD, ADHD)

Homeschooling is not for everyone, even if you can get help from other parents who are in the same boat. Parents are a child's first teacher, but they're not always the best teachers for all topics. There's also the issue of burnout. Parents don't like to bring it up, but spending all day, every day, with a bipolar child can be exhausting. There are many parents who send their child off to school each day knowing that he will learn little, but also knowing that getting a break will make it possible for the parent to help him stay safe after school. You don't have to feel bad if you are not emotionally able to homeschool your child.

If you do homeschool, decide in advance whether your child will be working toward a high school diploma (this is possible if you use certain homeschool curricula), a GED, or a portfolio of work. Experienced homeschooling parents can help you consider your options, and can be contacted through local groups or online.

Private schools

As noted earlier in this chapter, school districts sometimes contract with private schools and programs to provide services that the district does not. These programs are usually not religious in nature (there are a few exceptions, such as residential programs that are affiliated with a religious denomination), and they must be willing to comply with district regulations.

In a few areas, parents may be able to use school vouchers to lower the cost of private schools, making them one of several educational options. Depending on local regulations (and on the mood of the courts) these options may include parochial schools.

Sometimes parents have good reasons to opt for private school placement directly, at their own cost. Perhaps daily religious instruction is very important to you, or your child's siblings already attend a private school. Luckily, choosing a private school does not automatically disqualify your child from publicly funded Early Intervention and special education services.

Many parents of bipolar children have not had a rosy private school experience. The school that served your other children well may be horribly wrong for a child with a bipolar disorder. Educational programming for children with mental illness requires a certain level of knowledge and flexibility that not all schools have, public or private. You can advocate until you're blue in the face, but in the end, private schools do not *have* to work with your child.

To receive public special education services, you must have your child evaluated and qualified within the public system. Then you'll use an Individual Family Service Plan (IFSP) or IEP to determine which services will be delivered, where they will be delivered, and by whom.

This can get sticky, depending on your state or local district. Some districts are so cautious about maintaining separation of church and state that if several children in a parochial school need speech therapy they will send a speech van to park outside the school, then have children receive speech therapy in the van rather than allowing a public employee to help children inside the walls of a parochial school. Other districts have no qualms about sending employees to private school sites.

Unlike a public school, your private school itself will not be required to fulfill any academic promises made in an IEP. The IEP is a contract between you and the school district only. However, enlightened private schools that wish to better serve students with disabilities are well aware of how valuable the ideas in a well-written IEP can be. Some parochial and private schools encourage teachers to be part of the IEP process. In some cases, these private school representatives have entered their own goals into the IEP, usually under the aegis of the parent.

Private schools that accept any form of public funding may be subject to additional regulations. Many are also subject to the Americans with Disabilities Act. The ADA may prevent a school from discriminating against your child due to his disability. However, unlike Section 504 and IDEA, it will not give you tools to require the school to do anything specific to help him learn.

Mixing and matching

In between the placement options presented in this chapter are combination settings created to meet a student's specific needs. For example, one student might be able to handle a half-day inclusion program in the morning, then have home-based instruction for other subjects in the afternoon. Another child might be placed in a special class for everything but art and music.

The setting(s) listed in your child's IEP should be reviewed every year (or more often, if you request it) to ensure that the educational program is still meeting his needs, and that he is still in the least restrictive setting.

Be flexible, but not too flexible

Whenever possible, the current movement in US schools is toward full inclusion. Sometimes this is not appropriate. If a setting is proposed by the district, be open-minded enough to check it out, but don't say yes unless you're sure it's right. Inquire about supports, such as personal or classroom aides, that can be added to make inclusive settings more realistic.

It's important to remember that because your child's symptoms may wax and wane drastically, a school setting that once worked well may not work forever. And even though you may want your child to finish high school "on time," take college prep courses, or be in a special magnet program, she may not be able to handle it. At the same time, be a fierce advocate for allowing your child to get an education. Far too many bipolar kids are pushed out or sent to get a GED or an IEP diploma, when with appropriate support they could have made it through.

Lisa's story, which is very typical of the school histories provided by parents interviewed for this book, illustrates this point well:

> In her freshman year in school, Lisa started having difficulty attending classes. She had severe panic attacks plus the mood swings from bipolar disorder that as yet had not been diagnosed. She skipped a lot of school, but mainly had trouble just concentrating on school work. She admits now that the kids in school were afraid of her because of her black moods and dress. She was very intimidating at this point.

> Toward the end of her freshman year we finally had to hospitalize her because she was doing so bad mentally. By the time she got back to school, there were only a few weeks left in school. She was able to get through them, but only passed about three of her classes.

> During her sophomore year, things did not improve. This is when we started having more problems with the school administration and getting an education for her. We had several meetings with the administration and finally set up an Individualized Education Plan where Lisa would be taught one-on-one by a teacher outside the school setting. They ended up meeting at one of the school administration buildings every day. Lisa was still having trouble concentrating and missed some of the specialized school, but by the end of the year had turned things around quite a bit.

Unfortunately, with about three months left in the school year the school psychiatrist decided Lisa wasn't making enough progress. He felt that by this time Lisa should be back in school at least part-time. She was still having problems getting regulated on medications. When I tried explaining this to the psychiatrist, he felt that I should just push her into going back to school. Knowing Lisa as I do—this guy had not ever spent any time with Lisa to get to know her—I knew this would not work. You can't push a bipolar person who also has severe panic attacks into doing something they're not ready to do. And only Lisa can determine when she's ready for something.

They suggested we try an alternative school. In this area, alternative schools are for students who cannot make it in the regular school setting. It is usually because of behavior problems, trouble with the law, being kicked out of school for discipline problems. The best one they recommended wasn't too bad. Unfortunately, when I took Lisa there to look it over, we ran into a student who was being taken into another room by the principal because of disrupting the class he was in. This really set Lisa off. Also, a couple of kids that she was introduced to gave her gang signs. At this point in Lisa's life, the last thing that she needed was to be surrounded by kids in gangs. She was too afraid that she would be sucked into that lifestyle.

At the next meeting, I told the school administrators that alternative school was not going to work for Lisa. By the time we were through with this meeting, several of the people in attendance said maybe the best alternative for Lisa would be to drop out and get her GED. This was coming from educators who are responsible for her getting an education. After much discussion with Lisa and her dad, we decided that maybe it really would be best.

She did try and go back to school at the beginning of this school year, but it only lasted two days. It was still too much for her to cope with the crowded halls and kids giving her strange looks because she had been out of school so long.

Lisa is currently attending classes to get her GED. —Donna, mother of 16-year-old Lisa (diagnosed BPII, post-traumatic stress disorder, anxiety disorder)

GED programs

Because of the high drop-out rate among children with mental illness, and because of many school districts' unwillingness to serve these children, there is a possibility that your child may end up pursuing a General Equivalency Diploma (GED) rather than a regular high school diploma. The GED is earned by passing a test. The test includes a short essay and questions on a variety of topics. In most states, you must be 16 to take the GED.

If the school district forces your child out of school, the very least you should ask for is assistance for helping her pass the exam. This might mean homebound instruction geared to the GED, an alternative school program that has earning a GED as its goal, or help in obtaining study materials. There are books, videos, and software programs available to help people be successful on the GED.

Frankly, the GED is not a difficult test. If your child has successfully completed junior high and can apply a simple formula for writing a short essay, he can probably pass it already.

A GED is legally equal to a high school diploma. You can get a job or attend any community college or trade-school program with a GED. If your child wants to pursue a degree at a four-year college, he will probably be able to get in with a GED if he meets the school's other requirements, such as having an adequate score on college placement exams like the SAT and ACT. His chances of admission will be best if he can document his abilities through writing a persuasive admissions essay and building a portfolio of work. He may also want to complete a year or two of community college before applying, as this will be the best possible indicator of his ability to handle college-level work.

Monitoring school progress

Once you have an educational program in place, your next job is playing spy and enforcer. You can't rely totally on the school or the school district to monitor your child's progress, or to ensure compliance with his IEP. Keep a copy of this document and other important notes on hand, and check them against any communications notebooks, progress reports, report cards, and assignments that come home from the school.

Of course you'll want to attend all official meetings, but make a point of just dropping by occasionally on the pretext of bringing your child her coat or having paperwork due at the school office. If you can volunteer an hour a week or so in the school (not necessarily in your child's classroom), that's even better.

If the school is not complying with the IEP, start by talking to the teacher, and work your way up. Most compliance problems can be addressed at the classroom level.

One area that can be especially difficult is monitoring the delivery of therapy and other pull-out services. It seems like a relatively simple task, but parents across the country report that their school district refuses to provide any type of checklist that parents can see to make sure their child is receiving the services listed in the IEP.

Another problem area is the administration of medication at school. Some parents have reported refusal to deliver medication at the appointed time, mysteriously missing pills (especially Ritalin and other amphetamines), and missed or mistaken doses. Most self-contained classrooms have many children who take scheduled medications, and they tend to have processes in place. The worst medication problems seem to occur in full inclusion settings, especially if the student is not capable of monitoring medication delivery himself. You may need to insist on a daily checklist, and increase your own monitoring efforts.

If your IEP includes academic goals, see if there are standardized ways to monitor progress (grades aren't always enough). Too often parents are told that their child is participating well and learning, and then discover that he has not gained new skills or has actually regressed when an objective measure is used. Ask that your child be tested every year if possible. Get the results of standardized tests (you are entitled to these). Check the scores to make sure your child is progressing.

Many parents have found that their child is not only not learning, but is actually regressing. Lack of progress or regression give you firm grounds for demanding that your child's academic needs be included in the IEP. Several parents report that one of the best ways to get the rest of your IEP team to understand the problem is using visual aids, such as charts. If you aren't an artistic whiz, there are software programs that can make simple graphs from your numbers.

Taking on the school system

If your child's school persistently refuses to comply with her IEP, what can you do? A lot—the IEP is a type of legal contract, although far too many schools treat it like a nuisance that they can ignore at their leisure. Your options include:

- Sitting back and letting it happen (obviously not recommended)
- Advocating for your child within the classroom and the IEP process
- Bringing in an expert to help you advocate for your child
- Requesting a due process hearing
- Organizing with other parents to advocate for a group of students with similar problems
- Working with other advocates at a legislative level
- Going to court

While some schools and school districts have a well-deserved reputation for venality, most are simply hamstrung by low budgets and lack of knowledge. These are areas where an informed parent can make a difference. You can provide the teacher and administrators with information about educational possibilities, and you can let them know that their resource problems are something to take up with government funding sources, not something to unfairly penalize children with.

Remember that as a full member of the IEP team, you have the power to call an IEP meeting whenever one is needed. This will bring together all of the team members to review the document, and to compare its requirements with what your child is receiving.

There are times when you will need to bring in an expert. All over the country educational advocates and self-styled IEP experts are becoming available. Some of these people work for disability advocacy organizations or disability law firms. Others are freelance practitioners. Some are parents of children with disabilities who have turned their avocation into a vocation.

You will probably have to pay for expert services, unless they are available through your local NAMI chapter or another parent group. Expert services can include researching programs available in your area, connecting you with appropriate resources, helping you write a better IEP, and advocating for your child at IEP meetings and due process hearings.

Due process

The words "due process" make schools very nervous. This term refers to the processes that a child and his family are supposed to have access to while being evaluated for special education or provided with special education services. If you or the school has requested that your child be evaluated for special education services, whether or not he has been approved, you are entitled to due process.

When parents start talking about due process, they're usually referring to a due process hearing: an internal appeals procedure used by school districts to determine whether or not procedures have been handled properly. Due process hearings hinge on whether the district has followed federal and state-mandated procedures for evaluating a child for special education and setting up a program for that child. Violations can include small things, like notifying parents of a meeting over the phone rather in writing, or major issues, like using untrained or incompetent personnel to evaluate children or deliberately denying needed services to save money.

Issues that tend to end up in due process include disagreements over evaluations or educational labels, provision of inadequate therapeutic services, placement in inappropriate educational settings, noncompliance with the IEP, lack of extended school year services when appropriate, and poor transition planning.

Obviously, every due process case is unique. Each state also has its own due process system. Regulations that all of these systems have in common are:

- Parents must initiate a due process hearing in writing.

- The hearing must take place in a timely fashion.

- Hearings are presided over by an impartial person who does not work for the district.

- Children have the right to stay in the current placement until after the hearing (this is called the "stay put" rule).

- Parents can attend due process hearings and advocate for their child.

- Parents can hire an educational advocate or lawyer to represent them at the due process hearing.

- If the parents use a lawyer and they win, they are entitled to have their legal fees paid by the district.

Due process hearings resemble a court hearing before a judge. Both sides will be asked to argue their case and present evidence on their behalf. Both sides can call on experts or submit documents to buttress their statements. However, experienced advocates know that, despite the veneer of impartiality, if it comes down to your word against the district's on educational or placement issues, the district will probably have an edge.

Some districts offer arbitration or mediation, which are not as formal as a due process hearing. In an arbitration hearing, both parties agree in advance to comply with the arbitrator's ruling. You can't recover your legal fees in arbitration, and your rights are not spelled out in the law. Be very cautious before agreeing to waive your right to a due process hearing in favor of mediation.

However, you can try mediation without waiving your right to due process while you're waiting for your due process hearing date to come up. If mediation works, you're done; if it doesn't, you can continue with the due process proceeding.

Section 504 actions

You can bypass the cumbersome due process procedure if your child has a 504 plan rather than or in addition to an IEP. Assuming that the school and district administrators have not responded to your written complaints, take your case directly to your state Office of Civil Rights. This office is responsible for enforcing the Rehabilitation Act.

The state Office of Civil Rights is also charged with enforcing the Americans with Disabilities Act (see the section "The ADA and schools" later in this chapter).

Public advocacy

If your child is denied special education services, you'll soon find out that you have a lot of company. Some problems in special education are systemic. Parents in several states have banded together effectively to get better services for their children. The National Alliance for the Mentally Ill (NAMI) is just one of several national organizations that are actively trying to secure improvements in special education. (See the appendix, *Resources*, for a list of helpful groups.)

You may choose to form your own organization, join an existing group covering childhood mental health issues, or work with a larger group of special education parents. You may also find allies in teacher's unions and organizations, the PTA and other parents associations, and elsewhere in your community.

Parents can personally help improve school funding for the education of mentally ill students by lobbying their local school board or state legislature. They can help write and press for laws that require adequate support for these students and for others in the special education system.

If you're not the kind of person who enjoys conflict, advocacy and due process can be very draining. School districts count on endless meetings, criticism of your parenting skills, and constant references to their superior knowledge to wear down your defenses. You must always stay on guard, and yet be open to logical compromises and the possibility of beneficial alliances. It's not easy, but it's necessary.

Going to court

Due process is bad enough. Going to court is absolutely, positively your last recourse. It's something you do only when nothing else works, not even marching on a school board meeting with a bunch of disgruntled parents.

Going to court is time-consuming, exhausting, and expensive. The outcome is uncertain, and while the case drags on, your child may be languishing in an inappropriate setting. But if you've exhausted every other avenue, it may just have to happen.

Most court cases involving special education involve school districts that have lost a due process hearing, and yet persist in denying the services mandated for a child. A 1994 case, *W.B. v. Matula*, also established the right of parents to sue a school on constitutional grounds. The parent of a grade-schooler who was eventually diagnosed with multiple neurological disabilities took her district to court over violation of her child's due process rights and under the Fourteenth Amendment of the Constitution, which entitles all citizens to equal protection under the law. To the consternation of school districts everywhere, she won her case, which included a substantial financial judgment (she used the money to pay her massive legal bills and to get her son an appropriate education).

The ADA and schools

The Americans with Disabilities Act is a pioneering civil rights law. Patterned on civil rights laws that bar discrimination based on race, ethnicity, or gender, the ADA mandates access to all public and most private facilities for disabled citizens. It's usually invoked to make sure people with physical disabilities have access to wheelchair ramps, elevators, grab bars, and other aids to using public or private accommodations. It also prevents handicapped people from most forms of job discrimination.

Many people do not know that people with mental illnesses are included in the federal definition of disabled, and therefore eligible for protection under the ADA.

In schools, the ADA does more than force the district to install handicapped-accessible restrooms and wheelchair ramps for physical access. It mandates that children with disabilities have right to be involved in all school activities, not just classroom-based educational activities. This includes band, chess club, chorus, sports, camping trips, field trips, and any other activities of interest to your child that are school-sponsored or school-affiliated.

If your child will need accommodations or support to take advantage of these activities, the IEP is where these should be listed. If you do not have an IEP, a 504 plan can be used.

If your child's behavior is actually dangerous to himself or others, that's another issue, but under the ADA the school cannot discriminate based simply on his diagnosis or on assumptions they might have about his behavior.

Education in Canada

The Canadian special education process is very similar to that used in the US. Provincial guidelines are set by the national Ministry of Education and governed by the Education Act. However, most educational decisions are made at the regional, district, or school level. Bipolar children between the ages of six and twenty-two should qualify for special education assistance under the Targeted Behaviour Program (TBP).

Special education evaluations are done by a team that may include a school district psychologist, a behavior specialist, a special education teacher, other school or district personnel, and in some cases a parent, although inviting parents to participate is not required by law.

The evaluation is used as a basis for an IEP. Almost identical to the American document of the same name, the IEP is usually updated yearly, or more frequently if needed. A formal review is required every three years.

> We have IEPs, but they don't have quite the same clout here that they appear to have under the US legislation. What you have to trumpet here is the legal requirement, under human rights legislation, that disability be "accommodated." For us, the school counselor is being very helpful, as is the district behaviour specialist. I'm doing some research at the moment on the actual legal requirements so that I know just how much I can demand. I've found the most effective resource is to be a pleasant, informed, persistent, somewhat annoying, pest. —Rae, mother of 13-year-old D'Arcy

Placement options for Canadian students with bipolar disorders range from home-based instruction to full inclusion. Partial inclusion is increasingly common, as is supported mainstreaming. Students from rural or poorly served areas may be sent to a residential school, or funding may be provided for room and board to allow the student to attend a day program outside of their home area.

If disputes arise between the school or the district and the parents, there is a school division decision review process available for adjudicating them. The concept known as due process in the US is usually referred to as "fundamental justice" in Canada.

Education in the UK

When a child in the UK is judged eligible for special education services, he is said to be "statemented." This term refers to an IEP-like document called a Statement of Special Educational Needs, or Record of Needs. This document is developed at the council level by the Local Educational Authority (LEA), and lists the services that a statemented child needs. Usually the team that creates the statement includes an educational psychologist, a teacher, and the parents. It may also include the family's health visitor or other personnel, such as a psychiatrist or child development specialist. Each child's statement is reviewed and updated annually. Disability advocates strongly urge parents to get expert help with the statementing process.

Your LEA can limit services according to its budget, even if those services are listed as necessary on your child's statement. Service availability varies widely between LEAs. Some therapeutic services that would be delivered by schools in the US, such as psychiatric care and therapy, may be made available through National Health instead.

School placements in the UK run the gamut from residential schools to specialist schools to full inclusion in mainstream schools. There are more residential options available than in the US system due to the English tradition of public schools. (American readers may be confused by this term. In the UK, schools that are privately owned and run are known as public schools; schools run by the LEAs are called government schools.)

Schools working with statemented students operate under a government Code of Practice that is analogous to, but much weaker than, IDEA in the US. Parents and disability advocates can insist that LEAs follow this code when devising programs for statemented students, and have access to a formal appeals process.

The UK government has recently taken steps toward improving Early Intervention offerings. Currently, EI services are not mandated by law, although they are available in many areas.

Parents report that homeschooling a child with a disability is particularly hard in some parts of the UK. Regular inspection by an educational welfare officer is required, and some of these bureaucrats are not very knowledgeable about mental health issues. Parents should be prepared to provide detailed documentation of what they are teaching, and of how well their child is progressing.

Education in Australia

Australia's system is paradoxically looser and yet more accommodating to students with disabilities of all sorts. There is only a thin legal framework for the provision of special education services, but in the urban areas where most Australians live these services are apparently no harder to obtain than they are in the UK.

Early Intervention services are readily available in urban areas for children aged six and under. To obtain an EI evaluation, parents should contact the Specialist Children's Services Team at their local Department of Human Services.

Placement options for older children include residential schools (including placement in residential schools located in the UK, for some students), special schools for children with moderate to severe developmental delay or severe behavior disorders, special classrooms for disabled children within regular schools, and the full range of mainstreaming options. Mix and match placements that allow students to be mainstreamed for just part of the day are still rare, however. For students in rural areas, there is a traveling teacher service that can provide special education services and consultation to children learning in outback schools or at home.

Australia has federal special education regulations, but each state's Department of Education, Training and Employment (DETS, formerly called the Department of Education and Children's Services) is more important. Each DETS provides information, parent services, assistive technology, augmentative communication, special curricula, and many more services for students with disabilities. Individual school districts and schools themselves may also apply different rules, or offer special programs.

> We don't have anything like IEPs, and I think that there are some cultural factors involved in the way disability is approached here. I've been trying to put my finger on just what it is… I think it has to do with the fact that Australian society is less harsh than American society. There's a bit more sense of cooperation and caring for the underdog. People don't talk as much about rights, don't sue each other very often, etc. (though it is happening more). Perhaps there has been less need to label kids because there is somewhat less tendency to isolate and discriminate.

> I'm not saying that there aren't huge problems for kids with differences (especially subtle differences which aren't at all obvious); however, I think that people here tend to expect to talk things through with schools and teachers and make informal arrangements. There's an expectation of reasonableness, in many cases. I get to know teachers on a personal level and explain about Kim's differences. On the one hand we have less

bureaucratisation of services and more individual innovation, on the other hand we have less services altogether. —Kerry, mother of 12-year-old Kim

Education in New Zealand

Students who qualify for special education services in New Zealand are called "section nined" (old terminology) or "qualified for the Ongoing Resourcing Scheme" (ORS). ORS qualification is currently reserved for those children whose impairment is judged to be high or very high, with the most resources going to the latter group. As of this writing, special education services for early childhood centers and home-based programs are not funded. Nevertheless, special arrangements are made to provide services to some young children with disabilities in a clinical setting or in home-based programs.

The Ministry of Education sets qualifying guidelines for early childhood and school-age special education services.

Recent news reports indicate that limited local resources and a move to push for full inclusion under the Special Education 2000 program has eliminated many special education resources that were once available in New Zealand's schools. According to NZ parents, mentally ill children were never particularly well-served by the system anyway. There is a corresponding move to community-based services for children and adults with mental illness that advocates hope will eventually fill in the gaps, but as of yet services are neither widespread nor easy to obtain.

School placements include a few special schools, attached special education units within regular schools, and a range of inclusion options in mainstream settings. Some students are in residential settings. Under Special Education 2000, many more schools will have a resource room-like arrangement rather than self-contained special education units.

Special school problems

Certain problems that bipolar kids may have with school deserve special attention. These include issues of transitioning back into school after hospitalization, medications at school, and the serious problem of school violence.

Transition back to school

Imagine how it must feel to be sent to a hospital for a period of weeks, months, or even years, then dropped back into your old school as if nothing had happened. If it was a psychiatric facility, you may not want to talk to your friends about it. You may feel embarrassed. Your medications may make you feel different. Everything probably feels very strange.

And yet we expect children and teens to navigate properly despite this sudden transition.

It's best to ease from hospital to school, starting with a few days or weeks of homebound instruction, then going back to school in a resource room (perhaps with pull-outs for some inclusion activities), half days at school, or an intermediate period in day treatment. Making the transition gradual improves your child's chances for successful reintegration. Think of a best case scenario and one or more fall-back positions, just in case.

As soon as you begin planning a hospitalization, or when your child enters the hospital if it is a crisis hospitalization, start planning for this transition. Communication is the key. As discussed in the section "Hospital-based education" earlier in this chapter, the school and the hospital must be talking to each other (and to you) from the start. Ask the professionals working with your child in the hospital what they would recommend. They have seen many children your child's age and may have some good ideas about improving transition planning.

Identify one person at your child's school—a teacher, counselor, school psychologist, or perhaps an administrator—who can be in charge of the transition back to school. If you have to personally explain the situation to too many people, it's likely that someone will be missed, or that someone will miss out on important information. It's better to have someone fully informed right there at school. Preferably this person will be someone your child can confide in if problems crop up.

Make sure that both you and your child's school are fully informed about any medications he may be taking, how they should be administered, and side effects that school personnel should watch out for. You may also need to adjust the IEP, 504 plan, or behavior plan to fit new knowledge about your child, or the effects of medication (such as cognitive dulling, sleepiness, or agitation).

Medications at school

Some children and teens with bipolar disorder can take all their meds at home, and this is the best way to avoid school medication problems. Generally speaking, kids prefer not to take medicine at school. Some children will need to take daytime doses, though, and these will have to be administered at school.

In any school there are many, many children who have daily medication needs, ranging from Ritalin to migraine medicine. Your child will not be seen as unusual if he needs to take a pill every day—in fact, he'll probably have to wait in line.

Schools these days are very uptight about student drug use. Anti-drug policies usually include prescription medications and over-the-counter drugs, such as aspirin, as well as illicit drugs. Make sure you have a copy of your child's school's policy on using prescription and non-prescription medications at school to avoid problems. It is very rare for even a teenager to be allowed to self-administer medication at school. The usual exceptions to this rule are medications needed if life-threatening symptoms could emerge suddenly, such as asthma inhalers or emergency allergy medications for anaphylactic shock.

Medications should be properly stored. The pill bottle's label or pharmacy insert should tell you if a medication needs refrigeration or should simply be stored away from light or heat. For safety's sake, medications should be kept in a locked drawer or cabinet. This will prevent them from misuse, abuse, and theft. Ask to see where your child's medications will be kept.

If your school has an on-site health clinic or nurse's office, that's the best place for your child to get and take his medication. If it does not, medications will be given out by someone who is neither licensed nor trained in how to handle medication-related problems. This is a major problem for many families whose children need to take medication at school. School secretaries and teachers are frequently pressed into the role of pill-pushers, and it's rarely one that they relish. In hospitals and nursing homes, a certified medication aide (CMA) license is the minimum qualification required to give medications to patients.

If your child takes medication daily, make sure there is some sort of checklist used to monitor compliance. The person administering medications should actually *see* the child take them, not hand them out and let the child walk away. It may be necessary to check the child's mouth to make sure the pills were swallowed. Ask to see the medication compliance checklist at least one a semester, and talk to your child about whether he is getting his medications regularly.

Emergency or as-needed psychiatric medications are problematic for schools. Unless they have a medical person on staff, they will naturally be unsure of when to allow their use. If your doctor prescribes this kind of medication for your child, the pill bottle should say "use as needed" or "PRN" (for the Latin "pro re nata," meaning as circumstances dictate). Ask your physician to write a brief statement about when school personnel should give the medication out. Alternatively, you could write this statement yourself. Older children and teens should know the symptoms that these drugs can help with and be able to ask for them independently. The medications most commonly prescribed in this way are tranquilizers and other anti-anxiety drugs. When used properly, they can be very helpful.

Students may be prescribed medications by a psychiatrist working at the school, with parental permission. Occasionally someone without a license to practice medicine, such as a psychologist or school counselor, may tell parents that their child should take a certain medication. In either case, parents have the right to refuse medication for their child, and to ask for a second opinion.

School behavior and school violence

Due to recent episodes of violence, many US schools are taking a hard line on verbal threats, aggressive or assaultive behavior, and even on the presence of students with behavioral, emotional, or neurological disorders in schools. In some cases, this campaign has crossed over from prudent caution to violating the rights of special education students. For example, some districts have announced that all assaults (a category that includes hitting, biting, and even playground pushing) will result in police being called to actually arrest the student. Students have been suspended or threatened with expulsion for angrily saying things like "I wish this school would burn down" or for threatening the school bully with a stick hastily grabbed off the ground.

According to IDEA, students with disabilities are subject to discipline for infractions of school rules just like all other students—unless the problem is a result of the disability. For example, it would be unfair to suspend a child with Tourette syndrome for having a spitting tic, even though spitting would normally be a rule violation. Likewise, it would be wrong to expel or arrest a student with a bipolar disorder if he has a rage episode as a result of his illness.

At the same time, schools do have a duty to protect other students, faculty, and staff. Case law has upheld the idea that if a student cannot be safely maintained in a less restrictive setting, the district has the right to place the student in a more restrictive setting. The devil is in the details, of course. Parents in these situations find they carry the burden of proving that the district did not do all it could to keep the student in the least restrictive setting.

If you or the school suspects that your child's misbehavior is the result of her disability, a functional behavior assessment and a functional intervention plan are the correct response. The functional behavior assessment should include:

- A clear description of the problem behavior, including the pattern or sequence of behavior observed

- Time, place, and situation when the behavior occurs (setting and antecedents)

- The current consequences attached to the behavior

- A hypothesis about the cause and effect of the behavior

- Direct observation data

The functional intervention plan should derive from the functional behavior assessment, and consist of guidelines for modifying the student's environment to eliminate or improve behavior, as well as ideas for teaching the student positive alternative behavior. Creating a workable plan may require trying on several hypotheses about the behavior, and then testing different interventions. This procedure should be followed whenever a special education student has a long-lasting behavior problem, or if he has any behavior problem that puts him at danger for suspension, expulsion, or arrest.

For example, in the situation cited earlier where a child has a spitting tic, the plan could include several ideas for handling the problem. The child could go to the bathroom to spit, use a trash can, or spit into a handkerchief. Adults could see if stress is leading to increased ticcing and then reduce stress, or try a different medication for tic reduction. For the child who rages, the functional behavior assessment could be used to find out if there is an environmental trigger, and the functional intervention plan could provide ways to prevent the behavior. These might include removing the environmental trigger, designating a safe place for the child to go when he feels the warning signs of impending rage, training personnel in safe restraint techniques, or providing emergency medication.

Parents of a bipolar child who is sometimes aggressive, assaultive, or even just plain hateful often secretly worry that he could turn his rage on others, with serious or even deadly results. Especially after the rash of school killings in the late 1990s, this is a logical worry. When fifteen students and teachers were shot by students at Columbine High School in Littleton, Colorado in March of 1999, both the press and legislative arenas were filled with calls to remove problem students from schools.

Responsible parents can do much to ensure that their child does not become the perpetrator of such crimes. Almost every teen involved in a school killing has had several traits in common. They have been very depressed, usually suicidal, and they have had easy access to weapons, little parental oversight, and no special program of supports at school. Most had been the victims of teasing and mistreatment at school, with no intervention from school administrators. For example, Michael Carneal, the 14-year-old who shot classmates in ultra-conservative West Paducah, Kentucky, had been labeled a homosexual in the school newspaper. He had been the butt of jokes for many years before he allegedly snapped and became violent. He had actually been exhibiting psychotic behavior since eighth grade, but had not received any help. Carneal, who pled guilty though mentally ill, has since been variously diagnosed with a cyclic mood disorder and schizotypal personality disorder.

For those teens guilty of school shootings who were supposedly under the care of a psychiatrist, that care was generally cursory—perhaps a single visit and a quickly discarded prescription, as was apparently the case with Kip Kinkel in Oregon and Eric Harris in Colorado. Some may have been misdiagnosed or mismedicated—for example, given SSRIs when they actually suffered from bipolar disorder, theoretically causing mania or psychosis to emerge. The vast majority had never gotten any substantive help for their psychiatric or emotional problems.

If you are reading this book, you are the kind of involved, informed parent who will make sure that weapons are not easily available to your child, ensure that he is under proper medical care, and see to it that your child's school is part of the solution to his problems, not a problem itself.

If your child develops a fascination with weapons and violence, you must intervene immediately. Don't wait to get help—call on all possible resources in his school and in the community.

Suspension and expulsion

Some bipolar students will break school rules, and not necessarily as a result of their illness. When they do so, they must pay the price. However, if a student covered by an IEP is suspended for more than ten days in one school year or is expelled, the district is responsible for finding an appropriate alternative educational setting immediately, and for continuing to implement the IEP. Suspension of a disabled student for more than ten days requires parental permission or a court order. The district is also required to do a functional behavior assessment and create a functional intervention plan if this has not already been done, or to take a new look at the existing plan in light of the incident.

Suspensions of longer than ten days constitute a change of placement, and that means that an IEP meeting must be called immediately. IDEA does not spell out exactly how this procedure should work, so districts may not have a plan in place to deal with emergency placements. Parents have reported that many school districts respond by putting the student on homebound instruction until a new placement can be found. This may or may not be acceptable. Delivery of therapeutic services may be a problem on homebound instruction. Parents will probably have to get involved to prevent the search process from dragging on too long.

For the purpose of these protections, the category of disabled students includes not only those with a special education IEP or other formal agreement with the district, but also those students whose parents have requested a special education assessment or written a letter of concern about the child to school personnel (if the parent is illiterate or cannot write, a verbal inquiry will suffice) before the incident occurred, students whose behavior and performance should have indicated a disability to any objective observer, and children about whom district personnel have expressed concern before the incident.

Expulsion is an even more serious matter. Parents must be informed in writing about the district's intention to seek expulsion, and this document must include clear reasons for this action, evidence, and information about the child's procedural rights. There must be an assessment before expulsion can take place, and parents must also be informed about this in writing. Only if all safeguards are provided and all procedures are followed can a disabled student be expelled.

Expulsion for a disabled student does not mean the same thing as it does for a garden-variety miscreant, who may simply be kicked out to rot in front of the TV at home. It's more like a forced change of placement. By expelling the student, the district has determined that the current placement is not working. It must then find an appropriate placement, which means revisiting the IEP.

As a result of school violence, several states and the federal government are considering laws that would mandate the arrest and incarceration (pending a hearing before a judge) of any child who brings a gun to school. Under current circumstances, this seems like a logical response. If your child is ever in this situation, you should be able to use this opportunity to get him into a diversion program with psychiatric support.

Extended school year services

If your child needs to have a consistent educational and therapeutic program year round, most school districts will only provide services during summer vacations and other long breaks if you can document his need for extended school year (ESY) services. This requires monitoring how your child copes with breaks in the school routine. Teachers and your child's psychiatrist or therapist can help you gather the evidence you need to show that your child loses skills or regresses behaviorally after being out of school for more than a weekend. During breaks from school, keep your own log of behaviors and regressions, if any.

Some parents have also been able to qualify their children for ESY services by showing that services can be made available during the summer that satisfy parts of the IEP not addressed adequately during the school year. For example, a student might be able to get ESY funding approved for a special summer program geared toward teaching social skills or independent living skills.

Early intervention

It is very rare for a child to be diagnosed with bipolar disorder as a preschooler. However, if your child falls into this category, or if she has another disabling condition that emerges in early childhood, she should be eligible for Early Intervention (EI) services.

EI service offerings vary widely according to where you live. They should, however, be determined by the child's needs, not just what happens to be available or customary in your area. Evaluation is the first, and sometimes the most important, service provided through EI programs. Once an evaluation has been carried out, if your child is found to have bipolar disorder or another disability an Individual Family Service Plan (IFSP) is developed. The IFSP spells out the needs of the child and the family, and the services that will be provided to meet those needs.

The Individual Family Service Plan

This document should be created at an IFSP meeting, which you will be invited to attend and contribute to. Although it's a good idea for both parents and practitioners to write down their ideas for goals and interventions in advance, the IFSP itself should not be written in advance and simply handed to the parents to sign.

The cover page of the IFSP summarizes what's known about the child and his diagnosis, and lists the team members present at the IFSP meeting. It also lists the services to be provided, who will provide them, how often they will be provided, and where they will be delivered. Further details about these services are entered on goals and objectives pages, later in the IFSP. Accordingly, the cover page should be mostly blank until the goals and objectives pages have been filled out.

Goals and objectives will be developed by the team at the IFSP meeting. They can be written to cover any area where your child has a deficit, including cognition, behavior, coping strategies, fine and gross motor development, communication, social skills, and self-help skills. Goals should be finite, observable items rather than general concepts. For example, "Kim will learn to use counting to ten and breathing deeply as a response to frustration," is a workable goal, while "Kim will learn to deal with frustration," is not.

One or more pages of the IFSP describe your child's evaluation. These pages should cover medical information, psychiatric diagnosis, and the results of hearing, vision, and developmental screening, if any.

The IFSP can also include services needed by the whole family to help you care for your child. For example, these services might include parent education classes, the services of a behavior expert who can help you with home discipline problems, psychiatric consultation, and assistance in finding and accessing community resources.

The goals set in your child's IFSP will dictate what kind of setting services should be delivered in. Typical EI settings include:

- **Home-based services.** For very young children, home-based services often make the most sense. Home-based programs may include direct therapeutic and educational services, training and supervision for parents and volunteers working with the child, and assistance with medical procedures and care needed to allow education to take place.

- **Direct services.** This category includes all types of professional services, such as psychological therapy, that are delivered in a school setting (but not as part of the preschool program itself), clinic, or other setting outside the home. For example, the IFSP might specify that your child is to receive 45 minutes of play therapy twice a week at a nearby university's clinic. These services may be delivered by professionals or facilities under contract with Early Intervention, or by practitioners working directly for the EI program.

- **School-based services.** This category includes all services delivered as part of a public or private preschool program, at the school site. Therapeutic services may be integrated into a special or typical preschool program, or may be delivered as pull-out services for which your child leaves the class for one-on-one or small-group work.

A primarily home-based program goes the furthest to build a strong relationship between the child and his parents. It takes place in a familiar, non-distracting environment that has probably already been made appropriate for the child's sensory and safety needs. It eliminates lost time and problems related to transporting a preschool child to school (many EI programs actually bus infants and toddlers across town). It also provides the best stage for intensive, one-on-one intervention, such as floor-time play therapy.

It can also be extraordinarily difficult to get approval for. One tool that may help you win this battle is a thorough and accurate financial appraisal that compares the cost of an intensive home-based program in the early years to twelve years of residential or private placement. If your child has been diagnosed with a bipolar disorder at this early an age, it is likely that his symptoms are already very severe. That makes early, intensive intervention the most cost-effective solution, no matter how you cut it.

Early Intervention classrooms

A preschool setting with other children is often considered the best placement for a young child with a psychiatric condition, because it provides the child with the greatest number of opportunities to relate to others, play, and learn. Spending time with other children in a structured setting can be very beneficial for developing social skills. However, attention must be paid to your child's special needs, deficits, strengths, and so on—just any preschool class won't do.

Early Intervention preschools come in four basic flavors:

- **Regular preschool classroom, with or without special support.** Also called a full integration setting or mainstreaming, this might be a Head Start or similar preschool classroom. Your child would attend preschool with therapeutic services, classroom adaptations, and personal support, such as an aide, as needed. These services, adaptations, and supports must be written into the IFSP.

- **Supported integrated preschool classroom.** Also called a reverse integration setting, because it's the nondisabled students who are integrated into a special program rather than the other way around. This is a specially created preschool setting that brings together a small group of children with disabilities and children without disabilities. Therapeutic services, classroom adaptations, and personal support are provided to each child with a disability as per his IFSP. Children in a supported integrated classroom may have a variety of different disabilities, such as autism, Down syndrome, or mental illness.

- **Special preschool classroom.** This is a specially created preschool setting for children with disabilities only. The children may have a mix of various physical or emotional disabilities, or a mix of different behavior disorders only. The classroom may be part of a larger school with other types of classrooms.

- **Special preschool.** This is an entire preschool program created specifically to work with children who have disabilities. It may be within a larger school program that also educates school-age children. It may be owned and run by a public school district, or it may be a private school that contracts with the Early Intervention program to provide services. If it is private, EI and/or the school district should pay the full cost of tuition if it is judged to be the most appropriate setting for your child.

There are positive aspects to each of these typical settings. For children who can handle full, supported inclusion in a regular preschool classroom, there are ample opportunities to model the behavior of less-challenged peers.

Supported integrated classrooms offer similar benefits, with a daily program and structure that's more geared toward the child with special needs.

Special classrooms and schools generally have the most services, but provide few opportunities to interact with nondisabled peers. Your child's needs, abilities, and difficulties will dictate the right placement, as there is no workable one-size-fits-all approach.

Why school matters so much

School is your child's work, the most important thing he does outside of his relationships with family members. It is preparation for the rest of his life. And although many young people are not developmentally or emotionally ready for all of the challenges of school, it is a legal responsibility as well as a societal one.

One of the most devastating effects of childhood-onset bipolar disorders is the disruption of a child's education. It can affect your child's prospects for higher education, employment, and ability to function in the community as an adult. This is especially true when the onset of severe symptoms is sudden, as it so often is. The patient feels intense self-doubt, anxiety, and shame when she is unable to handle something that other kids seem to tackle with ease, and that was once a source of personal pride.

> *It was the end of my senior year in high school when I was devastated by my first down-swing. It lasted for months, and it wasn't long before the anxiety was so high I couldn't figure out what books I should*

bring to class. I was a 4.0 student and president of the student body, but the thought of attending school terrified me so much that I could only retreat into my bed and stay there all day. —Troy, 30 years old (diagnosed bipolar at age 17)

School failure and dropping out of school can be predictors for serious trouble in adult life—but only if the problem is not solved. There are so many options for young people with bipolar disorder that an inability to manage traditional schooling should not be a barrier to learning. Parents and their allies at school may have to be more creative and flexible than they have ever been before, but the outcome will be worth it.

CHAPTER 9

Transitions

THE MAIN GOAL OF TRANSITION PLANNING is the same for all students, regardless of their abilities or goals: preparation for the world of work. For most students, high school graduation marks a jumping-off point: some go straight to work, some to apprenticeships, some to community college, and some to college. But there's nothing magical about the number 18. When your child reaches the age of legal majority, he may still need your assistance. How much help he'll need will depend entirely on the severity of his symptoms, and on how well you have been able to plan for the future.

In this chapter, we'll look at transition planning: the process of smoothing your teenager's transition into the adult world through careful educational, vocational, financial, and medical preparation. There are two kinds of transition planning: a formal process that will be part of your child's IEP and that will concentrate on school and employment issues, and a family process that covers legal, financial, and personal concerns.

Transition planning as part of an IEP

Within the special education system, transition planning should begin by age 13 or 14, when your child's peers are beginning to gain basic work skills and amass credits toward high school graduation. Special education students have a right to also be prepared for graduation, higher education, and work in ways that fit their needs. For many, extra support will be needed.

Your teenager's transition plan should address high school graduation, higher education, and work skills and opportunities. It may also include preparing the young adult to apply for public assistance, supported housing, and other necessary benefits; helping her learn how to self-manage medical and psychiatric care; and instructing her in life skills such as budgeting, banking, driving, and cooking.

A high school student's IEP must include an area for transition planning. Because this is an area that has received little emphasis in the past, you may need to keep the IEP team on track. Make sure your child's transition plan involves all relevant life areas, not just education.

Preparing for work

Preparing for the world of work means gaining appropriate basic skills, such as typing, filing, driving, filling out forms, writing business letters, using tools, or cooking. These skills may be gained in school-based vocational-technical classes, in classes taken at a community college or vocational school while the student is still in high school, in a union- or employer-sponsored apprenticeship program, via job shadowing arrangements or internships, or on the job. Vocational planning is mandatory for special education students in the US by age 16, and should start much earlier.

Transition-to-work services may include moving into the public vocational rehabilitation system, which trains and places adults with disabilities into jobs. However, in many states the vocational rehabilitation system is severely overloaded, with wait times for placement ranging from three months to as much as three years. Typical opportunities range from sheltered workshop jobs (splitting kindling wood, sorting recyclables, light assembly work) under direct supervision, to supported placement in the community as grocery clerks, office helpers, chip-fabrication plant workers, and the like. Often the person works with a job coach who helps them handle workplace stresses and learn work skills. In some cases, the job coach actually comes to work with the person for awhile.

> We had never even heard of vocational rehabilitation when Jakob left the hospital. His therapist at community mental health sent him there. They had a job counselor who worked with him on his first resume, how to dress, and what interviews were like. They placed him in a part-time file clerk job with a hospital near the community college, and they checked up on him regularly for quite awhile. That was perfect: he's been there two years, and now he's taking classes part-time also. —Pam, mother of 20-year-old Jakob (diagnosed bipolar I disorder)

School districts may sponsor their own supported work opportunities for special education students, such as learning how to run an espresso coffee cart or working in a student-run horticultural business. Many schools have vocational programs that give students a chance to have a mentor in their chosen field, possibly including actual work experience with local employers. Not all vocational programs are for low-wage or blue-collar jobs. Vocational options in some urban districts include health and biotechnology careers, computing, and the fine arts.

Some public and private agencies may also be able to help with job training and placement. These include your state employment department; the Opportunities Industrialization Commission (OIC); the Private Industry Council (PIC); and job placement services operated by Goodwill Industries, St. Vincent dePaul, and similar service organizations for people with disbilities.

All students with disabilities should receive appropriate vocational counseling, including aptitude testing, discussion of their interests and abilities, and information about different employment possibilities. Parents need to ensure that capable students are not shunted into dead-end positions that will leave them financially vulnerable as adults.

Graduation

Most students with bipolar disorders will be headed for a regular high school diploma. This usually requires passing a certain number of specified courses. If the student needs changes in the graduation requirements—for example, if your child has been unable to develop proficiency in a foreign language due to cognitive deficits caused by medication, or if he was hospitalized during a required course and needs a waiver—now's the time to arrange for these changes.

Some students will need extra coursework to make it through high school, such as special instruction in keyboarding or study skills. These abilities will also help with higher education or work later on, and you can make them part of your child's transition plan.

Some students will need more than the usual four years to complete diploma requirements. This can be a problem—most teens have a strong desire to graduate with their class. It is sometimes possible for a student who is still short some requirements for graduation to participate in the commencement ceremony with her class, if a plan has been made to remedy the deficits over the next few months.

Katie had to be hospitalized during her senior year. She was only two classes away from graduating, so we worked out a deal with the school counselor for her to finish those classes by correspondence over the summer. She walked across the stage in a cap and gown just like her friends. After a year that had been very difficult, that really meant a lot.
—George, father of 18-year-old Katie (diagnosed bipolar I disorder, anxiety disorder)

Some students will not be able to earn a regular diploma. They may choose (or be forced) to pursue a GED, as noted in Chapter 8, *School*. A special form of graduation called an IEP diploma is also available. If a student earns an IEP diploma, that means she has completed all of the objectives set out in her IEP for graduation. This option is usually reserved for students who are unable to master high school level work, such as students with severe mental retardation. However, it could be the route to a creative graduation option for your child.

Students who are headed for college may want or need to go beyond the basic high school diploma. If your state has a special diploma for advanced students, such as Oregon's Certificate of Advanced Mastery or New York's Regents Diploma, check early on about any accommodations that may be needed for the examination or portfolio process. Some states (including Oregon, as of this writing, but not New York) have refused to permit accommodations. This is patently illegal, and will surely be successfully challenged. If you don't want to be the one to bring a lawsuit, ask instead for special tutoring in advance of the test.

In the UK, Australia, New Zealand, and Ireland, special help may be available to help teens pass their level exams, including modified exams in some cases. Talk to your LEA or education department for more information about options in your area.

Higher education

If your child has been evaluated and judged eligible for special education services, the school district's responsibility for his education does not end with the GED or high-school diploma. Students planning to attend trade school, a two-year community college program, or a four-year college program need information far in advance on which high school courses will be required for entry. This is especially important for those students with di sabilities who carry a lighter course load, as they may need to make up some credits in summer school or via correspondence courses.

Transition programs should address the move from high school to higher education. Disabled students are eligible for publicly funded education and/or services until age 22 if needed. In some cases this assistance will include tuition; in all cases it should include setting up mentoring and counseling services in advance at the student's new school. Special education services and help for students with learning disabilities are available on campus and in the dorms at many colleges.

It's against the law to deny admission to students based on disabilities; of course, other admission criteria generally must be met. Public universities and community colleges may waive some admission criteria for disabled students on a case-by-case basis if the student can show that they are capable of college-level work. Standardized test requirements might also be set aside if high school grades or the student's work portfolio look good.

Schools that normally require all freshmen to live on campus may waive this requirement for a student with special needs. If living at home is not an option, a group home or supervised apartment near campus might be. Before your child leaves for college in another city, make sure that you have secured safe and appropriate housing, and found competent local professionals to provide ongoing care. You'll also want to work out a crisis plan with your child, just in case things go wrong. She will want to know whom to call and where to go. The freshman year of college is a very common time for symptoms to flare, as well as for the first onset of obvious bipolar symptoms in previously undiagnosed teenagers. The stress, the missed sleep, and the attractions of newfound freedom (such as drug and alcohol use) all play a role.

Healthcare

Family therapy can be very useful for helping teens and parents balance issues of healthcare and independence. The ultimate goal should be ensuring that your teenager is well-informed about his diagnosis and treatment options, and capable of self-care by young adulthood.

The biggest factor of all is accepting the illness. I think many people have a really tough time doing this, and until they do they will never truly

be stable. It's really easy to deny all sorts of things around us and even
things going on in our own bodies, but if you do this with a mental illness,
the results can be deadly. —Troy, age 30 (diagnosed bipolar I disorder)

Parents need to start teaching their children as early as possible about using public transportation or driving, picking up prescriptions and reading their labels, making and keeping medical appointments, paying medical bills, and knowing where to go for help.

Some adults are never able to handle all of these tasks adequately, even though they may be perfectly competent in other areas of their life. These individuals will need support to help them get appropriate medical care. Case management services (see below) can help, but a personal aide or a self-care advocate may be even better.

You'll also need to identify adult healthcare providers in advance as your child nears the end of adolescence. Young women will need to see a gynecologist, for example, and both boys and girls will be leaving their pediatrician for a general practitioner.

If there will be changes in how your child's healthcare is paid for—for example, if she will be transitioning from private health insurance to Medicaid—you may have to prospect for knowledgeable doctors in an unfamiliar medical bureaucracy.

Hopefully you've been providing your child with reminders all along about symptom triggers and early warning signs that should send him in search of help. You might want to go over this information more formally with your teenager and his psychiatrist at this time. Sometimes getting the word from a doctor is more effective than parental advice, which many teens simply blow off as nagging.

Case management

You may continue to act as your adult child's informal case manager for many years, or you may wish to give this job to a professional. Case management services can encompass arranging for healthcare, connecting the client with community services, a certain amount of financial management (such as being the client's payee for SSI), and more.

Case managers can be hired privately, found within government mental health or community services departments, or accessed through advocacy agencies for the mentally ill. Some health insurance plans provide case management services as part of their behavioral health package, including coordination of outside services as well as managing the patient's medical needs.

> *What we opted for was the services of a caseworker with our county's Mental Health Department. He will continue to be a resource person for Lili as she transitions to adulthood. He signed her up for a supplemental mental health insurance program available through the state that will cover any needs that fall outside of our insurance plan, like mental health inpatient care or extra therapy sessions. When she reaches the age of 18 she'll be eligible for subsidized health insurance from the state, based on her own income from work. She has already submitted the paperwork for this insurance. —Sarah, mother of 17-year-old Lili (diagnosed bipolar II disorder, OCD)*

Especially for young women

By the time transition planning comes around, your daughter has weathered the worst storms of puberty. She has probably noticed if her symptoms change significantly before, during, or after her monthly period. It's important for her to understand that patterns she observes now will change as she continues to mature.

With luck, any monthly mood swings will become less prominent. However, changes in her hormonal balance due to birth control medication or pregnancy can cause symptoms to flare. If your daughter is a teenager, it may seem too early to discuss how her illness might impact on birth control and pregnancy, but it definitely isn't.

Many young women with bipolar disorders find that using birth control pills, Depo-Provera injections, or Norplant has a beneficial effect on their moods. However, a smaller group will find that some or all of these make their symptoms worse. Your daughter absolutely must inform any physician who is giving her birth control about her bipolar diagnosis. She may need to consider alternative methods of birth control, such as an IUD, diaphragm and spermicide, or condoms and spermicide. These have their own risks (including a higher risk of unwanted pregnancy with the latter two) that she will need to explore with her doctor and her partner.

Most pregnant women report some weepy and hypomanic moods, but bipolar women seem to be especially susceptible to mood swings during pregnancy. They may also be unable to take their regular medication while pregnant or trying to get pregnant. Emphasize the need for your daughter to work closely with her psychiatrist, gynecologist, and/or obstetrician during her childbearing years.

Postpartum psychosis is of special concern. This is the most severe version of postpartum depression or the "baby blues" experienced after delivery. The normal risk of postpartum psychosis is one in 500—but for women with manic-depression, it is one in five.[1] This is a very serious risk, and every woman with a bipolar disorder should take steps well in advance of delivery to deal with it. These may include researching the warning signs of psychosis and making sure her partner is also aware of them; resuming medication immediately after delivery, or even during the latter part of pregnancy (the risk to the fetus is greatest during the first trimester, and least during the third trimester); and having a relative or mother's helper at home during the first weeks or months after delivery.

Bipolar on the job

Few career options are off limits to people with bipolar disorders. If anything, they are over-represented in creative careers—art, acting, music, and writing.[2] Many also gravitate toward high-excitement occupations, including brokerage work, the top levels of marketing and sales, medicine, and other jobs that feed their need for excitement and variety.

Of course, the more exciting the job is, the greater its potential for stress and mood swings. That shouldn't (and won't) dissuade any young person from pursuing his dreams. As a parent, your role is simply to point out areas of concern and help your adult child find good coping strategies, from medication to meditation.

Off-limits occupations

One door that is barred to most people with bipolar disorder is the US military. Current regulations prohibit anyone who has ever taken a psychiatric drug from enlisting. This includes Ritalin, Prozac, and yes, lithium. For a teenager or adult who has never taken medication, the diagnosis may not preclude enlistment if he can pass the preliminary mental health screening.

There is ample reason to believe that people who took psychiatric medications as children or teens have entered the military, with varying degrees of success. Whether they did not divulge their medication use when enlisting, or whether the officers in charge simply chose to ignore this one "blemish" in an otherwise promising candidate, is an open question. With Ritalin and Prozac now topping the list of childhood prescriptions, it does seem likely that the military will have to take a second look at this policy to keep its ranks filled. Should the draft be reinstituted, the ban will almost certainly have to be lifted.

Other careers that involve firearms could also be off limits, including work as a police officer or armed security guard. That's because under some gun control laws, a person who has been found mentally ill by a court or who has a history of mental illness is legally prohibited from purchasing or being licensed to carry a gun. Most police departments also do mental health screening of applicants. A person whose bipolar disorder is well-controlled by medication could probably pass one of these, however.

Low-stress work options

The world of high-stress employment is not for every person with a bipolar disorder, including many who initially choose it. Your adult child may try several possible careers before finding one that suits both his moods and his needs.

For some, part-time, temporary, or on-call work will be the best option. Although these work styles may not offer the same level of financial security, they do provide more down time and flexibility.

Out at work or not?

To tell or not to tell...that's the big work issue for most bipolar adults. Some feel that their employers might see them as unworthy of responsibility or promotion, or that there will be worries about how their mental health could affect company operations. Although it's illegal to discriminate on the basis of mental illness, most bipolar adults have personal experiences with job discrimination or know someone else who has. Their reticence is natural.

> *Don't be embarrassed about it, but you don't have to tell everyone about it. A friend of mine told everyone when she got the diagnosis. It's*

not cool, it's not a status symbol, but it's not something to be ashamed of. It's who you are. —Carmen, age 17 (diagnosed bipolar II disorder and OCD)

If your child's symptoms are well-controlled, there's probably no reason for him to tell, unless it is required by company policy. People who need to take a pre-employment drug screen, or whose jobs require regular screening for drugs, will need to inform the tester about prescription medications they take. In most circumstances this information is not shared with the employer.

If your child occasionally has breakthrough symptoms, she may want to consider confiding in one key person at work. Surprisingly, that person may not be her direct supervisor. The personnel department might be a better choice. She could ask that a letter be placed in her personnel file outlining her diagnosis and any accommodations she might need should her symptoms worsen.

If she does have a sympathetic boss, urge your child to approach the topic with caution. She might try making a joking reference to the illness (on a particularly frantic day, "I think I'm having one of those manic mood swings my doctor warned me about," for instance) to break the ice. Some adults have simply left their medication in plain view one day—another conversation opener. You may be surprised at what you learn.

Bipolar? Oh, I think everybody in this business is on lithium—comes with the territory. The ones who aren't are either crazy or taking Prozac! —Editor of a major business news magazine, in reply to one very surprised bipolar job applicant

Bipolar adults who feel secure in their ability to manage on the job are often comfortable about addressing the issue forthrightly and openly. It would be wonderful if more people could do so.

When it comes to who you should and should not tell, honestly I am still unclear on what is best. All my immediate family and close friends know I am bipolar. Actually, I feel like my diagnosis has helped strengthen my relationship with my friends and family. Now that we have identified my symptoms, my family and friends know when it's me and not the bipolar talking.

Even though I have been working now at the same company for almost three years, I have not told any of my co-workers about my bipolar disorder. Whether or not that is the right decision, I am still unsure.
—Marcia, age 20 (diagnosed bipolar II disorder)

You can get more information about the legal rights of disabled people on the job, including tips on approaching employers, from the Job Assistance Network (800-ADA-WORK) or the US Department of Justice Hotline (800-514-0301).

Housing

Some disabled people in the US are eligible for financial assistance with housing, and for housing preference programs through Housing and Urban Development (HUD) programs, such as the Section 8 grant program. Section 8 is especially flexible, because the monthly grant can be used to reduce the cost of housing found on the open market, not just in a housing project or other government-owned building. Some charitable organizations and churches also manage low-income housing projects or voucher programs, and may have preferential treatment for people with disabilities.

Subsidized housing ranges from adult foster homes with full-time staff on up to private apartments with no support on site. The wait for housing can be long (three years or more for Section 8 vouchers), so it's important to apply before there's a pressing need. This may mean applying while a teenager is still in high school.

Some subsidized housing is substandard, especially in urban areas where the supply of low-cost units is tight. You'll need to pay special attention to security concerns, such as locking doors and windows, having a personal telephone in case of emergencies, and the safety of the surrounding neighborhood for a person who may be particularly vulnerable to crime. Some older housing projects and residential hotels are also very dirty, and may not have fully functional plumbing, lighting, and heating. Landlords can be made responsible for bringing units up to code, but they may not respond until the tenant's family or a social services agency gets involved.

Group homes that stress independent living, including self-managed group homes or co-ops, are also an option. Some of these programs may be covered by long-term care insurance, health insurance, funds placed in trust, or monthly payments made by you or your adult child. Your local NAMI chapter may have information about special housing options for adults with mental illness, or you can check in with a public or private social services agency. A number of innovative housing options are starting to spring up, including subsidized apartment buildings where each tenant has a maximum of personal autonomy despite having on-site medical management staff, therapy groups, AA and NA meetings, and the like.

Young adults with severe symptoms may need services to maintain themselves in a regular apartment or home, rather than a special housing arrangement. These are usually less expensive to boot, and may be available through government or private social services. Options include housekeeping assistance, self-care help, medication and case management, and special transportation arrangements to help the person handle shopping, medical appointments, and recreation needs.

There is a growing trend toward helping disabled adults purchase their own homes. Sometimes grants are available for down payment assistance, along with special loan programs, trust arrangements, and home buying and home ownership training.

In Canada, the UK, Ireland, Australia, and New Zealand, your local housing authority or council housing office can help you get on the waiting list, and inform you of any preference programs for the disabled and their careers that might move you up the queue faster. Charitable agencies and churches may also have low-income housing programs.

Legal and financial planning

If you or a grandparent plan to help your child financially, before or after death, you'll have to make special arrangements. Because of the laws surrounding public disability benefits—benefits your adult child could need if his symptoms require hospitalization or prevent him from working—inheriting money could end up being a terrible burden rather than a safety net.

Guardianship

When your child's 18th birthday occurs, you will no longer have the same legal control over him unless you've made prior arrangements. If your 18-year-old is still unable to safely care for himself, or if he becomes so at any time in the future, you will need to go to court to obtain legal guardianship.

In most US states there are three types of guardianship: full, limited, and temporary. Full guardianship is just what it sounds like: full authority over all decisions in the person's life. Limited guardians have authority only in certain areas where the court recognizes the need for oversight. In your child's case, this might be medical care, housing, or entering into financial contracts. Temporary guardianship is limited to a short period of time (usually 30 days) and for a specific purpose. You might be appointed as your adult child's temporary guardian when he is hospitalized. Conversely, the court might appoint someone else as his temporary guardian.

There are other forms of legal status that you or another responsible person might want to hold for an adult child with a mental illness. These include power of attorney and medical power of attorney status.

Your will

Even if you and your child are both young, you should have a will to protect your estate. It doesn't matter if you don't have much to leave. Even furniture, an old car, or a modest home can have tremendous value to an adult whose earning power could be limited by illness.

You'll want to consult a lawyer who understands disability inheritance issues. She can help you write a will that protects your child's interests and helps him retain eligibility for needs-based services.

Special needs trusts

Special needs trusts can be part of your will. These trusts can make funds or real property (such as a home) available to an adult with a disability. Formally established in the US by the Omnibus Budget Reconciliation Act, special needs trusts are set up to keep the recipient eligible for government assistance, publicly funded health insurance, and subsidized housing if needed.

Money held in trust can be used to pay for items other than food, clothing, and shelter, such as education, phone bills, and recreation, without reducing benefits. If these funds are used for food, clothing, or shelter, a limited amount can be deducted from the SSI check.

Another financial instrument that benefits adults with special needs is the pooled trust, in which several parents and perhaps other entities (such as a social services organization or charity) combine their resources. A pooled trust might be used to fund a group home, for example.

You can set up your estate to fund a special needs trust at your death, or you can set up an irrevocable special needs trust during your lifetime to tend to the needs of a disabled adult or child. It is also possible to purchase certain types of annuities, such as life insurance policies, and earmark the proceeds for a trust to be set up in the future.

You'll need to consult a financial planner and/or a lawyer with experience in working on disability issues to set up a trust. Special needs trusts require a trustee other than the recipient to be in charge. This might be a well sibling, another relative, a trusted friend, or a professional trust manager. For adults with mental illness, it's crucial that the trust administrator be someone who understands how the money should be used. You don't want it to be frittered away on whims, or worse yet, on substance abuse. Neither would you want the trust manager to use funds to keep your adult child in a hospital when she could safely be living in the community. The trust manager may need to be instructed to pay bills directly from the trust, and never to give funds directly to your adult child. Either the trust manager or a co-trustee should have full understanding of your adult child's needs, and how they might be met in the most inclusive, community-based way.

Letter of intent

This isn't a legal document, but it's an important one when it comes to how your child's affairs will be handled after you're gone. The letter of intent can serve as your voice to guide future caretakers, should you ever be out of the picture. It should be written as though intended for someone who knows nothing about your child or your family, and stored with your will and other legal documents.

The letter of intent should be comprised of at least four sections:

- **General information.** This section should include such things as your child's full name, date of birth, Social Security number, address, blood type, religion, and citizenship status. It should also include a list of all known family members, and any non-relatives (such as a family friend, clergy member, or caseworker) whose advice and help a caretaker could call on.

- **Medical history and care.** In this section, list all of your child's diagnoses, with a brief explanation of the symptoms of each that a caretaker might need to be aware of. List any hospitalizations and surgeries your child has had. Include complete contact information for all doctors involved in your child's care, as well as dentists and therapists, and provide insurance information.

- **Goals.** This is a section to work out with your child. It should state what his preferences are for living situation, daily activities, diet, social activities and hobbies, religious observance, etc. Should your child be unable to communicate his needs for any reason, this section will help guide his care.

- **Legal information.** List all assets, including bank accounts, annuities, property, life insurance policies, stocks, trusts, and safe deposit boxes, in this section. It should also include contact information for any financial advisor who handles your finances or assets held in trust for your child.

Other adult issues

During this time of transition, you can help your teen get informed about other adult issues involving bipolar disorders. These include:

- Legal adult activities that can become compulsions when depression, hypomania, or mania is involved, such as drinking, gambling, sexual activity, and spending.

- Gun ownership, legal prohibitions for people with mental illness (see the section "Off-limit occupations," earlier in this chapter), the consequences of possessing a firearm illegally, the increased danger of self-harm or danger to others from owning a gun.

- Once again (as if you haven't belabored the point enough already), the dangers of drug and alcohol use for a person with bipolar disorder.

- What role you hope to play in your bipolar child's adult life, level of personal involvement, financial support, whether your home is to automatically be a haven in crisis or if you would prefer that your adult child seek professional help first.

Building on strengths

Many brain disorders bring with them built-in limits. Bipolar disorders do not. Some would even argue that they may equip the affected person with certain strengths: a high energy level, strong verbal skills, sometimes an especially creative way of looking at the world and solving problems. All parents hope that their adult children will find a way to use their special talents, and for people with bipolar disorders, these talents can help make up for the down side of their illness.

> *Encourage the good sides that you see. There's nothing wrong with your child having a bunch of instant energy. They can take things that they really like and obsess on them, and maybe turn them into their careers. I think I'm a more creative person [because of this disorder]... sometimes, anyway.* —Carmen, age 17

As you consider helping your child to move from dependency to independence, know that he has many strengths to build a good future on. During this period, as it has been throughout your child's life, your goal should be to help him internalize personal rules and habits that will continue to keep him safe, sober, and level for life.

Parents share their hopes

Following are five parents' responses to the question, "What are your hopes for your child?"

> *I hope that he does not have to suffer the severe psychic pain of full-blown bipolar disorder. I hope he will be able to develop his talents and strengths and contribute to the world while enjoying life.* —Marlene, mother of 8-year-old Billy (diagnosed cyclothymic disorder)

· · · · ·

> *My main hope is that one day she'll be able to live on her own. As it is right now, I'm not certain that will happen. She's still afraid to be by herself for any length of time.* —Donna, mother of 16-year-old Lisa (diagnosed bipolar II disorder, post-traumatic stress disorder, anxiety disorder)

· · · · ·

I hope that she will be as successful as I have been. That she will eventually be able to self-regulate so she can marry and have children. I hope she will be a happy, loving wife and mother, and an adult friend to me. —Stephanie, mother of 7-year-old Cassidy (diagnosed bipolar disorder, Tourette syndrome, OCD, ADHD)

· · · · ·

I want her to get a handle on her mental health before she's in her thirties, like I was. I hope for her to be able to apply her many artistic talents (art, music, etc.) as part of her career. —Sue, mother of 16-year-old Vanessa (diagnosed bipolar disorder, OCD, borderline personality disorder, passive-aggressive personality disorder)

· · · · ·

I hope that he can go to college, get a good job, live independently, marry, and stay stable and happy. —Lynn, mother of 11-year-old Michael (diagnosed bipolar I disorder with mixed states and psychosis, OCD, tic disorder)

Dream for your child with bipolar disorder, just as you would for any child. Ground your dreams in reality as you must—for a child with severe symptoms, good health and safety are enough to want for now. But keep at least a little dream about a productive and happy life for your adult child alive, no matter what. Patients, their families, and the medical profession are learning so much that we all have reason to hope.

Resources

This appendix lists support and advocacy organizations, as well as books, pamphlets, videos, and online resources on topics related to bipolar disorders, related conditions, special-needs parenting, sibling issues, insurance and healthcare, and medications. Contact information for some of the most prominent diagnostic and treatment centers is included, as is a list of national and state agencies in charge of mental health care.

Advocacy and support groups

United States

The Child and Adolescent Bipolar Foundation (CABF)
1187 Wilmette Avenue, #331
Wilmette, IL 60091
(847) 256-8525
cabf@bpso.org
http://www.cabf.org/

A parent-led group providing education, support, and advocacy for children, adolescents, families and professionals.

Depression and Related Affective Disorders Association (DRADA)
Meyer 3-181
600 North Wolfe Street
Baltimore, MD 21287-7381
(410) 955-4647 (Baltimore, MD)
(202) 955-5800 (Washington, DC)
drada@jhmi.edu
http://www.med.jhu.edu/drada/index.html

Federation of Families for Children's Mental Health
1021 Prince Street
Alexandria, VA 22314-2971
(703) 684-7710
Fax (703) 836-1040
http://www.ffcmh.org/

A group for families, especially low-income families, who are caring for a child with a mental illness.

National Alliance for the Mentally Ill (NAMI)
200 N. Glebe Road, Suite 1015
Arlington, VA 22203-3754
(703) 524-7600
(800) 950-NAMI (Helpline)
Fax (703) 524-9094
TDD (703) 516-7227
http://www.nami.org/

NAMI is the largest organization for mentally ill people and their families in the US. It has state and local chapters around the country, sponsors legislation, advocates for mentally ill people, and provides excellent information via its web site and publications.

National Depressive and Manic-Depressive Association
730 N. Franklin Street, Suite 501
Chicago, IL 60610-3526
(800) 826-3632
Fax (312) 642-7243
http://www.ndmda.org/

This support and advocacy group specifically for people with depression or bipolar depression has chapters throughout the US and an informative web site.

Canada

Canadian Mental Health Association
2160 Yonge Street, 3rd Floor
Toronto, ON M4S 2Z3
(416) 484-7750
Fax (416) 484-4617
cmhanat@interlog.com
http://www.cmha.ca/

Integrated Network of Disability Information and Education
info@indie.ca
http://www.indie.ca/

Mood Disorders Association of British Columbia
2730 Commercial Drive, No. 201
Vancouver, BC V5N 5PN
(604) 873-0103
Fax (604) 873-3095
mda@lynx.bc.ca
http://www.lynx.bc.ca/~mda/

United Kingdom

Glasgow Association for Mental Health
Melrose House, First Floor
15/23 Cadogan Street
Glasgow, G2 6QQ
(01) 41-204 22 70
Fax (01) 41-204 27 70
GAMH@colloquium.co.uk
http://users.colloquium.co.uk/~GAMH/

Manic Depression Fellowship
8-10 High Street
Kingston-upon-Thames
Surrey KT1 1EY UK
(0181) 974 6550
http://www.mdfglmhmip.u-net.com/ (Greater London MDF)

This organization has regional offices in Wales, Greater London, and Manchester, as well as 125 local groups throughout the UK. It provides support, advice, and information for people with manic depression, their families, friends, and carers.

National Alliance of the Relatives of the Mentally Ill (NARMI)
Tydehams Oaks
Tydehams, Newbury
Berks RG14 6JT
(01635) 551923

National Disability Council
Caxton House, Level 4
Tothill Street
London SW1H 9NA
(0207) 273 5636
Fax (0207) 273 5929
Minicom (0207) 273 5645
http://www.open.gov.uk/ndc/ndchome.htm

Northern Ireland Association for Mental Health
80 University Street
Belfast BT7 1HE
(01232) 328474

SANE
Worthington House, 2nd Floor
199-205 Old Marylebone Road
London NW1 5QP
(0171) 724 6520 (office)
National Helpline 0345 678000 (daily from 2:00 pm until midnight)

UK Advocacy Network
Volserve House
14-18 West Bar Green
Sheffield S1 2DA
(0114) 272 8171

Young Minds
102-108 Clerkenwell Road, 2nd Floor
London EC1M 5SA
(0171) 336 8445 (office)
(0345) 626376 (Parents Information Service hotline)

Ireland

AWARE
147 Phipsborough Road
Dublin 7 Ireland
(01) 830 8449
(0) 679-1711 (Helpline)
http://www.mensana.org/Alliance/Aware.htm

AWARE offers help by phone, sponsors support groups in 38 locations around Ireland, provides information and literature, does public advocacy, and supports research.

Mental Health Association of Ireland
Mensana House, 6 Adelaide Street
Dun Laoghaire, County Dublin, Ireland
(01) 284-1166
Fax (01) 284-1736
http://www.mensana.org/

Australia

Action Resource Network Inc.
266 Johnston Street
Abbotsford, Victoria 3067
(03) 9416-3488 or (800) 808-126
Fax (03) 9416-3484
TTY (03) 9416-3491

Association of Relatives and Friends of the Mentally Ill (ARAFMI)
http://www.span.com.au/mhrc/arafmi.html

ARAFMI has chapters in most Australian states.

Disability Action Inc.
62 Henley Beach Road
Mile End, SA 5031
(08) 8352 8599, (800) 805 495
Fax (08) 8354 0049
TTY (08) 8352 8022
brad@disabilityaction.in-sa.com.au

Mood Disorders Association (SA) Inc./Self-Help (MDP) Inc.
MHRC Building, 1 Richmond Road
Keswick, SA 5035
(08) 8221-5170
Fax (08) 8221-5159
http://www.span.com.au/moodswing/index.html

Sponsors support groups and a center with trained volunteers and a library, and can link you with services.

SANE Australia
PO Box 226
South Melbourne, Victoria 3065
(61) 3 9682 5933
Fax (61) 3 9682 5944
sane@sane.org
http://www.vicnet.net.au/~sane/

New Zealand

Richmond Fellowship
249 Madras Street, Level 3
Christchurch, NZ
(64) 3 365-3211
Fax (64) 3 365-3905
national@richmond.org.nz
http://www.richmondnz.org/

Online support

BiPolar Children and Teens
http://hometown.aol.com/DrgnKpr1/BPCAT.html

This parent-run page features lots of supportive information and personal stories, including an incomplete list of support groups in the US and Canada for parents of children with mental illness, and links to an AOL chat room and several mailing lists.

BipolarKids list
http://www.bpparent.org/

This fabulous list for parents of bipolar children and teens is moderated by parent volunteers, and sponsored through the generosity of Active-Websites, owned by

Steve Worden. It's an excellent source of support and reliable information. To subscribe, see the requirements at the web site above.

BPSO list
http://www.bpso.org/BPKids.htm
For parents, spouses, siblings, and friends of people with bipolar disorder. To subscribe, send email to *majordomo@ipl.co.uk*. In the body of the message, write: subscribe bpso.

Harbor of Refuge
http://www.harbor-of-refuge.org/

WalkersWeb
http://www.walkers.org/
WalkersWeb is the home of several mailing lists geared toward people with bipolar disorders or depression. It also has excellent links to mental health sites, its own informational files, and online chat groups.

Books and publications

Berger, Diane, et al. *We Heard the Angels of Madness: A Family Guide to Coping with Manic Depression.* New York: Quill, 1992.

Bipolar Disorders Letter (online newsletter). *http://www.mhsource.com/bipolar/letter.html.* This is an online newsletter, mostly for professionals but of interest to parents as well. It summarizes recent studies on treatments. You'll need the free program Acrobat Reader to look at it.

Bipolar Network News (newsletter). Stanley Foundation Bipolar Network, Bethesda, Maryland. *http://www.bipolarnetwork.org/.*

Fieve, Ronald R. *Moodswing: Dr. Fieve on Depression* (revised edition). New York: Bantam Books, 1997.

Guiness, David. *Inside Out: A Guide to Self-Management of Manic Depression* (booklet). The Manic Depression Fellowship (UK), 1998.

Halebsky, Mark. *Surviving the Crisis of Depression and Bipolar Illness: Layperson's Guide to Coping with Mental Illness Beyond the Time of Crisis and Outside the Hospital.* Arvada, Colorado: Personal and Professional Growth Organization, 1997.

Jamison, Kay Redfield. *An Unquiet Mind.* New York: Random House, 1997. Dr. Jamison is one of the most prominent experts on bipolar disorders—and is herself a manic-depressive. This is her fascinating (and for worried parents, heartening) memoir.

Jamison, Kay Redfield. *Touched with Fire: Manic-Depressive Illness and the Artistic Temperament.* New York: Free Press,1996.

Web sites about bipolar disorders

BipolarKids
http://www.geocities.com/EnchantedForest/1068/

Especially for parents and other caregivers for bipolar children and teens. Also home to the BPKids mailing list (see "Online support" earlier in this appendix).

Bipolar (Mining Co.)
http://bipolar.miningco.com/

A collection of articles, links, and a Web chat group about bipolar disorders.

FyrenIyce
http://users.wantree.com.au/~fractal/

Information about bipolar disorders, and links to support and advocacy groups in Australia and elsewhere. There's also a FyrenIyce email list.

Massachusetts General Hospital Neurology Forums
http://neuro-www.mgh.harvard.edu/

This site features discussion groups (live and bulletin board style) on almost every known neurological disorder, including bipolar disorders.

Moodswing.org
http://www.moodswing.org/index.shtml

Home of the Bipolar FAQ (frequently asked questions list).

Pendulum Resources
http://www.pendulum.org/

You can find up-to-date information on bipolar disorders here, with a strong mental health consumer orientation.

Related conditions and symptoms

If your child has multiple diagnoses or simply shares symptoms with another condition, these books and online resources may help.

Hallowell, Edward. *When You Worry About the Child You Love: Emotional and Learning Problems in Children.* New York: Simon & Schuster, 1996. This book provides a good introduction to the whole spectrum of psychiatric, emotional, developmental, and learning disorders in young children. It's very readable.

ADD/ADHD

Hallowell, Edward. *Driven to Distraction: Recognizing and Coping with Attention Deficit Disorder from Childhood Through Adulthood.* Reading, Massachusetts: Addison-Wesley, 1994. The classic book on ADD/ADHD.

Hallowell, Edward, and John Ratey. *Answers to Distraction.* New York: Bantam Books, 1996. A companion to Dr. Hallowell's *Driven to Distraction*, this book provides behavior management and learning strategies to help the ADD/ADHD child.

ODD/Conduct disorders

Oppositional Defiant Disorder: What is it?
http://www.klis.com/chandler/pamphlet/oddcd/about.htm

A Place for Us
http://www.conductdisorders.com

This web site includes a parent message board, information, and links about conduct disorders, ODD, and related problems.

Eating disorders

Eating Disorders Shared Awareness (EDSA)
http://www.eating-disorder.com/

This site includes links to US and Canadian support and informational sites on anorexia and bulimia.

Eating Disorders Association
Wenson House, 1st Floor
103 Prince of Wales Road
Norwich NR1 1DW UK
(0160) 362-1414

Seasonal affective disorder

Rosenthal, Norman E., MD. *Winter Blues*. New York: The Guilford Press, 1993.

National Organization for Seasonal Affective Disorder (NOSAD)
PO Box 40190
Washington, DC 20016
(301) 762-0768

SAD Homepage
http://www.geocities.com/HotSprings/7061/sadhome.html

Environmental Health and Light Research Institute
16057 Tampa Palms Boulevard, Suite 227
Tampa, FL 33647
(800) 544-4878

Apollo Light Systems Inc.
352 West 1060 South
Orem, UT 84058
(801) 226-2370

Light system vendor.

Hughes Lighting Technologies
34 Yacht Club Drive
Lake Hopatcong, NJ 07849
(973) 663-1214

Light system vendor.

The SunBox Company
19217 Orbit Drive
Gaithersburg, MD 20870
(800) 548-3968

Light system vendor.

Self-injurious behavior (SIB)

Strong, Marilee. *A Bright Red Scream: Self-Mutilation and the Language of Pain.* New York: Viking Press, 1998.

Levenkron, Steven. *Cutting: Understanding and Overcoming Self-Mutilation.* New York: W. W. Norton & Company, 1998.

Alderman, Tracy. *The Scarred Soul: Understanding and Ending Self-Inflicted Violence.* Oakland, California: New Harbinger Publications, 1997.

Bodies-Under-Siege mailing list
http://www.palace.net/~llama/psych/busfaq.html

Bodies-Under-Siege is an online support group for people with self-injurious behavior. May not be appropriate for all teens with SIB, but some may find this therapeutic. To subscribe, send email to *majordomo@majordomo.pobox.com* with the message body text: subscribe bus.

Secret Shame
http://www.palace.net/~llama/psych/injury.html

Secret Shame is a web site about self-injury, offering information and support to people with SIB and their families.

Suicide prevention

The National Alliance for the Mentally Ill
(703) 524-7600
http://www.nami.org/

NAMI is the largest support group for people with mental illness in the US. Its national information line or web site can help you find local resources right away.

National suicide prevention hotline (US)
(800) 999-9999

Call this number to get information about the closest suicide prevention hotline.

Suicide Awareness/Voices of Education (SA/VE)
http://www.save.org/

Suicide Information and Education Centre (SEIC)
http://www.siec.ca/crisis.html
SEIC maintains a list of suicide prevention hotlines and services in the US and Canada.

Befrienders International Online
http://www.befrienders.org/centre.html
The Befrienders maintain a list of crisis and suicide counseling centers throughout the world.

Substance abuse

Adolescent Substance Abuse and Recovery Resources
http://www.winternet.com/~webpage/adolrecovery.html
Includes links to AA, NA, and many other groups that can help young people stop using drugs and alcohol.

Canadian Centre on Substance Abuse
75 Albert Street, Suite 300
Ottawa, ON K1P 5E7 Canada
(613) 235-4048
Fax (613) 235-8101
http://www.ccsa.ca/default.htm

Drugline Ltd.
9A Brockley Cross
Brockley, London SE4 2AB UK
(0181) 692-4975

Special-needs parenting

Bending the Rules: A Guide for Parents of Troubled Children. Michael McDonald Productions, 1996. Made by the Southern California chapter of the Tourette Syndrome Association, this is an excellent video on handling problem behaviors that are driven by brain dysfunction. It comes highly recommended by parents. Call (818) 881-3211 to order.

Bruun, Ruth Dowling, MD, et al. *Problem Behaviors and Tourette's Syndrome* (pamphlet). Bayside, New York: Tourette Syndrome Association, 1993. Contact information: 42-40 Bell Boulevard, Bayside, NY 11361-2820, (718) 224-2999, *http://neuro-www2.mgh.harvard.edu/TSA/allourstuff/catalogofpubs.html.*

Budman, Cathy, MD, and Ruth Dowling Bruun, MD. *Tourette Syndrome and Repeated Anger Generated Episodes (RAGE)* (pamphlet). Bayside, New York: Tourette Syndrome Association, 1998.

Greene, Ross. *The Explosive Child: A New Approach for Understanding and Parenting Easily Frustrated, "Chronically Inflexible" Children.* New York: HarperCollins, 1998. The title says it all: This may be the best book ever on raising a child with bipolar disorder, or even just a "difficult" temperament. Full of parent-tested strategies for defusing behavior problems.

Greenspan, Stanley I., with Jacqueline Salmon. *The Challenging Child*. Reading, Massachusetts: Addison-Wesley, 1995. Dr. Greenspan explains why some kids have a "challenging" temperament, and offers excellent ideas for turning down the volume of outbursts, anxiety, and other behavior problems.

Greenspan, Stanley I., with Jacqueline Salmon. *Playground Politics: Understanding the Emotional Life of Your School-Age Child*. Reading, Massachusetts: Addison-Wesley, 1993. Help for parents with children who don't fit in.

Greenspan, Stanley I., and Serena Wieder, with Robin Simons. *The Child with Special Needs*. Reading, Massachusetts: Addison-Wesley, 1998. This book concentrates on working with developmentally or emotionally challenged children from infancy through school age. Highly recommended, especially if your child has an additional diagnosis of PDD/autism, ADHD, etc.

Kurcinka, Mary Sheedy. *Raising Your Spirited Child*. New York: HarperPerennial, 1991. Covers handling sensory defensiveness and other contributors to "spirited" behavior.

Marsh, Diane T., Rex M. Dickens, and E. Fuller Torrey. *How to Cope with Mental Illness in Your Family: A Self-Care Guide for Siblings, Offspring, and Parents*. New York: Putnam Publishing Group, 1998.

Meyer, Donald, editor. *Uncommon Fathers: Reflections on Raising a Child with a Disability*. Rockville, Maryland: Woodbine House, 1995.

Naseef, Robert A. *Special Children, Challenged Parents: The Struggles and Rewards of Raising a Child with a Disability*. New York: Birch Lane Press, 1997.

Phelan, Thomas W. *1-2-3 Magic: Effective Discipline for Children 2-12*. Glen Ellyn, Illinois: Child Management Inc., 1996. Phelan has devised a workable system for managing behavior without getting physical, especially for strong-willed kids. Many parents swear by it. Also available on tape.

Wollis, Rebecca, and Agnes Hatfield. *When Someone You Love Has a Mental Illness: A Handbook for Family, Friends, and Caregivers*. Los Angeles: J. P. Tarcher, 1992.

Sibling issues

Meyer, Donald, and Patricia Vadasy. *Living with a Brother or Sister with Special Needs*. Seattle: University of Washington Press, 1996.

Meyer, Donald, editor. *Views from Our Shoes: Growing up with a Brother or Sister with Special Needs*. Rockville, Maryland: Woodbine House, 1997.

Sib Kids Club
http://mail.idt.net/~julhyman/sibkids.htm
A web site for kids who have a sibling with a disability.

SibShops/Sibling Support Project
Children's Hospital and Medical Center
PO Box 5371, CL-09
Seattle, WA 98105
(206) 368-4911
Fax (206) 368-4816
http://www.chmc.org/departmt/sibsupp/sibshoppage.htm

SibShops are special support groups for children dealing with a sibling's disability. This site provides information on SibShops and related topics, and can help you find a SibShop program in your area.

Special education

Anderson, Winifred, Stephen Chitwood, and Dierdre Hayden. *Negotiating the Special Education Maze: A Guide for Parents and Teachers,* Second Edition. Rockville, Maryland: Woodbine House, 1990. Well-written and very complete. A new edition with information on the changes wrought in IDEA 97 was said to be in production at press time.

Cutler, Barbara Coyne. *You, Your Child, and "Special" Education: A Guide to Making the System Work.* Baltimore: Paul H. Brookes Publishing, 1993. An uppity guide to fighting the system on your child's behalf.

Dornbush, Marilyn P., and Sheryl K. Pruitt. *Teaching the Tiger: A Handbook for Individuals Involved in the Education of Students With Attention Deficit Disorders, Tourette Syndrome, or Obsessive Compulsive Disorder.* Duarte, California: Hope Press, 1995. This is a wonderful book, full of practical suggestions, organizing aids, and ideas for teachers, parents, and students. Very applicable to children with bipolar disorders, with or without ADD/ADHD.

Advocating for the Child
http://www.crosswinds.net/washington-dc/~advocate/

Maintained by the mother of neurologically challenged children, this site is an purpose guide to advocating for your child's educational rights in the US. Information-rich, with great links and lots of inspiration.

The Special Ed Advocate/Wrightslaw
http://www.wrightslaw.com/

This is the place to find the actual text of special education laws, information on the latest court battles, and answers to your special education questions.

Special Education and Disabilities Resources
http://www.educ.drake.edu/rc/sp_ed_top.html

US information and links on special education law, assistive technology, and related topics.

Healthcare and insurance

Beckett, Julie. *Health Care Financing: A Guide for Families.* To order, contact: the National Maternal and Child Health Resource Center, Law Building, University of Iowa, Iowa City, IA 52242, (319) 335-9073. This overview of the healthcare financing system includes advocacy strategies for families, and information about public health insurance in the US.

How to Get Quality Care for a Child with Special Health Needs: A Guide to Health Services and How to Pay for Them. To order, contact: The Disability Bookshop, PO Box 129, Vancouver, WA 98666-0129, (206) 694-2462 or (800) 637-2256.

Larson, Georgianna, and Judith Kahn. *Special Needs/Special Solutions: How to Get Quality Care for a Child with Special Health Needs*. St. Paul: Life Line Press, 1991.

Neville, Kathy. *Strategic Insurance Negotiation: An Introduction to Basic Skills for Families and Community Mental Health Workers* (pamphlet). To order, contact: CAPP/NPRC Project, Federation for Children with Special Needs, 95 Berkeley Street, Suite 104, Boston, MA 02116. Single copies available at no cost.

Association of Maternal and Child Health Programs (AMCHP)
1220 19th Street, NW, Suite 801
Washington, DC 20036
(202) 775-0436

Call AMCHP to locate your state's Children with Special Health Care Needs Program.

National Association of Insurance Commissioners (NAIC)
444 National Capitol Street NW, Suite 701
Washington, DC 20001
(202) 624-7790

Call NAIC to locate your state insurance commissioner, who can tell you about health insurance regulations in your state regarding bipolar disorders.

Association for the Care of Children's Health
ACCH Publications
19 Mantua Road
Mt. Royal, NJ 08061
(609) 224-1742
http://www.acch.org/

This group offers a variety of publications on child healthcare, including guides to prepare a child for the hospital and many items for parents of special-needs children.

Mail order pharmacies

CanadaRx
http://www.canadarx.net/

This is a consortium of Canadian pharmacies set up specifically to provide discounted prescriptions to US customers, although Canadians and others can use the service as well. Mail-order arrangements must be made over the Net, or directly through one of the consortium members (their addresses are available on the web site).

Continental Pharmacy
PO Box 94863
Cleveland, OH 44101-4863
Phone (216) 459-2010 or (800) 677-4323
Fax (216) 459-2004

Farmacia Rex S.R.L.
Cordoba 2401
Esq. Azcuénaga 1120
Buenos Aires, Argentina
Phone (54-011) 4961-0338
Fax (54-011) 4962-0153
http://www.todoservicio.com.ar/farmacia.rex/rexmenu.htm

Deeply discounted prices, and they mail anywhere.

GlobalRx
4024 Carrington Lane
Efland, NC 27243
Phone (919) 304-4278 or (800) 526-6447
Fax (919) 304-4405
info@aidsdrugs.com
http://globalrx.com/

Masters Marketing Company, Ltd.
Masters House No. 1
Marlborough Hill
Harrow, Middlesex HA1 1TW
England
Phone (011) 44-181-424-9400
Fax (011) 4481 427 1994

Carries a limited selection of European pharmaceuticals, as well as a few American-made drugs, including Prozac.

No Frills Pharmacy
1510 Harlan Drive
Bellevue, NB 68005
Phone (800) 485-7423
Fax (402) 682-9899
refill@nofrillspharmacy.com
http://www.nofrillspharmacy.com/

Peoples Pharmacy
http://www.peoplesrx.com/

This Austin, Texas-based chain provides Net-only mail-order service, and can compound medications as well.

Pharmacy Direct
3 Coal Street
Silverwater, NSW 2128 Australia
Phone (02) 9648-8888 or (1300) 656-245
Fax (02) 9648 8999 or (1300) 656 329
pharmacy@pharmacydirect.com.au
http://www.pharmacydirect.com.au/home.htm

You must have a prescription from an Australian doctor to use this mail-order service.

The Pharmacy Shop (Drugs By Mail)
5007 N. Central
Phoenix, AZ 85012
Phone (602) 274-9956 or (800) 775-6888
Fax (602) 241-0104
sales@drugsbymail.com
http://www.pharmacyshop.com/ or *http://www.drugsbymail.com/*

Preferred Prescription Plan
2201 W. Sample Road, Building 9, Suite 1-A
Pompano Beach, FL 33073
Phone (954) 969-1230 or (800) 881-6325 or
Fax (800) 881-6990
cust-svc@prefrx.com
http://www.prefrx.com/

Stadtlanders Pharmacy
600 Penn Center Boulevard
Pittsburgh, PA 15235-5810
(800) 238-7828
enroll@stadtlander.com
http://stadtlander.com/

Stadtlanders Pharmacy has a stellar reputation in the disability community.

Victoria Apotheke (Victoria Pharmacy)
Bahnhofstrasse 71
Postfach CH-8021
Zurich, Switzerland
Fax (01) 221-2322 (Europe) or (011) 411-221-2322 (US)
Phone (01) 211-2432 (Europe) or (011) 411-211-24 32 (US)
victoriaapotheke@access.ch
http://www.access.ch/victoria_pharmacy

General medical information

Medscape
http://www.medscape.com/

Searchable, online index to hundreds of medical journals. Many articles are available in full, others as abstracts only.

PubMed
http://www.ncbi.nlm.nih.gov/PubMed/

Free interface for searching the MEDLINE medical database, which can help you find out about studies, medications, and more.

Information about medications

There are a number of books available that list side effects, cautions, and more regarding medications. The biggest and best is the *Physicians Desk Reference* (PDR), but its price is well out of the average parent's league. You may be able to find a used but recent copy at a good price.

If your child is allergic to food dyes, or to corn, wheat, and other materials used as fillers in pills, you should consult directly with the manufacturer of any medications he takes.

The British National Formulary (BNF). British Medical Association and the Royal Pharmaceutical Society of Great Britain, 1998. The standard reference for prescribing and dispensing drugs in the UK, updated twice yearly.

Preston, John D., John H. O'Neal, and Mary C. Talaga. *Consumer's Guide to Psychiatric Drugs*. Oakland, California: New Harbinger Publications, 1998.

Silverman, Harold M., editor. *The Pill Book*, Eighth Edition. New York: Bantam Books, 1998. A basic paperback guide to the most commonly used medications in the US.

Sullivan, Donald. *The American Pharmaceutical Association's Guide to Prescription Drugs*. New York: Signet, 1998.

Wilens, Timothy E., MD. *Straight Talk About Psychiatric Medications for Kids*. New York: Guilford Press, 1998.

Canadian Drug Product Database
http://www.hc-sc.gc.ca/hpb-dgps/therapeut/htmleng/dpd.html

Dr. Bob's Psychopharmacology Tips
http://uhs.bsd.uchicago.edu/dr-bob/tips/

Excellent information on psychiatric drugs, including things like the MAOI dietary restrictions and common SSRI interactions.

Federal Drug Administration (FDA)
http://www.fda.gov/cder/drug.htm

Official US information on new drugs and generic versions of old drugs, FDA warnings and recalls, etc.

The Internet Drug List
http://www.rxlist.com/

MedEc Interactive/PDR.net
http://www.pdrnet.com/

This medical info site includes a link to a Web-accessible version of the PDR.

Pharmaceutical Information Network
http://pharminfo.com/

PharmWeb
http://www.pharmweb.net/

The Royal Pharmaceutical Society's Technical Information Center
http://www.rpsgb.org.uk/300.htm

There is a nominal fee for use of the RPS database, but one might be able to have it waived.

RXmed
http://www.rxmed.com/

Medical facilities

Sometimes a child's symptoms are so challenging that your local psychiatrist may want to seek the help of experts. These facilities are among the world's best-known centers for treating bipolar disorders.

United States

KidsPeace: The National Hospital for Kids in Crisis
5300 KidsPeace Drive
Orefield, PA 18069-9101
(800) 334-4KID
admissions@kidspeace.org
http://www.kidspeace.org/

Mood Disorders Clinic
Children's Hospital
300 Longwood Avenue
Boston, MA 02115
(617) 355-6000

National Institutes of Mental Health (NIMH)
Biological Psychiatry Branch
Building 10, Room 3N212
9000 Rockville Pike
Bethesda, MD 20892
(301) 496-6827
(301) 402-0052

NIMH Patient Recruitment and Referral Service
(800) 411-1222
prcc@cc.nih.gov

Stanford Bipolar Disorders Clinic
401 Quarry Road
Stanford, CA 94305-5723
(650) 498-4689
bipolar.clinic@stanford.edu
http://www.stanford.edu/group/bipolar.clinic/

The Stanley Clinical Research Center
Case Western Reserve University/University Hospitals of Cleveland
Department of Psychiatry
11100 Euclid Avenue
Cleveland, OH 44106
(216) 844-3880
Fax (216) 844-1703

The Stanley Center for the Innovative Treatment of Bipolar Disorders
3811 O'Hara Street, Suite 279
Pittsburgh, PA 15213
(412) 624-2476 or (800) 424-7657
Fax (412) 624-0493.
http://www.wpic.pitt.edu/stanley/

Stanley Foundation Bipolar Network
5430 Grosvenor Lane, Suite 200
Bethesda, MD 20814
(800) 518-7326
Fax (301) 571-0768
info@bipolarnetwork.org
http://www.bipolarnetwork.org/

This is a multi-center research effort, including the Stanley Foundation Center at Johns Hopkins University, NIMH, and several other institutions.

University of Texas Southwestern Bipolar and Research Program
8267 Elmbrook Drive, Suite 250
Dallas, TX 75247
(214) 689-3765
Fax (214) 689-3751
Contact: Mary Ann Westlake, *mwestl@mednet.swmed.edu*

Canada

Canadian Network for Mood and Anxiety Treatments (CANMAT)
http://www.canmat.org/

This is a consortium of university medical schools and other research organizations concentrating on depression, bipolar disorders, and anxiety disorders. Their web site can link you with a CANMAT center near you, and also provides information about diagnosis and treatment options.

University of British Columbia Mood Disorders Clinic
Department of Psychiatry
Vancouver Hospital & Health Sciences Centre, UBC Site
2211 Wesbrook Mall
Vancouver, BC V6T 2A1 Canada
(604) 822-9745
Fax (604) 822-7922
http://www.psychiatry.ubc.ca/mood/md_home.html

Alternative medicine resources

Balch, James F., MD, and Phyllis A. Balch, CNC. *Prescription for Nutritional Healing.* Garden City Park, New York: Avery Publishing, 1997.

Baumel, Syd. *Dealing with Depression Naturally.* New Canaan, Connecticut: Keats Publishing, 1995.

Elkins, Rita. *Depression and Natural Medicine.* Pleasant Grove, Utah: Woodland Publishing, 1995.

Murray, Michael T., ND. *Natural Alternatives to Prozac.* New York: William Morrow and Company, 1996.

Norden, Michael J., MD. *Beyond Prozac.* New York: HarperCollins, 1995.

Stoll, Andrew L., MD. *Omega3 Fatty Acid User Guide.* 1998. Available from: Psychopharmacology Research Laboratory, McLean Hospital, 115 Mill Street, Belmont, MA 02478.

Supplement suppliers

Nordic Naturals
3040 Valencia Avenue, Suite 2
Aptos, CA 95003
(800) 662-2544
Fax (408) 662-0382
http://www.nordicnat.com/proomega.htm

Nordic Naturals is the original source of most Omega-3 fatty acid supplements sold in the US.

The Vitamin Connection
72 Main Street
Burlington, VT 05401
(802) 846-2026 or (800) 760-3020
Fax (802) 846-2027
http://www.vitaminconnection.com/

Martek Biosciences
6480 Dobbin Road
Columbia, MD 21045
(410) 740-0081 or (800) 662-6339
Fax (410) 740-2985
http://www.martekbio.com/neuromins.html

Sagami Chemical Research Center
Nishi-Ohnuma 4-4-1, Sagamihara
Kanagawa 229-0012, Japan
(011) 81-427-42-4791
Fax (011) 81-427-49-763
Contact: Dr. Kazunaga Yazawa

Source for Omega-3 fish oils.

Omega Protein
PO Box 1799
Hammond, LA 70404-1799
(504) 345-6234
Fax (504) 345-5744
http://www.buyomegaprotein.com/
Contact: Kelsey Short, *kshort@i-55.com*

Source for Omega-3 fish oils.

Public mental health agencies

United States

Alabama

Department of Mental Health and Mental Retardation
RSA Union
100 N. Union Street
PO Box 30140
Montgomery, AL 36130-1410
(334) 242-3417
Fax (334) 242-0684
http://www.asc.edu/archives/agencies/mental.html

Alaska

Alaska Division of Mental Health and Developmental Disabilities
350 Main Street, Room 217
PO Box 110620
Juneau, AK 99811-0620
(907) 465-3370
Fax (907) 465-2668
TDD/TTY (907) 465-2225
http://www.hss.state.ak.us/dmhdd/

Arizona

Arizona Department of Health Services
Behavioral Health Services
2122 E. Highland
Phoenix, AZ 85016
(602) 381-8999
Fax (602) 553-9140
http://www.hs.state.az.us/bhs/home.htm

Arkansas

Department of Human Services
PO Box 3781
7th & Main Streets
Little Rock, AR 72203
(501) 682-6708

Colorado

Mental Health Services
3824 W. Princeton Circle
Denver, CO 80236
(303) 866-7400
Fax (303) 866-7428
http://www.cdhs.state.co.us/ohr/mhs/index.html

District of Columbia

DC Commission on Mental Health Services
Child Youth Services Administration
2700 Martin Luther King Avenue SE
St. Elizabeth's Hospital, L Bldg.
Washington, DC 20032
(202) 373-7225

Florida

Children's Medical Services (CMS)
Department of Health and Rehabilitative Services
1311 Winewood Boulevard
Building 5, Room 215
Tallahassee, FL 32301
(904) 488-4257
http://www.doh.state.fl.us/

Georgia

Department of Human Resources
2 Peachtree Street NE, Suite 22-205
Atlanta, GA 30303
(404) 657-2260

Hawaii

Department of Human Services
1000 Bishop Street, No. 615
Honolulu, HI 96813
(808) 548-4769

Idaho

Department of Health and Welfare
450 W. State Street
Boise, ID 83720-0036
(208) 334-5500
http://www.state.id.us/dhw/hwgd_www/home.html

Illinois

Department of Mental Health and Developmental Disabilities
402 Stratten Office Building
Springfield, IL 62706
(217) 782-7395

Indiana

Department of Mental Health
402 W. Washington W353
Indianapolis, IN 46204-3647

Iowa

Department of Human Services
Hoover Building, 5th Floor
Des Moines, IN 50310
(515) 278-2502

Kansas

Child & Adolescent Mental Health Programs
506 N. State Office Building
Topeka, KS 66612
(913) 296-1808

Kentucky

Department of Mental Health and Mental Retardation Services
100 Fair Oaks Lane, 4th Floor
Frankfort, KY 40621
(502) 564-7610

Louisiana

Department of Health and Human Resources
PO Box 4049
655 N. 5th Street
Baton Rouge, LA 70821
(504) 342-2548

Maine

Department of Mental Health and Mental Retardation
State House
Station 40
Augusta, ME 04333
(207) 287-4200

Maryland

Department of Health and Mental Hygiene
201 W. Preston Street
O'Connor Building, 4th Floor
Baltimore, MD 21201
(410) 767-6860

Massachusetts

Department of Mental Health
24 Farnsworth Street
Boston, MA 02210
(617) 727-5600

Minnesota

Children's Mental Health
Minnesota Department of Human Services
444 Lafayette Road
St. Paul, MN 55155
(651) 297-5242

Minnesota Children with Special Health Needs
717 Delaware Street SE
PO Box 9441
Minneapolis, MN 55440-9441
(612) 676-5150 or (800) 728-5420
Fax (612) 676-5442
mcshn@kids.health.state.mn.us
http://www.health.state.mn.us/divs/fh/mcshn/mcshn.html

Mississippi

Department of Mental Health
1101 Robert E. Lee Building
239 N. Lamar Street
Jackson, MS 39201
(601) 359-1288
http://www.dmh.state.ms.us/

Missouri

Department of Mental Health
1706 East Elm Street
PO Box 687
Jefferson City, MO 65102
(573) 751-3070 or (800) 364-9687
dmhmail@mail.state.mo.us
http://www.modmh.state.mo.us/

Montana

Department of Public Health and Social Services
PO Box 4210
111 Sanders, Room 202
Helena, MT 59604
(406) 444-2995
http://www.dphhs.state.mt.us/

Nebraska

Nebraska Health and Human Services
Office of Community Mental Health
PO Box 95007
Lincoln, NE 68509
(402) 471-2330
http://www.hhs.state.ne.us/beh/behindex.htm

Nevada

Department of Human Resources
State Capitol Complex
505 E. King Street
Carson City, NV 98710
(702) 687-4440

New Hampshire

Division of Mental Health and Developmental Services
Department of Health and Welfare
State Office Park South
105 Pleasant Street
Concord, NH 03301
(603) 271-5013

New Jersey

Services for Children with Special Health Care Needs
New Jersey Department of Health and Senior Services
PO Box 364
Trenton, NJ 08625
(609) 984-0755
http://www.state.nj.us/health/fhs/schome.htm

New Mexico

Department of Health and the Environment
1190 St. Francis Drive
Santa Fe, NM 87503
(505) 827-2707

New York

New York State Office of Mental Health
44 Holland Street
Albany, NY 12229
(518) 473-3456
http://www.omh.state.ny.us/

North Carolina

Department of Human Resources
620 N. West Street
PO Box 26053
Raleigh, NC 27611
(919) 733-6566

North Dakota

Department of Human Services
State Capitol Building
Bismarck, ND 58505
(701) 328-2310
http://lnotes.state.nd.us/dhs/dhsweb.nsf

Ohio

Ohio Department of Mental Health
State Office Tower
30 E. Broad Street, 8th Floor
Columbus, OH 43266-0315
(614) 466-1483
http://www.mh.state.oh.us/

Oklahoma

Oklahoma Department of Mental Health and Substance Abuse Services
1200 NE 13th Street
PO Box 53277
Oklahoma City, OK 73152-3277
(405) 522-3908
http://www.odmhsas.org/

Oregon

Office of Mental Health Services
Department of Human Resources
2575 Bittern Street NE
Salem, OR 97310
(503) 975-9700
http://omhs.mhd.hr.state.or.us/

Pennsylvania

Special Kids Network
Pennsylvania Department of Health
PO Box 90
Harrisburg, PA 17108
(800) 986-4550
http://www.health.state.pa.us/php/special.htm

Rhode Island

Department of Mental Health, Retardation, and Hospitals
Aime J. Forand Building
600 New London Avenue
Cranston, RI 02920
(401) 464-3234

South Carolina

Department of Mental Health
2414 Bull Street, Room 304
Columbia, SC 29201
(803) 734-7859

South Dakota

Developmental Disabilities and Mental Health
700 N. Illinois Street
Pierre, SD 57501
(605) 733-3438

Tennessee

Department of Mental Health and Mental Retardation
3rd Floor, Cordell Hull Building
425 Fifth Avenue North
Nashville, TN 37243-0675
(615) 532-6500

Texas

Department of Mental Health and Mental Retardation
909 West 45th Street
PO Box 12668
Austin, TX 78711
(512) 465-4657

Utah

State Division of Mental Health
Department of Human Services
120 N. 200 W., Room 415
Salt Lake City, UT 84145
(801) 538-4270
http://www.hsmh.state.ut.us/

Vermont

Department of Developmental and Mental Health Services
103 S. Main Street
Weeks Building
Waterbury, VT 05671-1601
(802) 241-2609
http://www.state.vt.us/dmh/

Virginia

Department of Mental Health, Mental Retardation, and Substance Abuse Services
PO Box 1797
Richmond, VA 23214
(804) 786-0992

Washington

Mental Health Division
Health and Rehabilitative Services Administration
PO Box 1788, OB-42C
Olympia, WA 98504
(800) 446-0259
http://www.wa.gov/dshs/hrsa/hrsa2hp.html

West Virginia

Department of Health and Human Resources
1800 Washington Street E.
Charleston, WV 25305
(304) 348-0627

Wisconsin

Bureau of Community Mental Health
Department of Health and Family Services
1 W. Wilson Street, Room 433
PO Box 7851
Madison, WI 53707
(608) 261-6746
Fax (608) 261-6748
http://www.dhfs.state.wi.us/mentalhealth/index.htm

Canada

British Columbia

British Columbia Ministry of Health
Parliament Buildings
Victoria, BC V8V 1X4
(250) 952-1742 or (800) 465-4911
http://www.hlth.gov.bc.ca/

Manitoba

Manitoba Health
Legislative Building
Winnipeg, MB R3C 0V8
http://www.gov.mb.ca/health/

New Brunswick

New Brunswick Health and Community Services
PO Box 5100
Fredericton, NB E3B 5G8
(506) 453-2536
Fax (506) 444-4697
http://www.gov.nb.ca/hcs/

Newfoundland and Labrador

Newfoundland Department of Health and Community Services
Division of Family and Rehabilitative Services
Confederation Building, West Block
PO Box 8700
St. John's, NF A1B 4J6
(709) 729-5153
Fax (709) 729-0583
http://www.gov.nf.ca/health/

Nova Scotia

Nova Scotia Department of Health
PO Box 488
Halifax, NS B3J 2R8
(902) 424-5886 or (800) 565-3611
http://www.gov.ns.ca/health/

Prince Edward Island

Prince Edward Island Health and Social Services
Second Floor, Jones Building
11 Kent Street
PO Box 2000
Charlottetown, PE C1A 7N8
(902) 368-4900
Fax (902) 368-4969
http://www.gov.pe.ca/hss/index.asp

Quebec

Quebec Ministére de la Santé et Services Sociaux
1075 Chemin Sainte-Foy, R.-C.
Québec, QC G1S 2M1
(418) 643-3380 or (800) 707-3380
Fax (418) 644-4574
http://www.msss.gouv.qc.ca/

Saskatchewan

Saskatchewan Health
T.C. Douglas Building
3475 Albert Street
Regina, SK S4S 6X6
(306) 787-3475
Fax (306) 787-3761
http://www.gov.sk.ca/health/

United Kingdom

People in England, Scotland, Wales, and Northern Ireland will generally need to be referred to a specialist at a clinic or hospital by their general practitioner.

The National Health Service Confederation
http://www.nahat.net/gateway.htm

This site lists all local NHS authorities and boards, as well as specific sites for health-care (including mental health services).

Ireland

Eastern Health Board
Dr. Stephens Hospital
Dublin 8
(679) 0700

Midland Health Board,
Arden Road
Tullamore, County Offaly
(0506) 21868

North Eastern Health Board
Kells, County Meath
(046) 40341
http://www.nehb.ie/

North Western Health Board
Manorhamilton, County Leitrim
(072) 55123
Fax (072) 20431
http://www.nwhb.ie/

Southern Health Board
Wilton Road
County Cork
(021) 545011
Fax (021) 545748
http://www.shb.ie/

Western Health Board
Merlin Park Regional Hospital
Galway
(091) 751131

Australia

Australian Capitol Territory

Commonwealth Department of Health and Family Services
Child Health and Development Service
Weingarth Street at Blackwood Terrace
Holder, ACT 2611
(02) 6205-1277

New South Wales

Commonwealth Department of Health and Family Services
1 Oxford Street
Darlinghurst, NSW
(02) 9263-3555 or (800) 048-998
http://www.health.nsw.gov.au/

Northern Territory

Northern Territory Health Services
PO Box 40596
Casuarina, NT 0811
(08) 8999-2400
Fax (08) 8999-2700
http://www.nt.gov.au/nths/

Queensland

Commonwealth Department of Health and Family Services
340 Adelaide
Brisbane, Queensland
(07) 3360-2555

South Australia

Commonwealth Department of Health and Family Services
55 Currie Street
Adelaide, SA 5000
(08) 8237-6111
Fax (08) 8237-8000

Tasmania

Commonwealth Department of Health and Community Services
Child and Family Services
4 Farley Street
Glenorchy, Tasmania
(03) 6233-2921

Victoria

Department of Health and Family Services
Disability Programs
Casselden Place
2 Lonsdale Street
GPO Box 9848
Melbourne, Victoria 3001
(03) 9285-8888

Western Australia

Department of Health and Family Services
Central Park, 12th Floor
152 St. George Terrace
Perth, WA 6000
(08) 9346-5111 or (800) 198-008
Fax (08) 9346-5222
http://www.public.health.wa.gov.au/

New Zealand

New Zealand Ministry of Health
133 Molesworth Street
PO Box 5013
Wellington, NZ
(04) 496-2000
Fax (04) 496-2340
http://www.moh.govt.nz/

Notes

Chapter 1: *What Are Bipolar Disorders?*

1. Gary Spivack, MD, "When ADHD is not ADHD," *Treatment Today* (December 1993).
2. J. D. Lish et al., "The National Depressive and Manic-Depressive Association (DM-DA) Survey of Bipolar Members," *Journal of Affective Disorders* 31 (1994): 281-294.
3. Joseph Biederman et al., "Attention-Deficit Hyperactivity Disorder and Juvenile Mania: An Overlooked Comorbidity?" *Journal of the American Academy of Child and Adolescent Psychiatry* 35 (August 1996): 997-1008.
4. H. S. Akiskal, MD, "The Prevalent Clinical Spectrum of Bipolar Disorders: Beyond DSM-IV," *Journal of Clinical Psychopharmacology* 16, supplement 1 (1996): 4S-14S.
5. Stanley I. Greenspan, MD, et al., *The Child with Special Needs: Encouraging Intellectual and Emotional Growth.* (Reading, Massachusetts: Addison-Wesley, 1998), 10.
6. E. B. Weller, R. A. Weller, and M. A. Fristad, "Bipolar Diagnosis in Children: Misdiagnosis, Underdiagnosis, and Future Directions," *Journal of the American Academy of Child and Adolescent Psychiatry* 34, no. 6 (1995): 709-714.
7. Jon McClellan, MD, et al., "Practice Parameters for the Assessment and Treatment of Children and Adolescents with Bipolar Disorder," *Journal of the American Academy of Child and Adolescent Psychiatry* 36 (I) (1997): 138-157.
8. Ellen Leibenluft, MD, "Circadian Rhythms Factor in Rapid-Cycling Bipolar Disorder," *Psychiatric Times* 8, no. 5 (May 1996): *http://www.mhsource.com/edu/psytimes/p960533.html.*
9. J. Rice et al., "The Familial Transmission of Bipolar Illness," *Archives of General Psychiatry* 44 (1987): 441-447, and M. Strober, "Relevance of Early Age-of-Onset in Genetic Studies of Bipolar Affective Disorder," *Journal of the American Academy of Child and Adolescent Psychiatry* 31 (1992): 606-610.
10. D. F. Papolos, MD, et al., "Bipolar Spectrum Disorders in Patients Diagnosed with Velo-Cardio-Facial Syndrome: Does a Hemizygous Deletion of Chromosome 22q11 Result in Bipolar Affective Disorder?", *American Journal of Psychiatry* 153 (1996): 1541-1547.
11. Arline Kaplan, "Imaging Studies Provide Insights into Neurobiology of Bipolar Disorders," *Bipolar Disorders Letter* (February 1998): *http://www.mhsource.com/bipolar/bp9802image.html.*
12. Judith L. Rapoport, MD, et al., "Quantitative Brain Magnetic Resonance Imaging in Attention-Deficit Hyperactivity Disorder," *Archives of General Psychiatry* 53 (1996): 607-616.
13. J. Kerbeshian, L. Burd, and M. G. Klug, "Comorbid Tourette's Disorder and Bipolar Disorder: An Etiologic Perspective," *American Journal of Psychiatry* 152, no. 11 (November 1995): 1646-51.

14. E. H. Aylward et al., "Basal Ganglia Volumes and White Matter Hyperintensities in Bipolar Disorder," *American Journal of Psychiatry* 151 (1994): 687-693.
15. Katherine Brady, MD, and R. B. Lydiard, "Bipolar affective disorder and substance abuse," *Journal of Clinical Psychopharmacology* 12, no.1 (1992):17-22.
16. Elizabeth Costello, "Child Psychiatric Disorders and Their Correlates: A Primary Care Pediatric Sample," *Journal of the American Academy of Child and Adolescent Psychiatry* 28 (1989b): 851-855.
17. Anne Brown, "Mood Disorders in Children and Adolescents," *NARSAD Research Newsletter* (Winter 1996): *http://www.mhsource.com/advocacy/narsad/childmood.html*.
18. Jennifer Ianthe Downey, MD, "Recognizing the Range of Mood Disorders in Women," *Medscape Women's Health* 1, no. 8 (1996): *http://www.medscape.com/Medscape/WomensHealth/journal/1996/v01.n08/w159.downey/w159.downey.html*.

Chapter 2: *Getting a Diagnosis*

1. Elizabeth Costello, MD, et al., "The Great Smoky Mountains Study of Youth: Functional Impairment and Serious Emotional Disturbance (SED)," *Archives of General Psychiatry* (1988): 1107-1116.
2. Jane Wozniak et al., "Mania-like Symptoms Suggestive of Childhood Onset Bipolar Disorder in Clinically Referred Children," *Journal of the American Academy of Child and Adolescent Psychiatry* 34 (1995a): 867-876.
3. Brown, "Mood Disorders in Children."
4. Charles Popper, MD, "Diagnosing Bipolar vs. ADHD": *http://www.adhdnews.com/bipolar.htm*.
5. Spivack, "When ADHD is not ADHD."
6. B. A. Johnson et al., "Familial aggregation of adolescent personality disorders," *Journal of the American Academy of Child and Adolescent Psychiatry* 34 (1995): 798-804.

Chapter 3: *Living with Bipolar Disorders*

1. Todd Zwillich, "Battling Substance Abuse in Bipolar Youths," *Clinical Psychiatry News* 26 (1998): 8.

Chapter 4: *Medical Interventions*

1. Jay D. Amsterdam, MD, et al., "A Possible Anti-Viral Action of Lithium Carbonate in Herpes Simplex Virus Infections," *Biological Psychiatry* 27 (1990): 447-453.
2. National Institute on Alcohol Abuse and Alcoholism, "Clinical Use of Medications to Treat Alcoholism," *NIH Guide* 26, no. 35 (17 October 1997): *http://www.nih.gov/grants/guide/pa-files/PA-98-003.html*.
3. Terence Monmaney, "St. John's Wort: Regulatory Vacuum Leaves Doubt About Potency, Effects of Herb Used for Depression," *Los Angeles Times* (31 August 1998): A1.

Chapter 5: *Therapeutic Interventions*

1. Kristen Quigley and Ken Braiterman, "A Consumer Speaks Out: Talk Therapy and People with Bipolar Disorder," NAMI: *http://www.nami.org/medicat/971211091604.html*.

2. Gary Sachs, MD, "Bipolar Mood Disorder: Practical Strategies for Acute and Maintenance Phase Treatment," *Journal of Clinical Psychopharmacology* 16 (supplement 1) (April 1996): S32-S47.

3. D. J. Miklowitz, M. J. Goldstein, and L. C. Wynn, *Bipolar Disorder: A Family-Focused Treatment Approach* (New York: The Guilford Press, 1997).

4. Sally Kalson, "Clubhouse Helps the Mentally Ill Work Toward Independence," *Pittsburgh Post-Gazette* (28 January 1999): *http://www.post-gazette.com:80/magazine/19990128clubhouse1.asp*.

Chapter 6: *Other Interventions*

1. R. W. Lam, E. M. Tam, and A. J. Levitt, "Treatment of Seasonal Affective Disorder: A Review," *Canadian Journal of Psychiatry* 40 (1995): 457-466.

2. R. W. Lam et al., "Low Electrooculographic Ratios in Patients with Seasonal Affective Disorder," *American Journal of Psychiatry* 148 (1991): 1526-1529.

3. Leibenluft, "Circadian Rhythms."

4. Aziz Sancar and Yasuhide Miyamoto, "Vitamin B2-based Blue-light Photoreceptors in the Retinohypothalamic Tract as the Photoactive Pigments for Setting the Circadian Clock in Mammals," *Proceedings of the National Academy of Sciences* 95, no. 11 (26 May 1998): 6097-6102.

5. Andrew L. Stoll, MD, "Omega-3 Fatty Acids in Bipolar Disorder: A Preliminary Double-Blind, Placebo-Controlled Trail," *Archives of General Psychiatry* (in press).

6. Andrew L. Stoll, MD, "Omega-3 Fatty Acid User Guide" (Belmont, Massachusetts: Psychopharmacology Research Laboratory, McLean Hospital, 1998).

7. Robert H. Yolken, E. Fuller Torrey, "Viruses, Schizophrenia, and Bipolar Disorder," *Clinical Microbiology Reviews* (January 1995): 131-145.

8. I Dé et al./The Stanley Neuropathology Consortium, "Detection of Viral Particles in Glial Cells Inoculated with Brain Tissue from Individuals with Schizophrenia and Bipolar Disease" (1997): *http://www.med.jhu.edu/stanleylab/* (abstract).

CHapter 8: *School*

1. Laura Kann et al., "National Youth Risk Behavior Surveillance," Division of Adolescent and School Health, Centers for Disease Control and Prevention (1997): *http://www.cdc.gov/epo/mmwr/preview/mmwrhtml/00054432.htm* (summary).

2. "Twentieth Annual Report to Congress on the Implementation of the Individuals with Disabilities Education Act," Office of Special Education and Rehabilitation, US Department of Education (12 March 1999): *http://www.ed.gov/offices/OSERS/OSEP/OSEP98AnlRpt/*.

3. Quackenbush et al., "Premorbid and Postmorbid School Functioning in Bipolar Adolescents: Description and Suggested Academic Interventions," *Canadian Journal of Psychiatry* (February 1996): 16-22.

Chapter 9: *Transitions*

1. Downey, "Mood Disorders in Women."

2. Kay Redfield Jamison, MD, *Touched with Fire: Manic-Depressive Illness and the Artistic Temperament* (New York: The Free Press, 1993.)

Index

5-HTP (5-hydroxytryptophan), 249
5-hydroxytryptamine/5-HT, 21, 24, 126

A
absence seizures, 121
academic tests, 43–46
Acamprosate (calcium
    acetylhomotaurinate),
    180–181
accident prevention, 102–103
Achenbach Child Behavior Checklist
    (CBC), 41
acupressure, 239
acupuncture, 237–238
ADA (Americans with Disabilities Act),
    318, 355
Adaptive Behavior Inventory for
    Children (ABIC), 44
Adderall (dextroamphetimine/
    amphetamine), 174–175
ADHD
    compared to bipolar disorders, 3–4,
        18, 48–52
    hyperactivity, 49–50
    impulsivity, 50
    misdiagnoses as bipolar disorders,
        3–4, 16, 48
    occurrence with bipolar disorders,
        29
    resources, 395
    See also diagnosis of bipolar
        disorders
advocacy. See support and advocacy
African-American families, misdiagnoses
    in, 55
AIDS, 61

Akiskal, Hagop
    proposed definition of bipolar III, 7
akisthesia, 125
alcohol abuse. See substance abuse
Alexander Technique, 240
allergies, 256–258
"all or nothing" thinking, 80
alternative medicine
    acceptance of, 234
    considerations before choosing,
        192–193, 234–236
    effects on neurotransmitters
        possible, 26–27
    evaluating effectiveness of, 237
    misinformation about, 235
    practitioners of, 237–243
    resources, 406–408
    role of, 236–237
    types of, 237–277, 243
        acupressure, 239
        acupuncture, 237–238
        Alexander Technique, 240
        allergy tests and treatments,
            257–258
        antiviral treatments, 259–262
        Ayurvedic medicine, 238–239
        bodywork and massage, 239–
            240
        Chinese medicine, 238–239
        chiropractic, 239
        craniosacral therapy, 240
        diet/nutrition-based therapies,
            26–27, 242–243, 253–
            257
        essential fatty acids (EFAs),
            249–253
        Feldenkrais Method, 239–240

alternative medicine, types of (*continued*)
    fixing sleep problems, 245–249
    holistic psychology, 241–242
    homeopathy, 242
    hormonal treatments, 258–259
    humor, 276–277
    immunotherapy, 259–262
    light therapy, 243–245
    naturopathy, 241
    orthomolecular medicine, 243
    osteopathy, 243
    social skills instruction, 274–276
    stress-busters (stress reduction), 272–274
    supplements, 247–253, 263–272, 407–408
Americans with Disabilities Act, 318, 355
amygdala, 23
Anafranil (clomipramine), 143–144
anger and rage, 18, 50–51
anorexia, 68, 395–396
Antabuse (disulfiram), 181
antianxiety medications, 184–188
anti-Candida diets, 256
antidepressants, various, 152–155
antipsychotic medications, 163–173
antiseizure medications, 156–163
antisocial personality disorder, 57
antispasmodic medications, 156–163
antiviral treatments, 259–262
anxiety/anxiety disorders, 29, 55–56
Armour, 191–192
art therapy, 227
Asendin (amoxapine), 144–145
Ativan (lorazepam), 184
atonic seizures, 121
Attention Deficit Disorders Evaluation Scale, 41
attention deficit hyperactivity disorder. *See* ADHD
atypical neuroleptics, 171–173
auditory integration training, 226–227
auras, 64
    See also hallucinations
Aurorex (moclobemide), 150
Australia
    education in, 357–359
    finding housing in, 383
    insurance, financial assistance in, 303–305, 312
    resources, 389–421
autism, 29
autoimmune disorders, 29
Aventyl (nortriptyline), 145
aversives, 203
avoidant personality disorder, 58
axis system of diagnosis, 8–9
Ayurvedic medicine, 238–239

B

Battelle Developmental Inventory, 44
Behavior Assessment System for Children (BASC), 41
behavior modification/therapy, 27, 214, 223–224
bipolar I disorder (BPI), 5–6
bipolar II disorder (BPII), 6
bipolar III disorder (BPIII), 7–8
bipolar symptoms, specific medications for, 189–192
black cohosh (*Cimicifuga racemosa*), 266
blood tests, 119–120, 261–262
board certification, 32, 211
bodywork, 239–240
books and publications, 394
borderline personality disorder, 57
BPParent, 32, 113
bradyphrenia, 125
brain
    and ADHD, 23
    chemical messaging system of, 24–27
    differences as causes of bipolar disorders, 22–24
    electrical miswiring of, 27
    imaging technologies, 23–24
    neurotransmitters in, 21, 24–27
    role in nervous system, 22
    and Tourette syndrome, 23
    types of cells in, 23
breathing exercises, 272–273
bulemia, 68
BuSpar (buspirone), 185

C

Calan (verapamil), 181–182
calcium, 131, 269
Canada
  education in, 355–356
  finding housing in, 383
  finding therapists in, 210
  insurance, financial assistance in, 37–38, 299–301
  resources, 389–421
casein-free diets, 255–256
Catapres (clonidine), 189
catastrophizing, 79
CAT (computer tomography), 23
causes of bipolar disorders
  brain differences as, 22–24
  circadian rhythm disturbances, 20–21, 178
  exact cause not known, 1, 21
  genetic differences as, 22
  immune-system impairment possible, 28
  as medical problems, 4
Celexa (citalopram), 140–141
central nervous system. See brain
Centrax (prazepam), 185–186
Cerebyx (fosphenytoin), 157
chamomile (*Anthemis nobilis*), 248
children and adolescents
  bipolar disorders in different from adults, 19
  consequences of untreated bipolar disorders for, 19–20
  in criminal justice system, 107–110
  drop-in centers for teen use, 231–232
  drug and alcohol abuse in, 28
  family therapy useful to, 20, 218–221
  and lithium, 129–133
  mixed states in, 16
  play therapy for, 217–218
  positive characteristics of bipolar disorders in, 30
  rapid cycling in, 16
  signs and symptoms in, 17–19
  social skills instruction for, 274–276
  stress reduction for, 272–274
  teens in therapy, 224–226
  US public assistance for, 296–297
  violent behavior in, 88–90
  See also families; schools
Children's Memory Scale (CMS), 44
Chinese medicine, 238–239
chiropractic, 239
choline, 270
Christian counselors, 214
chromium picolinate, 269
chronic fatigue/chronic fatigue immune deficiency syndrome (CFIDS), 62
circadian rhythms, 20–21, 178
Classification of Mental and Behavioural Disorders, ICD-10, 4–5
clinical depression, 10–12
clinical trials of medications, 128, 311–312
Clozaril (clozapine), 171
Clusters A, B, C (I, II, III) personality disorders, 57–58
cognitive therapy, 216–217
communicating with specialists/experts, 38–40
compassionate use laws/programs, 127
complex partial seizures, 121
compounding pharmacies, 117
computer tomography (CAT), 23
conduct disorders, 56–57, 395
Connors Rating Scales (CRS), 41–42
consultation appointment, 33–35
coping with bipolar disorders. *See* taking charge of bipolar disorders
Costello, Elizabeth
  pediatricians' limited familiarity with psychiatric disorders, 31
counseling and counselors, 38–39, 213–215, 223
  See also therapies and therapists
craniosacral therapy, 240
criminal justice system, 107–110
crisis triage centers, 99
cultural issues as factors in diagnosis, 29–30, 64–65
Cushing's disease, 60
cyclothymic disorder (cyclothymia), 6–7, 8

Cylert (pemoline), 175
Cytomel, 191–192

D

damiana (*Turnera aphrodisiaca*), 266
dance therapy, 227
Das (dextroamphetamine sulfate), 175–176
day treatment facilities, 205
definitions of bipolar disorders, 4–5
delusional thinking, 18, 64, 80–82
dendrites, 24
Depakene (valproic acid), 134–135
Depakote/Depakote Sprinkles
    (divalproex sodium), 135
dependent personality disorder, 58
depression, 10–12
depressive personality disorder, 58
Desoxyn (methamphetamine (MTH)), 176–177
Desyrel (trazodone), 152–153
Developmental Assessment Screening
    Inventory II (DASI-II), 45
developmental delays, 29
Developmental Profile II, 45
development tests, 43–46
diabetes mellitus, 60
diagnosis of bipolar disorders
    African-American families,
        misdiagnoses in, 55
    axis system used in, 8–9
    and conditions with similar
        symptoms, 28–29
    cultural issues as factors in, 29–30,
        64–65
    definitions used in, 4–5
    differential diagnosis, 48–64
    dual/multiple diagnosis, 28–29
    gender as factor in, 29–30
    importance of, 3
    as medical problems, 4
    misdiagnoses as ADHD, 3–4, 16
    as ongoing process, 65
    pediatricians' limited familiarity
        with psychiatric disorders,
        31
    as recent development for children
        and teens, 3–4
    steps in getting

consultation appointment, 33–35
    diagnostic report, 46–47
    indentifying/choosing experts,
        31–40
    roadblocks to referral to
        experts, 36–38
    seeing specialists/experts, 38–40
    time needed for, 40
    tools/tests used in, 8–9, 35–36, 40–46
    See also differential diagnosis; signs
        and symptoms of bipolar
        disorders
*Diagnostic and Statistical Manual of
    Mental Disorders (DSM-IV)*, 4
diagnostic report, 46–47
diary of mood and behavior, 75–78, 77
    (figure)
diet/nutrition-based therapies, 26–27,
    242–243, 253–257
differential diagnosis
    conditions resembling or occurring
        with bipolar disorders
    ADHD, 48–52
    AIDS, 61
    anxiety/anxiety disorders, 55–56
    chronic fatigue syndrome, 62
    conduct disorder, 56–57
    Cushing's disease, 60
    diabetes mellitus, 60
    hepatitis, 63
    hormonal disorders, 58–60
    hypoglycemia, 60
    lupus, 61
    medication side effects, 52–53
    mononucleosis, 62
    multiple sclerosis (MS), 62–63
    oppositional defiant disorder,
        56–57
    personality disorders, 57–58
    psychosis/psychotic symptoms,
        63–65
    rheumatoid arthritis, 60
    schizoaffective disorder/
        depression, 55
    schizophrenia, 54–55

differential diagnosis (*continued*)
  substance abuse, 52
  Tay-Sachs disease, 63
  thyroid disorders, 58
  unipolar depression, 53–54
  defined, 48
  See also diagnosis of bipolar
    disorders
Dilantin (phenytoin), 157–158
disability income and insurance. *See*
    insurance and financial
    assistance
discipline
  after hospitalization, 204
  medications for emergencies, 85
  natural and logical consequences of,
    87–90
  physical abuse, reacting to, 88
  physical control of children and
    teens, 88–90
  physical punishments as, 88
  picking battles, 86–87
  proactive/preventative measures,
    84–85
  reacting to verbal abuse, 90
  self time-outs needed, 85–86
  support of friends and family
    helpful, 88
  token economy systems, 85
  using rewards to encourage, 85–86
discontinuing medications, 118–119
dopamine, 24
dosage considerations, 115–120
Draw-a-Person, 42
drop-in centers, 231–232
drug abuse. *See* substance abuse
drug and alcohol detox/dependency
    aids, 178–184
drugs (therapeutic). *See* medications,
    generally; medications,
    specific
DSM-IV (*Diagnostic and Statistical Manual
    of Mental Disorders*), 4
dual diagnosis, 28–29
dystonia, 125

E

Early Intervention (IE) services, 367–
    370

early signs and symptoms of bipolar
    disorders, 17–19
eating disorders, 68, 395–396
education. *See* schools
EEG (electroencephalogram), 27
Efalex, 252
Efamol, 252
Effexor/Effexor XR (venlafaxine), 153
EicoPro, 253
EKGs (electrocardiograms), 120
Elavil (amitriptyline), 145–146
electrical activity in brain. *See* brain
electrocardiograms (EKGs), 120
electroconvulsive therapy (ECT), 201–
    202
electroencephalogram (EEG), 27
elimination/re-introduction diets, 256–
    257
encephalopathic syndrome, 125
epilepsy. *See* seizures/seizure disorders
Eskalith, 129–130
Essential Balance/Essential Balance Jr.,
    253
essential fatty acids (EFAs), 249–253
esteem needs, 72–73
Etrafon (amitriptyline/perphenazine),
    164
Europe, insurance, financial assistance
    in, 37–38, 312
Euthroid, 191–192
exercise, 273–274
extrapyramidal side effects (EPS), 125

F

families
  and discipline, 88, 92
  history of bipolar disorders in, 18–
    19, 30
  maintaining sanity of, 110–114
  relationships with hospitals, 201
  respite care as help for, 111
  role of in life of adult children, 386
  siblings, issues for, 91–92
  strains on relationships in, 91–93
  therapeutic homes, 230–233
  therapy for, 20, 218–221
  See also children and adolescents
family therapy, 20, 218–221
Feingold Diet, 254–255

Feldenkrais Method, 239–240
financial issues. *See* insurance and
    financial assistance
finding experts, 31–40, 214
focal/local seizures, 121
Freud, Sigmund, 207–208, 225
friends, 88, 95–96
Functional Behavior Analysis plan, 224

G

GABA (gaba-amino butyric acid), 271
Gabitril (tiagabine hydrochloride), 136,
    158
gastrointestinal disorders, 29
gender as factor in diagnosis, 29–30
generalized seizures, 121
genetic differences, 22
gingko biloba, 266
ginseng (*Panax quinquefolium*), 266
glial cells, 23
gluten-free diets, 255–256
gotu kola (*Centella asiatica, Hydrocotyl
    asiatica*), 266
grandiosity, 79, 92
grand mal seizures, 121
grapeseed oil, 266
Greenspan, Stanley
    overlap of regulatory and bipolar
        disorders, 8
group therapy, 214, 221

H

Habitrol (nicotine), 189–190
Haldol/Haldol Decanoate (haloperidol),
    165
hallucinations, 16, 63–64
Halstead-Reitan Neuropsychological
    Test Battery for Children
    (HNTBC), 42
hepatitis, 63
herbal remedies/supplements, 26, 193,
    266–267
histrionic personality disorder, 58
HMOs. *See* insurance and financial
    assistance
holistic psychology, 241–242
home as therapeutic environment, 230–
    233

homeopathy, 242
hope, 113, 387–388
hops (*Humulus lupulus*), 248
hormones
    in females, 8, 29, 378
    hormonal disorders, 58–60
    hormonal treatments, 258–259
    and immune system, 28
    and premenstrual syndrome, 8
    See also neurotransmitters
hospitals and hospitalization
    admission to, 194–196
    conditions and regulations in, 197–
        201
    crisis triage centers, 99
    discharge from and considerations
        after, 204–205
    facilities, types of, 196–198
    hospital-based education, 341
    resources, 405–406
    school, return to following, 204–
        205
    situations requiring, 193, 195
    treatments, 201–204
House-Tree-Person Projective Drawing
    Technique, 42
humor as healing power, 276–277
hydrotherapy, 202–203
hyperactivity, 18, 49–50
hyperkinesia, 125
hyperventilation, 273
hypoglycemia, 60
hypomania, 13–15

I

ibuprofen, 132
*ICD-10 Classification of Mental and
    Behavioural Disorders*, 4–5
IEPs
    accommodations, 324–328, 325
        (figure), 355
    defined, 322
    and due process, 352–353
    goals and objectives of, 326
        (figure), 328–331
    meeting, 323–324
    participants in creation of, 322–323
    signing, 331–332
    in transition planning, 372–373

immune-system impairment, 28
immune system modulators/stimulants,
    262–263
immunotherapy, 259–262
impulsivity, 18, 50
indentifying/choosing experts, 31–40
Individual Family Service Plans (IFSPs),
    367–370
Individualized Education Plans (IEPs).
    See IEPs
Individuals with Disabilities Education
    Act (IDEA), 318
inositol, 132, 270
insulin shock, 202
insurance. *See* insurance and financial
    assistance
insurance and financial assistance
    in Australia, 303–305, 312
    in Canada, 37–38, 299–301
    in Europe, 37–38, 312
    in New Zealand, 305–307, 312
    in the Republic of Ireland, 303
    resources, 400–401
    in the United Kingdom (UK), 301–
        303, 308
    in the United States
        admission to hospitals, 196
        alternatives to insurance, 307–
            308
        case management, 377–378
        changing rules of, 313–315
        choice of plans, 279–280
        costs of care, 91–92
        denial of care, fighting, 285–
            289
        discount and access programs,
            312
        free/low-cost medications,
            309–312
        Katie Beckett Waiver, 293–294
        managed care and HMOs, 196,
            280–285
        Medicaid, 290–291
        medical savings accounts, 308–
            309
        Mental Health Parity Act, 313
        non-health/disability
            insurance, 315
        other public assistance, 296–
            297

        private healthcare, 278–279
        public healthcare, 290–297
        referral policies/procedures,
            32, 36–38
        SSI (Supplemental Security
            Income), 291–293
        state and local health plans,
            294–295
        tax benefits, 290–298
        and transition planning, 376–
            377
        transportation/lodging during
            care, 312
intelligence (IQ) tests, 43–46
interacting with specialists/experts, 38–
    40
interactions of medications, 52–53,
    124–127
Internet, xv, 32, 113
Inversine (mecamylamine
    hydrochloride), 190
Ireland, Republic of
    finding housing in, 383
    insurance, financial assistance in,
        303
    resources, 389–421
isolation, 203–204
Isoptin (verapamil), 181–182

J

Janimine (imipramine), 148–149

K

Katie Beckett Waiver, 293–294
kava-kava (*Piper methysticum*), 248
ketogenic diet, 255
Kiddie-SADS-Present and Lifetime
        Version (K-SADS-PL), 42
kindling, 27
Kinetic Family Drawing System for
        Family and School, 42
Klonopin (clonazepam), 159

L

Lamictal (lamotrigine), 136–137
language skills, 51

Learning Potential Assessment Device (LPAD), 45
lecithin, 270
Leiter International Performance Scale, Revised (Leiter-R), 45
Librium (chlordiazepoxide), 186
licensing boards and agencies, 210–215
licorice (*Glycyrrhiza glabra, Liquiritia officinalis*), 266
light therapy, 243–245
Limbitrol (amitriptyline/ chlordiazepoxide), 146
Lithane, 129–130
lithium
    brand names of, 129
    dietary considerations, 131–132
    possible antiviral effects, 28, 131
    side effects/interactions, 130–132
    substance abuse, impact on, 106
    tests prior to and during use, 130
    time before effective, 131
    tips for young people, 132–133
Lithobid/Lithonate/Lithotabs. *See* lithium
logical leaps, 80
Loxipax (loxapine), 165–166
Loxitane, 165–166
Luminol (phenobarbital), 159–160
lupus, 61
Luria-Nebraska Neuropsychological Battery, Children's Revision (LNNB-CR), 42–43
Luvox (fluvoxamine), 141

M

magical thinking, 79–80
magnesium, 269
magnetic resonance imaging (MRI), 23, 123
mail-order pharmacies, 311, 401–403
managed care. *See* insurance and financial assistance
Manerix (moclobemide), 150
manganese, 269
mania, 12–13
manic depression, 5–6
mannitol, 131

MAO inhibitors/MAOIs, 149–152
Maslow's hierarchy of needs, 66–67
massage, 239–240
Medicaid, 290–291
medical facilities. *See* hospitals and hospitalization
medical interventions, 115–205
medications, in general
    after hospitalization, 204
    antianxiety, 184
    antidepressants, various, 152
    antipsychotics, 163–164
    antiseizure/antispasmodics, 156–157
    assistance programs, directory of, 309–310
    for bipolar symptoms, various, 189
    brand and generic names of, 127
    clinical trials of, 128, 311–312
    compassionate use laws, 127
    compounding pharmacies, 117
    considerations while taking, 117–118, 128–129
    discontinuing, 118–119
    doctor's samples of, 310–311
    dosage considerations, 115–120
    drug and alcohol dependency aids, 178–180
    effectiveness of over time, 192
    for emergencies, 85
    forms of, 116–117
    free/low-cost, 309–312
    immune system modulators/ stimulants, 262–263
    interactions and side effects of, 52–53, 124–127
    mail-order availability of, 311, 401–403
    MAO inhibitors/MAOIs, 149–150
    mood stabilizers (non-lithium), 133–134
    neuroleptics/atypical neuroleptics, 163–164, 171
    pills, 116–117
    prescription abbreviations, 118 (chart)
    record keeping of, 192
    resources, 401–404
    SSRI antidepressants, 139–140

medications, in general (*continued*)
  stimulants, 174, 177
  tricyclic antidepressants, 143
  See also names of specific
    medications
medications, specific
  Acamprosate (calcium
    acetylhomotaurinate),
    180–181
  Adderall (dextroamphetimine/
    amphetamine), 174–175
  Anafranil (clomipramine), 143–144
  Antabuse (disulfiram), 181
  Armour, 191–192
  Asendin (amoxapine), 144–145
  Ativan (lorazepam), 184
  Aurorex (moclobemide), 150
  Aventyl (nortriptyline), 145
  BuSpar (buspirone), 185
  Calan (verapamil), 181–182
  Catapres (clonidine), 189
  Celexa (citalopram), 140–141
  Centrax (prazepam), 185–186
  Cerebyx (fosphenytoin), 157
  Clozaril (clozapine), 171
  Cylert (pemoline), 175
  Cytomel, 191–192
  Das (dextroamphetamine sulfate),
    175–176
  Depakene (valproic acid), 134–135
  Depakote/Depakote Sprinkles
    (divalproex sodium), 135
  Desoxyn (methamphetamine
    (MTH)), 176–177
  Desyrel (trazodone), 152–153
  Dilantin (phenytoin), 157–158
  Effexor/Effexor XR (venlafaxine),
    153
  Elavil (amitriptyline), 145–146
  Etrafon (amitriptyline/
    perphenazine), 164
  Euthroid, 191–192
  Gabitril (tiagabine hydrochloride),
    136, 158
  Habitrol (nicotine), 189–190
  Haldol/Haldol Decanoate
    (haloperidol), 165
  Inversine (mecamylamine
    hydrochloride), 190
  Isoptin (verapamil), 181–182

Janimine (imipramine), 148–149
Klonopin (clonazepam), 159
Lamictal (lamotrigine), 136–137
Librium (chlordiazepoxide), 186
Limbitrol (amitriptyline/
  chlordiazepoxide), 146
lithium (lithium carbonate, lithium
  citrate), 28, 106, 129–133
Loxipax (loxapine), 165–166
Loxitane, 165–166
Luminol (phenobarbital), 159–160
Luvox (fluvoxamine), 141
Manerix (moclobemide), 150
Mellaril (thioridazine
  hydrochloride), 166
Mesantoin (mephenytoin), 160–
  161
Moban (molindone), 166–167
Mysoline (primidone), 161
Narcan (naloxone hydrochloride),
  182
Nardil (phenelzine), 150–151
Navane (thiothixene), 167
Neurontin (gabapentin), 137
Nitoman (tetrabenzine, TDZ), 126–
  127
Norpramin (desipramine), 146–147
NTX (naltrexone hydrochloride),
  183–184
Orap (diphenylbutylpiperdine),
  167–168
Pamelor (nortriptyline), 145
Parnate (tranylcypromine sulfate),
  151–152
Paxil (paroxetine), 141–142
Peganone (ethotoin), 161–162
Pimozide (diphenylbutylpiperdine),
  167–168
Prolixin/Prolixin Decanoate
  (fluphenazine), 168–169
Prozac (fluoxetine), 142
Reboxetine (edronax), 153–154
Regulin (tetrabenzine, TDZ), 126–
  127
Remoron (mirtazapine), 154
ReVex (nalmefene hydrochloride),
  182–183
ReVia (naltrexone hydrochloride),
  183–184
Risperdal (risperidone), 171–172

medications, specific (*continued*)
    Ritalin (methylphenidate
        hydrochloride), 177
    Serax (oxazepam), 186–187
    Serentil (mesoridazine), 169
    Seroquel (quetiapine), 172
    Seroxat (paroxetine), 141–142
    Serzone (nefazodone), 154–155
    Sinequan (doxepin), 147
    S-P-T, 191–192
    Stelazine (trifluoperazine), 169–170
    Surmontil (trimipramine), 147–148
    Tegretol (carmazepine), 137–138
    Tenex (guanfacine), 190–191
    Thorazine (chlorpromazine), 170
    Thyrar, 191–192
    thyroid hormone replacements
        (levothyroxine,
        liothyronine, T3, T4),
        191–192
    Thyroid Strong, 191–192
    Tofranil (imipramine), 148–149
    Topomax (topiramate), 138–139,
        162
    Tranxene (clorazepate), 187
    Trexan (naltrexone hydrochloride),
        183–184
    Triavil, 164
    Trilafon, 164
    Valium (diazepam), 188
    Vesprin (trifluoperazine), 169–170
    Vivactil (protriptyline), 149
    Wellbutrin/Wellbutrin SR
        (buproprion), 155
    Xanax (alprazolam), 188–189
    Zarontin (ethosuximide), 162–163
    Zeldox (ziprasidone), 173
    Zoloft (sertraline), 142–143
    Zyban (buproprion), 155
    Zyprexa (olanzapine), 173
meditation, 272
melatonin, 20–21, 24, 247
Mellaril (thioridazine hydrochloride),
    166
Mental Health Parity Act, 313
Mesantoin (mephenytoin), 160–161
methionine, 271
migraines, 27, 29, 36, 64
milieu therapy, 222–223
minerals, 268–269

minimization, 79
mixed state (mixed mania), 15–16
Moban (molindone), 166–167
Monolaurin, 253
mononucleosis, 62
mood and behavior diary, 75–78, 77
    (figure)
mood disorder NOS (not otherwise
    specified), 7
mood stabilizers (non-lithium), 133–
    139
mood swings
    keeping diary of, 75–78, 77 (figure)
    normal, 1
    preventing, 76–78
    rapid cycling, 16
    as side effects of medications, 53
    as symptoms of bipolar disorders,
        18, 50
    viral causes of, 61
    See also types of bipolar disorders
morning energy levels, 51
MRI (magnetic resonance imaging), 23,
    123
multiple diagnosis, 28–29
multiple sclerosis (MS), 62–63
music therapy, 227
myoclonic seizures, 121
Mysoline (primidone), 161

N

NAMI (National Alliance for the
    Mentally Ill), 32, 112,
    128, 389
Narcan (naloxone hydrochloride), 182
narcissistic personality disorder, 58
Nardil (phenelzine), 150–151
naturopathy, 241
Navane (thiothixene), 167
needs of children with bipolar disorders
    for education and work, 73–74
    for food, shelter, medical care, 68
    for safety and security, 69–70
    for self-esteem, acceptance, love,
        72–73
    for social skills and interactions,
        70–72
    See also children and adolescents

neuroleptic malignant syndrome (NMS), 125
neuroleptics/atypical neuroleptics, 163–173
neurological assessments, 41–43
neurologists, 38–39
neurons, 23–24
Neurontin (gabapentin), 137
neuropsychologists, 38
neurotransmitters, 21, 24–27
New Zealand
    education in, 359
    finding housing in, 383
    insurance, financial assistance in, 305–307, 312
    resources, 389–421
nightmares, 51–52
Nitoman (tetrabenzine, TDZ), 126–127
non-talk therapies, 226–229
norepinephrine, 24
Norpramin (desipramine), 146–147
notes, 423–425
NTX (naltrexone hydrochloride), 183–184
nueroSPECT scans, 23, 123
nutritional supplements, 269–272, 407–408
nutrition-based therapies, 242–243
NutriVene-D, 253

O

obsessive-compulsive personality disorder, 29, 58
occupational therapy (OT), 227
oculogyric crisis, 125
ODD (oppositional defiant disorder), 56–57, 385
Omega 3/6 fatty acids, 249–253, 407–408
online support groups, xv, 13, 32, 393–394
    See also Internet
oppositional defiant disorder, 56–57, 385
Orap (diphenylbutylpiperdine), 167–168
orthomolecular medicine, 243
orthostatic hypotension, 125
osteopathy, 243

P

Pamelor (nortriptyline), 145
Papolos, Demetri
    velo-cardio-facial syndrome, 22
paranoia, 80
paranoid personality disorder, 57
Parent Effectiveness Training (PET), 87–88
parenting, 4, 30, 398–399
Parkinsonian symptoms, 126
Parnate (tranylcypromine sulfate), 151–152
partial seizures, 121
passion flower (Passiflora incarnata), 248
passive-aggressive personality disorder, 58
Paxil (paroxetine), 141–142
Peabody Developmental and Motor Scales (PDMS), 45
Peabody Individual Achievement Test (PIAT), 45
Pediatric Symptom Checklist, 43
peer support groups, 221
Peganone (ethotoin), 161–162
personality disorder, not otherwise specified, 58
personality disorders, 57–58
personalization, 79
pervasive developmental disorders, 29
petit mal seizures, 121
PET (positron emission tomography), 123
phenylalanine, 271
physical activity and exercise, 26
physiological needs, 68
pills, 116–117
Pimozide (diphenylbutylpiperdine), 167–168
play therapy, 217–218
PMS, 8, 29, 378
positive characteristics of bipolar disorders, 30
positron emission tomography (PET), 123
prayer, 272
premenstrual syndrome/dysphoric disorder, 8, 29, 378
prescriptions, abbreviations in, 118 (chart)

Professional Assault Response Training (PART), 88–89
prognosis, 47
Prolixin/Prolixin Decanoate (fluphenazine), 168–169
prosody, 229
Prozac (fluoxetine), 142
psychiatric assessments, 41–43
psychiatric nurses, 211
psychiatrists, 38–40, 211
psychoanalysis, 207–208
psychologists, 38–40, 212
psychosis/psychotic symptoms, 16–17, 61, 63–65
public mental health agencies, 408–421
pycogenol, 266

R

rapid cycling, 16
rebelliousness, 51
Reboxetine (edronax), 153–154
record keeping, 33–35, 111, 192, 281–282
referrals to experts, roadblocks to, 36–38
Regulin (tetrabenzine, TDZ), 126–127
religious beliefs, 64–65, 214
Remoron (mirtazapine), 154
resources, xv, 389–421
respite care, 111
restraints, 203
ReVex (nalmefene hydrochloride), 182–183
ReVia (naltrexone hydrochloride), 183–184
rheumatoid arthritis, 60
Risperdal (risperidone), 171–172
Ritalin (methylphenidate hydrochloride), 177
rotation diets, 256–257

S

SAD (seasonal affective disorder), 7, 396
safety needs, 69–70
SAMe (S-adenosyl-methionine), 271–272
sarsparilla (*Hemidesmus indicus*), 266
schizoaffective disorder/depression, 55

schizoid personality disorder, 57
schizophrenia, 54–55
schizotypal personality disorder, 57
schools
504 plans, 319–320, 353, 355
accommodations in, 324–328, 325 (figure), 355
alternative
GED programs, 349, 375
homeschooling, 343–345
hospital-based education, 341
mixing and matching alternatives, 346
private schools, 345–346
choice of, 332–334
Early Intervention (IE) services, 367–370
graduation from, 374–375
higher education, 375–376
IEPs (Individualized Education Plans), 322–332, 325–326 (figures), 353, 355, 372–373
ignorance and fear of bipolar disorders in, 316–318
importance of, 370–371
inclusion/inclusive classrooms, 332–333
Individual Family Service Plans (IFSPs), 367–370
laws effecting, 318
legal challenges to, 351–355
monitoring progress in, 349–350
need for, 73–74
resources, 399–400
return to after hospitalization, 204–205
special problems of students in, 359–366
disruption/violence, 362–365
need for extended school year services, 366
suspension/expulsion, 365–366
transition after hospitalization, 360–362
types of
alternative/charter schools, 337–338
diagnostic classrooms, 338

schools, types of (*continued*)
    residential schools, 340
    special classrooms, 334–337
    special schools, 338–339
seasonal affective disorder (SAD), 7, 396
Section 504 plans, 319–320, 353, 355
seizures/seizure disorders
    auras in, 64
    coping with, 123–124
    diagnosis of, 122–123
    and evening primrose oil, 250
    ketogenic diet, 255
    medications for, 124, 156–157
    occurrence with bipolar disorders,
        29, 36
    panic attacks, 124
    tests used to detect, 27, 121–122
    types of, 121–122
self-injurious behavior, 90, 103–104,
    396–397
sensory integration (SI), 228–229, 273
separation anxiety, 17
Serax (oxazepam), 186–187
Serentil (mesoridazine), 169
Seroquel (quetiapine), 172
serotonin (5-hydroxytryptamine, 5-HT),
    21, 24, 126
serotonin syndrome, 126
Seroxat (paroxetine), 141–142
Serzone (nefazodone), 154–155
sexual precociousness, 51
siblings, issues for, 91–92, 399
side effects of medications, 52–53, 124–
    127
signs and symptoms of bipolar disorders
    compared to symptoms of ADHD,
        50–52
    early signs, 17–19
    See also diagnosis of bipolar
        disorders
simple depression, 53–54
simple partial seizures, 121
Sinequan (doxepin), 147
single photon emission computed
    tomography (SPECT or
    neuroSPECT) scans, 23,
    123
skullcap (Scutellaria lateriflora), 248
sleep, 18, 51–52, 245–249

social needs, 70–72
social skills instruction, 274–276
social workers, 38–39, 212–213
sodium, 132
sodium bicarbonate, 131
Solfoton (phenobarbital), 159–160
special education. *See* schools
specialists, types of, 38–39, 210–215
SPECT (single photon emission
    computed tomography)/
    neuroSPECT scans, 23,
    123
speech therapy, 229
spiritual beliefs, 64–65
Spivack, Gary R.
    early treatment essential, 3
S-P-T, 191–192
SSI (Supplemental Security Income),
    291–293
SSRI antidepressants, 139–143
St. John's wort (*Hypericum perforatum*),
    266–267
Stanford-Binet Intelligence Test, Fourth
    Edition (S-B IV), 45
states of mind in bipolar disorders
    defined in *DSM-IV*, 9
    depression, 10–12
    hypomania, 13–15
    mania, 12–13
    mixed state (mixed mania), 15–16
    psychosis, 16–17
    rapid cycling of, 16
status epilepticus, 122
Stelazine (trifluoperazine), 169–170
stimulants, 174, 177
Stoll, Andrew
    essential fatty acids as mood
        stabilizers, 249–251
stress, ways to cope with, 110–114,
    272–274
substance abuse
    as cause of hallucinations, 63–64
    detox/dependency aids, 178–184
    effects of, 52
    impact of on diagnosis and
        treatment, 28
    resources, 398
    as safety issue, 69, 104–107
    as symptom of bipolar disorders, 52

suicide
  communicating with specialists
      about, 99
  crisis triage centers and, 99
  as outcome of untreated disorders,
      3
  preparing for crisis, 98–102
  preventing, 101–102, 397
  resources, 397
  warning signs of, 97–98
supplements, 247–253, 263–272, 407–
      408
support and advocacy
  groups, 112–113, 221–222, 389–
      394
  need for, 109–110, 112
  online, 109–110, 112–113, 393–
      394
Surmontil (trimipramine), 147–148
symptoms. See signs and symptoms of
      bipolar disorders
synaptic clefts, 24

T

taking charge of bipolar disorders
  adding structure to life, 82–84
  building/maintaining family
      relationships, 91–93
  coping with substance abuse, 104–
      106
  dealing with the criminal justice
      system, 107–110
  examining thinking and thought
      styles, 78–82
  handling self-injurious behavior,
      103–104
  helping children/adolescents
      understand, 74–76
  improving discipline, 84–90
  keeping diary of mood and
      behavior, 75–78
  maintaining hope/wishful thinking,
      113–114
  managing stress of parents, 110–
      112
  preventing accidents, 102–103
  preventing mood swings, 76–78
  preventing suicide, 97–102
  responding to choices of values/
      appearance/friends, 93–97
  seeking support and advocacy,
      112–113
  using the legal system to help, 110
talk therapies, 27, 216–225
tantrums, 17, 50–51
tardive dyskinesia (TD), 126–127
taurine, 271
Tay-Sachs disease, 63
teens. See children and adolescents
Tegretol (carmazepine), 137–138
Temporary Assistance for Needy
      Families (TANF), 296–
      297
Tenex (guanfacine), 190–191
Test of Nonverbal Intelligence 2 (TONI-
      2), 45–46
tests for bipolar disorders
  generally, 40–41
  intelligence (IQ), development,
      academic tests, specific
      Adaptive Behavior Inventory
          for Children (ABIC), 44
      Battelle Developmental
          Inventory, 44
      Children's Memory Scale
          (CMS), 44
      Developmental Assessment
          Screening Inventory II
          (DASI-II), 45
      Developmental Profile II, 45
      Learning Potential Assessment
          Device (LPAD), 45
      Leiter International
          Performance Scale,
          Revised (Leiter-R), 45
      Peabody Developmental and
          Motor Scales (PDMS), 45
      Peabody Individual
          Achievement Test (PIAT),
          45
      Stanford-Binet Intelligence
          Test, Fourth Edition (S-B
          IV), 45
      Test of Nonverbal Intelligence
          2 (TONI-2), 45–46
      Vineland Adaptive Behavior
          Scales, 46

tests for bipolar disorders (*continued*)
Weschler Intelligence Scale for Children, Revised (WISC-R)/Third Edition (WISC-III), 46
Wide Range of Asessment Test, Revision 3 (WRAT 3), 46
Woodcock-Johnson Psycho-Educational Battery, Revised (WJPEB-R, WJ-R), 46
psychiatric, neurological assessments, specific
Achenbach Child Behavior Checklist (CBC), 41
Attention Deficit Disorders Evaluation Scale, 41
Behavior Assessment System for Children (BASC), 41
Connors Rating Scales (CRS), 41–42
Draw-a-Person, 42
Halstead-Reitan Neuropsychological Test Battery for Children (HNTBC), 42
House-Tree-Person Projective Drawing Technique, 42
Kiddie-SADS-Present and Lifetime Version (K-SADS-PL), 42
Kinetic Family Drawing System for Family and School, 42
Luria-Nebraska Neuropsychological Battery, Children's Revision (LNNB-CR), 42–43
Pediatric Symptom Checklist, 43
Vineland Adaptive Behavior Scales, 43
therapeutic interventions, 206–233
therapies and therapists
finding in Canada, 210
licensing boards and agencies for, 210–215
non-talk, 226–229
overview of, 206–210

people who benefit from, 215
possible goals of, 209–210
self-esteem/skills, activities promoting, 232
styles of, 216–224
therapists, types of, 38–39, 210–215
thinking and thought styles
generally, 78–79, 80–82
specific problematic styles, 79–80
Thorazine (chlorpromazine), 170
Thyrar, 191–192
thyroid disorders, 58
thyroid hormone replacements (levothyroxine, liothyronine, T3, T4), 191–192
Thyroid Strong, 191–192
Tofranil (imipramine), 148–149
tonic/clonic seizures (grand mal), 121
Topomax (topiramate), 138–139, 162
Tourette syndrome, 23, 29
transition planning
building on strengths, 387
case management, 377–378
graduation from school, 374–375
healthcare and insurance, 376–377
higher education, 375–376
for housing, 382–383
legal and financial issues, 383–386
as part of IEP, 372–373
preparing for work, 373–374, 379–382
role of parents in adult life, 386
for young women, 378–379
Tranxene (clorazepate), 187
traveling for care, 312
Trexan (naltrexone hydrochloride), 183–184
Triavil, 164
tricyclic antidepressants, 143–149
Trilafon, 164
tryptophan, 248–249
types of bipolar disorders
bipolar I (BPI), 5–6
bipolar II (BPII), 6
bipolar III (BPIII), 7–8
cyclothymic disorder (cyclothymia), 6–7, 8

types of bipolar disorders (*continued*)
 manic depression, 5–6
 mood disorder NOS (not otherwise
  specified), 7
 other mood disorders
  premenstrual syndrome (PMS)/
   premenstrual dysphoric
   disorder, 8
  seasonal affective disorder
   (SAD), 7
tyrosine, 271

U

ultra-rapid cycling, 15
unipolar depression, 53–54
United Kingdom
 education in, 356–357
 finding housing in, 383
 insurance, financial assistance in,
  301–303, 308
 resources, 389–421
urea, 131–132

V

valerian (*Valeriana officinalis*), 248
Valium (diazepam), 188
value clashes, 93–97
velo-cardio-facial syndrome (VCFS), 22
Vesprin (trifluoperazine), 169–170
Vineland Adaptive Behavior Scales, 43,
 46
violent behavior, responding to, 88–90
viruses and viral infections. *See*
  immunotherapy
vitamins, 26, 248, 267–268
Vivactil (protriptyline), 149

W

web sites about bipolar disorders, 394–
 395
Wellbutrin/Wellbutrin SR (buproprion),
 155
Weschler Intelligence Scale for Children,
 Revised (WISC-R)/Third
 Edition (WISC-III), 46

Wide Range of Asessment Test, Revision
 3 (WRAT 3), 46
wishful thinking, 113–114
Woodcock-Johnson Psycho-Educational
 Battery, Revised (WJPEB-
 R, WJ-R), 46
World Wide Web, xv, 32, 113
Wozniak, Jane
 overlap in symptoms of ADHD and
  bipolar disorders, 48–49

X

Xanax (alprazolam), 188–189

Z

Zarontin (ethosuximide), 162–163
Zeldox (ziprasidone), 173
zinc, 269
Zoloft (sertraline), 142–143
Zyban (buproprion), 155
Zyprexa (olanzapine), 173

About the Author

Mitzi Waltz has been an author, journalist, and editor for more than a decade, covering topics from computers to health care. As the parent of a daughter diagnosed with bipolar disorder II, and a son diagnosed with pervasive developmental disorder not otherwise specified (PDD-NOS), she has been heavily involved in parent support work, and has also advocated for special-needs children within the medical, insurance, and education systems.

"When bipolar disorders strike in childhood or the teen years, the results can be especially devastating. Without appropriate and timely treatment, families are torn apart, many young people are unable to finish school, and the future can look grim. This situation isn't helped by the fact that few physicians understand what these illnesses look like at various ages, and frequently miss or misdiagnose them. This book was written to help parents and professionals recognize, treat, and cope with bipolar disorders in children and adolescents. With early intervention, the possibilities for these kids are limitless."

Ms. Waltz has also authored *Pervasive Developmental Disorders: Finding a Diagnosis and Getting Help* for O'Reilly's Patient-Centered Guides series, among other books.

Colophon

Patient-Centered Guides are about the experience of illness. They contain personal stories as well as a mixture of practical and medical information. The faces on the covers of our Guides reflect the human side of the information we offer.

The cover of *Bipolar Disorders: A Guide to Helping Children and Adolescents* was designed using Adobe Photoshop 5.0 and QuarkXPress 3.32 with Onyx BT and Berkeley fonts from Bitstream. The cover photos are from Rubberball Productions, and are used with that company's permission. The cover mechanical was prepared by Kathleen Wilson.

The interior layout for the book was designed by Alicia Cech, based on a series design by Nancy Priest and Edie Freedman. The interior fonts are Berkeley and Franklin Gothic. The text was prepared by Alicia Cech and Mike Sierra using QuarkXPress 3.32 and FrameMaker 5.5. Illustrations were created by Rhon Porter and Robert Romano using Adobe Photoshop 5.0 and Macromedia FreeHand 8.0. The text was copyedited by Lunaea Hougland and proofread by Sarah Jane Shangraw. Maureen Dempsey and Claire Cloutier provided quality assurance. The index was written by Kate Wilkinson. Interior composition was done by Sarah Jane Shangraw and Anna Snow.

Patient-Centered Guides™

Questions Answered
Experiences Shared

We are committed to empowering individuals to evolve into informed consumers armed with the latest information a heartfelt support for their journey.

When your life is turned upside down, your need for information is great. You to make critical medical decisions, often with information that seems little to g Plus you have to break the news to family, quiet your own fears, cope with symp or treatment side effects, figure out how you're going to pay for things, and son times still get to work or get dinner on the table.

Patient-Centered Guides provide authoritative information for intelligent info mation seekers who want to become advocates for their own health. The bc cover the whole impact of illness on your life. In each book, there's a mix o

- **Medical background for treatment decisions**
  We can give you information that can help you work with your doctor to come to a decision. We start from the viewpoint that modern medicii has much to offer and we discuss complementary treatments. Where th are treatment controversies, we present differing points of view.

- **Practical information**
  Once you've decided what to do about your illness, you still have to deal w treatments and changes to your life. We cover day-to-day practicalities, sucl those you'd hear from a good nurse or a knowledgeable support group.

- **Emotional support**
  It's normal to have strong reactions to a condition that threatens your life or changes how you live. It's normal that the whole family is affected. We cove issues such as the shock of diagnosis, living with uncertainty, and communic with loved ones.

Each book also contains stories from both patients and doctors—medical "frequent flyers" who share, in their own words, the lessons and strategies t have learned while maneuvering through the often complicated maze of me information that's available.

We provide information online, including updated listings of the resources appear in this book. This is freely available for you to print out and copy to share with others, as long as you retain the copyright notice on the printoui

www.patientcenters.com

Other Books in the Series

Child/Adolescent Health

Adolescent Drug & Alcohol Abuse
How to Spot It, Stop It, and Get Help for Your Family
By Nikki Babbit
ISBN 1-56592-755-9, Paperback, 6"x 9", 304 pages, $17.95 US, $26.95 CAN

"The clear, concise, and practical information, backed up by personal stories from
people who have been through these problems with their own children or clien
will have readers keeping this book within easy reach for use on a regular basis.
> —*James F. Crowley, MA President, Community Intervention, Inc.*
> *Author,* Alliance for Change: A Plan for Community Action on Ado
> Drug Abuse

Obsessive-Compulsive Disorder
Help for Children and Adolescents
By Mitzi Waltz
ISBN 1-56592-758-3, Paperback, 6" x 9", 408 pages, $24.95 US, $36.95 CAN

"More than a self-help manual…a wonderful resource for patients and profession
alike. Highly recommended."
> —*John S. March, MD, MPS, Author,* OCD in Children and Adolescents:
> A Cognitive-Behavioral Treatment Manual

Pervasive Developmental Disorders
Finding a Diagnosis and Getting Help
By Mitzi Waltz
ISBN 1-56592-530-0, Paperback, 6" x 9", 592 pages, $24.95 US, $36.95 CAN

"Mitzi Waltz's book provides clear, informative, and comprehensive information on
relevant aspect of PDD. Her in-depth discussion will help parents and professional
develop a clear understanding of the issues and, consequently, they will be able to a
informed decisions about various interventions. A job well done!"
> —*Stephen M. Edelson, PhD, Director, Center for the Study of Autism, Salem,*

Patient-Centered Guides
Published by O'Reilly & Associates, Inc.
Our products are available at a bookstore near you.
For information: **800-998-9938** • **707-829-0515** • **info@oreilly.com**
101 Morris Street • Sebastopol • CA • 95472-9902
www.patientcenters.com

Partial Seizure Disorders
Help for Patients and Families
By Mitzi Waltz
ISBN 0-596-50003-3, Paperback, 6" x 9", 325 pages, $19.95 US, $29.95 CAN

"Mitzi Waltz has provided people with epilepsy and their families a compassiona
yet supremely practical book. She explains complicated medical information in
detailed language, and provides an excellent guide to navigating the maze of
educational and healthcare bureaucracies. *Partial Seizure Disorders* is a book to l
referred to often and shared with others."
— *Patricia Murphy, Editor,* Epilepsy Wellness Newsletter

Hydrocephalus
A Guide for Patients, Families & Friends
By Chuck Toporek and Kellie Robinson
ISBN 1-56592-410-X, Paperback, 6" x 9", 384 pages, $19.95 US, $28.95 CAN

"In this book, the authors have provided a wonderful entry into the world of
hydrocephalus to begin to remedy the neglect of this important condition.
We are immensely grateful to them for their groundbreaking effort."
— *Peter M. Black, MD, PhD, Franc D. Ingraham Professor of Neurosurge
Harvard Medical School, Neurosurgeon-in-Chief, Brigham and Womer
Hospital, Children's Hospital, Boston, Massachusetts*

Making Informed Medical Decisions
Where to Look and How to Use What You Find
By Nancy Oster, Lucy Thomas & Darol Joseff, MD
ISBN 1-56592-459-2, Paperback, 6" x 9", 392 pages, $17.95 US, $26.95 CAN

"I will buy this book for all of our clinic sites and our patient library. It is a terrifi
reference."
— *Laurie Lyckholm, MD, Medical Oncologist, Massey Cancer Center,
Medical College of Virginia*

Your Child in the Hospital
A Practical Guide for Parents, Second Edition
By Nancy Keene and Rachel Prentice
ISBN 1-56592-573-4, Paperback, 5" x 8", 176 pages, $11.95 US, $17.95 CAN

"When your child is ill or injured, the hospital setting can be overwhelming. He1
terrific 'road map' to help keep families 'on track.'"
— *James B. Fahner, MD, Division Chief, Pediatric Hematology/Oncology,
DeVos Children's Hospital, Grand Rapids, Michigan*

Patient-Centered Guides
Published by O'Reilly & Associates, Inc.
Our products are available at a bookstore near you.
For information: **800-998-9938 • 707-829-0515 • info@oreilly.com**
101 Morris Street • Sebastopol • CA • 95472-9902
www.patientcenters.com

Childhood Cancer Survivors
A Practical Guide to Your Future
By Nancy Keene, Wendy Hobbie & Kathy Ruccione
ISBN 1-56592-460-6, Paperback, 6" x 9", 512 pages, $27.95 US, $40.95 CAN

"Every survivor of childhood cancer should read this book."
> —*Debra Friedman, MD, Assistant Professor of Pediatrics, Division of Hematology/Oncology, Children's Hospital and Regional Medical Cent∍ Seattle, WA*

Childhood Cancer
A Parent's Guide to Solid Tumor Cancers
By Honna Janes-Hodder & Nancy Keene
ISBN 1-56592-531-9, Paperback, 6"x 9", 544 pages, $24.95 US, $36.95 CAN

"I recommend [this book] most highly for those in need of high-level, helpful knowledge that will empower and help parents and caregivers to cope."
> —*Mark Greenberg, MD, Professor of Pediatrics, University of Toronto*

Childhood Leukemia
A Guide for Families, Friends & Caregivers, Second Edition
By Nancy Keene
ISBN 1-56592-632-3, Paperback, 6" x 9", 520 pages, $24.95 US, $36.95 CAN

"What's so compelling about *Childhood Leukemia* is the amount of useful medica͘ information and practical advice it contains. Keene avoids jargon and lays out ᴡ needed to deal with the medical system."
> —The Washington Post

Patient-Centered Guides
Published by *O'Reilly & Associates, Inc.*
Our products are available at a bookstore near you.
For information: 800-998-9938 • 707-829-0515 • info@oreilly.com
101 Morris Street • Sebastopol • CA • 95472-9902
www.patientcenters.com